Introduction to Business Writing

Eng W232

Erinn Kelley

INDIANA UNIV-SOUTH BEND

ENGLISH

create.mheducation.com

ISBN-13: 9781307708004

ISBN-10: 1307708005

Contents

CHAPTER

1

Succeeding in Business Communication

Chapter Outline

Benefits of Good Communication Skills

"I'll Never Have to Write Because . . ."

Communicating on the Job

The Cost of Communication

Costs of Poor Communication

- Wasted Time
- Wasted Efforts
- Lost Goodwill
- Legal Problems

Basic Criteria for Effective Messages

Following Conventions

Understanding and Analyzing Business Communication Situations

Ethics

Corporate Culture

How to Solve Business Communication Problems

- Gather Knowledge and Brainstorm Solutions.
- Answer the Five Questions for Analysis.
- Organize Your Information to Fit Your Audiences, Your Purposes, and the Situation.
- Make Your Document Visually Inviting.
- Revise Your Draft to Create a Friendly, Businesslike, Positive Style.
- Edit Your Draft for Standard English; Double-Check Names and Numbers.
- Use the Response You Get to Plan Future Messages.

Summary by Learning Objectives

©DrAfter123/Getty Images

NEWSWORTHY COMMUNICATION

Costly Miscommunications: Trouble at Netflix

©pixinoo/Shutterstock.com

Poorly done business communications can have severe consequences. Netflix learned this lesson the hard way when it chose to split its DVD and streaming services. The poorly communicated plan led Netflix to suffer in the following ways:

- The loss of approximately 800,000 subscriptions.

- The loss of 77% of its stock value in four months.

- Internal restructuring that led to a never-materialized spin-off company, Qwikster.

- A significant loss of reputation and customer goodwill.

A large part of the issue was the means of delivery of the message. A poorly worded blog post failed to minimize the negatives of the message. Indeed, the blog post invited members to cancel their subscriptions in its closing line.

Further, the comments section of the blog post was filled with unhappy customer comments about the plan. As a result, the chief executive officer (CEO) wrote an apologetic blog post as well as co-authored a shareholder statement that reassured investors while revising projected domestic-customer subscriptions down by 1,000,000.

Sources: Nick Wingfield and Brian Stelter, "How Netflix Lost 800,000 Members, and Good Will," *The New York Times*, October 24, 2011, http://www.nytimes.com/2011/10/25/technology/netflix-lost-800000-members-with-price-rise-and-split-plan.html?mcubz=1.

Greg Sandoval, "Netflix's Lost Year: The Inside Story of the Price-Hike Train Wreck," *CNET*, July 11, 2012., https://www.cnet.cm/news/netflixs-lost-year-the-inside-story-of-the-price-hike-train-wreck/.

"5 Business Lessons from the Netflix Pricing Debacle," *Forbes*, December 28, 2011, https://www.forbes.com/sites/theyec/2011/12/28/5-business-lessons-from-the-netflix-pricing-debacle/#32c4020ed2a7.

James B. Stewart, "Netflix Looks Back on Its Near-Death Spiral," *The New York Times*, April 26, 2013, https://www.nytimes.com/2013/04/27/business/netflix-looks-back-on-its-near-death-spiral.html.

Rian Barrett, Jason Parham, Brian Raftery, Peter Rubin, and Angela Watercutter, "Netflix Is Turning 20—But Its Birthday Doesn't Matter," *Wired*, August 29, 2017, https://www.wired.com/story/netflix-20th-anniversary/.

"15 Years After IPO, Netflix Has Changed Drastically—And Is Worth Nearly 22,000% More," *MarketWatch*, May 24, 2017, https://www.marketwatch.com/story/15-years-after-ipo-netflix-has-changed-drasticallyand-is-worth-nearly-22000-more-2017-05-23.

Learning Objectives

After studying this chapter, you will know

LO 1-1 What the benefits of good communication are.

LO 1-2 Why you need to be able to communicate well.

LO 1-3 What the costs of communication are.

LO 1-4 What the costs of poor communication are.

LO 1-5 What the basic criteria for effective messages are.

LO 1-6 What role conventions play in business communication.

LO 1-7 Why ethics are so important in business communication.

LO 1-8 How corporate culture affects the business environment.

LO 1-9 How to solve business communication problems.

Communication is a vital part of business. As you will see in this and later chapters, missteps in handling business communications can cost organizations millions, and even billions, of dollars.

The amount of business communication is staggering. The U.S. Postal Service processed 160 billion pieces of mail in 2012, more than half of which were business communications. Advertising mail accounted for 79.5 billion pieces; first-class mail accounted for 68.7 billion,[1] many of which were business communications such as bills and insurance documents. When you consider that most of your business communications are electronic or oral, you can start to imagine the staggering number of business communications that people compose, hear, and read.

More and more, communications—both professional and personal—are moving to electronic media.

- According to the *Harvard Business Review,* "In the past decade the world has gone from a total of 12 billion emails a day to 247 billion."[2]

- In June 2014, people around the world sent 561 billion text messages.[3]

- In 2017, Twitter passed 330 million monthly users.[4]

Business depends on communication. People must communicate to plan products and services; hire, train, and motivate workers; coordinate manufacturing and delivery; persuade customers to buy; and bill them for the sale. Indeed, for many businesses and nonprofit and government organizations, the "product" is information or services rather than something tangible. Information and services are created and delivered by communication. In every organization, communication is the way people get work done.

Communication takes many forms: face-to-face or phone conversations, informal meetings, presentations, email messages, letters, memos, reports, blogs, tweets, text messaging, social media, and websites. All of these methods are forms of **verbal communication,** or communication that uses words. **Nonverbal communication** does not use words. Pictures, computer graphics, and company logos are nonverbal. Interpersonal nonverbal signals include how people sit at meetings, how office spaces are used, and how long someone keeps a visitor waiting.

Benefits of Good Communication Skills

Good communication is worth every minute it takes and every penny it costs. Recently, the communication practices of 335 U.S. and Canadian companies with an average of 13,000 employees each and median annual revenues of $1.8 billion were analyzed. The study found those companies that best communicated with their employees enjoyed "greater employee engagement and commitment, higher retention and productivity, and—ultimately—better financial performance . . .

- They boasted a 19.4% higher market premium (the degree to which the company's market value exceeds the cost of its assets).

- They were 4.5 times more likely to report high levels of employee engagement.

- They were 20% more likely to report lower turnover rates."[5]

Good communication skills also will benefit you. You may have wonderful ideas for your workplace, but unless you can communicate them to the relevant people, they will get you nowhere. In fact, many experts call communication skills—the ability to persuade, explain complex material, and adapt information to particular audiences—one of the most crucial skills of the new workplace, and a skill that is unlikely to be replaced by a computer.

Even in your first job, you'll communicate. You'll listen to instructions; you'll ask questions; you may solve problems with other workers in teams. Even entry-level jobs require high-level skills in reasoning, mathematics, and communicating. As a result, communication ability consistently ranks first among the qualities that employers look for in college graduates.[6] Warren Buffett, chairman of Berkshire Hathaway and ranked among the world's wealthiest people, told Columbia Business School students that they could increase their value 50% by learning communication skills, and that many of them did not yet have those skills.[7]

The National Commission on Writing surveyed 120 major corporations, employing nearly 8 million workers. Almost 70% of respondents said that at least two-thirds of their employees have specific writing responsibilities included in their position descriptions. These writing responsibilities include

- Email (100% of employees).

- Presentations with visuals, such as PowerPoint slides (100%).

- Memos and correspondence (70%).

- Formal reports (62%).

- Technical reports (59%).

Respondents also noted that communication functions were least likely to be outsourced.[8]

Because communication skills are so important, good communicators earn more. Research has shown that among people with two- or four-year degrees, workers in the top 20% of writing ability earn, on average, more than three times as much as workers whose writing falls into the worst 20%.[9] Jeffrey Gitomer, business consultant and author of best-selling business books, says there are three secrets to getting known in the business world; all of them are communication skills: writing, e-zining (he reaches more than 130,000 subscribers each week), and speaking. He states, "Writing leads to wealth."[10]

"I'll Never Have to Write Because . . ."

LO 1-2

Despite the frequency of on-the-job writing and the importance of overall communication skills, college graduates often don't demonstrate the necessary writing skills as they enter the workforce. A survey of employers conducted on behalf of the Association of American Colleges and Universities found that writing was one of the weakest skills of college graduates.[11] In another large survey, respondents noted that a lack of "effective business communication skills appears to be a major stumbling block among new [job] entrants—even at the college level."[12]

Some students think that an administrative assistant will do their writing, that they can use form letters if they do have to write, that only technical skills matter, or that they'll call or text rather than write. Each of these claims is fundamentally flawed.

Claim 1:   An administrative assistant will do all my writing.

Reality: Because of automation and restructuring, job responsibilities in offices have changed. Today, many offices do not have typing pools. Most secretaries have become administrative assistants with their own complex tasks such as training, research, and database management for several managers. Managers are likely to take care of their own writing, data entry, and phone calls.

Claim 2:   I'll use form letters or templates when I need to write.

Reality: A form letter is designed to cover only routine situations, many of which are computerized or outsourced. Also, the higher you rise, the more frequently you'll face situations that aren't routine, that demand creative solutions.

Claim 3:   I'm being hired as an accountant, not a writer.

Reality: Almost every entry-level professional or managerial job requires you to write email messages, speak to small groups, write documents, and present your work for annual reviews. People who do these things well are likely to be promoted beyond the entry level. Employees in jobs as diverse as firefighters, security professionals, and construction project managers all are being told to polish their writing and speaking skills.[13]

Claim 4:   I'll just pick up the phone.

Reality: Important phone calls require follow-up letters or emails. People in organizations put things in writing to make themselves visible, to create a record, to convey complex data, to make things convenient for the reader, to save money, and to convey their own messages more effectively. "If it isn't in writing, it didn't happen" is a maxim at many companies. Writing is an essential way to record agreements, to make yourself visible, and to let your accomplishments be known.

Communicating on the Job

Communication—oral, nonverbal, and written—goes to both internal and external audiences. **Internal audiences** are other people in the same organization: subordinates, superiors, and peers. **External audiences** are people outside the organization: customers, suppliers, distributors, unions, stockholders, potential employees, trade associations, special interest groups, government agencies, the press, and the general public.

People in organizations produce a large variety of documents. Figures 1.1 and 1.2 list a few of the specific documents produced at Ryerson, a company that fabricates and sells steel, aluminum, other metals, and plastics to a wide variety of industrial clients and has sales offices across the United States, Canada, and China.

All of the documents in Figures 1.1 and 1.2 have one or more of the three basic purposes of organizational writing: to inform, to request or persuade, and to build

Figure 1.1	Internal Documents Produced in One Organization	
Document	**Description of document**	**Purpose(s) of document**
Transmittal	Memo accompanying document, telling why it's being forwarded to the receiver	Inform; persuade reader to read document; build image and goodwill
Monthly or quarterly report	Report summarizing profitability, productivity, and problems during period; used to plan activity for next month or quarter	Inform; build image and goodwill (report is accurate, complete; writer understands company)
Policy and procedure bulletin	Statement of company policies and instructions (e.g., how to enter orders, how to run fire drills)	Inform; build image and goodwill (procedures are reasonable)
Request to deviate from policy and procedure bulletin	Persuasive message arguing that another approach is better for a specific situation than the standard approach	Persuade; build image and goodwill (request is reasonable; writer seeks good of company)
Performance appraisal	Evaluation of an employee's performance	Inform; persuade employee to improve
Memo of congratulations	Congratulations to employees who have won awards, been promoted	Build goodwill

Figure 1.2	External Documents Produced in One Organization	
Document	**Description of document**	**Purpose(s) of document**
Quotation	Letter giving price for a specific product or service	Inform; build goodwill (price is reasonable)
Claims adjustment	Letter granting or denying customer request to be given credit for defective goods or service	Inform; build goodwill
Job description	Description of qualifications and duties of job; used for performance appraisals, salaries, and hiring	Inform; persuade good candidates to apply; build goodwill (job duties match level, pay)
10-K report	Report filed with the Securities and Exchange Commission detailing financial information	Inform
Annual report	Report to stockholders summarizing financial information for year	Inform; persuade stockholders to retain stock and others to buy; build goodwill (company is a good corporate citizen)
Thank-you letter	Letter to suppliers, customers, or other people who have helped individuals or the company	Build goodwill

goodwill. In fact, most messages have multiple purposes. When you answer a question, for instance, you're informing, but you also want to build goodwill by suggesting that you're competent and perceptive and that your answer is correct and complete.

The Cost of Communication

LO 1-3

Writing costs money. The annual Social Security statements cost $70 million a year to mail, even with huge economies of scale.[14] The cost does not include employee time in the writing and processing, a major expense.

Business communication involves paper documents, electronic communications, and interpersonal abilities.

©Rawpixel.com/Shutterstock.com

Document cycling processes also increase costs. In many organizations, all external documents must be approved before they go out. *ISO 9000 Quality Systems Handbook* requires approval procedures of both internal and external documents.[15] A major document may *cycle* from writer to superior to writer to another superior to writer again 10 or more times before final approval. Longer documents can involve large teams of people and take months to write.

Large organizations handle so much paper that even small changes to their communication practices amount to millions of dollars. Xerox Global Services Europe touts contractual annual savings of up to 1 million euros for organizations with 4,000 or more employees who switch to its printing services.[16] The Federal Electronics Challenge developed a list of formatting guidelines to reduce paper waste and increase savings.[17]

Another significant cost of communication is email storage. In addition to their exponential increase in frequency, emails also are growing in size. Many more of them also come with attachments. And businesses are storing much of this huge load on their servers. But the cost of the hardware is only some of the storage cost; a larger cost is administering and maintaining the archives. These costs include downtime when storage systems crash and time spent retrieving lost or corrupted messages.[18]

Costs of Poor Communication

LO 1-4

Poor communication can cost billions of dollars.

- Hurricane Katrina caused billions of dollars of damage—damage that was worsened by horrendous miscommunications between federal, state, and private relief organizations. The Federal Emergency Management Agency (FEMA) claimed it was days before the relief agency knew about the thousands of people stranded in the New Orleans Convention Center. The lack of coordination and communication caused by these systems put even more lives at risk by delaying assistance where it was most needed. Some rescuers in helicopters were unable to communicate with rescuers in boats. Some National Guard units actually used runners to communicate. State and local agency teams received conflicting messages, which led to confusion.[19] The massive communication problems led to an entire chapter on communication in the U.S. House of Representatives report on the Hurricane Katrina disaster.

- Internal and external communication problems contributed greatly to delays in Boeing's 787 Dreamliner, delays that cost Boeing billions in penalties and caused some customers to switch their orders to Airbus.[20]

- GlaxoSmithKline was fined $3 billion, the largest payment ever by a drug company, for failing to communicate accurately safety data on some of its popular drugs and for misdirecting the use of others.[21]

- British Petroleum agreed to a $4 billion fine for its role in the Gulf of Mexico oil spill. That sum is in addition to the $36.5 billion BP already had spent, or committed to spend, in additional fines, cleanup costs, and settlements to individuals and businesses. According to the presidential commission, inadequate communication among British Petroleum, Halliburton, and Transocean, as well as within their own companies, was a contributing factor in BP's massive oil spill, which caused extensive damage, as well as fatalities, in the Gulf of Mexico.[22]

Costs of poor communication are not just financial. People died in the explosion of British Petroleum's oil well. In the aftermath of Hurricane Katrina, inaccurate media reports of looting convinced some residents to stay to protect their property instead of evacuating; false reports of shootings at helicopters resulted in some states refusing to send trained emergency workers.

Not all communication costs are so dramatic, however. When communication isn't as good as it could be, you and your organization pay a price in wasted time, wasted effort, lost goodwill, and legal problems.

Wasted Time

Bad writing takes longer to read as we struggle to understand what we're reading. How quickly we can comprehend written material is determined by the difficulty of the subject matter and by the document's organization and writing style.

Communication failures increased the damage caused by Hurricane Katrina.

Source: USCG

Second, bad writing needs to be rewritten. Poorly written documents frequently cycle to others for help, thus wasting time of people other than the original writer.

Third, ineffective communication may obscure ideas so that discussions and decisions are needlessly drawn out.

Fourth, unclear or incomplete messages may require the receiver to gather more information. Some receivers may not bother to do so, leading to wrong decisions or a refusal to act.

Wasted Efforts

Ineffective messages don't get results. A receiver who has to guess what the sender means may guess wrong. A reader who finds a letter or email unconvincing or insulting simply won't do what the message asks.

Like many business projects, the *Mars Climate Orbiter* involved a wide range of people in a range of locations. The programmers who wrote the software that controlled the spacecraft's engines worked in Great Britain and used metric measurements in their calculations, while the engineers who made the satellite's engines worked in the United States and used English measurements. Both teams assumed they were using the same measurement standards, neither team made any attempt to check, and no one else caught the error. With that failure, NASA lost a $125 million satellite and years of effort, while gaining a major public embarrassment.[23]

Lost Goodwill

Whatever the literal content of the words, every communication serves either to build or to undermine the image the audience has of the communicator.

Part of building a good image is taking the time to write correctly. Even organizations that have adopted casual dress still expect writing to appear professional and to be free from typos and grammatical errors.

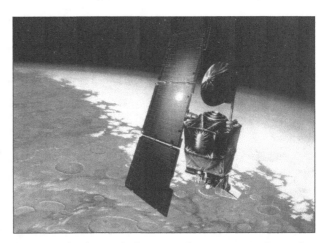

One example of wasted effort arising from communication problems occurred when the *Mars Climate Orbiter* spacecraft lost contact with NASA mission control just after it arrived at Mars. A subsequent investigation revealed the main problem was a minor software-programming error caused by communication errors.

Source: NASA

Figure 1.3	A Form Letter That Annoyed Customers

Nelson Manufacturing

600 N. Main Street   317-281-3000
Indianapolis, IN   46204   fax 317-281-3001
www.nelson.comv

*Where are date,
Inside address?
No excuse for not adding these!*

Gentlemen: *Sexist!*

Stuffy   *Emphasizes the writer, not the reader.*

Main point is buried.

Please be advised that upon reviewing your credit file with *us*, *we* find the information *herein* outdated. In an effort to *expedite* the handling of your future orders with *us*, and to allow *us* to open an appropriate line of credit for your company, *we ask* that you send an updated list of vendor references. Any other additional financial information that you can supply would be to both of our benefits.

Wrong word (also stuffy).

Prove it!   *What information?*

May we hear from you soon?

Sincerely,

Messages also can create a poor image because of poor audience analysis and inappropriate style. The form letter printed in Figure 1.3 failed because it was stuffy and selfish. The comments in red show specific problems with the letter:

- **The language is stiff and legalistic.**   Note the sexist "Gentlemen:" and obsolete "Please be advised" and "herein."

- **The tone is selfish.**   The letter is written from the writer's point of view; there are no benefits for the reader. (The writer says there are, but without a shred of evidence, the claim isn't convincing.)

- **The main point is buried.**   The main point is in the middle of the long first paragraph. The middle is the least emphatic part of a paragraph.

- **The request is vague.**   How many references does the supplier want? Are only vendor references OK, or would other credit references, such as banks, work too? Is the name of the reference enough, or is it necessary also to specify the line of credit, the average balance, the current balance, the years credit has been established, or other information? What "additional financial information" does the supplier want? Annual reports? Bank balance? Tax returns? The request sounds like an invasion of privacy, not a reasonable business practice.

- **Words are misused.**   The use of *herein* for *therein* suggests either an ignorant writer or one who doesn't care enough about the subject and the reader to use the right word.

Legal Problems

Poor communication choices can lead to legal problems for individuals and organizations. The news is full of examples. Papa John's pizza was hit with a lawsuit of a quarter billion dollars for text advertisements that customers claimed were spam.[24] Capital One Financial, the large credit card company, agreed to pay $210 million to settle allegations that its call center pressured customers into buying credit-protection products such as credit monitoring.[25]

Individual communications also can have legal consequences. Text messages revealed an affair between Detroit Mayor Kwame Kilpatrick and one of his aides; both the messages and the affair contradicted testimony the mayor had given under oath. Consequences included loss of office, jail time, and a $1 million fine.

U.S. Representative Mark Foley of Florida resigned after his instant messages to House pages were published. Emails have helped bring about the fall of many executives, including

- Senior Enron executives.

- Hewlett-Packard chair Patricia Dunn.

- Walmart Vice Presidents Julie Roehm and Sean Womack.

- CIA Director David Petraeus.

One San Francisco law firm says 70% of its routine evidence now comes from emails.[26]

In particular, letters, memos, emails, and instant messages create legal obligations for organizations. When a lawsuit is filed against an organization, the lawyers for the plaintiffs have the right to subpoena documents written by employees of the organization. These documents then may be used as evidence, for instance, that an employer fired an employee without adequate notice or that a company knew about a safety defect but did nothing to correct it.

These documents also may be used as evidence in contexts the writer did not intend. This means a careless writer can create obligations that the organization does not mean to assume. For instance, a letter from a manager telling scouts they may not visit a factory floor because it is too dangerous could be used in a worker's compensation suit.[27]

Careful writers and speakers think about the larger social context in which their words may appear. What might those words mean to other people in the field? What might they mean to a judge and jury? What might they mean to an unintended audience in the general public?

Basic Criteria for Effective Messages

LO 1-5

Good business and administrative communication meets five basic criteria: it's clear, complete, and correct; it saves the audience's time; and it builds goodwill.

- **It's clear.** An effective message clearly imparts its intended meaning. The audience doesn't have to work to figure out what the author means. Inaccurate and imprecise word choices impede comprehension. Often, you'll need to revise an entire sentence to incorporate more accurate or more precise words:

    Imprecise: The first problem with the incentive program is that middle managers do not use good interpersonal skills in implementing it. For example, the hotel chef openly ridicules the program.

    Better: The first problem with the incentive program is that some middle managers undercut it. For example, the hotel chef openly ridicules the program.

- **It's complete.** All of the audience questions are answered. The audience has enough information to evaluate the message and act on it.

- **It's correct.** The message is free from errors in spelling, capitalization, word choice, and grammar.

- **It saves the audience's time.** The style, organization, and visual or aural impact of the message help the audience read or hear, understand, and act on the information as quickly as possible. For example, effective messages use forecasting statements for organization, "Employee stock ownership programs (ESOPs) provide four benefits." Such statements tell readers what information will follow. Effective messages also use transition words, phrases, and sentences (such as "The second factor . . ." and "An alternative to this plan is . . .") to tell audiences whether the discussion is continuing on the same point or shifting.

- **It builds goodwill.** The message presents a positive image of the communicator and his or her organization. It treats the message recipient as a person, not a number. It cements a good relationship between the communicator and the audience.

Whether a message meets these five criteria depends on the interactions among the communicator, the audience, the purposes of the message, and the situation. No single set of words will work in all possible situations.

Following Conventions

LO 1-6

Conventions are widely accepted practices you routinely encounter. Common business communications have conventions. These conventions help people recognize, produce, and interpret different kinds of communications. Each chapter in this textbook presents conventions of traditional business documents. For example, Chapter 11 discusses conventions of job application letters and Chapter 16 talks about conventions of delivering oral presentations.

Conventions change over time. Consider how the conventions governing movies and television have changed just during your lifetime, allowing more explicit sex and violence. Similarly, conventions change in business. Paper memos have mostly given way to emails, and some emails are being replaced by text messaging.

The key to using conventions effectively, despite their changing nature, is to remember that they always need to fit the rhetorical situation—they always need to be adjusted for the particular audience, context, and purpose. For instance, Chapter 9 provides guidelines on constructing negative messages. However, you will need to adapt these guidelines based on the way your organization presents its negative messages. Some organizations will use a more formal tone than others; some present negative news bluntly, while others ease into it more gently.

Because every organization will be unique in the conventions it follows, the information presented in this text will provide a basic understanding of common elements for particular genres. You always will need to adjust the basics for your particular needs.

The best way to learn conventions in a particular workplace is to see what other workers are doing. How do they communicate with each other? Do their practices change when they communicate with superiors? What kinds of letters and emails do they send? How much do they email? What tone is preferred? Close observation will help your communications fit the conventions of your employer.

Understanding and Analyzing Business Communication Situations

The best communicators are conscious of the context in which they communicate; they're aware of options.

Ask yourself the following questions:

- **What's at stake—to whom?**   Think not only about your own needs, but also about the concerns your boss and your audience will have. Your message will be most effective if you think of the entire organizational context—and the larger context of shareholders, customers, and regulators. When the stakes are high, you'll need to take into account people's feelings as well as objective facts.

- **Should you send a message?**   Sometimes, especially when you're new on the job, silence is the most tactful response. However, be alert for opportunities to learn, to influence, to make your case.

- **What channel should you use?**   Paper documents and presentations are formal and give you considerable control over the message. Email, texting, tweeting, phone calls, and stopping by someone's office are less formal. Oral channels are better for group decision making, allow misunderstandings to be cleared up more quickly, and seem more personal. Sometimes you may need more than one message, in more than one channel.

- **What should you say?**   Content for a message may not be obvious. How detailed should you be? Should you repeat information that the audience already knows? The answers will depend on the kind of message, your purposes, audiences, and the corporate culture. And you'll have to figure these things out for yourself, without detailed instructions.

- **How should you say it?**   How you arrange your ideas—what comes first, second, and last—and the words you use shape the audience's response to what you say.

Ethics

LO 1-7

See Figure 1.4 for an explanation of this and another icon used throughout this textbook.

Ethics concerns have become a major part of the business environment. Financial giants such as AIG, Bear Stearns, Lehman Brothers, Merrill Lynch, Wachovia, and Washington Mutual had to be bailed out or went bankrupt. Banks, corporate officials, and rating agencies all were accused of unethical behavior. The Securities and Exchange Commission (SEC) charged Goldman Sachs with fraud on securities linked to subprime mortgages; the firm settled out of court for more than half a billion dollars.

In a much larger lawsuit, Credit Suisse was sued for $11.2 billion in losses from bundled mortgage securities. According to New York's attorney general, Credit Suisse "kept its investors in the dark about the inadequacy of its review procedures and defects in the loans," a major lapse in business communication. The bank also was accused of misrepresenting information in its SEC filings regarding when problem loans would be repurchased.[28]

Figure 1.4	An explanation of the I and E icons used throughout this text to mark particular types of content.

	= Intercultural communication	Marks content related to considerations for communicating across different cultural groups.
	= Ethics	Marks content related to principles that develop and sustain ethical communicative behavior.

Ethics breaches have cost other organizations millions and even billions of dollars.

- GlaxoSmithKline incurred a $3 billion fine for failing to report drug safety data. Previously, the company had pleaded guilty to charges that it knowingly sold adulterated drugs, including the antidepressant Paxil, and paid fines of $750 million.[29]

- Siemens settled with the government for $800 million in a bribery case; the document review alone cost an additional $100 million.[30]

- In 2013, the credit-rating agency Standard & Poor's was sued by the U.S. government for $5 billion; the suit alleged the agency inflated credit ratings for bundled mortgage securities.[31]

- In 2015, Volkswagen admitted to cheating American emissions standards on their diesel vehicles.[32] In 2016, a judge approved a $14.7 billion settlement.[33]

The Ethics Resource Center, America's oldest nonprofit organization devoted to ethical practice, reported in its 2011 National Business Ethics Survey that 45% of employees surveyed personally witnessed unethical or illegal behavior; 35% of those witnesses did not report it. The most frequent misconducts were misusing company time, displaying abusive behavior, lying, abusing company resources, violating company Internet use policies, discriminating, displaying conflicts of interest, inappropriately using social networking, violating health or safety regulations, stealing, falsifying time reports, violating use of benefits, and sexually harassing others.[34]

Some common reasons for not reporting ethical misconduct are the following: it's standard practice here, it's not a big deal, it's not my responsibility (a particularly common reason for junior employees), and I want to be loyal to my colleagues/manager/company. (Stated negatively, this reason is "fear of consequences.")[35]

On the other side of the coin, positive ethical efforts also are getting attention. The United Nations Global Compact, "the world's largest corporate citizenship and sustainability initiative," focuses on human rights, labor, environment, and anticorruption measures. More than 7,000 businesses in 145 countries participate.[36] The Clinton Global Initiative has brought together 150 heads of state, 20 Nobel laureates, and hundreds of CEOs, who collectively have committed $63 billion. This money already has had an impact on the lives of 400 million people in 180 countries.[37]

Business ethics include far more than corporate greed, international pacts, and philanthropy, of course. Much of business ethics involves routine practices, and many of these practices involve communication. How can we make our contracts with our clients and suppliers easier to understand? How can we best communicate with our employees? How much should our hospital disclose about infection rates?

Many basic, daily communication decisions involve an ethics component.

- Am I including all the information my audience needs?

- Am I expressing it in ways they will understand?

- Am I putting it in a format that helps my audience grasp it quickly?

- Am I including information for all segments of my audience?

- Am I taking information from other sources accurately?

- Am I acknowledging my sources?

Figure 1.5 elaborates on ethical components of communication. As it suggests, language, graphics, and document design—basic parts of any business document—can be

Figure 1.5	Ethical Issues in Business Communications	
Manner of conveying the message	**Qualities of the message**	**Larger organizational context of the message**
• Is the language clear to the audience? Does it respect the audience?	• Is the message an ethical one that is honest and sensitive to all stakeholders?	• How does the organization treat its employees? How do employees treat each other?
• Do the words balance the organization's right to present its best case with its responsibility to present its message honestly?	• Have interested parties been able to provide input?	• How sensitive is the organization to stakeholders such as the people who live near its factories, stores, or offices and to the general public?
• Do graphics help the audience understand? Or are graphics used to distract or confuse?	• Does the audience get all the information it needs to make a good decision or is information withheld?	• Does the organization support employees' efforts to be honest, fair, and ethical?
• Does the design of the document make reading easy? Does document design attempt to make readers skip key points?	• Is information communicated so the audience can grasp it or are data "dumped" without any context?	• Do the organization's actions in making products, buying supplies, and marketing goods and services stand up to ethical scrutiny?
	• Are the arguments logical? Are they supported with adequate evidence?	• Is the organization a good corporate citizen, helpful rather than harmful to the community in which it exists?
	• Are the emotional appeals used fairly? Do they supplement logic rather than substitute for it?	• Are the organization's products or services a good use of scarce resources?
	• Does the organizational pattern lead the audience without undue manipulation?	
	• Does the message use good sources? Are the sources used honestly? Are they documented?	

ethical or manipulative. Persuading and gaining compliance—activities at the heart of business and organizational life—can be done with respect or contempt for customers, co-workers, and subordinates.

In these days of instant communication, you, like the organization in which you work, always must act in an ethical manner. Consequences for not doing so are becoming more common as disgruntled colleagues and employees now have ample means for whistle-blowing.

There are also positive reasons—moral and business—for ethical behavior. As the Ethics Resource Center notes, customers and employees are attracted to ethical businesses. Rosabeth Moss Kanter, a professor at Harvard Business School, argues in her book *SuperCorp: How Vanguard Companies Create Innovation, Profits, Growth, and Social Good* that companies desiring to do good have a competitive advantage. In fact, a benevolent viewpoint provides a wider view of society and thus awareness of new opportunities for growth and innovation by solving the problems of unmet needs.

Many religions and philosophers have offered advice on how to be ethical. Some of the more familiar advice are the Golden Rule (do unto others as you would have them do unto you) and the utilitarian principle that an action should produce the greatest happiness for the greatest number of people. Business leaders also have given advice. For example, Tony Hsieh, the founder and CEO of Zappos, offer this useful ethics guideline in his book *Delivering Happiness: A Path to Profits, Passion, and Purpose*:

> As a guiding principle in life for anything I do, I try to ask myself, *What would happen if everyone in the world acted in the same way? What would the world look like? What would the net effect be on the overall happiness in the world?* [Hsieh's italics]
>
> This thought experiment has been useful to me when thinking about whether to share how we do things at Zappos, or whether to get upset at the waitress who accidentally got my order wrong, or whether to hold the door open for a stranger who's a slightly inconvenient distance away.

Corporate Culture

LO 1-8

Another strong influence on the business environment is corporate culture (see Chapter 2 for ways to analyze corporate culture). Corporate cultures vary widely. They range from formal—with individual offices, jackets, and hierarchical lines of command—to informal—with open office space, casual attire, and individually empowered workers. Characteristics of popular corporate cultures include flexible work arrangements, profit sharing, information sharing, good training, health insurance, and wellness programs.

Both large and small companies get positive publicity for their corporate cultures.

- Google is known for company gyms, well-stocked snack rooms, restaurants, and casual work attire.

- Ogilvy & Mather's Canton, China, office has a carnival theme to remind employees of the company's mission to "stay fresh." The décor includes a full-size carousel, carousel horses throughout the office, circus lights, and a fake Ferris wheel, whose carriages serve as small meeting rooms.[38]

- Dealer.com offers subsidized meals at its café, with organic and locally grown food, wellness seminars on exercise and stress management, chair massages, bike rentals, tennis and basketball courts, fitness center, and half-price ski passes. The company supports its sports teams, including softball, volleyball, soccer, bowling, and dragon-boat racing.[39]

Some employees use exercise balls as desk chairs. The balls require employees to use core muscles to maintain posture. Employees say they are also fun because they can bounce.

©Seth Joel/Getty Images

Two companies in the same field may have very different cultures. When Procter & Gamble bought Gillette, the company expected a smooth marriage between the world's number-one toothbrush, Oral-B, and the world's number-two toothpaste, Crest. But cultural differences caused problems. Gillette employees found P&G's culture rigid, its decision making slow. Gillette employees also had to learn P&G's famous acronyms, such as CIB (consumer is boss) and FMOT (first moment of truth, when consumers notice the product). P&G people sent memos; Gillette people called meetings.[40]

Wise companies also use effective corporate cultures to retain hourly workers. Joie de Vivre Hospitality has a turnover rate that is half the industry average. The CEO attributes the low rate to a corporate culture that listens to employees, enacts some of their suggestions, and tries to make work fun. In addition to awards, the company offers free classes on subjects such as English as a second language and sponsors parties, annual retreats, and regularly scheduled dinners.[41]

How to Solve Business Communication Problems

LO 1-9

When you're faced with a business communication problem, you need to develop a solution that will both solve the organization's problem and meet the psychological needs of the people involved. The strategies in this section will help you solve the problems in this book. Almost all of these strategies also can be applied to problems you encounter on the job. Use this process to create good messages.

- Gather knowledge and brainstorm solutions.

- Answer the five questions for analysis in Figure 1.6.

- Organize your information to fit your audiences, your purposes, and the context.

- Make your document visually inviting.

- Revise your draft to create a friendly, businesslike, positive style.

- Edit your draft for standard spelling, punctuation, and grammar; double-check names and numbers.

- Use the response you get to plan future messages.

Gather Knowledge and Brainstorm Solutions.

Problem solving usually starts by gathering knowledge. What are the facts? What can you infer from the information you're given? What additional information might be helpful? Where could you get it? What emotional complexities are involved? This information will usually start to suggest some solutions, but the first solution you think of may not be best. Develop several. Then evaluate them in terms of your audience and purposes. You will learn more about gathering knowledge in Chapter 15 and more about brainstorming in Chapter 8.

Answer the Five Questions for Analysis.

The five questions in Figure 1.6 help you analyze your audience(s), purpose(s), and the organizational context.

1. Who Is (Are) Your Audience(s)?   What audience characteristics are relevant for this particular message? If you are writing or speaking to more than one person, how do the people in your audience differ? How much does your audience know about your topic? How will they respond to your message? What objections might they have?

Some characteristics of your audience will be irrelevant; focus on ones that matter *for this message.* Whenever you address several people or a group, try to identify the economic, cultural, or situational differences that may affect how various subgroups may respond to what you have to say. For a more complete audience analysis, see the questions in Chapter 2.

Figure 1.6	Questions for Analysis
1. Who is (are) your audience(s)?	
2. What are your purposes in communicating?	
3. What information must your message include?	
4. How can you build support for your position? What reasons or benefits will your audience find convincing?	
5. What aspects of the total situation may be relevant?	

2. What Are Your Purposes in Communicating?   What must this message do to meet the organization's needs? What must it do to meet your own needs? What do you want your audience to do? To think or feel? List all your purposes, major and minor.

Even in a simple message, you may have several related purposes: to announce a new policy; to make the audience aware of the policy's provisions and requirements; and to have them feel that the policy is a good one, that the organization cares about its employees, and that you are a competent communicator and manager.

3. What Information Must Your Message Include?   Make a list of the points that must be included; check your draft to make sure you include them all. To include information without emphasizing it, put it in the middle of a paragraph or document and present it as briefly as possible.

4. How Can You Build Support for Your Position? What Reasons or Benefits Will Your Audience Find Convincing?   Brainstorm to develop reasons for your decision, the logic behind your argument, and possible benefits to the audience if they do as you ask. Reasons and audience benefits do not have to be monetary. Making the audience's job easier or more pleasant is a good benefit. In an informative or persuasive message, identify multiple audience benefits. In your message, use those that you can develop most easily and effectively.

Be sure the benefits are adapted to your audience. Many people do not identify closely with their organizations; the fact that the organization benefits from a policy will help the individual only if the saving or profit is passed directly on to the employees. Instead, savings and profits often are eaten up by returns to stockholders, bonuses to executives, and investments in plants and equipment or in research and development.

5. What Aspects of the Total Situation May Be Relevant?   Should you consider the economy? The time of year? Morale in the organization? Any special circumstances? The organization may be prosperous or going through hard times; it may have just been reorganized or may be stable. All these different situations will affect what you say and how you say it.

Think about the news, the economy, the weather. Think about the general business and regulatory climate, especially as it affects the organization specified in the problem. Use the real world as much as possible. Think about interest rates, business conditions, and the economy. Is the industry doing well? Is the government agency enjoying general support? Think about the time of year. If it's fall when you write, is your business in a seasonal slowdown after a busy summer? Gearing up for the Christmas shopping rush? Or going along at a steady pace unaffected by seasons?

To answer these questions, draw on your experience, your courses, and your common sense. Read the *Wall Street Journal* or look at a company's website. Sometimes you even may want to phone a local businessperson to get information.

Organize Your Information to Fit Your Audiences, Your Purposes, and the Situation.

You'll learn different psychological patterns of organization in Chapters 8, 9, and 10. For now, remember these three basic principles:

- Put good news first.

- In general, put the main point or question first. In the subject line or first paragraph, make it clear that you're writing about something that is important to the reader.

- Disregard the above point and approach the subject indirectly when you must persuade a reluctant audience.

Make Your Document Visually Inviting.

A well-designed document is easier to read and builds goodwill. To make a document visually attractive:

- Use subject lines to orient the reader quickly.
- Use headings to group related ideas.
- Use lists and indented sections to emphasize subpoints and examples.
- Number points that must be followed in sequence.
- Use short paragraphs—usually eight typed lines or fewer.

If you plan these design elements before you begin composing, you'll save time and the final document will probably be better.

The best medium for a document depends on how it will be used. For example, a document that will be updated frequently may need to be on a website so the reader easily can obtain the most current information. Chapters 5 and 13 will provide more information on the design of documents and visuals.

Revise Your Draft to Create a Friendly, Businesslike, Positive Style.

In addition to being an organizational member or a consumer, your audience has feelings just as you do. Communication that keeps the audience in mind uses **you-attitude** (see Chapter 3). Read your message as if you were in your audience's shoes. How would you feel if *you* received it?

Good business and administrative communication is both friendly and businesslike. If you're too stiff, you put extra distance between your audience and yourself. If you try to be too chummy, you'll sound unprofessional. When you communicate with strangers, use simple, everyday words and make your message as personal and friendly as possible. When you write to friends, remember that your message may be read by people you've never even heard of: avoid slang, clichés, and "in" jokes.

Sometimes you must mention limitations, drawbacks, or other negative elements, but don't dwell on them. People will respond better to you and your organization if you seem confident. Expect success, not failure. If you don't believe that what you're writing about is a good idea, why should they?

You emphasize the positive when you

- Put positive information first, give it more space or time, or set it off visually in an indented list.
- Eliminate negative words whenever possible.
- Focus on what is possible, not what is impossible.

Edit Your Draft for Standard English; Double-Check Names and Numbers.

Businesspeople care about correctness in spelling, grammar, and punctuation. If your grasp of mechanics is fuzzy, if standard English is not your native dialect, or if English is not your native language, you'll need to memorize rules and perhaps find a good book or a tutor to help you. Even software spelling and grammar checkers require the writer to make decisions. If you know how to write correctly but rarely take the time to do so, now is the time to begin to edit and proofread to eliminate careless errors. Correctness in usage, punctuation, and grammar is covered in Appendix B.

Always proofread your document before you send it out. Double-check the reader's name, any numbers, and the first and last paragraphs. Chapter 5 will provide more tips on revising and editing communication.

Use the Response You Get to Plan Future Messages.

Evaluate the **feedback,** or response, you get. The real test of any message is "Did you get what you wanted, when you wanted it?" If the answer is *no,* then the message has failed—even if the grammar is perfect, the words elegant, the approach creative, the document stunningly attractive. If the message fails, you need to find out why.

Analyze your successes, too. You want to know *why* your message worked. There has to be a reason, and if you can find what it is, you'll be more successful more often.

Summary by Learning Objectives

LO 1-1   **What the benefits of good communication are.**

Communication helps organizations and the people in them achieve their goals. People put things in writing to create a record, to convey complex data, to make things convenient for the reader, to save money, and to convey their own messages more effectively.

LO 1-2   **Why you need to be able to communicate well.**

- The three basic purposes of business and administrative communication are to inform, to request or persuade, and to build goodwill. Most messages have more than one purpose.

- The ability to write and speak well becomes increasingly important as you rise in an organization.

LO 1-3   **What the costs of communication are.**

Common communication costs include writing time, document cycling, printing, mailing, and electronic storage of copies.

LO 1-4   **What the costs of poor communication are.**

Poor writing wastes time, wastes effort, and jeopardizes goodwill.

LO 1-5   **What the basic criteria for effective messages are.**

Good business and administrative writing meets five basic criteria: it's clear, complete, and correct; it saves the reader's time; and it builds goodwill.

LO 1-6   **What role conventions play in business communication.**

Common business communications have conventions, as do organizations. Business communicators need to know how to adjust conventions to fit a particular audience, context, and purpose.

LO 1-7   **Why ethics are so important in business communication.**

The economic news continues to create concern over lapses in business ethics. On the other hand, positive ethical efforts also are increasing.

LO 1-8   **How corporate culture impacts the business environment.**

Corporate cultures range from informal to formal and impact such widely diverse areas as worker performance and sales.

LO 1-9   **How to solve business communication problems.**

- To evaluate a specific document, we must know the interactions among the writer, the reader(s), the purposes of the message, and the context. No single set of words will work for all readers in all situations.

- To understand business communication situations, ask the following questions:
  - What's at stake—to whom?
  - Should you send a message?
  - What channel should you use?
  - What should you say?
  - How should you say it?

- The following process helps create effective messages:
  - Gather knowledge and brainstorm solutions.
  - Answer the analysis questions in Figure 1.6.
  - Organize your information to fit your audiences, your purposes, and the context.
  - Make your document visually inviting.
  - Revise your draft to create a friendly, businesslike, positive style.
  - Edit your draft for standard English; double-check names and numbers.
  - Use the response you get to plan future messages.

Exercises and Cases

1.1   Reviewing the Chapter

1. Why do businesses need to be able to communicate well? (LO 1-1)
2. Why do you need to be able to communicate well? (LO 1-1)
3. What are some flawed assumptions about workplace communication? What is the reality for each myth? (LO 1-2)
4. What are the costs of communication? (LO 1-3)
5. What are the costs of poor communication? (LO 1-4)
6. What are the basic criteria for effective messages? (LO 1-5)
7. What role do conventions play in business communication? (LO 1-6)

8. What are some positive ethical efforts that are getting attention? (LO 1-7)
9. What are some ethical components of communication? (LO 1-7)
10. What are some elements of corporate culture? How do they affect business? (LO 1-8)
11. What are the components of a good problem-solving method for business communication opportunities? (LO 1-9)

1.2   Assessing Your Punctuation and Grammar Skills

To help you see where you need to improve in grammar and punctuation, take the Diagnostic Test, B.1, Appendix B.

1.3   Messages for Discussion I—Asking for a Class

The following are emails from various students to Dr. Violet Sands, who is a professor in the English Department. These students are wondering if Dr. Sands would let them register for her already-full class (English 320: Business Communication).

Each email shows a different way a student could make a request of Dr. Sands. How well does each message meet the needs of the reader and the writer? Is the message clear, complete, and correct?

1.
Hi Violet,

My name is Jake and I was wondering if you had any extra seats in your English 320 class. See, I'm a senior and I really need to take your class so I can graduate. I don't know what else to do. I didn't take it last year cuz I really didn't want to.

I'm desperate. Help me out.

Jake

2.
Hello Sands,

I'm sorry to bother you, but I really, really need to get into your English 320 class. My advisor totally screwed up my schedule and I didn't know I needed to take this class. It's so weird because I shouldn't have to take this class anyway, but whatever. So, if you could just add me into your class, that would be great.

Thanks,

Ally

3.
Dr. Sands,

Good morning. I hate to email you right before the semester begins, but I have a request. When I tried to register for your Eng 320 course, the website stated the course was full. I was wondering if I could possibly be put on a list to add the course just in case someone drops it? I am very interested in this course and would love to take it this semester if at all possible.

Thank you so much for your time,

Christine

4.

Dear Dr. Sands,

Do u have anymore seats open in your class? I think its 302 or 320 or something like that. Anyways, it would be cool if you would let me into the class. Sorry for emailing right at the last minute, but I didn't know what else to do.

You are the best,

Andrew

1.4   Messages for Discussion II—Responding to Rumors

The Acme Corporation has been planning to acquire Best Products, and Acme employees are worried about how the acquisition will affect them. Ed Zeplin, Acme's human resource manager, has been visiting the Acme chat sites and sees a dramatic rise in the number of messages spreading rumors about layoffs. Most of the rumors are false.

The following messages are possible responses that Ed can post to the chat sites. How well does each message meet the needs of the reader, the writer, and the organization? Is the message clear, complete, and correct? Does it save the reader's time? Does it build goodwill?

1.

It Will Be Great!

Author: L. Ed Zeplin, HR

Date: Tuesday, May 23

I am happy to tell you that the HR news is good. Two months ago, the CEO told me about the merger, and I have been preparing a human resource plan ever since.

I want you to know about this because morale has been bad, and it shouldn't be. You really should wait for the official announcements, and you'll see that the staffing needs will remain strong. My department has been under a lot of pressure, but if you'll be patient, we'll explain everything—the staffing, the compensation.

Our plan should be ready by Monday, and then if you have any questions, just contact your HR rep.

2.

HR Staffing

Author: HR Boss

Date: Tuesday, May 23

The rumors are false. Just ask anyone in HR. There will be no layoffs.

3.

Don't Believe the Rumors

Author: lezeplin@acme.com

Date: Tuesday, May 23

Acme has 475 employees, and Best Products has 132 employees. Our human resource plan for next year calls for 625 employees. If you do the math, you can see that there will be no layoffs. Rather, we will be hiring 18 employees. Of course, as we consolidate operations with Best, there will be some redeployments. However, our plan indicates that we will be able to retain our current staff. All employees are valued at Acme, as our current benefits package testifies.

Our HR plan is based on the best analytic techniques and a business forecast by a top consulting firm. If you're an employee, you should review our business plan, at the Our Goals page on Acme's intranet. Everyone should read Acme's mission statement on our home page, www.acme.com/homepage.html.

4.   Layoff Rumors Do Acme a Disservice

Author: Zeplin in HR

Date: Tuesday, 23 May

If you come here to get your company information, you aren't getting the straight story. The people posting to this discussion board are spreading false rumors, not the truth. If you want to know the truth about Acme, ask the people who have access to the information.

As HR manager, I can assure you we won't be laying off employees after the merger with Best Products. I'm the one who approves the staffing plan, so I should know. If people would ask me, instead of reading the negative, whining lies at this site, they would know the facts, too.

If people really cared about job security, they would be working and exceeding their goals, rather than wasting their time in rumor-mongering on message boards. Hard work: that's the key to success!

5.   The True Story about Layoffs

Author: lezeplin@acme.com

Date: Tuesday, 23 May

Whenever there is a merger or acquisition, rumors fly. It's human nature to turn to rumors when a situation seems uncertain. The case of Acme acquiring Best Products is no exception, so I'm not surprised to see rumors about layoffs posted on this message board.

Have no fear! I am working closely with our CEO and with the CEO and human resource manager at Best Products, and we all agree that our current staff is a valuable asset to Acme, to Best, and to our combined companies in the future. We have no plans to lay off any of our valued people. I will continue monitoring this message board and will post messages as I am able to disclose more details about our staffing plans. In the meantime, employees should watch for official information in the company newsletter and on our intranet.

We care about our people! If employees ever have questions about our plans and policies, they should contact me directly.

L. Ed Zeplin, HR Manager

1.5   Discussing Communication Barriers

With a small group, discuss some of the communication barriers you have witnessed in the workplace or classroom. What confuses audiences? What upsets them? What creates ill will? What causes loss of interest? Try to pinpoint exactly how the communication broke down.

1.6   Identifying Poor Communicators

Almost everyone has come in contact with someone who is a poor communicator. With a small group, discuss some of your experiences with poor communicators either in the workplace or in the classroom. Why was the communicator ineffective? What would have made communication clearer? After your discussion, develop a list of poor communication traits and what can be done to overcome them.

1.7   Identifying Changing Conventions

This chapter talks about the need to be aware of conventions and how they shift with time. What are some changing classroom communication conventions you have observed in your classes? What are some changing communication conventions you have observed at your workplace, or those of your family and friends? With a small group, discuss your examples.

1.8   Understanding the Role of Communication in Your Organization

Interview your work supervisor to learn about the kinds and purposes of communication in your organization. Your questions could include the following:

- What kinds of communication (e.g., emails, presentations) are most important in this organization?
- What communications do you create? Are they designed to inform, to persuade, to build goodwill—or to do a combination?
- What communications do you receive? Are they designed to inform, to persuade, to build goodwill—or to do a combination?
- Who are your most important audiences within the organization?

- Who are your most important external audiences?
- What are the challenges of communicating in this organization?
- What kinds of documents and presentations does the organization prefer?

As your instructor directs,

a. Share your results with a small group of students.
b. Present your results in an email to your instructor.
c. Join with a group of students to make a group presentation to the class.
d. Post your results online to the class.

1.9   Protecting Privacy Online

As companies demand ever more accurate audiences to whom they can pitch their products and services, the debate over online tracking versus privacy continues. For example, e-books allow sellers to track not only which books you buy, but how often you open them, how many hours you spend reading them, how far you get in them, and what you underline in them.[42]

1. Working in small groups, discuss some of the challenges you see to protecting your privacy on the Internet.

   - Should companies be allowed to track your online activity? Is it OK if they notify you they are tracking you? Do you like targeted placement ads, similar to Google's recommendations for you? Where do you find a balance between allowing Internet sites to use your information to provide better service and protecting your privacy?
   - Are employers justified in monitoring employees' email, Twitter, and Internet usage on company machines?

   - Are employers justified in monitoring employees' Facebook accounts? Do you think it is fair when employees get fired for comments they post on their Facebook site?
   - What do you think of companies such as Google tracking searches to produce sites like Google Flu Trends, which shows where people are getting sick during flu season?

2. The Federal Trade Commission is considering a "Do Not Track" option. Like the Do Not Call Registry, it would offer consumers a way to avoid some electronic marketing. See http://www.ftc.gov/opa/reporter/privacy/donottrack.shtml for more information. If such an option becomes available, would you use it? Suppose that big websites such as Google or Facebook started dropping Do Not Track customers. How would that action influence your opinion? Write an email to your instructor explaining your decision.

Chapter 1   Succeeding in Business Communication   25

1.10   Making Ethical Choices

Indicate whether you consider each of the following actions ethical, unethical, or a gray area. Which of the actions would you do? Which would you feel uncomfortable doing? Which would you refuse to do?

Discuss your answers with a small group of classmates. In what ways did knowing you would share with a group change your answers?

1. Taking home office supplies (e.g., pens, markers, calculators, etc.) for personal use.
2. Inflating your evaluation of a subordinate because you know that only people ranked *excellent* will get pay raises.
3. Updating your Facebook page and visiting the pages of friends during business hours.

4. Writing a feasibility report about a new product and de-emphasizing test results that show it could cause cancer.
5. Designing an ad campaign for a cigarette brand.
6. Working as an accountant for a company that makes or advertises cigarettes.
7. Telling a job candidate that the company "usually" grants cost-of-living raises every six months, even though you know that the company is losing money and plans to cancel cost-of-living raises for the next year.
8. Laughing at the racist or sexist jokes a client makes, even though you find them offensive.

1.11   Analyzing Business Ethics

New Oriental Education & Technology Group offers Chinese students intensive courses to prepare for SAT, GRE, and TOEFL exams. The object of the courses is to enable the students to achieve scores that will get them into American colleges and universities. The courses provide traditional prep help, such as cramming vocabulary words, but they also offer more controversial techniques.

- The courses avail themselves of websites where students download the test questions they remember immediately after the exam. Because the tests do recycle some questions to ensure score consistency over time, the courses can prep students for actual exam questions.
- They provide tricks (e.g., females in the test passages are always smarter than males) that help students choose correct answers just by looking at the choices, without understanding the passages.
- Because many of the students are good at math, they recommend that five minutes into the math section, their students should flip back to the reading section and finish it. Flipping is prohibited, but this timing helps students

escape the attention of the proctors, who look for it at the beginning and end of each test section.
- They help students prepare essays and speeches on topics—such as biographies of famous Americans—that can be memorized and adapted to many situations, thus avoiding extemporaneous performances.

The upside of these efforts is that many of the students do fulfill dreams of getting into American schools. The downside is that many of these same students have such poor English skills that they cannot understand the lectures or participate in class discussions. Nor can they write class papers without help. Unfortunately, they score so well that they even sometimes test out of the transitional programs many schools have to help students with shaky English skills.[43]

1. Is New Oriental an ethical business?
2. What are New Oriental's effects on its students?
3. Why do American schools accept these students?
4. What could be done to make the situation more ethical?

1.12   Introducing Yourself to Your Collaborative Writing Group

Write an email (about a single-spaced page if printed) introducing yourself to the other students in your collaborative writing group. (See Appendix A for examples of email format.) Include the following topics:

Background: What is your major? What special areas of knowledge do you have? What have you done in terms of school, extracurricular activities, jobs, and family life?

Previous experience in groups: What groups have you worked in before? Are you usually a leader, a follower, or a bit of both? Are you interested in a quality product? In maintaining harmony in the group? In working efficiently? What do you like most about working in groups? What do you like least?

Work and composing style: Do you like to talk out ideas while they're in a rough stage or work them out on paper before you discuss them? Would you rather have a complete outline before you start writing or just a general idea? Do you want to have a detailed schedule of everything that

has to be done and who will do it, or would you rather "go with the flow"? Do you work best under pressure, or do you want to have assignments ready well before the due date?

Areas of expertise: What can you contribute to the group in terms of knowledge and skills? Are you good at brainstorming ideas? Researching? Designing charts? Writing? Editing? Word processing? Managing the flow of work? Maintaining group cohesion?

Goals for collaborative assignments: What do you hope to accomplish this term? Where does this course fit into your priorities?

Use appropriate headings and a conversational writing style; edit your final draft for mechanical and grammatical correctness. A good email will enable others in your group to see you as an individual. Use details to make your writing vivid and interesting. Remember that one of your purposes is to make your readers look forward to working with you!

Describing Your Writing Experiences and Goals

Write an email (about a single-spaced page if printed) to your instructor describing the experiences you've had writing and what you'd like to learn about writing during this course. (See Appendix A for examples of email format.)

Answer several of the following questions:

- What memories do you have of writing? What made writing fun or frightening in the past?

- What have you been taught about writing? List the topics, rules, and advice you remember.

- What kinds of writing have you done in school? How long have the papers been?

- How has your school writing been evaluated? Did the instructor mark or comment on mechanics and grammar? Style? Organization? Logic? Content? Audience analysis and adaptation? Have you gotten extended comments on your papers? Have instructors in different classes had the same standards, or have you changed aspects of your writing for different classes?

- What voluntary writing have you done—journals, poems, stories, essays? Has this writing been just for you or has some of it been shared or published?

- Have you ever written on a job or in a student or volunteer organization? Have you ever edited other people's writing? What have these experiences led you to think about real-world writing?

- What do you see as your current strengths and weaknesses in writing skills? What skills do you think you'll need in the future? What kinds of writing do you expect to do after you graduate?

Use appropriate headings and a conversational writing style; edit your final draft for mechanical and grammatical correctness.

Notes

1. U.S. Postal Service, "Postal Facts 2013," https://about.usps.com/who-we-are/postal-facts/welcome.htm#H2.

2. Cathy Davidson, "Dividing Attention Deliberately," *Harvard Business Review* 90, no. 1–2 (January–February 2012): 142.

3. Kenneth Burke, "How Many Texts Do People Send Every Day?," *Text Request,* May 18, 2016, https://www.textrequest.com/blog/many-texts-people-send-per-day.

4. Statista: The Statistics Portal, "Number of Monthly Active Twitter Users Worldwide from 1st Quarter 2010 to 3rd Quarter 2017 (in millions)," accessed January 5, 2018, https://www.statista.com/statistics/282087/number-of-monthly-active-twitter-users.

5. Eric Krell, "The Unintended Word," *HRMagazine* 51, no. 8 (2006): 52.

6. National Association of Colleges and Employers, "Top 10 Skills for Job Candidates," April 3, 2013, http://www.naceweb.org/Publications/Spotlight_Online/2013/0403/Top_10_Skills_for_Job_Candidates.aspx.

7. Alex Crippen, "Warren Buffett's $100,000 Offer and $500,000 Advice for Columbia Business School Students," *CNBC,* November 12, 2009, http://www.cnbc.com/id/33891448/Warren_Buffett_s_100_000_Offer_and_500_000_Advice_for_Columbia_Business_School_Students.

8. The National Commission on Writing for America's Families, Schools, and Colleges, "Writing: A Ticket to Work . . . or a Ticket Out: A Survey of Business Leaders," *College Board* (2004): 7–8.

9. Anne Fisher, "The High Cost of Living and Not Writing Well," *Fortune,* December 7, 1998, 244.

10. Jeffrey Gitomer, *Jeffrey Gitomer's Little Black Book of Connections: 6.5 Assets for Networking Your Way to Rich Relationships* (Austin, TX: Bard Press, 2006), 128–31.

11. Peter D. Hart Research Associate Inc., *How Should Colleges Assess and Improve Student Learning? Employers' Views on the Accountability Challenge: A Survey of Employers Conducted on Behalf of the Association of American Colleges and Universities* (Washington, DC: The Association of American Colleges and Universities, 2008), 3.

12. The Conference Board et al., *Are They Really Ready to Work? Employers' Perspectives on the Basic Knowledge and Applied Skills of New Entrants to the 21st Century U.S. Workforce,* accessed April 10, 2013, http://www.conference-board.org/pdf_free/BED-06-workforce.pdf.

13. Tom DeMint, "So You Want to Be Promoted," *Fire Engineering* 159, no. 7 (2006); Karen M. Kroll, "Mapping Your Career," *PM Network* 19, no. 11 (2005): 28; and Jeff Snyder, "Recruiter: What It Takes," *Security* 43, no. 11 (2006): 70.

14. Emily Brandon, "Social Security Statements Now Available Online," *USNews Money,* May 1, 2012, http://money.usnews.com/money/blogs/planning-to-retire/2012/05/01/social-security-statements-now-available-online.

15. David Hoyle, *ISO 9000 Quality Systems Handbook* (New York: Elsevier, 2006).

16. Xerox, *The Optimum Office: How to Achieve Immediate and Guaranteed Cost Savings via a Managed Print Service,* April 2009, http://www.xerox.com/downloads/gbr/en/x/XGS_Optimum_Office_en.pdf.

17. https://www.epa.gov/sites/production/files/documents/paper_usage.pdf.

18. Pui-Wing Tam, "Cutting Files Down to Size: New Approaches Tackle Surplus of Data," *Wall Street Journal,* May 8, 2007, B4.

19. *A Failure of Initiative: Final Report of the Select Bipartisan Committee to Investigate the Preparation for and Response to Hurricane Katrina,* 109th Cong., 2d sess. (Washington, DC, February 15, 2006), http://www.gpoaccess.gov/katrinareport/mainreport.pdf.

20. Peter Sanders, "Boeing Has New Delay for Dreamliner," *Wall Street Journal,* August 28, 2010, B6.

21. Charles Riley and Emily Jane Fox, "GlaxoSmithKline in $3 Billion Fraud Settlement," *CNNMoney.com,* July 2, 2012, http://money.cnn.com/2012/07/02/news/companies/GlaxoSmithKline-settlement/index.htm.

22. Selina Williams, "For BP, the Cleanup Isn't Entirely Over," *Wall Street Journal,* February 4, 2013, B2.

23. NASA MCO Mission Failure Mishap Investigation Board, *Mars Climate Orbiter Mishap Investigation Board Phase I Report,* November 10, 1999, ftp://ftp.hq.nasa.gov/pub/pao/reports/1999/MCO_report.pdf.

24. Olivia Smith, "Papa John's Faces $250 Million Spam Lawsuit," *CNNMoney,* November 13, 2012, http://money.cnn.com/2012/11/13/technology/mobile/papa-johns/index.html?iid=obinsite.

25. Matthias Rieker, Andrew R. Johnson, and Alan Zibel, "Capital One Dealt Fine for Pitch to Customers," *Wall Street Journal,* July 19, 2012, C1.

26. Stephen Baker, "A Painful Lesson: Email Is Forever," *BusinessWeek,* March 21, 2005, 36; Gary McWilliams, "Wal-Mart Details Roehm Firing," *Wall Street Journal,* March 21, 2007, B11; Peter Waldman and Don Clark, "California Charges Dunn, 4 Others in H-P Scandal; Action Sends Strong Message to Business about Privacy; Precedents for the Web Age?," *Wall Street Journal,* October 5, 2006, A1; and "Will 'Love Factor' Help Make S. C.'s Sanford More Forgivable?," *Des Moines Register,* June 29, 2009, 12A.

27. Elizabeth A. McCord, "The Business Writer, the Law, and Routine Business Communication: A Legal and Rhetorical Analysis," *Journal of Business and Technical Communication* 5, no. 3 (1991): 173–99.

28. James O'Toole, "New York Sues Credit Suisse in Latest Mortgage Lawsuit," *CNNMoney,* November 20, 2012, http://money.cnn.com/2012/11/20/investing/credit-suisse-new-york/index.html?eref=mrss_igoogle_business.

29. Charles Riley and Emily Jane Fox, "GlaxoSmithKline in $3 Billion Fraud Settlement," *CNNMoney,* July 2, 2012, http://money.cnn.com/2012/07/02/news/companies/GlaxoSmithKline-settlement/index.htm; and Peter Loftus and Jon Kamp, "Glaxo to Pay $750 Million in Pact; Whistleblower Due Big Payment," *Wall Street Journal,* November 27, 2010, B3.

30. Joe Palazzolo, "FCPA Inc.: The Business of Bribery," *Wall Street Journal,* October 2, 2012, B1.

31. Mary Williams Walsh and Ron Nixon, "S.&P. Emails on Mortgage Crisis Show Alarm and Gallows Humor," *DealBook,* February 5, 2013, http://dealbook.nytimes.com/2013/02/05/case-details-internal-tension-at-s-p-amid-subprime-problems/.

32. http://www.bbc.com/news/business-34324772.

33. http://www.npr.org/sections/thetwo-way/2016/10/25/499301280/judge-approves-vws-14-7-billion-settlement-over-emissions-scandal.

34. Ethics Resource Center, *2011 National Business Ethics Survey,* 12, 39, accessed April 11, 2013, http://www.ethics.org/nbes/files/FinalNBES-web.pdf.

35. Mary C. Gentile, "Keeping Your Colleagues Honest," *Harvard Business Review* 88, no. 2 (February 2010): 114–15.

36. "United Nations Global Compact Participants," *United Nations Global Compact,* October 23, 2012, http://www.unglobalcompact.org/ParticipantsAndStakeholders/index.html.

37. "About Us," *Clinton Global Initiative,* accessed April 12, 2013, http://www.clintonglobalinitiative.org/aboutus/default.asp.

38. M. Rose, "Three-Ring Ad Circus: Ogilvy & Mather's Surreal Canton Fun House," *Bloomberg Businessweek,* October 8, 2012, 88–89.

39. Leigh Buchanan, "Learning from the Best: Smart Strategies from the Top Small Company Workplaces," *Inc.,* June 2010, 92.

40. Ellen Byron, "Merger Challenge: Unite Toothbrush, Toothpaste: P&G and Gillette Find Creating Synergy Can Be Harder Than It Looks," *Wall Street Journal,* April 24, 2007, A1.

41. Phred Dvorak, "Hotelier Finds Happiness Keeps Staff Checked In," *Wall Street Journal,* December 17, 2007, B3.

42. Andrew McAfee and Erik Brynjolfsson, "Big Data: The Management Revolution," *Harvard Business Review,* October 2012, 60–68.

43. Daniel Golden, "U.S. College Test Prep in China Is: [sic]" *Bloomberg Businessweek,* May 9, 2011, 58–63.

CHAPTER

2 Adapting Your Message to Your Audience

Chapter Outline

Identifying Your Audiences

Analyzing Your Audience

- Analyzing Individuals
- Analyzing Members of Groups
- Analyzing the Organizational Culture and the Discourse Community

Choosing Channels to Reach Your Audience

Using Audience Analysis to Adapt Your Message

1. How Will the Audience Initially React to the Message?
2. How Much Information Does the Audience Need?
3. What Obstacles Must You Overcome?
4. What Positive Aspects Can You Emphasize?
5. What Are the Audience's Expectations about the Appropriate Language, Content, and Organization of Messages?
6. How Will the Audience Use the Document?

Audience Analysis Works

Characteristics of Good Audience Benefits

1. Adapt Benefits to the Audience.
2. Stress Intrinsic as Well as Extrinsic Motivators.
3. Prove Benefits with Clear Logic and Explain Them in Adequate Detail.
4. Phrase Benefits in You-Attitude.

Identifying and Developing Audience Benefits

1. Identify the Need, Wants, and Feelings That May Motivate Your Audience.
2. Identify the Objective Features of Your Product or Policy That Could Meet the Needs You've Identified.
3. Show How the Audience Can Meet Their Needs with the Features of the Policy or Product.

Audience Benefits Work

Writing or Speaking to Multiple Audiences with Different Needs

Summary by Learning Objectives

©DrAfter123/Getty Images

NEWSWORTHY COMMUNICATION

Retweet Record for Free Nuggets

©mrwebhoney/shutterstock

Social media sites and applications offer a unique platform that allows organizations to interact directly with millennial audiences, the largest demographic of social media users. In the United States alone, 90% of 18- to 29-year-olds use social media.[1]

Organizations can respond to individual customer complaints or inquiries, and also promote their brands or products, through digital versions of traditional advertisements or by injecting humor and personality into otherwise faceless conglomerates. Specifically, the purposeful usage of humor in social media is directed at younger demographics, providing a new way for organizations to capture the attention of a notoriously difficult-to-reach audience.

In April 2017, teenager Carter Wilkerson tweeted at the fast-food chain Wendy's asking how many retweets he would need for a year of free chicken nuggets. Wendy's responded tongue-in-cheek with "18 million," and Wilkerson appealed to his fellow Twitter users and nugget lovers to help him meet his goal. He also sold t-shirts with "#NuggsforCarter" and pledged to donate the proceeds to the Dave Thomas Foundation for Adoption. While not reaching 18 million retweets, he did break the record for most retweets on Twitter with more than 3,470,000 retweets at the time. Wendy's publically acknowledged Carter's achievement by giving him the "nuggs" and donating $100,000 to the Dave Thomas Foundation for Adoption themselves.

Source: Laura Roman, "Quest for Free Chicken Nuggets Inspires Twitter's Most Retweeted Tweet," *NPR*, May 9 2017, http://www.npr.org/sections/thetwo-way/2017/05/09/527597422/quest-for-free-chicken-nuggets-inspires-twitters-most-retweeted-tweet.

Learning Objectives

After studying this chapter, you will know

LO 2-1 How to identify your audience.

LO 2-2 How to analyze different kinds of audiences.

LO 2-3 How to choose channels to reach your audience.

LO 2-4 How to adapt your message to your audience.

LO 2-5 How to characterize good audience benefits.

LO 2-6 How to create audience benefits.

LO 2-7 How to communicate with multiple audiences.

Knowing who you're talking to is fundamental to the success of any message. You need to identify your audiences, understand their motivations, and choose the most effective and appropriate channel or medium to send your message.

Identifying Your Audiences

LO 2-1

The first step in analyzing your audience is to decide who your audience is. Organizational messages have multiple audiences:

1. A **gatekeeper** has the power to stop your message instead of sending it on to other audiences. The gatekeeper therefore controls whether your message even gets to the primary audience. Sometimes the supervisor who assigns the message is the gatekeeper; sometimes the gatekeeper is higher in the organization. In some cases, gatekeepers may exist outside the organization.

2. The **primary audience** decides whether to accept your recommendations or act on the basis of your message. You must reach the primary audience to fulfill your purposes in any message.

3. The **secondary audience** may be asked to comment on your message or to implement your ideas after they've been approved. Secondary audiences also include lawyers who may use your message—perhaps years later—as evidence of your organization's culture and practices.

4. An **auxiliary audience** may encounter your message but will not have to interact with it. This audience includes the "read-only" people.

5. A **watchdog audience,** though it does not have the power to stop the message and will not act directly on it, has political, social, or economic power. The watchdog pays close attention to the transaction between you and the primary audience and may base future actions on its evaluation of your message.

As the following examples show, one person can be part of two audiences. Frequently, a supervisor is both the primary audience and the gatekeeper.

Dawn is an assistant account executive in an ad agency. Her boss asks her to write a proposal for a marketing plan for a new product the agency's client is introducing. Her *primary audience* is the executive committee of the client company, who will decide whether to adopt the plan. The *secondary audience* includes the marketing staff of the client company, who will be asked for comments on the plan, as well as the artists, writers, and media buyers who will carry out details of the plan if it is adopted. Her boss, who must approve the plan before it is submitted to the client, is the *gatekeeper.* Her office colleagues who read her plan are her *auxiliary audience.*

Joe works in the information technology department of a large financial institution. He must write an email explaining a major software change. His boss is the *gatekeeper;* the software users in various departments are the *primary audience.* The *secondary audience* includes the tech people who will be helping the primary audience install and adjust to the new software. The *auxiliary audience* includes department program assistants who forward the e-mail to appropriate people in each department. A *watchdog audience* is the board of directors.

Analyzing Your Audience

LO 2-2

The most important tools in audience analysis are common sense and empathy. **Empathy** is the ability to put yourself in someone else's shoes, to feel with that person. Use what you know about people and about organizations to predict likely responses. These questions from the online Connect chapter exercise are a great starting point:

These questions will help you analyze your audience:

1. How will the audience initially react to the message?
2. How much information does the audience need?
3. What obstacles must you overcome?
4. What positive aspects can you emphasize?
5. What are the audience's expectations about the appropriate language, content, and organization of messages?
6. How will the audience use the document?

Analyzing Individuals

When you write or speak to people in your own organization and in other organizations you work closely with, you may be able to analyze your audience as individuals. You already may know them, or probably can get additional information easily. You may learn that one manager may dislike phone calls, so you will know to write your request in an email. Another manager may have a reputation for denying requests made on a Friday, so you will know to get yours in earlier.

A useful schema for analyzing people is the **Myers-Briggs Type Indicator®**. This instrument uses four pairs of dichotomies to identify ways that people differ.[2] The Extraversion (the Myers-Briggs term)-Introversion dichotomy measures how individuals prefer to focus their attention and get energy. Extraverted types are energized by interacting with other people. Introverted types get their energy from within.

The other three dichotomies in Myers-Briggs® typology are Sensing-Intuition, Thinking-Feeling, and Judging-Perceiving. The Sensing-Intuition dichotomy measures the way an individual prefers to take in information. Sensing types gather information through their senses, preferring what is real and tangible. Intuitive types prefer to gather information by looking at the big picture, focusing on the relationships and connections between facts.

The Thinking-Feeling dichotomy measures the way an individual makes decisions. Thinking types prefer to use thinking in decision making to consider the logical consequences of a choice or action. Feeling types make decisions based on the impact to people, considering what is important to them and to others involved.

The Judging-Perceiving dichotomy measures how individuals orient themselves to the external world. Judging types like to live in a planned, orderly way, seeking closure. Perceiving types prefer to live in a flexible, spontaneous way, enjoying possibilities.

The descriptors on each of the scales' dichotomies represent a preference, just as we have a preference for using either our right or our left hand to write. If necessary, we can use the opposite style, but we have less practice in it and use it less easily.

You can find your own personality type by taking the Myers-Briggs Type Indicator® instrument at your college's counseling center or student services office. Some businesses administer the Myers-Briggs Type Indicator® instrument to all employees to assist with team building.

Analyzing Members of Groups

In many organizational situations, you'll analyze your audience not as individuals, but as members of a group. When creating your message, first determine the relationship between the audience and your organization, what separates them from the public: "taxpayers who must be notified that they owe more income tax," "customers who use our accounting services," or "employees with small children." Focus on what group members have in common. After determining the relationship between the audience and your organization, focus on what these audience members have in common.[3] Although generalizations won't be true for all members of the group, generalization is necessary when you must appeal to a large group of people with one message. In some cases, no research is necessary: It's easy to guess the attitudes of people who must be told they owe more taxes. In other cases, databases may yield useful information. In still other cases, you may want to do original research.

Demographic Characteristics Databases enable you to map demographic and psychographic profiles of customers or employees. **Demographic characteristics** are measurable features that can be counted objectively: age, sex, race, religion, education level, income, and so on.

Sometimes demographic information is irrelevant; sometimes it's important. Does education matter? The fact that the reader has a degree from Eastern State rather than from Harvard may not matter, but how much the reader knows about accounting may. Does literacy matter? Roughly 30 million, or 14%, of adults in the United States possess below basic reading skills.[4] Does family structure matter? Sometimes. Some hotels and resorts offer family packages that include babysitting, multiple bedrooms, and children's activities.

Age certainly matters. One aspect of age that gets much press is the differences between generations in the office. Many older people believe younger workers have a sense of entitlement, that they expect great opportunities and perks without working for them. On the other hand, many younger workers see their older colleagues as rigid. Figure 2.1 shows some of the frequently mentioned differences between baby boomers

Group membership sometimes gives clues about your audience.
©kali9/Getty

Figure 2.1	Some Generational Differences in the Office	
	Baby boomers	**Generation X and millennials**
Birth dates	1946–1964	1965 and on
Work ethic	Long hours in office	Flexible hours in office
	Respect corporate confidentiality	Apt to blog or tweet corporate negatives
	Long-term commitment to company	Expectation of multiple employers
Values	Hard work	Work/life balance
	Consistency	Flexibility
	Privacy	Sharing
	Hierarchy	Social equality, autonomy
	Clearly defined roles	Variety of challenges
	Confident in proven abilities	Overconfidence in abilities
	Serious about work	Want work to be fun
Preferred channels	Face-to-face, email	Texting, social networks
Motivators	Duty to company	What's in it for them; want important tasks
Communication style	Through channels and hierarchy; accept annual evaluation	Freely offer opinions, both laterally and upward; want great amounts of attention and praise; want faster feedback
Decorum	Follow basic business decorum	May need to be reminded about basic business decorum

Sources: "Millennials, Gen X and Baby Boomers: Who's Working at Your Company and What Do They Think about Ethics?" Ethics Resource Center, 2010, http://ethics.org/files/u5/Gen-Diff.pdf; and Jen Wieczner, "10 Things Millennials Won't Tell You," *Market Watch*, June 24, 2013, http://finance.yahoo.com/news/10-things-millennials-won-t-113327583.html?page=all.

and millennials. While awareness of generational differences may help in some communication situations, such lists are also a good place to attach mental warnings against stereotypes. Plenty of baby boomers also like frequent positive feedback and almost everyone likes a chance to make a difference.

For most companies, income is a major demographic characteristic. In 2011, Walmart quietly returned to its "everyday low prices" after experimenting with low-priced sale products balanced by slightly higher prices elsewhere. The new pricing had not appealed to Walmart's financially strapped customers. The chain also returned guns and fishing equipment to the shelves of many of its stores in an attempt to attract more male customers.[5]

Location is yet another major demographic characteristic. You can probably think of many differences among regional audiences or between urban and rural audiences in the United States. See Chapter 6 for more information on communicating across cultures.

Psychographic Characteristics   **Psychographic characteristics** are qualitative rather than quantitative: values, beliefs, goals, and lifestyles. Knowing what your audience finds important allows you to choose information and benefits that the audience will find persuasive.

Marketing companies are combining consumers' web surfing records with personal offline data from sources such as the Census Bureau, consumer research firms such as Nielsen, credit card and shopping histories, and real estate and motor vehicle records. The combined data allow marketers to reach narrowly defined audiences.

Analyzing the Organizational Culture and the Discourse Community

Be sensitive to the culture in which your audiences work and the discourse community of which they are a part. **Organizational culture** is a set of values, attitudes, and philosophies. An organization's culture is revealed verbally in the organization's myths, stories, and heroes, as well as in documents such as employee manuals. It is revealed nonverbally through means such as dress codes; behavior standards; or the allocation of space, money, and power. A **discourse community** is a group of people who share assumptions about what channels, formats, and styles to use for communication; what topics to discuss and how to discuss them; and what constitutes evidence.

In an organization that values equality and individualism, you can write directly to the CEO and address him or her as a colleague. In other companies, you'd be expected to follow a chain of command. Some organizations prize short messages; some expect long, thorough documents. Messages that are consistent with the organization's culture have a greater chance of succeeding.

You can begin to analyze an organization's culture by asking the following questions:

- Is the organization tall or flat? Are there many levels between the CEO and the lowest worker, or only a few?

- How do people get ahead? Are the organization's rewards based on seniority, education, being well-liked, saving money, or serving customers? Are rewards available only to a few top people or is everyone expected to succeed?

- Does the organization value diversity or homogeneity? Does it value independence and creativity or being a team player and following orders?

- What stories do people tell? Who are the organization's heroes and villains?

- How important are friendship and sociability? To what extent do workers agree on goals and how intently do they pursue them?

Some companies are beginning to accept visible body art and long hair in traditional workplace cultures.

©LWA-Dann Tardif/CORBIS/Getty Images

- How formal are behavior, language, and dress?

- What does the work space look like? Do employees work in offices, cubicles, or large rooms?

- What are the organization's goals? Making money? Serving customers and clients? Advancing knowledge? Contributing to the community?

To analyze an organization's discourse community, ask the following questions:

- What media, formats, and styles are preferred for communication?

- What do people talk about? What topics are not discussed?

- What kind of and how much evidence is needed to be convincing?

Choosing Channels to Reach Your Audience

LO 2-3

A communication **channel** is the means by which you convey your message. Communication channels vary in speed, accuracy of transmission, cost, number of messages carried, number of people reached, efficiency, and ability to promote goodwill.

Electronic channel usage is growing phenomenally every second. At the time of this writing, there are more than

- 3.7 billion Internet users worldwide.

- 1.25 billion websites.

- 185 billion emails sent today alone.[6]

Evolving channels can have enormous impacts on businesses. Online retailer Amazon has recently become a massive competitor to traditional brick-and-mortar retail and grocery stores. From easy ordering via the Amazon digital assistant Alexa, to same-day Prime deliveries in some areas or free two-day shipping, to plans for grocery stores without cashiers, Amazon is leading other retailers to find creative solutions to remain competitive and viable in a predominantly digital economy. Amazon's market share is larger than most brick-and-mortar retailers put together.[7]

Depending on the audience, your purposes, and the situation, one channel may be better than another. Marketers frequently use both the Internet and television because they believe the two channels do different things. The Internet excels at selling when customers know what they want, such as a book or airline ticket; television is good at getting people to want to buy something and then remembering to do so.[8] Procter & Gamble has a website, BeingGirl.com, where girls can share experiences and questions about feminine hygiene products. P&G says this channel is four times more effective, dollar for dollar, than television commercials.[9]

A written message makes it easier to

- Present extensive or complex data.

- Present many specific details.

- Minimize undesirable emotions.

- Track details and agreements.

Oral messages make it easier to

- Use emotion to help persuade the audience.
- Focus the audience's attention on specific points.
- Resolve conflicts and build consensus.
- Modify plans.
- Get immediate action or response.

Choosing the right channel can be tricky sometimes. As Hurricane Katrina approached the Gulf Coast, the National Hurricane Center found its electronic communications about the looming wallop were not enough; officials at the center then phoned Gulf Coast mayors and governors to hasten disaster preparations.[10]

Even in the office, you will have to decide if your message will be more effective as an email, text message, phone call, visit, or sticky note posted on a colleague's computer. In nonstandard situations, choosing a channel can be challenging.

- If you are the head of a small, nonprofit literacy agency that helps adults learn to read, how do you reach your clients? You cannot afford TV ads and they cannot read print channels such as flyers.
- If you are a safety officer for a manufacturer, how do you send out product recall notifications? How many people file the contact-information cards when they purchase an item?
- If you are the benefits manager in a large manufacturing plant, how will you get information about your new benefits plan out to the thousand people on the floor? They don't use computers at work and may not have computer access at home.

Businesses are becoming savvier about using the array of channels. Ad money has been moving out of print and TV channels and into online advertising, which topped $39.5 billion in 2012.[11]

Businesses use Facebook, Twitter, YouTube, and Flickr to highlight new products and services. Many companies have interactive websites and forums where customers can get product information and chat about products; Amazon is a prime example. Manufacturers give perks to bloggers to talk about their products. Police departments are posting pictures of wanted people on Pinterest. Nonprofits advertise events, connect with volunteers, and schedule volunteer service on their Facebook pages. And all that social network communication now can be mined by software that performs semantic analyses, providing feedback to advertisers about both products and audiences.

Even traditional paper channels are moving online. Publishers are making their travel books into e-books and cell phone apps. Magazines and newspapers are expanding from paper copies to include electronic copies as well as blogs, podcasts, and chat rooms as more people receive their news on mobile platforms and social networking sites. In fact, Warren Buffett warned the *Washington Post,* on whose board he served, that the paper-only model would no longer work.[12]

According to the Pew Research Center for the People & the Press, in the past 20 years, the percentage of Americans who regularly

- Watch local TV news has dropped from about 80% to 48%.
- Watch evening network news has dropped from 60% to 27%.
- Regularly read a daily newspaper has dropped from almost 60% to 38%.[13]

Prime-time television viewing in general is declining, as people turn to DVRs, streaming, and video on demand; prime-time ads also are losing some of their appeal for companies.[14]

Preferred channels reflect age categories. Americans 50 and older prefer traditional channels—television, radio, and print newspapers. Americans under 30 prefer digital sources. Comedy news shows such as *The Daily Show with Trevor Noah* attract younger audiences; cable talk shows, such as *Hannity,* attract viewers 65 and older.[15]

Some channels also reflect gender difference. Audiences for business publications such as the *Wall Street Journal, Economist,* and *Bloomberg Businessweek* are more than 70% male, while audiences for daytime talk shows such as Ellen DeGeneres's show and *The View* are more than 70% female.[16]

Creative uses of channels are appearing everywhere:

- Ads are appearing on subway tunnels, fire hydrants, grocery checkout conveyors, sidewalks, toilet stall doors, and cardboard shirt hangers used by cleaners.[17]

- Toy maker Mattel used Facebook, Twitter, and a series of eight webisodes to celebrate the 50th birthday of Ken, Barbie's boyfriend. The webisodes allowed Mattel to extend the audience to teenagers and adults who have an emotional tie with the toy and may be collectors.[18]

- CBS used 35 million eggs printed with show logos and related puns; they called the endeavor "egg-vertising."[19]

- The USA Network used 50,000 $1 bills bearing stickers for one of its miniseries.[20]

- Scientists are using computer games to enlist the help of nonscientists. EyeWire enlists players to map neural connections in the eye; Foldit enlists players to help solve the question of how proteins fold.[21]

- Vienna, Austria, raised money for the main public library with a phone sex hotline. Pay by the minute and you got to hear a famous Austrian actress reading passages from the library's collection of erotic fiction from the eighteenth through the twentieth centuries.[22]

Using Audience Analysis to Adapt Your Message

LO 2-4

Zeroing in on the right audience with the right message is frequently a formula for success. If you know your audience well and if you use words well, much of your audience analysis and adaptation will be unconscious. If you don't know your audience or if the message is very important, take the time to analyze your audience formally and to revise your message with your analysis in mind. Remember that audiences change, sometimes drastically, over time. Just think how much college students have changed since the 1950s and 1960s. The questions in Figure 2.2 will help guide a careful audience analysis.

Figure 2.2	Analyzing Your Audience

These questions will help you analyze your audience:

1. How will the audience initially react to the message?
2. How much information does the audience need?
3. What obstacles must you overcome?
4. What positive aspects can you emphasize?
5. What are the audience's expectations about the appropriate language, content, and organization of messages?
6. How will the audience use the document?

As you answer these questions for a specific audience, think about the organizational culture in which the person works. At every point, your audience's reaction is affected not only by his or her personal feelings and preferences but also by the political environment of the organization, the economy, and current events.

1. How Will the Audience Initially React to the Message?

a. **Will the audience see this message as important?** Audiences will read and act on messages they see as important to their own careers; they may ignore messages that seem unimportant to them.

   When the audience may see your message as unimportant, you need to

---

- Use a subject line or first paragraph that shows your reader this message is important and relevant.

- Make the action as easy as possible.

- Suggest a realistic deadline for action.

- Keep the message as short as possible.

---

b. **How will the fact that the message is from you affect the audience's reaction?** The audience's experience with you and your organization shapes the response to this new message. Someone who thinks well of you and your organization will be prepared to receive your message favorably; someone who thinks poorly of you and the organization will be quick to find fault with what you say and the way you say it.

   When your audience has negative feelings about your organization, your position, or you personally, you need to

---

- Make a special effort to avoid phrases that could seem condescending, arrogant, rude, hostile, or uncaring.

- Use positive emphasis (see Chapter 3) to counteract the natural tendency to sound defensive.

- Develop logic and benefits fully.

---

2. How Much Information Does the Audience Need?

a. **How much does the audience already know about this subject?** It's easy to overestimate the knowledge an audience has. People outside your own immediate unit may not really know what it is you do. Even people who once worked in your unit may have forgotten specific details now that their daily work is in management. People outside your organization won't know how *your* organization does things.

   When some of your information is new to the audience, you need to

---

- Make a special effort to be clear. Define terms, explain concepts, use examples, and avoid acronyms.

- Link new information to old information that the audience already knows.

- Use paragraphs and headings to break up new information into related chunks so that the information is easier to digest.

- Test a draft of your document with your reader or a subset of your intended audience to see whether the audience can understand and use what you've written.

---

b. **Does the audience's knowledge need to be updated or corrected?** Our personal experience guides our expectations and actions, but sometimes it needs to be corrected. If you're trying to change someone's understanding of something, you need to

- Acknowledge the audience's initial understanding early in the message.
- Use examples, statistics, or other evidence to show the need for the change, or to show that the audience's experience is not universal.
- Allow the audience to save face by suggesting that changed circumstances call for new attitudes or action.

c. **What aspects of the subject does the audience need to be aware of to appreciate your points?** When the audience must think of background or old information to appreciate your points, you can

- Preface information with "As you know" or "As you may remember" to avoid suggesting that you think the audience does not know what you're saying.
- Put old or obvious information in a subordinate clause: for example, "Because we have recently expanded delivery into Central America, we need to consider a change to heat-resistant packaging."

3. What Obstacles Must You Overcome?

a. **Is your audience opposed to what you have to say?** People who have already made up their minds are highly resistant to change. When the audience will oppose what you have to say, you need to

- Start your message with any areas of agreement or common ground that you share with your audience.
- Make a special effort to be clear and unambiguous. Points that might be clear to a neutral audience can be misinterpreted by someone opposed to the message.
- Make a special effort to avoid statements that will anger the audience.
- Limit your statement or request to the smallest possible area. If parts of your message could be delivered later, postpone them.
- Show that your solution is the best solution currently available, even though it isn't perfect.

b. **Will it be easy for the audience to do as you ask?** Everyone has a set of ideas and habits and a mental self-image. If we're asked to do something that violates any of those, we first have to be persuaded to change our attitudes or habits or self-image—a change we're reluctant to make.

When your request is time-consuming, complicated, or physically or psychologically difficult, you need to

- Make the action as easy as possible.
- Break down complex actions into a list, so the audience can check off each step as it is completed. This list also will help ensure complete responses.
- Show that what you ask is consistent with some aspect of what the audience believes.
- Show how the audience (not just you or your organization) will benefit when the action is completed.

4. What Positive Aspects Can You Emphasize?

a. **From the audience's point of view, what are the benefits of your message?** Benefits help persuade the audience that your ideas are good ones. Make the most of the good points inherent in the message you want to convey.

- Put good news first.
- Use audience benefits that go beyond the basic good news.

---

b. **What experiences, interests, goals, and values do you share with the audience?** A sense of solidarity with someone can be an even more powerful reason to agree than the content of the message itself. When everyone in your audience shares the same experiences, interests, goals, and values, you can

---

- Consider using a vivid anecdote to remind the audience of what you share. The details of the anecdote should be interesting or new; otherwise, you may seem to be lecturing the audience.
- Use a salutation and close that remind the audience of their membership in this formal or informal group.

---

5. What Are the Audience's Expectations about the Appropriate Language, Content, and Organization of Messages?

a. **What style of writing does the audience prefer?** Good writers adapt their style to suit the reader's preferences. A reader who sees contractions as too informal needs a different style from one who sees traditional business writing as too stuffy. As you write:

- Use what you know about your reader to choose a more or less formal, more or less friendly style.
- Use the reader's first name in the salutation only if both of you are comfortable with a first-name basis.

---

b. **Are there hot buttons or "red flag" words that may create an immediate negative response?** You don't have time to convince the audience that a term is broader or more neutral than his or her understanding. When you need agreement or approval, you should

---

- Avoid terms that carry emotional charges for many people: for example, *criminal, un-American, feminist, fundamentalist, liberal.*
- Use your previous experience with individuals to replace any terms that have particular negative meanings for them.

---

c. **How much detail does the audience want?** A message that does not give the audience the desired amount or kind of detail may fail. Sometimes you can ask your audience how much detail they want. When you write to people you do not know well, you can

- Provide all the detail needed to understand and act on your message.

- Group chunks of information under headings so that readers can go directly to the parts of the message they find most interesting and relevant.

- Be sure that a shorter-than-usual document covers the essential points; be sure that a longer-than-usual document is free from wordiness and repetition.

d. **Does the audience prefer a direct or indirect organization?** Individual personality or cultural background may lead someone to prefer a particular kind of structure. You'll be more effective if you use the structure and organization your audience prefers.

6. How Will the Audience Use the Document?

a. **Under what physical conditions will the audience use the document?** Reading a document in a quiet office calls for no special care. But suppose the audience will be reading your message on the train commuting home or on a ladder as he or she attempts to follow instructions. Then the physical preparation of the document can make it easier or harder to use.

When the reader will use your document outside an office:

- Use a lot of white space.

- Make the document small enough to hold in one hand.

- Number items so readers can find their place after an interruption.

b. **Will the audience use the document as a general reference? As a specific guide?** Understanding how your audience will use the document will enable you to choose the best pattern of organization and the best level of detail.

If the document will serve as a general reference:

- Use a specific subject line to aid in filing and retrieval. If the document is online, consider using several key words to make it easy to find the document in a database search program.

- Use headings within the document so that readers can skim it.

- Give the office as well as the person to contact so that the reader can get in touch with the appropriate person some time from now.

- Spell out details that may be obvious now but might be forgotten in a year.

If the document will be a detailed guide or contain instructions:

- Check to be sure that all the steps are in chronological order.

- Number steps so that readers can easily see which steps they've completed.

- Group steps into five to seven categories if there are many individual steps.

- Put any warnings at the beginning of the document; then repeat them just before the specific step to which they apply.

Audience Analysis Works

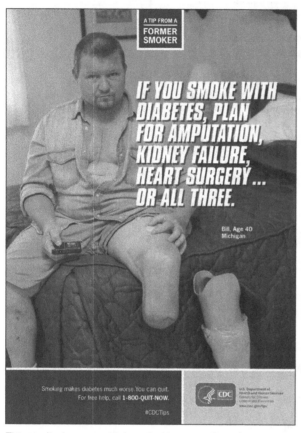

IF YOU SMOKE WITH DIABETES, PLAN FOR AMPUTATION, KIDNEY FAILURE, HEART SURGERY ... OR ALL THREE.

A TIP FROM A FORMER SMOKER

Bill, Age 40
Michigan

Smoking makes diabetes much worse. You can quit.
For free help, call **1-800-QUIT-NOW.**

#CDCTips

CDC

U.S. Department of Health and Human Services Centers for Disease Control and Prevention www.cdc.gov/tips

This medical message is targeted to a specific audience: smokers with diabetes.

Source: U.S. Department of Health and Human Services Centers for Disease Control and Prevention. www.cdc.gov/tips

Audience analysis is a powerful tool. Amazon.com tracks users' online histories to make suggestions on items they might like. PetFlow carved out a niche in the pet supply business by delivering pet food ordered online. The company's audience consists mostly of people who have grown tired of lugging home heavy bags of pet food.[23]

Nintendo believes that much of its success is extending its concept of audience. An important part of its audience is hard-core gamers, a very vocal group: they love to blog. But if Nintendo listened just to them, they would be the only audience Nintendo had. Instead, Nintendo extended its audience by creating the Wii, a new system that the hard-core gamers had not imagined and one that is collecting new users who never imagined owning a system.[24] With the introduction of Wii Fit, Nintendo expanded its audience to more women and more senior citizens.

Tesco PLC, Britain's largest retailer, signs up customers for its Clubcard. The card gives customers discounts, and it gives Tesco audience data. When Tesco added Asian herbs and ethnic foods in Indian and Pakistani neighborhoods, the data showed the products were also popular with affluent white customers, so Tesco expanded the rollout. When customers buy diapers the first time, they get coupons for usual baby products such as wipes and toys. They also get coupons for beer because the data show that new fathers buy more beer.[25]

Characteristics of Good Audience Benefits

LO 2-5

Use your analysis of your audience to create effective **audience benefits,** advantages that the audience gets by using your services, buying your products, following your policies, or adopting your ideas. In informative messages, benefits give reasons to comply with the information you announce and suggest that the information is good. In persuasive messages, benefits give reasons to act and help overcome audience resistance. Negative messages do not use benefits.

Good benefits meet four criteria. Each of these criteria suggests a technique for writing good benefits.

1. Adapt Benefits to the Audience.

When you write to different audiences, you may need to stress different benefits. Suppose that you manufacture a product and want to persuade dealers to carry it. The features you may cite in ads directed toward customers—stylish colors, sleek lines, convenience, durability, good price—won't convince dealers. Shelf space is at a premium, and no dealer carries all the models of all the brands available for any given product. Why should the dealer stock your product? To be persuasive, talk about the features

Figure 2.3	Extrinsic and Intrinsic Motivators	
Activity	**Extrinsic motivator**	**Intrinsic Motivator**
Making a sale	Getting a commission	Pleasure in convincing someone; pride in using your talents to think of a strategy and execute it
Turning in a suggestion to a company suggestion system	Getting a monetary reward when the suggestion is implemented	Solving a problem at work; making the work environment a little more pleasant
Writing a report that solves an organizational problem	Getting praise, a good performance appraisal, and maybe a raise	Pleasure in having an effect on an organization; pride in using your skills to solve problems; solving the problem itself

that are benefits from the dealer's point of view: turnover, profit margin, the national advertising campaign that will build customer awareness and interest, the special store displays you offer that will draw attention to the product.

2. Stress Intrinsic as Well as Extrinsic Motivators.

Intrinsic motivators come automatically from using a product or doing something. **Extrinsic motivators** are "added on." Someone in power decides to give them; they do not necessarily come from using the product or doing the action. Figure 2.3 gives examples of extrinsic and intrinsic motivators for three activities.

Intrinsic motivators or benefits are better than extrinsic motivators for two reasons:

- There just aren't enough extrinsic motivators for everything you want people to do. You can't give a prize to every customer every time he or she places an order or to every subordinate who does what he or she is supposed to do.

- Research shows that extrinsic motivators actually may make people *less* satisfied with the products they buy or the procedures they follow.

In a groundbreaking study of professional employees, Frederick Herzberg found that the things people said they liked about their jobs were all intrinsic motivators—pride in achievement, an enjoyment of the work itself, responsibility. Extrinsic motivators—pay, company policy—were sometimes mentioned as things people disliked, but they were never cited as things that motivated or satisfied them. People who made a lot of money still did not mention salary as a good point about the job or the organization.[26]

3. Prove Benefits with Clear Logic and Explain Them in Adequate Detail.

An audience benefit is a claim or assertion that the audience will benefit if they do something. Convincing the audience, therefore, involves two steps: making sure the benefit really will occur and explaining it to the audience.

If the logic behind a claimed benefit is faulty or inaccurate, there's no way to make that particular benefit convincing. Revise the benefit to make it logical.

Faulty logic:	Moving your account information into Excel will save you time.
Analysis:	If you have not used Excel before, in the short run it will probably take you longer to work with your account information using Excel. You may have been pretty good with your old system!
Revised benefit:	Moving your account information into Excel will allow you to prepare your monthly budget pages with a few clicks of a button.

If the logic is sound, making that logic evident to the audience is a matter of providing enough evidence and showing how the evidence proves the claim that there will be a benefit. Always provide enough detail to be vivid and concrete. You'll need more detail in the following situations:

- The audience may not have thought of the benefit before.

- The benefit depends on the difference between the long run and the short run.

- The audience will be hard to persuade, and you need detail to make the benefit vivid and emotionally convincing.

The apparel industry, which is actively seeking a middle-aged and baby boomer audience, is using details to attract them. Slacks may offer slimming panels and jeans may offer stretch waists and room for padded hips and thighs. Tops may cover upper arms. The potential market is huge. Women's apparel sales are more than $100 billion annually, and women over 35 account for more than half of those sales.[27]

Sometimes customers are willing to pay more for a product with desired benefits. Starbucks charges a high price for coffee but lets you linger for hours at your table. However, customers are not always willing to pay for benefits they like or even need. Bank attempts to charge for using tellers often fail miserably. Customers resent paying to talk to someone about their own money, even when most would be better off economically paying per teller visit rather than paying for everyone's visits through some other fee or lower interest rates.[28]

4. Phrase Benefits in You-Attitude.

If benefits aren't worded with you-attitude (see Chapter 3), they'll sound selfish and won't be as effective as they could be. It doesn't matter how you phrase benefits while you're brainstorming and developing them, but in your final draft, check to be sure that you've used you-attitude.

Lacks you-attitude:	We have the lowest prices in town.
You-attitude:	At Havlichek Cars, you get the best deal in town.

Identifying and Developing Audience Benefits

LO 2-6

Brainstorm benefits for your audience—perhaps twice as many as you'll need. Then you can choose the ones that are most effective for your audience or that you can develop most easily. The first benefit you think of may not be the best.

Sometimes benefits will be easy to think of and to explain. When they are harder to identify or to develop, use the following steps to identify and then develop good benefits.

1. Identify the Needs, Wants, and Feelings That May Motivate Your Audience.

All of us have basic needs, and most of us supplement those needs with possessions or intangibles we want. We need enough food to satisfy nutritional needs, but we may want our diet to make us look sexy. We need basic shelter, but we may want our homes to be cozy, luxurious, or green. And our needs and wants are strongly influenced by our feelings. We may feel safer in a more expensive car, even though research does not show that car as being safer than cheaper models.

2. Identify the Objective Features of Your Product or Policy That Could Meet the Needs You've Identified.

Sometimes just listing the audience's needs makes it obvious which feature meets a given need. Sometimes several features together meet the need. Try to think of all of them.

Suppose that you want to persuade people to come to the restaurant you manage. It's true that everybody needs to eat, but telling people they can satisfy their hunger needs won't persuade them to come to your restaurant rather than going somewhere else or eating at home. Depending on what features your restaurant offered, you could appeal to one or more of the following subgroups:

Subgroup	Features to meet the subgroup's needs
People who work outside the home	A quick lunch; a relaxing place to take clients or colleagues
Parents with small children	High chairs, children's menus, and toys to keep the kids entertained while they wait for their order
People who eat out a lot	Variety both in food and in decor
People on tight budgets	Economical food; a place where they don't need to tip (cafeteria or fast food)
People on special diets	Low-sodium and low-carb dishes; vegetarian food; kosher or halal food
People to whom eating out is part of an evening's entertainment	Music or a floor show; elegant surroundings; reservations so they can get to a show or event after dinner; late hours so they can come to dinner after a show or game

Whenever you're communicating with customers or clients about features that are not unique to your organization, it's wise to present both benefits of the features themselves and benefits of dealing with your company. If you talk about the benefits of the new healthy choices in children's menus but don't mention your own revised menu, people may go somewhere else.

3. Show How the Audience Can Meet Their Needs with the Features of the Policy or Product.

Features alone rarely motivate people. Instead, link the feature to the audience's needs and provide details that make the benefit vivid.

Weak: You get quick service.

Better: If you only have an hour for lunch, try our Business Buffet. Within minutes, you can choose from a variety of main dishes, vegetables, and a make-your-own-sandwich-and-salad bar. You'll have a lunch that's as light or filling as you want, with time to enjoy it—and still be back to the office on time.

Audience Benefits Work

Appropriate audience benefits work so well that organizations spend much time and money identifying them and then developing them.

- Hotels study which benefits are worth the money and which are not. Holiday Inn keeps restaurants and bars in all its hotels, even though they are not moneymakers, but does not have bellhops. Staybridge Suites cleans less often but has "Sundowner receptions," which give guests a free meal and a chance to socialize.[29]

- The reviewing site Yelp offers its best reviewers exclusive social events ranging from museum cocktail parties to Mardi Gras parties. These elite reviewers, who continue to write reviews to maintain their status, produce about 100 more reviews than nonelite reviewers and about 25% of Yelp's reviews.[30]

- American Express maintains Connectodex, a social network for holders of its OPEN credit cards (for small-business owners). More than 15,000 small businesses have joined. Members—who post profiles, list services and needs, and make business connections—say they prefer Connectodex to LinkedIn because the small businesses with which they connect have been vetted by American Express.[31] American Express benefits because the service has significantly reduced customer churn.

- To fight online purchasing, many retail chains offer loyalty programs that offer buyers rewards such as coupons, free purchases, or money back. Some chains offer buyers an elite status: bigger spenders get better rewards, but the status lasts only one year to encourage continual shopping.

- Automakers know that brand loyalty is money in the bank. In addition to purchase loyalty discounts, many are now turning to service to reward and keep customers. General Motors offers the "GM Preferred Owner" program. Those customers get credits for having their cars serviced at the dealership, credits that count toward discounts on repair work or new vehicles. BMW offers its buyers four years of free maintenance, years that give dealers time to nurture relationships with customers.[32]

Remember that audience benefits must be appropriate for the audience before they work. Tylenol tried a new ad campaign that said, "We put our love into Tylenol." Upset customers who remembered the Tylenol cyanide poisonings wrote in saying they didn't want anyone putting anything into their Tylenol.[33]

Sometimes it is hard to know what your audience wants. A classic example is "feature creep" in electronic goods. Unfortunately, consumers seem to want lots of features in their electronics when they buy them, but then become frustrated trying to use them and return the devices. In the United States, product returns cost more than $100 billion.[34] Research has shown that over half the wares are in complete working order; consumers just cannot operate them.[35]

Writing or Speaking to Multiple Audiences with Different Needs

LO 2-7

Many business and administrative messages go not to a single person, but to a larger audience. When the members of your audience share the same interests and the same level of knowledge, you can use the principles outlined above for individual readers or for members of homogeneous groups. But, often, different members of the audience have different needs.

Researcher Rachel Spilka has shown that talking to readers both inside and outside the organization helped corporate engineers adapt their documents successfully. Talking to readers and reviewers helped writers involve readers in the planning process, understand the social and political relationships among readers, and negotiate conflicts orally rather than depending solely on the document. These writers were then able to think about content as well as about organization and style, appeal to common grounds (such as reducing waste or increasing productivity) that multiple readers shared, and reduce the number of revisions needed before documents were approved.[36]

When it is not possible to meet everyone's needs, meet the needs of gatekeepers and decision makers first. Figure 2.4 offers strategies for creating documents for multiple audiences.

Figure 2.4	Strategies for Documents with Multiple Audiences

Content and number of details

- Provide an overview or executive summary for readers who want just the main points.
- In the body of the document, provide enough detail for decision makers and for anyone else who could veto your proposal.
- If the decision makers don't need details that other audiences will want, provide those details in appendixes—statistical tabulations, earlier reports, and so forth.

Organization

- Use headings and a table of contents so readers can turn to the portions that interest them.
- Organize your message based on the decision makers' attitudes toward it.

Level of formality

- Avoid personal pronouns. *You* ceases to have a specific meaning when several different audiences use a document.
- If both internal and external audiences will use a document, use a slightly more formal style than you would in an internal document.
- Use a more formal style when you write to international audiences.

Technical level

- In the body of the document, assume the degree of knowledge that decision makers will have.
- Put background and explanatory information under separate headings. Then readers can use the headings and the table of contents to read or skip these sections, as their knowledge dictates.
- If decision makers will have more knowledge than other audiences, provide a glossary of terms. Early in the document, let readers know that the glossary exists.

Although you will probably use different styles, and sometimes include different content, when communicating with multiple audiences, you need to keep your core message consistent. Engineers might need more technical information than managers, but the core messages they receive should not be conflicting in any way.

Summary by Learning Objectives

LO 2-1　How to identify your audience.

The primary audience will make a decision or act on the basis of your message. The secondary audience may be asked by the primary audience to comment on your message or to implement your ideas after they've been approved. The auxiliary audience encounters the message but does not have to interact with it. A gatekeeper controls whether the message gets to the primary audience. A watchdog audience has political, social, or economic power and may base future actions on its evaluation of your message.

LO 2-2　How to analyze different kinds of audiences.

The most important tools in audience analysis are common sense and empathy. The Myers-Briggs Type Indicator can help you analyze individuals. Demographic and psychographic characteristics can help you analyze groups.

LO 2-3　How to choose channels to reach your audience.

A communication channel is the means by which you convey your message to your audience. Different channels have different strengths and weaknesses, which need to be matched to the audience.

LO 2-4　How to adapt your message to your audience.

The following questions help guide a careful audience analysis:

- What will the audience's initial reaction be to the message?
- How much information does the audience need?
- What obstacles must you overcome?
- What positive aspects can you emphasize?

- What expectations does the audience have about the appropriate language, contents, and organization of messages?

- How will the audience use the document?

LO 2-5   How to characterize good audience benefits.

Audience benefits are advantages that the audience gets by using your services, buying your products, following your policies, or adopting your ideas. Benefits can exist for policies and ideas as well as for goods and services.

Good benefits are adapted to the audience, based on intrinsic rather than extrinsic motivators, supported by clear logic, explained in adequate detail, and phrased in you-attitude. Extrinsic benefits simply aren't available to reward every desired behavior; further, they reduce the satisfaction in doing something for its own sake.

LO 2-6   How to create audience benefits.

To create audience benefits,

- Identify the feelings, fears, and needs that may motivate your audience.

- Identify the features of your product or policy that could meet the needs you've identified.

- Show how the audience can meet their needs with the features of the policy or product.

LO 2-7   How to communicate with multiple audiences.

When you write to multiple audiences, use the primary audience to determine level of detail, organization, level of formality, and use of technical terms and theory.

Exercises and Cases

2.1   Reviewing the Chapter

1. Who are the five different audiences your message may need to address? (LO 2-1)

2. What are some characteristics to consider when analyzing individuals? (LO 2-2)

3. What are some characteristics to consider when analyzing groups? (LO 2-2)

4. What are some questions to consider when analyzing organizational culture? (LO 2-2)

5. What is a discourse community? Why will discourse communities be important in your career? (LO 2-2)

6. What are standard business communication channels? (LO 2-3)

7. What kinds of electronic channels seem most useful to you? Why? (LO 2-3)

8. What are considerations to keep in mind when selecting channels? (LO 2-3)

9. What are 12 questions to ask when considering how to adapt your message to your audience? (LO 2-4)

10. What are four characteristics of good audience benefits? (LO 2-5)

11. What are three ways to identify and develop audience benefits? (LO 2-6)

12. What are considerations to keep in mind when addressing multiple audiences? (LO 2-7)

2.2   Reviewing Grammar

Good audience analysis requires careful use of pronouns. Review your skills with pronoun usage by doing grammar exercise B.5, Appendix B.

2.3   Identifying Audiences

In each of the following situations, label the audiences as gatekeeper, primary, secondary, auxiliary, or watchdog audiences (all audiences may not be in each scenario) and explain your reasoning:

1. Kent, Carol, and Jose are planning to start a website design business. However, before they can get started, they need money. They have developed a business plan and are getting ready to seek funds from financial institutions for starting their small business.

2. Barbara's boss asked her to write a direct-mail letter to potential customers about the advantages of becoming a preferred member of their agency's travel club. The letter will go to all customers of the agency who are more than 65 years old.

3. Paul works for the mayor's office in a big city. As part of a citywide cost-cutting measure, a blue-ribbon panel has recommended requiring employees who work more than 40 hours in a week to take compensatory time off rather than

being paid overtime. The only exceptions will be the police and fire departments. The mayor asks Paul to prepare a proposal for the city council, which will vote on whether to implement the change. Before they vote, council members will hear from (1) citizens, who will have an opportunity to read the proposal and communicate their opinions to the city council; (2) mayors' offices in other cities, who may be asked about their experiences; (3) union representatives, who may be concerned about the reduction in

income that will occur if the proposal is implemented; (4) department heads, whose ability to schedule work might be limited if the proposal passes; and (5) the blue-ribbon panel and good-government lobbying groups. Council members come up for reelection in six months.

4. Sharon, Steven's boss at Bigster Corporation, has asked him to write an email for everyone in her division, informing them of HR's new mandatory training sessions on new government regulations affecting Bigster's services.

2.4   Analyzing Multiple Audiences

Like most major corporations, the U.S. Census Bureau has multiple, conflicting audiences, among them the president, Congress, press, state governments, citizens (both as providers and users of data), statisticians, and researchers.

- For the bureau, who might serve as gatekeeper, primary, secondary, auxiliary, and watchdog audiences?
- What kinds of conflicting goals might these audiences have?

- What would be appropriate benefits for each type of audience?
- What kinds of categories might the bureau create for its largest audience (citizens)?
- How do some of the posters at the website below differ for different audiences? "In-Language Fact Sheets, Posters and Key Dates," U.S. Census Bureau, http://www.census. gov/2010census/partners/materials/inlangfacts.php#arabic.

2.5   Choosing a Channel to Reach a Specific Audience

Suppose your organization wants to target a product, service, or program for each of the following audiences. What would be the best channel(s) to reach that group in your city? To what extent would that channel reach all group members?

1. Parents of autistic children.
2. Ballroom dancers.
3. Nontraditional college students.
4. Parents whose children play basketball.
5. People who are blind.
6. Mothers who are vegan.
7. People who are interested in improvisation.
8. Dog owners.

2.6   Identifying and Developing Audience Benefits

Listed here are several things an organization might like its employees to do:

1. Write fewer emails.
2. Volunteer at a local food pantry.
3. Volunteer to recruit interns at a job fair.
4. Attend team-building activities every other Friday afternoon.
5. Attend HR seminars on health policy changes.

As your instructor directs,

a. Identify the motives or needs that might be met by each of the activities.

b. Develop each need or motive as an audience benefit in a full paragraph. Use additional paragraphs for the other needs met by the activity. Remember to use you-attitude.

2.7   Identifying Objections and Audience Benefits

Think of an organization you know something about and answer the following questions for it:

1. Your organization is thinking about developing a knowledge management system that requires workers to input their knowledge and experience in their job functions into the organizational database. What benefits could the knowledge management system offer your organization? What drawbacks are there? Who would be the easiest to convince? Who would be the hardest?

2. New telephone software would efficiently replace your organization's long-standing human phone operator, who has been a perennial welcoming voice to incoming callers. What objections might people in your organization have to replacing the operator? What benefits might your organization receive? Who would be easiest to convince? Who would be the hardest?

3. Your organization is thinking of outsourcing one of its primary products to a manufacturer in another country where the product can be made more cost-efficiently. What fears or objections might people have? What benefits might your organization receive? Who would be easiest to convince? Who would be hardest?

As your instructor directs,

a. Share your answers orally with a small group of students.

b. Present your answers in an oral presentation to the class.

c. Write a paragraph developing the best audience benefit you identified. Remember to use you-attitude.

2.8   Analyzing Benefits for Multiple Audiences

The U.S. Census Bureau lists these benefits from cooperating with the census:

> "Census information affects the numbers of seats your state occupies in the U.S. House of Representatives. And people from many walks of life use census data to advocate for causes, rescue disaster victims, prevent diseases, research markets, locate pools of skilled workers and more.
>
> "When you do the math, it's easy to see what an accurate count of residents can do for your community. Better infrastructure. More services. A brighter tomorrow for everyone. In fact, the information the census collects helps to determine how more than $400 billion of federal funding each year is spent on infrastructure and services like:
>
> - Hospitals
> - Job-training centers
> - Schools
> - Senior centers
> - Bridges, tunnels and other public works projects
> - Emergency services"[37]

How well do these benefits meet the four characteristics of good audience benefits discussed in this chapter?

2.9   Analyzing Individuals

Review this chapter's discussion of the Myers-Briggs Type Indicator. On the web, take one of the free tests similar to the Myers-Briggs. Read about your personality type and consider how accurate the description may be. Print your results.

As your instructor directs,

a. Share your results orally with a small group of students and discuss how accurately the type indicator describes you. Identify some of the differences among your personality types and consider how the differences would affect efforts to collaborate on projects.

b. Identify other students in the classroom with the same combination of personality traits. Create a brief oral presentation to the class that describes your type indicator and explains how the pros and cons of your personality will affect group dynamics in collaborative work.

c. Write a brief email to your instructor describing your results, assessing how well the results reflect your personality, and suggesting how your personality traits might affect your work in class and in the workplace.

2.10   Getting Customer Feedback

Smart businesses want to know what their customers and clients are saying about their products and services. Many websites can help them do so.

Check some of the common sites for customer comments. Here is a list to get you started:

http://www.amazon.com
http://www.angieslist.com
http://www.my3cents.com

http://www.thesqueakywheel.com

http://www.yelp.com

What does each site do? What are good features of each site? What are drawbacks?

As your instructor directs,

a. Discuss your findings in an email to your instructor.

b. Share your findings in small groups.

c. As a group, make a presentation to your classmates.

2.11 Evaluating a New Channel

To combat software piracy, Microsoft tried an unusual communication channel. A new software update turned screens black on computers using pirated software; the update also posted a message to switch to legitimate software copies. The update did not prevent people from using their machines, and they could manually change their wallpaper back to its previous design. But the black screen returned every 60 minutes. Microsoft said there was little protest except in China, where the software piracy problem is greatest.[38]

In small groups, discuss this practice.

1. What do you think of this channel?

2. Is it ethical?

3. Do you think it helped or hurt Microsoft profits in China?

4. How do you think receivers of the black screen reacted?

As your instructor directs,

a. Post your findings electronically to share with the class.

b. Present your findings in an email to your instructor.

c. Present your findings in an oral presentation to the class.

2.12 Discussing Ethics

1. What do you think about the practice of companies giving perks such as free samples to bloggers to discuss their products? Does your opinion change according to the expense of the perk (free tissues versus tablet computers, for instance)? How can you tell if bloggers have been influenced by the companies whose products they discuss?

2. What do you think about the practice of law firms using social media to find plaintiffs? Is it any worse to use social media than print or TV ads? Why? Look at some of the sites provided by law firms. As a start, try http://www.oil-rig-explosions.com and http://www.consumerwarningnetwork.com. How persuasive is the content?

3. What do you think about the practice of tracking consumers' Internet surfing and selling the information to marketers? Does the tracking seem more intrusive when it is combined with offline records such as shopping and credit card records?

4. What do you think about the practice of companies asking their employees to take health screenings and then giving them hundreds of dollars off their health insurance if they do so? What benefits do you see for employees? Drawbacks? Is this just a way to penalize employees who refuse by making them pay more for health insurance?

2.13 Banking on Multiple Audiences

Bruce Murphy, an executive at KeyBank, tackled a new problem: how to extend banking services to a new audience—people who use banks intermittently or not at all. It is a large group, estimated at 73 million people. Together, they spend an estimated $11 billion in fees at places such as check-cashing outlets, money-wire companies, and paycheck lenders (companies offering cash advances on future paychecks).

However, they are a tough audience. Many of them have a deep distrust of banks or believe banks will not serve them. Murphy also faced another tough audience: bank managers who feared attracting forgeries and other bad checks and thus losing money. One manager actually said, "Are you crazy? These are the very people we're trying to keep out of the bank!"

To attract the new customers, KeyBank cashes payroll and government checks for a 1.5% fee, well below the 2.44% average

for check-cashing outlets. The bank also started offering free financial education classes. In fact, the bank even has a program to help people with a history of bounced checks to clear their records by paying restitution and taking the financial education class.

The program is growing, among both check-cashing clients and branches offering the services, to the satisfaction of both audiences.[39]

- What are some other businesses that could expand services to underserved populations?

- What services would they offer?

- What problems would they encounter?

- What audience appeals could they use to attract clients or customers?

2.14   Analyzing a Discourse Community

Analyze the way a group you are part of uses language. Possible groups include

1. Work teams.
2. Sports teams.
3. Sororities, fraternities, and other social groups.
4. Churches, mosques, synagogues, and temples.
5. Geographic or ethnic groups.
6. Groups of friends.

Questions to ask include the following:

1. What specialized terms might not be known to outsiders?
2. What topics do members talk or write about? What topics are considered unimportant or improper?
3. What channels do members use to convey messages?

4. What forms of language do members use to build goodwill? To demonstrate competence or superiority?
5. What strategies or kinds of proof are convincing to members?
6. What formats, conventions, or rules do members expect messages to follow?
7. What are some nonverbal ways members communicate?

As your instructor directs,

a. Share your results orally with a small group of students.
b. Present your results in an oral presentation to the class.
c. Present your results in an email to your instructor.
d. Share your results with a small group of students and write a joint email reporting the similarities and differences you found.

Notes

1. "Social Media Update 2016," Pew Research Center, November 11, 2016, http://www.pewinternet.org/2016/11/11/social-media-update-2016/.
2. Isabel Briggs Myers, *Introduction to Type* (Palo Alto, CA: Consulting Psychologists Press, 1980). The material in this section follows Myers's paper.
3. Mary Anne Moffitt, *Campaign Strategies and Message Design: A Practitioner's Guide from Start to Finish* (Connecticut: Praeger Publishers, 1999), 12–13.
4. "National Assessment of Adult Literacy," National Center for Education Statistics, 2016, https://nces.ed.gov/naal/kf_demographics.asp.
5. Miguel Bustillo, "Wal-Mart Adds Guns Alongside Butter," *Wall Street Journal,* April 28, 2011, B1; and Karen Talley and Shelly Banjo, "With More on Shelves, Wal-Mart Profit Rises," *Wall Street Journal,* May 18, 2012, B3.
6. "Internet Live Stats," Internet Live Stats, accessed September 8, 2017, http://www.internetlivestats.com/.
7. Jeff Desjardins, "Amazon Is Now Bigger Than Most Brick and Mortar Retailers Put Together," *Business Insider,* January 3, 2017, http://www.businessinsider.com/the-extraordinary-size-of-amazon-in-one-chart-2017-1.
8. Jessica E. Vascellaro and Sam Schechner, "TV Lures Ads but Viewers Drop Out," *Wall Street Journal,* September 21, 2011, B1.
9. Frances Frei and Anne Morriss, *Uncommon Service: How to Win by Putting Customers at the Core of Your Business* (Boston: Harvard Business Review Press, 2012), 152.
10. Nate Silver, *The Signal and the Noise: Why So Many Predictions Fail—But Some Don't* (New York: Penguin, 2012), 139–40.
11. "Statistics and Facts on Online Advertising in the U.S.," *Statista,* accessed March 6, 2013, http://www.statista.com/topics/1176/online-advertising/.
12. Marc Gunther, "Hard News," *Fortune,* August 6, 2007, 82.
13. Pew Research Center for the People & the Press, "In Changing News Landscape, Even Television Is Vulnerable: Trends in News Consumption: 1991–2012," September 27, 2012, http://www.people-press.org/files/legacy-pdf/2012%20News%20Consumption%20Report.pdf.
14. Christopher S. Stewart, "King of TV for Now, CBS Girds for Digital Battle," *Wall Street Journal,* November 30, 2012, A1.
15. Pew Research Center for the People & the Press, "In Changing News Landscape, Even Television Is Vulnerable."
16. Ibid.
17. Suzanne Vranica, "Hanger Ads Ensure Message Gets Home," *Wall Street Journal,* March 12, 2007, B4; and Curtis Peters, "Your Ad Here: As Marketers Fight for Consumer Eyeballs, Everything Has Become a Billboard," *Bloomberg Businessweek,* August 6, 2012, 73.
18. Elizabeth Olson, "The Ken Doll Turns 50, and Wins a New Face," *New York Times,* March 21, 2011, http://www.nytimes.com/2011/03/22/business/media/22adco.html.
19. Peters, "Your Ad Here."
20. Ibid.
21. Joe Palca, "Wanna Play? Computer Gamers Help Push Frontier of Brain Research," *NPR,* March 5, 2013, http://www.npr.org/2013/03/05/173435599/wanna-play-computer-gamers-help-push-frontier-of-brain-research?ft=1&f=1001.
22. "Steamy Hot Line Raises Pulses, Library Funds," *Des Moines Register,* May 9, 2007, 4A.
23. Elaine Pofeldt, "David vs. Goliath," *Fortune,* July 4, 2011, 30.
24. Lev Grossman, "A Game for All Ages," *Time,* May 15, 2006, 39.
25. Cecilie Rohwedder, "Store of Knowledge: No. 1 Retailer in Britain Uses 'Clubcard' to Thwart Wal-Mart: Data from Loyalty Program Help Tesco Tailor Products as It Resists U.S. Invader," *Wall Street Journal,* June 6, 2006, A1.
26. Frederick Herzberg, "One More Time: How Do You Motivate Employees?" *Harvard Business Review* 65, no. 5 (1987), 109–20.
27. Teri Agins, "Over-40 Finds a Muse," *Wall Street Journal,* December 6, 2008, W4.
28. Frei and Morriss, *Uncommon Service,* 57–58.
29. Ryan Chittum, "Price Points: Good Customer Service Costs Money. Some Expenses Are Worth It—and Some Aren't," *Wall Street Journal,* October 30, 2006, R7.
30. Mikotaj Jan Piskorski, "Social Strategies That Work," *Harvard Business Review* 90, no. 11 (November 2012): 119.
31. Ibid.
32. Joseph B. White, "How Auto Makers Keep You Coming Back," *Wall Street Journal,* January 23, 2013, D3.

33. Richard M. Smith, "Stay True to Your Brand: Ad Guru Rance Crain Says the Rules Are Eternal," *Newsweek,* May 5, 2008, E18.

34. James Surowiecki, "The Financial Page Feature Presentation," *The New Yorker,* May 28, 2007, 28.

35. Reuters, "Scientist: Complexity Causes 50% of Product Returns," *Computer World,* May 6, 2006, http://www.computerworld.com/s/article/109254/Scientist_Complexity_causes_50_of_product_returns.

36. Rachael Spilka, "Orality and Literacy in the Workplace: Process- and Text-Based Strategies for Multiple Audience Adaptation," *Journal of Business and Technical Communication* 4, no. 1 (1990): 44–67.

37. Quoted from "Why It's Important," U.S. Census Bureau: United States Census 2010, accessed March 6, 2013, http://www.census.gov/2010census/about/why-important.php.

38. Loretta Chao and Juliet Ye, "Microsoft Tactic Raises Hackles in China: In Antipiracy Move, Software Update Turns Screens Black and Urges Users to Buy Legal Windows Copies," *Wall Street Journal,* October 23, 2008, B4.

39. Ann Carrns, "Banks Court a New Client: The Low-Income Earner: KeyCorp Experiments with Check Cashing," *Wall Street Journal,* March 16, 2007, A1, A14.

CHAPTER

3 Building Goodwill

©DrAfter123/Getty Images

NEWSWORTHY COMMUNICATION

Amazon's Relationship with Customers

©Hadrlan/Shutterstock

Reliability, convenience, and high-quality customer service are paramount features of goodwill, or the relationship that companies develop with their audience. Few businesses can compete with the quality of these traits that Amazon offers to consumers. Amazon's reputation for having a variety of products and services, easy and convenient returns, fast and free shipping, and competitive pricing insulates the mega-company from otherwise damaging concerns like unfair working conditions of the warehouse workers and the potential sale of counterfeit items from the third-party marketplace. Stories about worker exploitation or counterfeit items might seriously damage similar businesses, and yet roughly 55% of online shoppers begin their search for goods on Amazon's website, regardless of whether or not they end up ultimately purchasing from Amazon.

In addition to free two-day shipping, Amazon Prime subscriptions offer access to media, as well as subscription services like grocery delivery or unlimited free audiobooks, which makes the $99 subscription fee seem like a bargain. In fact, giving away free shipping to Prime members costs the company more than the revenue accrued from membership dues. That, however, doesn't concern CEO Jeff Bezos, whose business model is driven by growth rather than profit margin. All of these conveniences add to the goodwill that Amazon has established with consumers, a goodwill that is both strong enough to persevere in what may be times of crisis for companies with a less established rapport and strong enough to enable the company to generate excitement over the retailer's Prime Day holiday.

Sources: Noah Robischon, "Why Amazon Is the World's Most Innovative Company of 2017," *Fast Company,* February 13, 2017, https://www.fastcompany.com/3067455/why-amazon-is-the-worlds-most-innovative-company-of-2017; Krystina Gustafson, "More Shoppers Are Starting Their Online Search on Amazon," *CNBC,* September 27, 2016, https://www.cnbc.com/2016/09/27/amazon-is-the-first-place-most-online-shoppers-visit.html; and Nanette Byrnes, "How Amazon Loses on Prime and Still Wins," *MIT Technology Review,* July 12, 2016, https://www.technologyreview.com/s/601889/how-amazon-loses-on-prime-and-still-wins/.

Learning Objectives

After studying this chapter, you will know

LO 3-1   How to create you-attitude.

LO 3-2   How to create positive emphasis.

LO 3-3   How to improve tone in business communications.

LO 3-4   How to reduce bias in business communications.

Goodwill eases the challenges of business and administration. Companies have long been aware that treating customers well pays off in more sales and higher profits. Today we work in a service economy: The majority of jobs are in service, where goodwill is even more important.[1]

- Amazon's corporate mission says, "We seek to be Earth's most customer-centric company for four primary customer sets: consumers, sellers, enterprises, and content creators." Jeff Bezos, Amazon's founder and CEO, has a video on YouTube titled "Everything I Know." It has three points: obsess over customers, invent on behalf of customers, and think long term because doing so allows you to serve customers better.[2]

- Tony Hsieh built Zappos around customer service, including a service attitude toward vendors.

- A study by Vanderbilt University found that a portfolio of companies whose ACSI (American Consumer Satisfaction Index) scores were above the national average far outperformed the market. Over a 10-year period, the portfolio gained 212%; the Standard & Poor's 500 stock index rose 105% over the same period.[3]

Goodwill is important both internally as well as externally. More and more organizations are realizing that treating employees well is both financially wise and ethically sound. Happy employees result in less staff turnover, reducing hiring and training costs. Research indicates prioritizing employee satisfaction can lead to a 6.6% increase in productivity per hour.[4] In 2015, Dan Price, CEO of Gravity Payments, a credit card processing company, made headlines for raising the minimum wage at his business to $70,000, while taking a salary cut to fund the increase. This increase in worker salary directly led to an increase in retention and worker happiness rates, as well as a boost in sales and nearly double profits in 2016.[5]

You-attitude, positive emphasis, trust, and bias-free language are four ways to help build goodwill. All four help you achieve your purposes and make your messages friendlier, more persuasive, more professional, and more humane. They suggest that you care not just about money, but also about the needs and interests of your customers, employees, and fellow citizens.

You-Attitude

LO 3-1

You-attitude is a communication style that looks at things from the audience's point of view, emphasizing what the audience wants or needs to know, respecting the audience's intelligence, and protecting the audience's ego. We see this often in terms of customer service. In fact, companies are increasingly focusing on improving customer relationships over efficiency. For instance, Walgreens is training pharmacists to work closely with patients with chronic illnesses, replacing 3- to 5-minute meetings with 20- to 45-minute meetings to help patients manage their illnesses; American Express is training call-center agents to focus on building customer loyalty rather than processing phone calls quickly; and Comcast is giving its 24,000 call-center agents additional training to repair and avoid the negative customer service issues it has suffered in the past.[6] These changes are not about improving profits, but improving customer experience and happiness by anticipating customers' needs, thus improving customer retention and satisfaction. Satisfied, happy customers are more likely to recommend the organization to their friends and families, and word-of-mouth recommendations from trusted sources are more effective than any advertising or marketing campaign.[7]

Here's another example: For years, Microsoft fought lax enforcement of intellectual property laws in China. The software company finally started making progress when it looked at the problem from the Chinese point of view. Government officials were ignoring the problem because many of their people made a living from illegal copies and because Microsoft prices put the products beyond the reach of most citizens. With this new perspective, Microsoft began creating jobs in China and lowering the prices of its products—in return for better law enforcement.[8]

Consider Cultural Differences with International Audiences

When you communicate with international audiences, familiarize yourself with the differences in social norms. Simple actions such as greetings easily can be taken for granted but should be researched to ensure that you do not alienate an audience with your message. Different countries, and even different regions of the same country, have different greetings. They may shake hands, bow, hug, kiss, or a combination of these actions as a method of professional greetings.[9]

In addition to different greetings, measurement systems are likely to be different. The United States, along with Liberia and Myanmar, clings to the Imperial measurement system, which has been abandoned by the rest of the world in favor of the metric system.[10] When you write for international audiences, use the metric system.

Even pronouns and direction words need attention. *We* may not feel inclusive to readers with different assumptions and backgrounds. *Here* won't mean the same thing to a reader in Bonn, Germany, as it does to one in Boulder, Colorado.

How to Create You-Attitude

Expressing what you want to say with you-attitude is a crucial step in communicating your concern to your audience.

To apply you-attitude on a sentence level, use the following techniques:

1. Talk about the audience, not about yourself.
2. Refer specifically to the customer's request or order.
3. Don't talk about feelings, except to congratulate or offer sympathy.
4. In positive situations, use *you* more often than *I.* Use *we* when it includes the audience.
5. In negative situations, avoid the word *you.* Protect the audience's ego. Use passive verbs and impersonal expressions to avoid assigning blame.

Revisions for you-attitude do not change the basic meaning of the sentence. However, revising for you-attitude often makes sentences longer because the revision is more specific and has more information. Long sentences need not be wordy. **Wordiness** means having more words than the meaning requires. You can add information and still keep your writing concise.

1. Talk about the audience, not about yourself.

Your audience wants to know how they benefit or are affected. When you provide this information, you make your message more complete and more interesting.

Lacks you-attitude:	We have negotiated an agreement with Apex Rent-a-Car that gives you a discount on rental cars.
You-attitude:	As a Sunstrand employee, you can now get a 20% discount when you rent a car from Apex.

2. Refer specifically to the customer's request or order.

A specific referral, rather than a generic *your order* or *your policy,* helps show that your customer is important to you. If your customer is an individual or a small business, it's friendly to specify the content of the order. If you're dealing with a company with which you do a great deal of business, give the invoice or purchase order number.

Lacks you-attitude:	Your order . . .
You-attitude (to individual):	The desk chair you ordered . . .
You-attitude (to a large store):	Your invoice #783329 . . .

3. Don't talk about feelings, except to congratulate or offer sympathy.

In most business situations, your feelings are irrelevant and should be omitted.

Lacks you-attitude:	We are happy to extend you a credit line of $15,000.
You-attitude:	You can now charge up to $15,000 on your American Express card.

It *is* appropriate to talk about your own emotions in a message of congratulations or condolence.

You-attitude:	Congratulations on your promotion to district manager! I was really pleased to read about it.

Don't talk about your audience's feelings, either. It's distancing to have others tell us how we feel—especially if they are wrong.

Lacks you-attitude:	You'll be happy to hear that Open Grip Walkway Channels meet OSHA requirements.
You-attitude:	Open Grip Walkway Channels meet OSHA requirements.

Maybe the audience expects that anything you sell would meet government regulations (OSHA—the Occupational Safety and Health Administration—is a federal agency). The audience may even be disappointed if they expected higher standards. Simply explain the situation or describe a product's features; don't predict the audience's response.

When you have good news, simply give the good news.

Lacks you-attitude:	You'll be happy to hear that your scholarship has been renewed.
You-attitude:	Congratulations! Your scholarship has been renewed.

4. In positive situations, use *you* more often than *I*. Use *we* when it includes the audience.

Talk about the audience, not you or your company.

Lacks you-attitude:	We provide health insurance to all employees.
You-attitude:	You receive health insurance as a full-time Procter & Gamble employee.

Most readers are tolerant of the word *I* in email messages, which seem like conversation. But edit paper documents to use *I* rarely if at all. *I* suggests that you're concerned about personal issues, not about the organization's problems, needs, and opportunities. *We* works well when it includes the reader. Avoid *we* if it excludes the reader (as it would in a letter to a customer or supplier or as it might in an email about what *we* in management want *you* to do).

5. In negative situations, avoid the word *you*. Protect your audience's ego. Use passive verbs and impersonal expressions to avoid assigning blame. When you report bad news or limitations, use a noun for a group of which your audience is a part instead of *you* so people don't feel that they're singled out for bad news.

Lacks you-attitude:	You must get approval from the director before you publish any articles or memoirs based on your work in the agency.
You-attitude:	Agency personnel must get approval from the director to publish any articles or memoirs based on their work at the agency.

Use passive verbs and impersonal expressions to avoid blaming people. **Passive verbs** describe the action performed on something, without necessarily saying who did it. A verb is in **passive voice** if the subject is acted upon. Passive voice is usually made up of a form of the verb *to be* plus a past participle:

were obtained	(in the past)
is endorsed	(in the present)
will be fulfilled	(in the future)

In most cases, active verbs are better, but when your audience is at fault, passive verbs may be useful to avoid alienation by assigning blame.

Impersonal expressions omit people and talk only about things. Normally, communication is most lively when it's about people—and most interesting to audiences when it's about them. When you have to report a mistake or bad news, however, you can protect your audience's ego by using an impersonal expression, one in which things, not people, do the acting.

Lacks you-attitude:	You made no allowance for inflation in your estimate.
You-attitude (passive):	No allowance for inflation has been made in this estimate.
You-attitude (impersonal):	This estimate makes no allowance for inflation.

A purist might say that impersonal expressions are illogical: An estimate, for example, is inanimate and can't "make" anything. In the pragmatic world of business writing, however, impersonal expressions help you convey criticism tactfully.

You-Attitude beyond the Sentence Level

Good messages apply you-attitude beyond the sentence level by using content and organization as well as style to build goodwill.

To create goodwill with content:

- Be complete. When you have lots of information to give, consider putting some details in an appendix, which may be read later.

- Anticipate and answer questions your audience is likely to have.

- Show why information your audience didn't ask for is important.

- Show your audience how the subject of your message affects them.

To organize information to build goodwill:

- Put information your audience is most interested in first.

- Arrange information to meet your audience's needs, not yours.

- Use parallel-structure headings and lists so readers can find and understand key points quickly.

Creating parallel structure in headings and lists facilitates readers' comprehension of your message. Headings and list items in parallel structure share the same grammatical structure, such as the verbal-first phrases (*-ing* verbs) in a report titled, "Ways to Increase Volunteer Commitment and Motivation":

- Increasing Training Opportunities
- Improving Supervision
- Providing Emotional Support
- Establishing and Maintaining a Two-Way Information Flow

These headings are in parallel structure when written as noun phrases as well:

- Increased Training Opportunities
- Improved Supervision
- More Emotional Support
- A Two-Way Information Flow

Consider the email in Figure 3.1. As the red marginal notes indicate, many individual sentences in this message lack you-attitude. Fixing individual sentences could improve the email. However, it really needs to be totally rewritten.

Figure 3.2 shows a possible revision of this email. The revision is clearer, easier to read, and friendlier. Note that the list items are all in simple present tense: *give, have,* and *give.*

Positive Emphasis

LO 3-2

With some bad news—announcements of layoffs, product defects and recalls, salary cuts—straightforward negatives build credibility. (See Chapter 9 for how to present bad news.) Sometimes negatives are needed to make people take a problem seriously. In some messages, such as disciplinary notices and negative performance appraisals, one of your purposes is to make the problem clear. Even here, avoid insults or attacks on your audience's integrity or sanity.

In most situations, however, it's better to be positive. Researchers have found that businesspeople responded more positively to positive language than to negative language, and were more likely to say they would act on a positively worded request.[11] In groundbreaking research for Met Life, Martin Seligman found that optimistic salespeople sold 37% more insurance than pessimistic colleagues. As a result, Met Life began hiring optimists even when they failed to meet the company's other criteria. These "unqualified" optimists outsold pessimists 21% in their first year and 57% in the next.[12]

Positive emphasis is a way of looking at things. Is the bottle half empty or half full? You can create positive emphasis with the words, information, organization, and layout you choose. "Part-time" may be a negative phrase for someone seeking full-time employment, but it may be a positive phrase for college students seeking limited work hours while they pursue their education. It may become even more positive if connected with flexible hours.

| **Figure 3.1** | An Email Lacking You-Attitude |

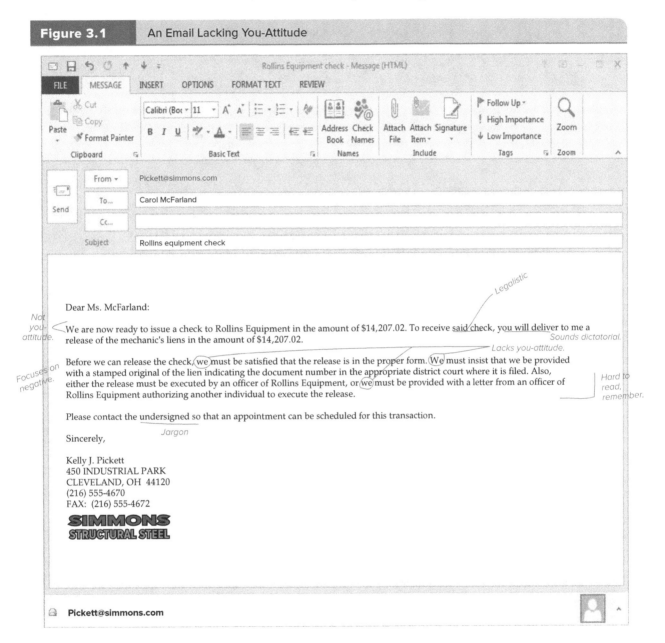

How to Create Positive Emphasis
================================

Create positive emphasis by using the following techniques:

1. Avoid negative words and words with negative connotations.
2. Beware of hidden negatives.
3. Focus on what the audience can do rather than on limitations.
4. Justify negative information by giving a reason or linking it to an audience benefit.
5. Put the negative information in the middle and present it compactly.

Choose the technique that produces the clearest, most accurate communication.

Figure 3.2	An Email Revised to Improve You-Attitude

Dear Ms. McFarland:

Let's clear up the lien in the Allen contract.

Starts with main point from the reader's point of view.

Rollins will receive a check for $14,207.02 when you give us a release for the mechanic's lien of $14,207.02. To assure us that the release is in the proper form,

Focuses on what reader gets.

1. Give us a stamped original of the lien indicating the document's district court number, and

2. Either
   a. Have an officer of Rollins Equipment sign the release
      or
   b. Give us a letter from a Rollins officer authorizing someone else to sign the release.

List makes it easy to see that reader needs to do two things—and that the second can be done in two ways.

Please call to tell me which way is best for you.

Emphasizes reader's choice.

Sincerely,

Kelly J. Pickett
450 INDUSTRIAL PARK
CLEVELAND, OH 44120
(216) 555-4670 Ext. 5318
FAX: (216) 555-4672

Extension number makes it easy for reader to phone.

SIMMONS STRUCTURAL STEEL

Pickett@simmons.com

1. Avoid negative words and words with negative connotations.

Figure 3.3 lists some common negative words. If you find similar words in a draft, try to substitute a more positive word. When you must use a negative, use the least negative term that will convey your meaning:

Negative:	We have failed to finish taking inventory.
Better:	We haven't finished taking inventory.
Still better:	We will be finished taking inventory Friday.
Negative:	If you can't understand this explanation, feel free to call me.
Better:	If you have further questions, just call me.
Still better:	Omit the sentence.

Figure 3.3	Negative Words to Avoid		
afraid	impossible	**Some dis- words:**	**Many un- words:**
anxious	lacking	disapprove	Unclear
avoid	loss	dishonest	Unfair
bad	neglect	dissatisfied	Unfortunate
careless	never		Unfortunately
damage	no		Unpleasant
delay	not	**Many in- words:**	Unreasonable
delinquent	objection	inadequate	Unreliable
deny	problem	incomplete	Unsure
difficulty	reject	inconvenient	
eliminate	sorry	insincere	
error	terrible	injury	
except	trivial		
fail	trouble		
fault	wait	**Some mis- words:**	
fear	weakness	misfortune	
hesitate	worry	missing	
ignorant	wrong	mistake	
ignore			

Omit double negatives.

Negative:	Never fail to back up your documents.
Better:	Always back up your documents.

When you must use a negative term, use the least negative word that is accurate.

Negative:	Your balance of $835 is delinquent.
Better:	Your balance of $835 is past due.

Getting rid of negatives has the added benefit of making what you write easier to understand. Sentences with three or more negatives are hard to interpret correctly.[13]

2. Beware of hidden negatives.

Some words are not negative in themselves but become negative in context. *But* and *however* indicate a shift, so, after a positive statement, they are negative. *I hope* and *I trust that* suggest that you aren't sure. *Patience* may sound like a virtue, but it is a necessary virtue only when things are slow. Even positives about a service or product may backfire if they suggest that in the past the service or product was bad.

Negative:	I hope this is the information you wanted. [Implication: I'm not sure.]
Better:	Enclosed is a brochure about road repairs scheduled for 2019.
Still better:	The brochure contains a list of all roads and bridges scheduled for repair during 2019, specific dates when work will start, and alternate routes.
Negative:	Please be patient as we switch to the automated system. [Implication: You can expect problems.]
Better:	If you have questions during our transition to the automated system, please call Melissa Morgan.
Still better:	You'll be able to get information instantly about any house on the market when the automated system is in place. If you have questions during the transition, please call Melissa Morgan.
Negative:	Now Crispy Crunch tastes better. [Implication: it used to taste terrible.]
Better:	Now Crispy Crunch tastes even better.

Removing negatives does not mean being arrogant or pushy.

Negative:	I hope that you are satisfied enough to place future orders.
Arrogant:	I look forward to receiving all of your future business.
Better:	Whenever you need computer chips, a call to Mercury is all it takes for fast service.

When you eliminate negative words, be sure to maintain accuracy. Words that are exact opposites will usually not be accurate. Instead, use specifics to be both positive and accurate.

Negative:	The exercycle is not guaranteed for life.
Not true:	The exercycle is guaranteed for life.
True:	The exercycle is guaranteed for 10 years.

Legal phrases also have negative connotations for most readers and should be avoided whenever possible.

3. Focus on what the audience can do rather than on limitations.

When there are limits, or some options are closed, focus on the alternatives that remain.

Negative:	We will not allow you to charge more than $5,000 on your Visa account.
Better:	You can charge $5,000 on your new Visa card.
or:	Your new Visa card gives you $5,000 in credit that you can use at thousands of stores nationwide.

As you focus on what will happen, check for *you-attitude*. In the previous example, "We will allow you to charge $5,000" would be positive, but it lacks you-attitude.

When you have a benefit and a requirement the audience must meet to get the benefit, the sentence is usually more positive if you put the benefit first.

Negative:	You will not qualify for the student membership rate of $55 a year unless you are a full-time student.
Better:	You get all the benefits of membership for only $55 a year if you're a full-time student.

4. Justify negative information by giving a reason or linking it to an audience benefit.
A reason can help your audience see that the information is necessary; a benefit can suggest that the negative aspect is outweighed by positive factors. Be careful, however, to make the logic behind your reason clear and to leave no loopholes.

Negative:	We cannot sell individual pastel sets.
Loophole:	To keep down packaging costs and to help you save on shipping and handling costs, we sell pastel sets in packages of 12.

Suppose the customer says, "I'll pay the extra shipping and handling. Send me six." If you truly sell only in packages of 12, you need to say so:

Better:	To keep down packaging costs and to help customers save on shipping and handling costs, we sell pastel sets only in packages of 12.

If you link the negative element to a benefit, be sure it is a benefit your audience will acknowledge. Avoid telling people that you're doing things "for their own good." They may have a different notion of what their own good is. You may think you're doing customers a favor by limiting their credit so they don't get in over their heads and go bankrupt. They may think they'd be better off with more credit so they could expand in hopes of making more sales and more profits.

5. Put the negative information in the middle and present it compactly.

Put negatives at the beginning or end only if you want to emphasize the negative. To de-emphasize a written negative, put it in the middle of a paragraph rather than in the first or last sentence and in the middle of the message rather than in the first or last paragraph.

When a letter or memo runs several pages, remember that the bottom of the first page is also a position of emphasis, even if it is in the middle of a paragraph, because of the extra white space of the bottom margin. (The first page gets more attention because it is on top and the reader's eye may catch lines of the message even when he or she isn't consciously reading it; the tops and bottoms of subsequent pages don't get this extra attention.) If possible, avoid placing negative information at the bottom of the first page.

Giving a topic lots of space emphasizes it. Therefore, you can de-emphasize negative information by giving it as little space as possible. Give negative information only once in your message. Don't list negatives with bulleted or numbered lists. These lists take space and emphasize material.

How to Check Positive Emphasis

All five of the strategies just listed help create positive emphasis. However, you always should check to see that the positive emphasis is appropriate, sincere, and realistic.

As you read at the beginning of this section, positive emphasis is not always *appropriate.* Some bad news is so serious that presenting it with a positive tone is insensitive, if not unethical. Layoffs, salary cuts, and product defects are all topics in this category.

Some positive emphasis is so overdone that it no longer seems *sincere.* The used-car sales rep selling a rusting auto is one stereotype of insincerity. A more common example for most businesspeople is the employee who gushes praise through gritted teeth over your promotion. Most of us have experienced something similar, and we know how easy it is to see through the insincerity.

Positive emphasis also can be so overdone that it clouds the reality of the situation. If your company has two finalists for a sales award, and only one award, the loser does not have second place, which implies a second award. On the other hand, if all sales reps win the same award, top performers will feel unappreciated. Too much praise also can make mediocre employees think they are doing great. Keep your communications *realistic.*

Restraint can help make positive emphasis more effective. Conductor Otto Klemperer was known for not praising his orchestra. One day, pleased with a particularly good rehearsal, he spoke a brusque "good." His stunned musicians broke into spontaneous applause. Klemperer rapped his baton on his music stand to silence them and said, "Not *that* good."[14]

Positive Psychology

Positive psychology is a branch of psychology that studies how to help people thrive. Its goal is to increase thriving, also called flourishing, well-being, and happiness. This goal connects closely with goodwill, you-attitude, and positive tone, all of which help employee happiness. A workplace that looks at its culture from its employees' perspectives, a culture where praise and goodwill are part of daily communications, will help increase thriving in employees. According to the *Harvard Business Review,* which devoted an entire issue to positive psychology, research from various fields "makes the link between a thriving workforce and better business performance absolutely clear."[15] Even former Federal Reserve Chairman Ben Bernanke has called happiness an important gauge for measuring economic progress.[16]

Why should companies care if their employees are happy? Happy employees help improve corporate profits, as well as other corporate goals.

■ A University of Michigan study found that thriving employees had 125% less burnout, 46% more job satisfaction, and 32% more commitment to the company than their peers who weren't thriving. They also had 16% better performance, according to their managers. These findings were true across industries and job types.[17]

■ A University of Illinois meta-analysis of 225 studies found that happy employees are 31% more productive, have 37% higher sales, and are three times more creative than unhappy ones.[18]

■ Researchers studying a retail chain found that stores with thriving employees earned $21 more per square foot of retail space than the other stores, resulting in $32 million additional profit for the chain.[19]

Thriving employees also are healthier and more energetic, go beyond the call of duty, and attract other good workers.[20]

How do organizations boost happiness among their employees? One major way is to provide meaningful, challenging work with a variety of tasks. Allow employees to continue to learn on the job and to make decisions that affect their work.[21] Use you-attitude to help all employees see that what they do daily makes a difference.

Another major way to boost happiness is to facilitate social support. Social factors such as teamwork or mentoring, plus environmental factors such as break rooms and exercise areas, help enhance social connections among workers. Social support doesn't have to be time-consuming. One large health care provider with 11,000 employees instituted a 10/5 rule to increase social support for both employees and patients. Anyone within 10 feet of another person had to make eye contact and smile; anyone within 5 feet had to say hello. Adopting this rule led to an increase in patient satisfaction and significant improvement in medical practice provider scores.[22]

On the job, as well as in individual lives, the frequency of positive experiences is a better predictor of happiness than the intensity of such experiences. Job happiness may depend more on daily experiences—such as interesting work projects, pleasant interactions with colleagues, and positive feedback from managers—than with big-ticket items such as salary and job title.[23]

Tone, Power, and Politeness

LO 3-3

Tone is the implied attitude of the communicator toward the audience. If the words of a document seem condescending or rude, tone is a problem. Norms for politeness are cultural and generational; they also vary from office to office.

Tone is tricky because it interacts with context and power. Language that is acceptable within one group may be unacceptable if used by someone outside the group. Words that might seem friendly from a superior to a subordinate may seem uppity if used by the subordinate to the superior. Similarly, words that may be neutral among peers may be seen as negative if sent by a superior to a subordinate.

Using the proper tone with employees can have a huge economic impact for a business. Disgruntled employees are suing more than ever before and disputes over wages or hours frequently can be brought as class action suits, making them even more expensive.[24]

The desirable tone for business writing is businesslike but not stiff, friendly but not phony, confident but not arrogant, polite but not groveling. Several guidelines will help you achieve the tone you want.

Use Courtesy Titles for People You Don't Know Well

Most U.S. organizations use first names for everyone, whatever their age or rank. But many people don't like being called by their first names by people they don't know or by someone much younger. When you talk or write to people outside your organization, use first names only if you've established a personal relationship. If you don't know someone well, use a courtesy title (discussed later in this chapter).

Be Aware of the Power Implications of Word Choice

"Thank you for your cooperation" is generous coming from a superior to a subordinate; it's not appropriate in a message to your superior. Different ways of asking for action carry different levels of politeness.[25]

Order: (lowest politeness)	Turn in your time card by Monday.
Polite order: (midlevel politeness)	Please turn in your time card by Monday.
Indirect request: (higher politeness)	Time cards should be turned in by Monday.
Question: (highest politeness)	Would you be able to turn in your time card by Monday?

Higher levels of politeness may be unclear. In some cases, a question may seem like a request for information to which it's acceptable to answer, "No, I can't." In other cases, it will be an order, simply phrased in polite terms.

You need more politeness if you're asking for something that will inconvenience the audience and help you more than the person who does the action. Generally, you need less politeness when you're asking for something small, routine, or to the audience's benefit. Some discourse communities, however, prefer that even small requests be made politely.

Trust

Financial crises, Internet scams, and shoddy goods and services all have contributed to a lack of trust of the commercial world. Trust is a vital element in goodwill and is necessary on the personal level as well as the corporate level. Robert Hurley, author of *The Decision to Trust: How Leaders Can Create High Trust Companies,* says, "Trust comes from delivering every day on what you promise—as a manager, an employee, and a company. It involves constant teamwork, communication and collaboration."[26]

A large part of trust comes from honesty and ethics, but by themselves, these qualities are not enough. As Hurley notes, trust is also delivering on our commitments. This delivery is important for you when you start a new job and then move up the organizational rungs. Do you do what you are expected to do? What you say you will do? Or do you say yes to more than you can possibly deliver? Honoring commitments is also important for the organization: Does it deliver the expected quality and quantity of goods and services in a timely fashion?

Trust also comes from the goodwill communication skills described in this chapter, and especially from skill with you-attitude. Are you good at discerning the interests of others and fulfilling or promoting those interests fairly and ethically?

Clear, open, and timely communication helps build and maintain trust.

Using Technology to Build Goodwill

Most organizations use a variety of technology-based communications to create and sustain goodwill with their customers, clients, and employees. Companies have long used technologies such as electronic newsletters for employees and e-mail addresses where customers could ask questions.

Now most organizations also have websites and Facebook pages featuring new products and services, tips on using products and services, and customer forums. Toy companies offer creative ways to use their products. News organizations use blogs to provide commentary. Many companies use Facebook to enter into dialogues with customers, Twitter to solve customer complaints quickly, or YouTube clips to offer instructions, or even humorous content about their products and services. In 2013, even the staid Securities and Exchange Commission started allowing corporate news postings on Twitter and corporate Facebook sites, as long as companies have informed their investors which channels will be used.[27]

Many companies are getting creative in their efforts to use technology to increase goodwill.

- Charmin launched its SitOrSquat app that helps people find a nearby public restroom, and then allows them to rate it for cleanliness. They also created the hashtag #tweetfromtheseat.[28]

- Energy drink Red Bull, sponsor of extreme sports, broadcast on YouTube Felix Baumgartner's enormous skydive that broke the sound barrier.[29]

- April Fools' Day traditionally finds jokes on social media. Past jokes include an IKEA self-assembly lawn mower, posted on Facebook; glass-bottomed airplanes for a new flying experience, posted on Virgin Atlantic Airways' founder Richard Branson's blog; and an announcement by Twitter that it was banishing vowels unless users paid a fee.[30]

As one advertising consultant says, "If you can give someone a laugh, you can create good will for your brand."[31]

Reducing Bias in Business Communication

LO 3-4

The makeup of the U.S. population is changing. According to the U.S. Census Bureau:

- Women outnumber men.

- More women than men are attaining associate's, bachelor's, and master's degrees.

- For people 16 and older, more women (41.7%) than men (35.11%) work in management, professional, and related occupations.

- The Hispanic population is the fastest growing in the country; it numbered 50.5 million in the 2010 census. Four states (California, Hawaii, New Mexico, and Texas) plus the District of Columbia have a "majority-minority" population, where more than 50% are part of a minority group.

- Projections show non-Hispanic whites becoming a minority soon after 2040.

- The number of people 65 and older also is growing; that population now numbers more than 41 million, and 6.5 million of them are still in the workforce.[32]

These figures highlight the growing diversity of the workplace and the need to communicate with appropriate, unbiased language.

Bias-free language is language that does not discriminate against people on the basis of sex, physical condition, race, ethnicity, age, religion, or any other category. It includes all audience members, helps to sustain goodwill, is fair and friendly, and complies with the law.

Check to be sure that your language is bias-free. Doing so is ethical; it also can avoid major problems and lawsuits.

- Josef Ackermann, chief executive of Deutsche Bank, was mocked in the international news when he said at a news conference that including women on the bank's all-male executive board would make it "more colorful and prettier too." The publicity added to mistrust of the bank at an awkward time when it was lobbying to dissuade German policy makers from imposing restrictions.[33]

- Conservative advice expert Dr. Laura Schlessinger resigned abruptly from her syndicated radio show after a controversy arising from her multiple use of a racial epithet while talking to an African American caller.

- Famous radio personality Don Imus was fired by CBS after making racist comments about the Rutgers University women's basketball team.

Making Language Nonsexist

Nonsexist language treats both sexes neutrally. Check to be sure your messages are free from sexism in four areas: job titles, courtesy titles and names, pronouns, and other words and phrases.

Job Titles   Use neutral titles that do not imply a job is held only by men or only by women. Many job titles are already neutral: *accountant, banker, doctor, engineer, inspector, manager, nurse, pilot, secretary, technician,* to name a few. Other titles reflect gender stereotypes and need to be changed.

Instead of	Use
Businessman	A specific title: executive, accountant, department head, owner of a small business, men and women in business, businessperson
Chairman	Chair, chairperson, moderator
Fireman	Firefighter
Foreman	Supervisor
Mailman	Mail carrier
Salesman	Salesperson, sales representative
Waitress	Server
Woman lawyer	Lawyer
Workman	Worker, employee. Or use a specific title: crane operator, bricklayer, etc.

Courtesy Titles and Names   Emails to people you know normally do not use courtesy titles. However, letters and emails to people with whom you have a more formal relationship require courtesy titles in the salutation *unless* you're on a first-name basis with your reader. (See Appendix A for examples of email and letter formats.)

When you know your reader's name and gender, use courtesy titles that do not indicate marital status: *Mr.* for men and *Ms.* for women. *Ms.* is particularly useful when you do not know what a woman's marital status is. However, even when you happen to know that a woman is married or single, you still use *Ms.* unless you know that she prefers another title. There are, however, two exceptions:

1. If the woman has a professional title, use that title if you would use it for a man.

   Dr. Kristen Sorenson is our new company physician.

   The Rev. Elizabeth Townsley gave the invocation.

Part 1 The Building Blocks of Effective Messages

2. If the woman prefers to be addressed as *Mrs.* or *Miss,* use the title she prefers rather than Ms. (You-attitude takes precedence over nonsexist language: address the reader as the reader prefers to be addressed.) To find out if a woman prefers a traditional title:

- Check the signature block in previous correspondence. If a woman types her name as *(Miss) Elaine Anderson* or *(Mrs.) Kay Royster,* use the title she designates.

- Notice the title a woman uses in introducing herself on the phone. If she says, "This is Robin Stine," use Ms. when you write to her. If she says, "I'm Mrs. Stine," use the title she specifies.

- When you're writing job letters or crucial correspondence, call the company and ask the receptionist which title your reader prefers.

In addition to using parallel courtesy titles, use parallel forms for names.

Not Parallel	Parallel
Members of the committee will be Mr. Jones, Mr. Yacone, and Lisa.	Members of the committee will be Mr. Jones, Mr. Yacone, and Ms. Melton.
	or
	Members of the committee will be Irving, Ted, and Lisa.

When you know your reader's name but not the gender, either

- Call the company and ask the receptionist or

- Use the reader's full name in the salutation:
  Dear Chris Crowell:
  Dear J. C. Meath:

When you know neither the reader's name nor gender, you have three options:

- Omit the salutation and use a subject line in its place. (See Figure A.2, Simplified Format, in Appendix A.)
  SUBJECT: RECOMMENDATION FOR BEN WANDELL

- Use the reader's position or job title:
  Dear Loan Officer:
  Dear Registrar:

- Use a general group to which your reader belongs:
  Dear Investor:
  Dear Admissions Committee:

Pronouns When you refer to a specific person, use the gender pronouns preferred by the audience:

In his speech, Pat Jones said . . .

In her speech, Alex Jones said . . .

When you are referring not to a specific person but to anyone who may be in a given job or position, traditional gender pronouns are sexist.

Sexist: a. Each supervisor must certify that the time sheet for his department is correct.

Sexist: b. When the nurse fills out the accident report form, she should send one copy to the Central Division Office.

Business communication uses four ways to eliminate sexist generic pronouns: use plurals, use second-person *you,* revise the sentence to omit the pronoun, or use pronoun pairs. Whenever you have a choice of two or more ways to make a phrase or sentence nonsexist, choose the alternative that is the smoothest and least conspicuous.

The following examples use these methods to revise sentences *a* and *b* above.

1. Use plural nouns and pronouns.

    Nonsexist: a. Supervisors must certify that the time sheets for their departments are correct.

    Note: When you use plural nouns and pronouns, other words in the sentence may need to be made plural too. In the example above, plural supervisors have plural time sheets and departments.

    Avoid mixing singular nouns and plural pronouns.

    Nonsexist but lacks agreement: b. When the nurse fills out the accident report, they should send one copy to the Central Division Office.

    Because *nurse* is singular, it is incorrect to use the plural *they* to refer to it. The resulting lack of agreement is acceptable orally but is not yet acceptable in writing. Instead, use one of the other ways to make the sentence nonsexist.

2. Use *you.*

    Nonsexist: a. You must certify that the time sheet for your department is correct.

    Nonsexist: b. When you fill out an accident report form, send one copy to the Central Division Office.

    You is particularly good for instructions and statements of the responsibilities of someone in a given position.

3. Substitute an article (*a, an,* or *the*) for the pronoun, or revise the sentence so that the pronoun is unnecessary.

    Nonsexist: a. The supervisor must certify that the time sheet for the department is correct.

    Nonsexist: b. The nurse will

         1. Fill out the accident report form.

         2. Send one copy of the form to the Central Division Office.

4. When you must focus on the action of an individual, use pronoun pairs.

    Nonsexist: a. The supervisor must certify that the time sheet for his or her department is correct.

    Nonsexist: b. When the nurse fills out the accident report form, he or she should send one copy to the Central Division Office.

Other Words and Phrases   If you find any terms similar to those in the first column in Figure 3.4 in your messages or your company's documents, replace them with terms similar to those in the second column.

Not every word containing *man* is sexist. For example, *manager* is not sexist. The word comes from the Latin *manus* meaning *hand;* it has nothing to do with maleness.

Figure 3.4	Getting Rid of Sexist Terms and Phrases	
Instead of	**Use**	**Because**
The girl at the front desk	The woman's name or job title: "Ms. Browning," "Rosa," "the receptionist"	Call female employees *women* just as you call male employees *men*. When you talk about a specific woman, use her name, just as you use a man's name to talk about a specific man.
The ladies on our staff	The women on our staff	Use parallel terms for males and females. Therefore, use *ladies* only if you refer to the males on your staff as *gentlemen*. Few businesses do because social distinctions are rarely at issue.
Manpower Manhours Manning	Personnel Hours or worker hours Staffing	The power in business today comes from both women and men.
Managers and their wives	Managers and their guests	Managers may be female; not everyone is married.

Avoid terms that assume that everyone is married or is heterosexual.

Biased: You and your husband or wife are cordially invited to the reception.

Better: You and your guest are cordially invited to the reception.

Making Language Nonracist and Nonageist

Language is **nonracist** and **nonageist** when it treats all races and ages fairly, avoiding negative stereotypes of any group. Use the following guidelines to check for bias in documents you write or edit.

Give someone's race or age only if it is relevant to your story.   When you do mention these characteristics, give them for everyone in your story—not just the non-Caucasian, non-young-to-middle-aged adults you mention.

Refer to a group by the term it prefers. As preferences change, change your usage.   Fifty years ago, *Negro* was a more dignified term than *colored* for African Americans. As times changed, both *Negro* and *colored* are offensive, while *black* and *African American* replaced the terms. Gallup polls show that the majority of black Americans (about 60%) have no preference between *black* or *African American;* however, among those who do care, polls show a slight trend toward African American.[34]

Oriental has now been replaced by *Asian*.

The term *Latinx* is the most acceptable gender-neutral group term to refer to Mexican Americans, Cuban Americans, Puerto Ricans, Dominicans, Brazilianos, and other people with Central and Latin American backgrounds (*Latino* is masculine, while *Latina* is feminine).[35] Better still is to refer to the precise group. The differences among various Latinx groups are at least as great as the differences among Italian Americans, Irish Americans, Armenian Americans, and others descended from various European groups.

Baby boomers, older people, and *mature customers* are more generally accepted terms than *senior citizens* or *golden agers*.

Organizations are making their business sites more accommodating to people with disabilities.

©Image Source/PunchStock

Avoid terms that suggest competent people are unusual. The statement "She is an intelligent purple woman" suggests the writer expects most purple women to be stupid. "He is an asset to his race" suggests excellence in the race is rare. "He is a spry 70-year-old" suggests the writer thinks anyone that old has mobility issues.

Talking about People with Disabilities and Diseases

A disability is a physical, mental, sensory, or emotional impairment that interferes with the major tasks of daily living. According to the U.S. Census Bureau, 19% of Americans currently have a disability; of those, about 71% who were 21 to 64 years old and had a "nonsevere disability" were employed.[36] The number of people with disabilities will rise as the population ages.

To keep trained workers, more and more companies are making disability accommodations such as telecommuting, flexible hours, work shift changes, and assignment changes.

When talking about people with conditions and disabilities, use **people-first language.** People-first language names the person first. Use it instead of the traditional noun phrases that imply the condition defines the person, for example, "people being treated for cancer" rather than "cancer patients." In 2010, President Obama signed Rosa's Law, which replaces "mentally retarded" with "an individual with an intellectual disability" in most federal statutes.[37] Figure 3.5 lists more examples.

Avoid negative terms, unless the audience prefers them. You-attitude takes precedence over positive emphasis: use the term a group prefers. People who lost their hearing as infants, children, or young adults often prefer to be called *deaf,* or *Deaf* in recognition of Deafness as a culture. But people who lose their hearing as older adults often prefer to be called *hard of hearing,* even when their hearing loss is just as great as that of someone who identifies him- or herself as part of the Deaf culture.

Using the right term requires keeping up with changing preferences. If your target audience is smaller than the whole group, use the term preferred by that audience, even if the group as a whole prefers another term.

Figure 3.5	Using People-First Language	
Instead of	**Use**	**Because**
Confined to a wheelchair	Uses a wheelchair	Wheelchairs enable people to escape confinement.
AIDS victim	Person with AIDS	Someone can have a disease without being victimized by it.
Abnormal	Atypical	People with disabilities are atypical but not necessarily abnormal.

Some negative terms, however, are never appropriate. Negative terms such as *afflicted, suffering from,* and *struck down* also suggest an outdated view of any illness as a sign of divine punishment.

Choosing Bias-Free Photos and Illustrations

When you produce a document with photographs or illustrations, check the visuals for possible bias. Do they show people of both sexes and all races? Is there a sprinkling of various kinds of people (younger and older, people using wheelchairs, etc.)? It's OK to have individual pictures that have just one sex or one race; the photos as a whole do not need to show exactly 50% men and 50% women. But the general impression should suggest that diversity is welcome and normal.

Check relationships and authority figures as well as numbers. If all the men appear in business suits and the women in jeans, the pictures are sexist even if an equal number of men and women are pictured. If the only nonwhites pictured are factory workers, the photos support racism even when an equal number of people from each race are shown. The 2013 *Sports Illustrated* swimsuit issue aroused controversy for its use of natives as "props" and laborers.[38]

Summary by Learning Objectives

LO 3-1   How to create you-attitude.

You-attitude is a style of communication that looks at things from the audience's point of view, emphasizing what the audience wants to know, respecting the audience's intelligence, and protecting the audience's ego. To create you-attitude:

1. Talk about the audience, not about yourself.
2. Refer to the audience's request or order specifically.
3. Don't talk about feelings except to congratulate or offer sympathy.
4. In positive situations, use *you* more often than *I.* Use *we* when it includes the audience.
5. In negative situations, avoid the word *you.* Protect the audience's ego. Use passive verbs and impersonal expressions to avoid assigning blame.

Apply you-attitude beyond the sentence level by using organization and content as well as style to build goodwill.

LO 3-2   How to create positive emphasis.

Positive emphasis means focusing on the positive rather than the negative aspects of a situation. To create positive tone:

1. Avoid negative words and words with negative connotations.
2. Beware of hidden negatives.
3. Focus on what the audience can do rather than on limitations.
4. Justify negative information by giving a reason or linking it to an audience benefit.
5. Put the negative information in the middle and present it compactly.

Check to see that your positive emphasis is appropriate, sincere, and clear.

Studies in positive psychology show that using goodwill within the organization leads to increases in well-being for employees and better business performance.

Many companies are using social media such as Twitter, Facebook, and YouTube to increase positive emphasis and goodwill.

LO 3-3　How to improve tone in business communications.

The desirable tone for business communication is businesslike but not stiff, friendly but not phony, confident but not arrogant, polite but not groveling.

LO 3-4　How to reduce bias in business communications.

Bias-free language is fair and friendly; it complies with the law; it includes all members of your audience; and it helps sustain goodwill.

- Check to be sure your language is nonsexist, nonracist, and nonageist.

- Communication should be free from sexism in four areas: job titles, courtesy titles and names, pronouns, and other words and phrases.

- *Ms.* is the nonsexist courtesy title for women. Whether or not you know a woman's marital status, use *Ms.* unless the woman has a professional title or unless you know she prefers a traditional title.

- Four ways to make pronouns nonsexist are to use plurals, to use *you,* to revise the sentence to omit the pronoun, and to use pronoun pairs.

- When you talk about people with disabilities or diseases, use the term they prefer.

- When you produce newsletters or other documents with photos and illustrations, picture a sampling of the whole population, not just part of it.

Exercises and Cases

3.1　Reviewing the Chapter

1. What are five ways to create you-attitude? (LO 3-1)
2. What are five ways to create positive emphasis? (LO 3-2)
3. How can you improve the tone of business messages? (LO 3-3)
4. What are different categories to keep in mind when you are trying to reduce bias in business messages? (LO 3-4)
5. What techniques can you use when you are trying to reduce bias in business messages? (LO 3-4)

3.2　Evaluating the Ethics of Positive Emphasis

The first term in each pair is negative; the second is a positive term that is sometimes substituted for it. Which of the positive terms seem ethical? Which seem unethical? Briefly explain your choices.

cost	investment	nervousness	adrenaline
second mortgage	home equity loan	problem	challenge
tax	user fee	price increase	price change
		for-profit hospital	tax-paying hospital
		used car	pre-owned car
		credit card fees	usage charges

3.3　Eliminating Negative Words and Words with Negative Connotations

Revise each of the following sentences to replace negative words with positive ones. Be sure to keep the meaning of the original sentence.

1. You will lose the account if you make a mistake and the customer is dissatisfied.
2. Avoid errors on customer reports by carefully proofreading.
3. Your account, #82654, is delinquent. If you neglect to pay this balance, your account will be sent to collections.
4. When you write a report, do not make claims that you cannot support with evidence.
5. Don't drop in without an appointment. Your counselor or caseworker may be unavailable.
6. I am anxious to discuss my qualifications in an interview.

3.4   Focusing on the Positive

Revise each of the following sentences to focus on the options that remain, not those that are closed off.

1. Applications that are postmarked after January 15 will not be accepted.
2. All new employees will not be able to receive benefits for 90 days.
3. I will not be available by phone on Saturdays and Sundays.
4. Overtime cannot be processed without the supervisor's signature.
5. Travel reimbursement forms will only be processed at the end of the month.

3.5   Identifying Hidden Negatives

Identify the hidden negatives in the following sentences and revise to eliminate them. In some cases, you may need to add information to revise the sentence effectively.

1. The seminar will help you become a better manager.
2. Thank you for the confidence you have shown in us by ordering one of our products. It will be shipped to you soon.
3. This publication is designed to explain how your company can start a recycling program.
4. I hope you find the information in this brochure beneficial to you and a valuable reference as you plan your move.
5. In thinking about your role in our group, I remember two occasions where you contributed something.
6. [In job letter] This job in customer service is so good for me; I am so ready to take on responsibility.

3.6   Improving You-Attitude and Positive Emphasis

Revise these sentences to improve you-attitude and positive emphasis. Eliminate any awkward phrasing. In some cases, you may need to add information to revise the sentence effectively.

1. You'll be happy to learn that the cost of tuition will not rise next year.
2. Although I was only an intern and didn't actually make presentations to major clients, I was required to prepare PowerPoint slides for the meetings and to answer some of the clients' questions.
3. At DiYanni Homes we have more than 30 plans that we will personalize just for you.
4. Please notify HR of your bank change as soon as possible to prevent a disruption of your direct deposit.
5. I'm sorry you were worried. You did not miss the deadline for signing up for a flexible medical spending account.
6. You will be happy to hear that our cell phone plan does not charge you for incoming calls.
7. The employee discount may only be used for purchases for your own use or for gifts; you may not buy items for resale. To prevent any abuse of the discount privilege, you may be asked to justify your purchase.
8. I apologize for my delay in answering your inquiry. The problem was that I had to check with our suppliers to see whether we could provide the item in the quantity you say you want. We can.
9. If you mailed a check with your order, as you claim, we failed to receive it.
10. This job sounds perfect for me.

3.7   Eliminating Biased Language

Explain the source of bias in each of the following and revise to remove the bias.

1. Mr. Brady, Mr. Barnes, and the new intern, Jodi, will represent our company at the job fair.
2. All sales associates and their wives are invited for cocktails.
3. Although he is blind, Mr. Morin is an excellent group leader.
4. Please join us for the company potluck! Ladies, please bring a main dish. Men, please bring chips and dip (store bought is fine).
5. Lee Torsad
   Pacific Perspectives
   6300 West Coronado Blvd.
   Los Angles, CA
   Dear Sir:
6. Please stop by and say "hi" to our new IT guy. Be very polite; he is oriental.
7. I would prefer if you hired a female secretary; women are typically friendlier than men.
8. Please do not use the side elevator because it is reserved for people who can't walk.

9. Sue Corcoran celebrates her 50th birthday today. Stop by her cubicle at noon to get a piece of cake and to help us sing "The Old Grey Mare Just Ain't What She Used to Be."

10. Because older customers tend to be really picky, we will need to give a lot of details in our ads.

3.8   Analyzing Goodwill Ethics

A study by a law professor shows that credit card companies make offers to people fresh out of bankruptcy. In the study of 341 families, almost 100% received credit card offers within a year after completing bankruptcy proceedings, and 87% of those offers mentioned the bankruptcy proceedings. In fact, 20% of the offers came from companies the family had owed before the bankruptcy.[39]

In small groups, discuss whether you think this practice is ethical. Why or why not? What reasons exist for not offering new credit to people who have just gone through bankruptcy? Why might such people need new credit cards?

3.9   Advising a Hasty Subordinate

Three days ago, one of your subordinates forwarded to everyone in the office a bit of email humor he'd received from a friend. Titled "You know you're Southern when . . . ," the message poked fun at Southern speech, attitudes, and lifestyles. Today you get this message from your subordinate:

> Subject: Should I Apologize?
>
> I'm getting flamed left and right because of the Southern message. I thought it was funny, but some people just can't take a joke. So far I've tried not to respond to the flames, figuring that would just make things worse. But now I'm wondering if I should apologize. What do you think?

Answer the message.

3.10   Responding to a Complaint

You're the director of corporate communications and the employee newsletter is produced by your office. Today you receive this email message from Tonya Freira:

> Subject: Complaint
>
> The section on the back of the employee newsletter referred to Mindy Kelso and me as "the girls at the front desk." We are not "girls," and we don't see why our gender was even pointed out in the first place. We are customer service representatives and would like to be referred to that way.

Write a response to Tonya Freira. Also, draft a message to your staff, reminding them to edit newsletter stories as well as external documents to replace biased language.

3.11   Dealing with Negative Clients

An executive at one of your largest client companies is known for his negative attitude. He is feared for his sharp tongue and scathing attacks, and he bullies everyone. Everyone you know, including yourself, is afraid of him. Unfortunately, he is also the one who decides whether or not you get your annual contract. Your contract is up for renewal and you have some new services you think his company would like.

In small groups, discuss at least four ways to handle Mr. Bully. Write up your two best to share with the whole class. Also write up the reasons you think these two approaches will work. Share your two approaches with the whole class, as a short oral presentation or online.

As a class, select the two best approaches from those offered by the small groups. Discuss your criteria for selection and rejection.

3.12   Writing Business Thank-You Notes

Some businesses make a practice of sending goodwill messages to some of their customers.

Pick a business you patronize that might logically send some thank-you notes. Write a suitable note and design a tasteful visual for it. In a separate document, write an email to your instructor explaining your design and content decisions.

Questions you might want to consider:

- Who is your audience? Will you write to everyone? Will you target big spenders? Trendsetters? People who might

become long-term customers? How will you identify your categories?

- What tone did you select? What words and phrases help produce that tone? What words and phrases did you avoid? What diction choices did you make to convey sincerity?

- What content did you choose? Why? What content choices did you discard?

- What design features did you choose? Why? What design features did you discard?

Notes

1. Frances Frei and Anne Morriss, *Uncommon Service: How to Win by Putting Customers at the Core of Your Business* (Boston: Harvard Business Review Press, 2012), 1.
2. "Amazon Investor Relations," Amazon.com, May 6, 2013, http://phx.corporate-ir.net/phoenix.zhtml?c=97664&p=irol-irhome; and "Video from Jeff Bezos about Amazon and Zappos," YouTube video, July 22, 2009, http://www.youtube.com/watch?v=hxX_Q5CnaA.
3. Aaron Pressman, "When Service Means Survival," *BusinessWeek,* March 2, 2009, 62.
4. Petri Böckerman and Pekka Ilmakunnas, "The Job Satisfaction-Productivity Nexus: A Study Using Matched Survey and Register Data," *Cornell University Industrial & Labor Relations Review* 65, no. 2 (2012): 259.
5. Rheana Muray, "Gravity Payments' $70K Minimum Salary: CEO Dan Price Shares Results over a Year Later," *Today,* August 11, 2016, https://www.today.com/money/gravity-payments-70k-minimum-salary-ceo-dan-price-shares-results-t101678.
6. Dana Mattioli, "Customer Service as a Growth Engine," *Wall Street Journal,* June 7, 2010, B6.
7. "Word-of-Mouth Recommendations Remain the Most Credible," *Nielsen,* October 7, 2015, http://www.nielsen.com/id/en/press-room/2015/word-of-mouth-recommendations-remain-the-most-credible.html.
8. Pino G. Audia, "Train Your People to Take Others' Perspectives," *Harvard Business Review* 90, no. 10 (November 2012): 28.
9. Tim Gibson, "A Guide to Business Greetings around the World," *The Telegraph,* September 7, 2015, http://www.telegraph.co.uk/sponsored/business/business-etiquette/11834830/business-greetings.html.
10. "Appendix G: Weights and Measures," *The World Factbook,* 2017, https://www.cia.gov/library/publications/the-world-factbook/appendix/appendix-g.html.
11. Annette N. Shelby and N. Lamar Reinsch, "Positive Emphasis and You-Attitude: An Empirical Study," *Journal of Business Communication* 32, no. 4 (1995): 303–27.
12. Martin E. P. Seligman, *Learned Optimism: How to Change Your Mind and Your Life,* 2nd ed. (New York: Pocket Books, 1998), 96–107.
13. Mark A. Sherman, "Adjectival Negation and Comprehension of Multiply Negated Sentences," *Journal of Verbal Learning and Verbal Behavior* 15 (1976): 143–57.
14. Jeffrey Zaslow, "In Praise of Less Praise," *Wall Street Journal,* May 3, 2007, D1.
15. "The Happiness Factor," *Harvard Business Review* 90, no. 1-2 (January–February 2012): 77.
16. "How Happy Are You? That Could Be Key to Measuring Economic Progress," *NJ.com,* August 7, 2012, http://www.nj.com/news/index.ssf/2012/08/how_happy_are_you_that_could_b.html.
17. Gretchen Spreitzer and Christine Porath, "Creating Sustainable Performance: If You Give Your Employees the Chance to Learn and Grow, They'll Thrive—and So Will Your Organization," *Harvard Business Review* 90, no. 1-2 (January–February 2012): 94.
18. Shawn Achor, "Positive Intelligence: Three Ways Individuals Can Cultivate Their Own Sense of Well-Being and Set Themselves Up to Succeed," *Harvard Business Review* 90, no. 1-2 (January–February 2012): 102.
19. Ibid.
20. Spreitzer and Porath, "Creating Sustainable Performance," 93.
21. Clayton M. Christensen, James Allworth, and Karen Dillon, *How Will You Measure Your Life?* (New York: Harper Business, 2012), 34.
22. Achor, "Positive Intelligence," 100–02.
23. Matthew Killingsworth, "The Future of Happiness Research," *Harvard Business Review* 90, no. 1-2 (January–February 2012): 89.
24. Stephen C. Dillard, "Litigation Nation," *Wall Street Journal,* November 25, 2006, A9.
25. Margaret Baker Graham and Carol David, "Power and Politeness: Administrative Writing in an 'Organized Anarchy,'" *Journal of Business and Technical Communication* 10, no. 1 (1996): 5–27.
26. Robert Hurley, "Trust Me," *Wall Street Journal,* October 24, 2011, R4.
27. Jessica Holzer and Greg Bensinger, "SEC Embraces Social Media: New Way to Make Disclosures Gets Go-Ahead if Investors Are Told Where to Look," *Wall Street Journal,* April 3, 2013, A1.
28. Danielle Sacks, "Can You Hear Me Now? The Art of Dialogue," *Fast Company,* February 2013, 37–43.
29. Ibid.
30. Bruce Horovitz, "Bacon Mouthwash? April Fools' Marketing Jokes Go Viral," *USA Today,* April 1, 2013, http://www.usatoday.com/story/money/business/2013/04/01/april-fools-day-pranks-scope-virgin-atlantic-ikea/2042451/.
31. Ibid.
32. "Women's History Month: March 2013," U.S. Census Bureau Newsroom, February 7, 2013, http://www.census.gov/newsroom/releases/archives/facts_for_features_special_editions/cb13-ff04.html; "2010 Census Shows America's Diversity," U.S. Census Bureau Newsroom, March 24, 2011, http://www.census.gov/2010census/news/releases/operations/cb11-cn125.html; "Rise of Latino Population Blurs US Racial Lines," Associated Press, May 17, 2013, http://www.npr.org/templates/story/story.php?storyId=174546756; and "Older Americans Month: May 2013," U.S. Census Bureau Newsroom, March 7, 2013, http://www.census.gov/newsroom/releases/archives/facts_for_features_special_editions/cb13-ff07.html.
33. Laura Stevens, "German CEO's Remark on Women Draws Fire," *Wall Street Journal,* February 8, 2011, A9.

34. Frank Newport, "Black or African American?" Gallup, September 28, 2007, http://www.gallup.com/poll/28816/black-african-american.aspx.

35. Amy Molina, "Latina, Latino, Latinx. What Is This New Term, Latinx?" *NASPA,* August 31, 2016, https://www.naspa.org/constituent-groups/posts/latina-latino-latinx.-what-is-this-new-term-latinx

36. "20th Anniversary of Americans with Disabilities Act: July 26," U.S. Census Bureau Newsroom, May 26, 2010, http://www.census.gov/newsroom/releases/archives/facts_for_features_special_editions/cb10-ff13.html.

37. Clark Ansberry, "Erasing a Hurtful Label from the Books," *Wall Street Journal,* November 30, 2010, A6.

38. Ann Oldenburg, "'SI' Swimsuit Issue Courts Controversy," *USA Today,* February 14, 2013, http://www.usatoday.com/story/life/people/2013/02/14/sports-illustrated-kate-upton-swimsuit-prop-controversy/1920311/.

39. Marie Beaudette, "Study: Credit Card Offers Flood Once-Bankrupt Consumers," *Des Moines Register,* August 10, 2007, 6D.

CHAPTER

4

Planning, Composing, and Revising

Chapter Outline

The Ways Good Writers Write
- Ethics and the Writing Process

Activities in the Composing Process

Using Your Time Effectively

Brainstorming, Planning, and Organizing Business Documents
- Overcoming Writer's Block

Writing Good Business and Administrative Documents
- Business Styles
- The Plain Language Movement
- Individualized Styles

Half-Truths about Business Writing
- Half-Truth 1: "Write as You Talk."
- Half-Truth 2: "Never Use *I*."
- Half-Truth 3: "Never Use *You*."
- Half-Truth 4: "Never Begin a Sentence with *And* or *But*."
- Half-Truth 5: "Never End a Sentence with a Preposition."

- Half-Truth 6: "Never Have a Sentence with More Than 20 Words, or a Paragraph with More Than 8 Lines."
- Half-Truth 7: "Big Words Impress People."
- Half-Truth 8: "Business Writing Does Not Document Sources."

Ten Ways to Make Your Writing Easier to Read
- As You Choose Words
- As You Write and Revise Sentences
- As You Write and Revise Paragraphs

Organizational Preferences for Style

Revising, Editing, and Proofreading
- What to Look for When You Revise
- What to Look for When You Edit
- How to Catch Typos

Getting and Using Feedback

Using Boilerplate

Readability Formulas

Summary by Learning Objectives

NEWSWORTHY COMMUNICATION

©AP Images/Nati Harnik

In September 2012, Beef Products Inc. (BPI) sued ABC News for $1.2 billion over two words: *Pink Slime*.

For more than 30 years, BPI has produced "lean, finely textured beef," a product made from beef trimmings treated with ammonia and added as filler in some ground beef. Although cleared by the U.S. Department of Agriculture (USDA), its safety came into question from some 2011 news reports.

ABC News reports described BPI's product as *pink slime*, a term coined by a USDA microbiologist in 2002. The term caught on and quickly spread through social media.

The effect of *pink slime* was swift. Restaurant chains, grocery stores, and school cafeterias eliminated products that contained it. In 28 days, BPI's business dropped by 80%, and the company was forced to shut three of its plants and lay off more than 700 employees. One facility remains operational as of 2017.

BPI's attorney blamed the losses on ABC News: "To call a food product slime is the most pejorative term that could be imagined. ABC's constant repetition of it . . . had a huge impact on the consuming public." ABC's lawyers disagreed, calling *pink slime* "the sort of 'loose, figurative, or hyperbolic

language' that courts recognize demands protection under the First Amendment."

ABC settled the lawsuit in June 2017. While the terms of the settlement were not disclosed, Walt Disney Co., ABC's parent company, indicated in its August 2017 financial statement that it spent $177 million to settle the case. A lawyer for BPI indicated that the settlement was even costlier than that amount as Disney had insurance that covered some of the cost.

Two small but powerful words nearly destroyed BPI's business and cost ABC a lot of money. In preparing documents, professionals always should be careful of the wording they use and the impression it conveys to an audience.

Sources: Bill Tomson, "ABC Sued for 'Pink Slime' Defamation," *Wall Street Journal,* September 14, 2012, B3; Daniel P. Finney, "'Pink Slime': Two Small Words Trigger Big Lawsuit," *Des Moines Register,* September 14, 2012, 1A; Jonathan Stempel, "ABC News Sued for Defamation over 'Pink Slime' Reports," *Reuters,* September 13, 2012, http://www.reuters.com/article/2012/09/13/us-usa-beef-pinkslime-lawsuit-idUSBRE88C0R720120913; Martha Graybow, "ABC News Seeks Dismissal of Beef Products' Defamation Lawsuit," *Reuters,* October 31, 2012, http://www.reuters.com/article/2012/11/01/us-usa-beef-pinkslime-abclawsuit-idUSBRE8A002F20121101; Timothy Mclaughlin and P. J. Huffstutter, "Meat Packer Blames ABC's 'Pink Slime' for Nearly Killing Company," *Reuters,* June 5, 2017, https://www.reuters.com/article/us-abc-pinkslime/meat-packer-blames-abcs-pink-slime-for-nearly-killing-company-idUSKBN18W0KJ; and Christine Hauser, "ABC's 'Pink Slime' Report Tied to $177 Million in Settlement Costs," *New York Times,* August 10, 2017, https://www.nytimes.com/2017/08/10/business/pink-slime-disney-abc.html?mcubz=1.

Learning Objectives

After studying this chapter, you will know

LO 4-1   **Activities involved in the composing process and how to use these activities to your advantage.**

LO 4-2   **Guidelines for effective word choice, sentence construction, and paragraph organization.**

LO 4-3   **Techniques to revise, edit, and proofread your communications.**

Skilled performances look easy and effortless. In reality, as every dancer, musician, and athlete know, they're the products of hard work, hours of practice, attention to detail, and intense concentration. Like skilled performances in other arts, writing rests on a base of work.

The Ways Good Writers Write

No single writing process works for all writers all of the time. However, good writers and poor writers seem to use different processes.[1] Good writers are more likely to

- Realize that the first draft can be revised.
- Write regularly.
- Break big jobs into small chunks.
- Have clear goals focusing on purpose and audience.
- Have several different strategies to choose from.
- Use rules flexibly.
- Wait to edit until after the draft is complete.

Research also shows that good writers differ from poor writers in identifying and analyzing the initial problem more effectively, understanding the task more broadly and deeply, drawing from a wider repertoire of strategies, and seeing patterns more clearly. Good writers also are better at evaluating their own work.

Thinking about the writing process and consciously adopting the processes of good writers will help you become a better writer.

 ### Ethics and the Writing Process

As you plan a message:

- Identify all audiences of the message.
- In difficult situations, seek allies in your organization and discuss your options with them.

As you compose:

- Provide accurate and complete information.

- Use reliable sources of material. Document when necessary.

- Warn your readers of limits or dangers in your information.

- Promise only what you can deliver.

As you revise:

- Check to see that your language is clear to the audience and bias-free.

- Use feedback to revise text and visuals that your audience may misunderstand.

- Check your sources.

- Assume that no document is confidential. Email documents, texts, and IMs (instant messages) can be forwarded and printed without your knowledge; both electronic and paper documents, including drafts, can be subpoenaed for court cases.

- Assume that your public discourse can be subverted from your intended message. Members of the public frequently augment and repurpose tweets, blogs, and other social media posts from organizations.

Activities in the Composing Process

LO 4-1

Composing can include many activities: planning, brainstorming, gathering, organizing, writing, evaluating, getting feedback, revising, editing, and proofreading. The activities do not have to come in this order. Not every task demands all activities.

Planning

- Analyzing the problem, defining your purposes, and analyzing the audience.

- Brainstorming information to include in the document.

- Gathering the information you need—from the message you're answering, a person, printed sources, or the web.

- Selecting the points you want to make and the examples, data, and arguments to support them.

- Choosing a pattern of organization, making an outline, creating a list.

Writing

- Putting words on paper or a screen. Writing can be lists, possible headings, fragmentary notes, stream-of-consciousness writing, and partial drafts.

- Creating rough drafts.

- Composing a formal draft.

Revising

- Evaluating your work and measuring it against your goals and the requirements of the situation and audience. The best evaluation results from *re-seeing* your draft as if someone else had written it. Will your audience understand it? Is it complete? Convincing? Friendly?

- Getting feedback from someone else. Is all the necessary information there? Is there too much information? Is your pattern of organization appropriate? Does a revision solve an earlier problem? Are there obvious mistakes?

- Adding, deleting, substituting, or rearranging. Revision can be changes in single words or in large sections of a document.

Editing

- Checking the draft to see that it satisfies the requirements of standard English. Here you'd correct spelling and mechanical errors and check word choice and format. Unlike revision, which can produce major changes in meaning, editing focuses on the surface of writing.

- Proofreading the final copy to see that it's free from typographical errors.

Note the following points about these activities:

- **The activities do not have to come in this order.** Some people may gather data *after* writing a draft when they see that they need more specifics to achieve their purposes.

- **You do not have to finish one activity to start another.** Some writers plan a short section and write it, plan the next short section and write it, and so on through the document. Evaluating what is already written may cause a writer to do more planning or to change the original plan.

- **Most writers do not use all activities for all the documents they write.** You'll use more activities when you write more complex or difficult documents about new subjects or to audiences that are new to you.

For many workplace writers, pre-writing is not a warm-up activity to get ready to write the "real" document. It's really a series of activities designed to gather and organize information, take notes, brainstorm with colleagues, and plan a document before writing a complete draft. And for many people, these activities do not include outlining. Traditional outlining may lull writers into a false sense of confidence about their material and organization, making it difficult for them to revise their content and structure if they deviate from the outline developed early in the process.

Using Your Time Effectively

To get the best results from the time you have, spend about one-third of your time actually "writing." Spend about another one-third of your time analyzing the situation and your audience, gathering information, and organizing what you have to say. Spend the final third evaluating what you've said, revising the draft(s) to meet your purposes and

Not all writing has to be completed in office settings. Some people work better outside, in coffee shops, or from home.

©Nicolas McComber/Getty Images

the needs of the audience and the organization, editing a late draft to remove any errors in grammar and mechanics, and proofreading the final copy.

Do realize, however, that different writers, documents, and situations may need different time divisions to produce quality communications, especially if documents are produced by teams. Geographic distance will add even more time to the process.

Brainstorming, Planning, and Organizing Business Documents

Spend substantial time planning and organizing before you begin to write. The better your ideas are when you start, the fewer drafts you'll need to produce a good document. Start by using the analysis questions from Chapter 1 to identify purpose and audience. Use the strategies described in Chapter 2 to analyze audience and identify benefits. Gather information you can use for your document. Select the points you want to make—and the examples and data to support them.

Overcoming Writer's Block

These actions help overcome writer's block:

1. **Prepare for writing.** Collect and arrange material. Talk to people; interact with some of your audiences. The more you learn about the company, its culture, and its context, the easier it will be to write—and the better your writing will be.
2. **Practice writing regularly and in moderation.** Write daily. Keep sessions to a moderate length; an hour to an hour and a half is ideal for many people.
3. **Talk positively to yourself:** "I can do this." "If I keep working, ideas will come." "It doesn't have to be perfect; I can make it better later."
4. **Talk to other people about writing.** Value the feedback you get from them. Talking to other people expands your repertoire of strategies and helps you understand your writing community.

Sometimes the situation will determine your content. Sometimes, even when it's up to you to think of information to include in a report, you'll find it easy to think of ideas. If ideas won't come, try the following techniques:

- **Brainstorming.** Think of all the ideas you can, without judging them. Consciously try to get at least a dozen different ideas before you stop. Good brainstorming depends on generating many ideas.

- **Freewriting.**[2] Make yourself write, without stopping, for 10 minutes or so, even if you must write "I will think of something soon." At the end of 10 minutes, read what you've written, identify the best point in the draft, then set it aside, and write for another 10 uninterrupted minutes. Read this draft, marking anything that's good and should be kept, and then write again for another 10 minutes. By the third session, you will probably produce several sections that are worth keeping—maybe even a complete draft that's ready to be revised.

- **Clustering.**[3] Write your topic in the middle of the page and circle it. Write down the ideas the topic suggests, circling them, too. (The circles are designed to tap into the nonlinear half of your brain.) When you've filled the page, look for patterns or repeated ideas. Use different colored pens to group related ideas. Then use these ideas to develop your content.

- **Talking to your audiences.** As research shows, talking to internal and external audiences helps writers to involve readers in the planning process and to understand the social and political relationships among readers. This preliminary work helps reduce the number of revisions needed before documents are approved.[4]

Thinking about the content, layout, or structure of your document also can give you ideas. For long documents, write out the headings you'll use. For short documents, jot down key points—information to include, objections to answer, benefits to develop. For an oral presentation, a meeting, or a document with lots of visuals, try creating a **storyboard,** with a rectangle representing each page or unit. Draw a box with a visual for each main point. Below the box, write a short caption or label.

Writing Good Business and Administrative Documents

After you have a collection of ideas, it is time to put them in a draft of your document. In *Bird by Bird: Some Instructions on Writing and Life,* writer Anne Lamott calls this first draft the "down draft": you just get your ideas down—without worrying about writing skills such as supporting detail, organization, or mechanics.[5] Don't even worry about completeness at this point.

If even a very rough draft seems daunting, try finding one small piece to write. Perhaps you can write up the information in a table or create some audience benefits. Just getting something on paper will help. Lamott tells the story of her 10-year-old brother trying to write his report on birds. He had had three months to write it, it was due the next day, and he had not started:

> He was at the kitchen table close to tears, surrounded by binder paper and pencils and unopened books on birds, immobilized by the hugeness of the task ahead. Then my father sat down beside him, put his arm around my brother's shoulder, and said, "Bird by bird, buddy. Just take it bird by bird.[6]

Lamott calls the second draft the "up draft": you start fixing up the first draft.[7] It is at this stage that you start turning your writing into professional writing.

Figure 4.1	Different Levels of Style		
Feature	**Conversational style**	**Good business style**	**Traditional term paper style**
Formality	Highly informal	Conversational; sounds like a real person talking	More formal than conversation would be but retains a human voice
Use of contractions	Many contractions	Okay to use occasional contractions	Few contractions, if any
Pronouns	Uses first- and second-person pronouns	Uses first- and second-person pronouns	First- and second-person pronouns kept to a minimum
Level of friendliness	Friendly	Friendly	No effort to make style friendly
How personal	Personal; refers to specific circumstances of conversation	Personal; may refer to reader by name; refers to specific circumstances of audiences	Impersonal; may generally refer to readers but does not name them or refer to their circumstances
Word choice	Short, simple words; slang	Short, simple words but avoids slang	Many abstract words; scholarly, technical terms
Sentence and paragraph length	Incomplete sentences; no paragraphs	Short sentences and paragraphs	Longer sentences and paragraphs
Grammar	Can be ungrammatical	Uses standard English	Uses more formal standard English
Visual impact	Not applicable	Attention to visual impact of document	No particular attention to visual impact

Good business and administrative writing is closer to conversation and less formal than the style of writing that has traditionally earned high marks in college essays and term papers (see Figure 4.1).

Business Styles

Most people have several styles of talking, which they vary instinctively depending on the audience. Good writers have several styles, too. An email to your boss about the delays from a supplier will be informal, perhaps even chatty; a letter to the supplier demanding better service will be more formal.

Reports tend to be more formal than letters, memos, and emails because they may be read many years in the future by audiences the writer can barely imagine. Reports tend to avoid contractions, personal pronouns, and second person (because so many people read reports, *you* doesn't have much meaning). See Chapter 15 for more about report style.

Keep the following points in mind as you choose a level of formality for a specific document:

- Use a friendly, informal style to someone you've talked with.

- Avoid contractions, slang, and even minor grammatical lapses in paper documents to people you don't know. Abbreviations are okay in email messages if they're part of the group's culture.

■ Pay particular attention to your style when you write to people you fear or when you must give bad news. Research shows our style changes in stressful contexts. We tend to rely on nouns rather than on verbs and deaden our style when we are under stress or feel insecure.[8] Confident people are more direct. Edit your writing so that you sound confident, whether you feel that way or not.

The Plain Language Movement

More and more organizations are trying to simplify their communications. In the financial world, the U.S. Securities and Exchange Commission's *A Plain English Handbook: How to Create Clear SEC Disclosure Documents* asks for short sentences, everyday words, active voice, bullet lists, and descriptive headings. It cautions against legal and highly technical terms. Warren Buffett wrote the preface, saying the handbook was good news for him because, too often, he had been unable to decipher the documents filed by public companies. He offers his own writing tip: Write to a specific person. He says he pretends he is writing to his sisters when he writes his Berkshire Hathaway annual reports. The SEC has more recently applied the handbook standards to the brochures investment advisers give to clients and has urged them on hedge funds.[9]

In 2010, the Plain Writing Act became law. It requires all federal agencies to use clear prose that the public can readily understand. The website www.plainlanguage.gov explains the law, provides a detailed manual to help agencies use plain language, and offers examples of good federal communication.

Of course, the news is full of examples where these efforts have failed. The same negative examples, however, also show the great need for clear, simple style. A major factor in the subprime mortgage disaster that precipitated the global recession of 2008 was material written in prose so complex that even experts couldn't understand the content. Many homeowners who signed adjustable-rate mortgages and subsequently lost their homes claim they did not understand all the consequences of what they were signing. Experts outside the mortgage business agree with the homeowners that the language was too complex for most people to understand.[10]

Individualized Styles

Good business style allows for individual variation. Warren Buffett is widely known for the style of his shareholder letters in the Berkshire Hathaway annual reports. He began the letters in 1966, and they have gotten better—and longer—ever since. In addition to intelligence, they are known for humor, colorful language, and originality. Carol Loomis, a senior editor at *Fortune* who has been the editor of Buffett's letters since 1977, notes she makes few changes to the letters.[11] Figure 4.2 shows excerpts from his 2012 letter. Buffett's direct style suggests integrity and openness. Later in the letter, Buffett adds some of the colorful prose for which he is famous:

■ "Charlie and I have again donned our safari outfits and resumed our search for elephants."

■ "Berkshire's year-end employment totaled a record 288,462 (see page 106 for details), up 17,604 from last year. Our headquarters crew, however, remained unchanged at 24. No sense going crazy."

■ "Berkshire's ownership interest in all four companies is likely to increase in the future. Mae West had it right: 'Too much of a good thing can be wonderful.' "

■ "If you are a CEO who has some large, profitable project you are shelving because of short-term worries, call Berkshire. Let us unburden you."

■ "But wishing makes dreams come true only in Disney movies; it's poison in business."[12]

Figure 4.2	Excerpts from Warren Buffett's 2012 Letter to Shareholders

BERKSHIRE HATHAWAY INC.

To the Shareholders of Berkshire Hathaway Inc.:

Buffett's letter starts with a short financial summary of the past year.

In 2012, Berkshire achieved a total gain for its shareholders of $24.1 billion. We used $1.3 billion of that to repurchase our stock, which left us with an increase in net worth of $22.8 billion for the year. The per-share book value of both our Class A and Class B stock increased by 14.4%. Over the last 48 years (that is, since present management took over), book value has grown from $19 to $114,214, a rate of 19.7% compounded annually.*

A number of good things happened at Berkshire last year, but let's first get the bad news out of the way.

If this is the bad news, think how great the good news will be.

When the partnership I ran took control of Berkshire in 1965, I could never have dreamed that a year in which we had a gain of $24.1 billion would be subpar, in terms of the comparison we present on the facing page.

. . .

Contextualizes good news to make it even more impressive.

Despite tepid U.S. growth and weakening economies throughout much of the world, our "powerhouse five" had aggregate earnings of $10.1 billion, about $600 million more than in 2011.

. . .

Todd Combs and Ted Weschler, our new investment managers, have proved to be smart, models of integrity, helpful to Berkshire in many ways beyond portfolio management, and a perfect cultural fit. We hit the jackpot with these two. In 2012 each outperformed the S&P 500 by double-digit margins. They left me in the dust as well.

Uses humor (plus tiny type) and humility to underscore his point.

. . .

Supports green initiatives.

MidAmerican's electric utilities serve regulated retail customers in ten states. Only one utility holding company serves more states. In addition, we are the leader in renewables: first, from a standing start nine years ago, we now account for 6% of the country's wind generation capacity. Second, when we complete three projects now under construction, we will own about 14% of U.S. solar-generation capacity.

---

* All per-share figures used in this report apply to Berkshire's A shares. Figures for the B shares are 1/1500th of those shown for A.

Source: Warren Buffett, "Letters 2012," Berkshire Hathaway Inc., accessed March 4, 2013, http://www.berkshirehathaway.com/letters/2012ltr.pdf.

Half-Truths about Business Writing

Many generalizations about business writing are half-truths and must be applied selectively, if at all.

Half-Truth 1: "Write as You Talk."

Most of us use a colloquial, conversational style in speech that is too informal for writing. We use slang, incomplete sentences, and even grammatical errors.

Unless our speech is exceptionally fluent, "writing as we talk" can create awkward, repetitive, and badly organized prose. It's okay to write as you talk to produce your first draft, but edit to create a good written style.

Half-Truth 2: "Never Use *I*."

Using *I* too often can make your writing sound self-centered; using it unnecessarily will make your ideas seem tentative. However, when you write about things you've done or said or seen, using *I* is both appropriate and smoother than resorting to awkward passives or phrases like *this writer*.

Half-Truth 3: "Never Use *You*."

Certainly writers should not use *you* in formal reports, as well as other situations where the audience is not known or *you* may sound too informal. But *you* is widely used in situations such as writing to familiar audiences like our office mates, describing audience benefits, and writing sales text.

Half-Truth 4: "Never Begin a Sentence with *And* or *But*."

Beginning a sentence with *and* or *also* makes the idea that follows seem like an afterthought. That's okay when you want the effect of spontaneous speech in a written document, as you may in a sales letter. If you want to sound as though you have thought about what you are saying, put the *also* in the middle of the sentence or use another transition such as *moreover* or *furthermore*.

But tells the reader that you are shifting gears and that the following point not only contrasts with but also is more important than the preceding ideas. Presenting such verbal signposts to your reader is important. Beginning a sentence with *but* is fine if doing so makes your paragraph read smoothly.

Half-Truth 5: "Never End a Sentence with a Preposition."

Prepositions are those useful little words that indicate relationships: *with, in, under, to, at.* In job application letters, business reports, and important presentations, avoid ending sentences with prepositions. Most other messages are less formal; it's okay to end an occasional sentence with a preposition. Noting exceptions to the rule, Sir Winston Churchill famously scolded an editor who had presumptuously corrected a sentence ending with a preposition, "This is the kind of impertinence up with which I will not put."[13] Analyze your audience and the situation and use the language that you think will get the best results.

Half-Truth 6: "Never Have a Sentence with More Than 20 Words, or a Paragraph with More Than 8 Lines."

While it is true that long sentences and paragraphs may sometimes be hard to read, such is not always the case. Long sentences with parallel clauses may be quite clear, and a longer paragraph with a bulleted list may be quite readable. Your audience, purpose, and context should guide length decisions. Instructions for complicated new software may need shorter sentences and paragraphs, but an instruction paragraph on the six criteria for legitimate travel expenses may be longer than eight lines and still quite clear.

If your audience, however, believes in rigid guidelines, then you should follow them also.

Half-Truth 7: "Big Words Impress People."

Learning an academic discipline requires that you master its vocabulary. After you get out of school, however, no one will ask you to write just to prove that you understand something. Instead, you'll be asked to write or speak to people who need the information you have.

Sometimes you may want the sense of formality or technical expertise that big words create. But much of the time, big words just distance you from your audience and increase the risk of miscommunication. If you feel you need to use big words, make sure you use them correctly. When people misuse big words, they look foolish.

Half-Truth 8: "Business Writing Does Not Document Sources."

It is true that much business writing does not use sources and that many businesses frequently use their own boilerplate. However, if you borrow the words or ideas of someone outside your business, you must acknowledge your source or you will be plagiarizing. Even inside a business, if the source is not widely known or the material was particularly good or controversial, it is common to acknowledge the source.

Ten Ways to Make Your Writing Easier to Read

LO 4-2

Direct, simple writing is easier to read. One study tested two versions of a memo report. The "high-impact" version was written with the "bottom line" (the purpose of the report) in the first paragraph, simple sentences in normal word order, active verbs, concrete language, short paragraphs, headings and lists, and first- and second-person pronouns. The high-impact version took 22% less time to read. Readers said they understood the report better, and tests showed that they really did.[14] Another study showed that high-impact instructions were more likely to be followed.[15]

Building a good style takes energy and effort, but it's well worth the work. Good style can make every document more effective; good style can help make you the good writer so valuable to every organization.

As You Choose Words

The best word depends on context: the situation, your purposes, your audience, the words you already have used.

1. Use words that are accurate, appropriate, and familiar. Accurate words mean what you want to say. Appropriate words convey the attitudes you want and fit well with the other words in your document. Familiar words are easy to read and understand.

Sometimes choosing the accurate word is hard. Most of us have word pairs that confuse us. Grammarian Richard Lederer tells Toastmasters that these 10 pairs are the ones you are most likely to see or hear confused.[16]

Affect/Effect	Disinterested/Uninterested
Among/Between	Farther/Further
Amount/Number	Fewer/Less
Compose/Comprise	Imply/Infer
Different from/Different than	Lay/Lie

For help using the pairs correctly, see Appendix B.

Some meanings are negotiated as we interact with another person, attempting to communicate. Individuals are likely to have different ideas about value-laden words such as *fair* or *rich*. Some word choices have profound implications.

- Because Super Storm Sandy was not labeled a hurricane by the National Weather Service or the National Hurricane Center (technically, it made landfall as a post-tropical depression), some officials and residents did not take it seriously enough, leading to damaging inaction. But once it hit, officials such as New Jersey's governor hastened to keep it labeled as a post-tropical depression so their residents could get more insurance money (many insurance policies limit hurricane payments).[17]

- Many hospitals are labeled as charities, a status that enables them to avoid millions of dollars in taxes. A survey of charity hospitals in one state found that in one-third of them, less than 1% of expenditures went to charity care.[18]

- In 2012, the American Psychiatric Association approved the fifth edition of its diagnostic manual for mental disorders, dropping and adding some categories, changes that will impact the billions of dollars spent on mental health insurance payments and subsidized treatments.[19]

As the last example indicates, some word choices have major health repercussions. Smokers have sued tobacco companies for duping them into believing that "light" cigarettes were less harmful. *Recall,* when used in warnings about defective pacemakers and defibrillators, causes patients to ask for replacements, even though the replacement surgery is riskier than the defective device. For this reason, some physician groups prefer *safety advisory* or *safety alert.*[20]

Accurate Denotations   To be accurate, a word's **denotation** must match the meaning the writer wishes to convey. Denotation is a word's literal or dictionary meaning. Most common words in English have more than one denotation. The word *pound,* for example, means, or denotes, a unit of weight, a place where stray animals are kept, a unit of money in the British system, and the verb *to hit.* Coca-Cola spends millions each year to protect its brand names so that *Coke* will denote only that brand and not just any cola drink.

When two people use the same word or phrase to mean, or denote, different things, **bypassing** occurs. For example, a large mail-order drug company notifies clients by email when their prescription renewals get stopped because the doctor has not verified the prescription. Patients are advised to call their doctors and remind them to verify. However, the company's website posts a sentence telling clients that the prescription is *being processed.* The drug company means the renewal is in the system, waiting for the doctor's verification. The patients believe the doctor has checked in and the renewal is moving forward. The confusion results in extra phone calls to the company's customer service number, delayed prescriptions, and general customer dissatisfaction.

Problems also arise when writers misuse words.

> Three major divisions of Stiners Corporation are poised to strike out in opposite directions.

(Three different directions can't be opposite each other.)

> Stiners has grown dramatically over the past five years, largely by purchasing many smaller, desperate companies.

This latter statement probably did not intend to be so frank. More likely, the writer relied on a computer's spell checker, which accepted *desperate* for *disparate,* meaning "fundamentally different from one another."

Appropriate Connotations   Words are appropriate when their **connotations,** that is, their emotional associations or colorings, convey the attitude you want. A great many words carry connotations of approval or disapproval, disgust or delight. Consider *firm* or *obstinate, flexible* or *wishy-washy.* Some businesses offer a cash discount; you rarely hear of a credit surcharge. Some companies offer an insurance discount if their employees follow specified good-health practices; the employees who do not follow those practices are paying a penalty, although it is not publicized that way.

A supervisor can "tell the truth" about a subordinate's performance and yet write either a positive or a negative performance appraisal, based on the connotations of the words in the appraisal. Consider an employee who pays close attention to details. A positive appraisal might read, "Terry is a meticulous team member who takes care of details that others sometimes ignore." But the same behavior might be described negatively: "Terry is hung up on trivial details."

Advertisers carefully choose words with positive connotations.

- In this youth-conscious society, hearing aids become personal communication assistants.[21]

- Expensive cars are never *used;* instead, they're *pre-owned, experienced,* or even *previously adored.*[22]

- Insurers emphasize what you want to *protect* (your home, your car, your life), rather than the losses you are insuring against (fire damage, auto accident, death).

Words also may connote categories. Some show status. Both *salesperson* and *sales representative* are nonsexist job titles. But the first sounds like a clerk in a store; the second suggests someone selling important items to corporate customers. Some words connote age: *adorable* generally connotes young children, not adults. Other words, such as *handsome* or *pretty,* connote gender.

Connotations change over time. The word *charity* had acquired such negative connotations by the 19th century that people began to use the term *welfare* instead. Now, *welfare* has acquired negative associations. Most states have *public assistance programs* instead.

Ethical Implications of Word Choice   How positively can we present something and still be ethical? We have the right to package our ideas attractively, but we have the responsibility to give the public or our superiors all the information they need to make decisions.

Word choices have ethical implications in technical contexts as well. When scientists refer to 100-year floods, they mean a flood so big that it has a 1% chance of happening in any given year. However, a "1% annual chance flood" is awkward and has not become standard usage. On the other hand, many nonscientists believe a 100-year flood will happen only once every hundred years. After a 100-year flood swamped the Midwest in 1993, many people moved back into flood-prone homes; some even dropped their flood insurance. Unfortunately, both actions left them devastated by a second 100-year flood in 2008.[23]

Perhaps one of the best-known examples of ethical implications deals with the interrogation technique of waterboarding. President George W. Bush's attorney general said waterboarding was not torture; President Obama's attorney general said it was.[24]

Familiar Words   Use familiar words, words that are in almost everyone's vocabulary. Use the word that most exactly conveys your meaning, but whenever you can choose between two words that mean the same thing, use the shorter, more common one. Some writers mistakenly believe that using long, learned words makes them seem smart. However, experimental evidence shows the opposite is usually true: Needlessly pretentious diction is generally taken as a sign of lower intelligence—and causes low credibility.[25] Try to use specific, concrete words. They're easier to understand and remember.[26]

The following list gives a few examples of short, simple alternatives:

Formal and stuffy	Short and simple
ameliorate	improve
commence	begin
enumerate	list
finalize	finish, complete
prioritize	rank
utilize	use
viable option	choice

There are some exceptions to the general rule that "shorter is better."

- Use a long word if it is the only word that expresses your meaning exactly.

- Use a long word—or phrase—if it is more familiar than a short word: *a word in another language for a geographic place or area* is better than *exonym*.

- Use a long word if its connotations are more appropriate. *Exfoliate* is better than *scrape off dead skin cells.*

- Use a long word if your audience prefers it.

---

2. Use technical jargon sparingly; eliminate business jargon.   There are two kinds of **jargon**. The first is the specialized terminology of a technical field. Many public figures enjoy mocking this kind of jargon. Even the *Wall Street Journal* does its share, mocking quotes like this one from a computer industry press release announcing a new "market offering":

> [The] offerings are leading-edge service configuration assurance capabilities that will help us to rapidly deploy high-demand IP services, such as level 3 virtual private networks, multi-cast and quality of service over our IP/MPLS network.[27]

A job application letter is one of the few occasions when it's desirable to use technical jargon: Using the technical terminology of the reader's field helps suggest that you're a peer who also is competent in that field. In other kinds of messages, use technical jargon only when the term is essential and known to the reader. If a technical term has a "plain English" equivalent, use the simpler term.

The second kind of jargon is the **businessese** that some writers still use: *as per your request, enclosed please find, please do not hesitate.* None of the words in this second category of jargon are necessary. Indeed, some writers call these terms *deadwood* because they are no longer living words. If any of the terms in the first column of Figure 4.3 appear in your writing, replace them with more modern language.

As You Write and Revise Sentences

At the sentence level, you can do many things to make your writing easy to read.

3. Use active voice most of the time.   "Who does what" sentences with active voice make your writing more forceful.

A verb is in **active voice** if the grammatical subject of the sentence does the action the verb describes. A verb is in **passive voice** if the subject is acted upon. Passive voice is

Figure 4.3	Getting Rid of Business Jargon	
Instead of	**Use**	**Because**
At your earliest convenience	The date you need a response	If you need it by a deadline, say so. It may never be convenient to respond.
As per your request; 65 miles per hour	As you requested; 65 miles an hour	*Per* is a Latin word for *by* or *for* each. Use *per* only when the meaning is correct; avoid mixing English and Latin.
Enclosed please find	Enclosed is; Here is	An enclosure isn't a treasure hunt. If you put something in the envelope, the reader will find it.
Hereto, herewith	Omit	Omit legal jargon.
Please be advised; Please be informed	Omit—simply start your response	You don't need a preface. Go ahead and start.
Please do not hesitate	Omit	Omit negative words.
Pursuant to	According to; or omit	*Pursuant* does not mean *after.* Omit legal jargon in any case.
This will acknowledge receipt of your letter.	Omit—start your response	If you answer a letter, the reader knows you got it.
Trusting this is satisfactory, we remain	Omit	Eliminate *-ing* endings. When you are through, stop.

usually made up of a form of the verb *to be* plus a past participle. *Passive* has nothing to do with *past.* Passive voice can be past, present, or future:

were received	(in the past)
is recommended	(in the present)
will be implemented	(in the future)

To spot a passive voice, find the verb. If the verb describes something that the grammatical subject is doing, the verb is in active voice. If the verb describes something that is being done to the grammatical subject, the verb is in passive voice.

Active voice	**Passive voice**
The customer received 500 widgets.	Five hundred widgets were received by the customer.
I recommend this method.	This method is recommended by me.
The state agencies will implement the program.	The program will be implemented by the state agencies.

To change from passive voice to active voice, you must make the agent the new subject. If no agent is specified in the sentence, you must supply one to make the sentence active.

Passive voice	**Active voice**
The request was approved by the plant manager.	The plant manager approved the request.
A decision will be made next month. No agent in sentence.	The committee will decide next month.
A letter will be sent informing the customer of the change. No agent in sentence.	[You] Send the customer a letter informing her about the change.

Passive voice has at least three disadvantages:

- If all the information in the original sentence is retained, passive voice makes the sentence longer and thus more time-consuming to understand.[28]
- If the agent is omitted, it's not clear who is responsible for doing the action.
- Using much passive voice, especially in material that has a lot of big words, can make the writing boring and pompous.

Passive voice is desirable in these situations:

a. Use passive voice to emphasize the object receiving the action, not the agent.

> Your order was shipped November 15.

The customer's order, not the shipping clerk, is important.

b. Use passive voice to provide coherence within a paragraph. A sentence is easier to read if "old" information comes at the beginning of a sentence. When you have been discussing a topic, use the word again as your subject even if that requires passive voice.

> The bank made several risky loans in the late 1990s. These loans were written off as "uncollectible" in 2001.

Using *loans* as the subject of the second sentence provides a link between the two sentences, making the paragraph easier to read.

c. Use passive voice to avoid assigning blame.

> The order was damaged during shipment.

Active voice would require the writer to specify *who* damaged the order. The passive voice is more tactful here.

According to PlainLanguage.gov, changing writing to active voice is the most powerful change that can be made to government documents.[29] But even the self-proclaimed prescriptivist style editor Bill Walsh, a copy chief at the *Washington Post,* admits that sometimes passive voice is necessary—although not as often as many writers think.[30]

4. Use verbs—not nouns—to carry the weight of your sentence.

Put the weight of your sentence in the verb to make your sentences more forceful and up to 25% easier to read.[31] When the verb is a form of the verb *to be,* revise the sentence to use a more forceful verb.

Weak: The financial advantage of owning this equipment instead of leasing it is 10% after taxes.

Better: Owning this equipment rather than leasing it will save us 10% after taxes.

Nouns ending in *-ment, -ion,* and *-al* often hide verbs.

Weak	Better
make an adjustment	adjust
make a payment	pay
make a decision	decide
reach a conclusion	conclude
take into consideration	consider
make a referral	refer
provide assistance	assist

Use verbs to present the information more forcefully.

Weak: We will perform an investigation of the problem.

Better: We will investigate the problem.

Weak: Selection of a program should be based on the client's needs.

Better: Select the program that best fits the client's needs.

5. Eliminate wordiness.

Writing is **wordy** if the same idea can be expressed in fewer words. Unnecessary words increase writing time, bore your reader, and make your meaning more difficult to follow because the reader must hold all the extra words in mind while trying to understand your meaning.

Good writing is concise, but it still may be lengthy. Concise writing may be long because it is packed with ideas. Chapter 3 shows how revisions to create you-attitude and positive emphasis and to develop benefits are frequently *longer* than the originals because the revision adds information not given in the original.

Sometimes you may be able to look at a draft and see immediately how to condense it. When the solution isn't obvious, try the following strategies to condense your writing:

a. Eliminate words that add nothing.

b. Combine sentences to eliminate unnecessary words.

c. Put the meaning of your sentence into the subject and verb to cut the number of words.

You eliminate unnecessary words to save the reader's time, not simply to see how few words you can use. You aren't writing a telegram, so keep the little words that make sentences complete. (Incomplete sentences are fine in lists where all the items are incomplete.)

The following examples show how to use these methods.

a. **Eliminate words that add nothing.** Cut words if the idea is already clear from other words in the sentence. Substitute single words for wordy phrases.

Wordy: Keep this information on file for future reference.

Better: Keep this information for reference.

or: File this information.

Wordy: The reason we want to see changing our hardware manager to Hanson's is because Hanson's is able to collect hardware from a larger number of vendors than our current supplier.

Better: We recommend changing our hardware manager to Hanson's for their larger number of vendors.

Phrases beginning with *of, which,* and *that* often can be shortened.

Wordy: the question of most importance

Better: the most important question

Wordy: the estimate that is enclosed

Better: the enclosed estimate

Wordy: We need to act on the suggestions that our customers offer us.

Better: We need to act on customer suggestions.

Sentences beginning with *There are* or *It is* often can be tighter.

Wordy: There are three reasons for the success of the project.

Tighter: Three reasons explain the project's success.

Wordy: It is the case that college graduates earn more money.

Tighter: College graduates earn more money.

Figure 4.4	Words to Cut		
Cut the following words	**Cut redundant words**	**Substitute a single word for a wordy phrase**	
quite	~~a period of~~ three months	~~at the present time~~	now
really	during ~~the course of~~ the negotiations	~~due to the fact that~~	because
very	during ~~the year of~~ 2013	~~in order to~~	to
	maximum ~~possible~~	~~in the event that~~	if
	~~past~~ experience	~~in the near future~~	soon (or give the date)
	plan ~~in advance~~	~~on a regular basis~~	regularly
	refer ~~back~~	~~prior to the start of~~	before
	~~the color~~ blue	~~until such time as~~	until
	~~the month of~~ November		
	~~true~~ facts		

Check your draft. If you find these phrases, or any of the unnecessary words shown in Figure 4.4, eliminate them.

b. **Combine sentences to eliminate unnecessary words.** In addition to saving words, combining sentences focuses the reader's attention on key points, makes your writing sound more sophisticated, and sharpens the relationship between ideas, thus making your writing more coherent.

Wordy: I conducted this survey by telephone on Sunday, April 21. I questioned two groups of upperclass students—male and female—who, according to the Student Directory, were still living in the dorms. The purpose of this survey was to find out why some upperclass students continue to live in the dorms even though they are no longer required by the University to do so. I also wanted to find out if there were any differences between male and female upperclass students in their reasons for choosing to remain in the dorms.

Tighter: On Sunday, April 21, I phoned upperclass men and women living in the dorms to find out (1) why they continue to live in the dorms even though they are no longer required to do so and (2) whether men and women gave the same reasons.

c. **Put the meaning of your sentence into the subject and verb to cut the number of words.** Put the core of your meaning into the subject and verb of your main clause.

Wordy: The reason we are recommending the computerization of this process is because it will reduce the time required to obtain data and will give us more accurate data.

Better: Computerizing the process will give us more accurate data more quickly.

Wordy: The purpose of this letter is to indicate that if we are unable to mutually benefit from our seller/buyer relationship, with satisfactory material and satisfactory payment, then we have no alternative other than to sever the relationship. In other words, unless the account is handled in 45 days, we will have to change our terms to a permanent COD basis.

Better: A good buyer/seller relationship depends upon satisfactory material and payment. You can continue to charge your purchases from us only if you clear your present balance in 45 days.

6. Vary sentence length and sentence structure. Readable prose mixes sentence lengths and varies sentence structure. A short sentence (under 10 words) can add punch to your prose. Long sentences (over 30 words) can be danger signs.

The first-place Golden Gobbledygook Award goes to a 1,000-word sentence in a legal document filed in Oklahoma.[32]

You can vary sentence patterns in several ways. First, you can mix simple, compound, and complex sentences. (See Appendix B for more information on sentence structure.) **Simple sentences** have one main clause:

> We will open a new store this month.

Compound sentences have two main clauses joined with *and, but, or,* or another conjunction. Compound sentences work best when the ideas in the two clauses are closely related.

> We have hired staff, and they will complete their training next week.

> We wanted to have a local radio station broadcast from the store during its grand opening, but the DJs were already booked.

Complex sentences have one main and at least one subordinate clause; they are good for showing logical relationships.

> When the stores open, we will have specials in every department.

> Because we already have a strong customer base in the northwest, we expect the new store to be just as successful as the store in the City Center Mall.

You also can vary sentences by changing the order of elements. Normally the subject comes first.

> We will survey customers later in the year to see whether demand warrants a third store on campus.

To create variety, occasionally begin the sentence with some other part of the sentence.

> Later in the year, we will survey customers to see whether demand warrants a third store on campus.

Use these guidelines for sentence length and structure:

- Always edit sentences for conciseness. Even a short sentence can be wordy.

- When your subject matter is complicated or full of numbers, make a special effort to keep sentences short.

- Use longer sentences to show how ideas are linked to each other; to avoid a series of short, choppy sentences; and to reduce repetition.

- Group the words in long and medium-length sentences into chunks that the reader can process quickly.

- When you use a long sentence, keep the subject and verb close together.

Let's see how to apply the last three principles.

Use long sentences to show how ideas are linked to each other; to avoid a series of short, choppy sentences; and to reduce repetition. The following sentence is hard to read not simply because it is long, but because it is shapeless. Just cutting it into a series of short, choppy sentences doesn't help. The best revision uses medium-length sentences to show the relationship between ideas.

> Too long: It should also be noted in the historical patterns presented in the summary, that though there were delays in January and February which we realized were occurring, we are now back where we were about a year ago, and that we are not off line in our collect receivables as compared to last year at this time, but we do show a considerable over-budget figure because of an ultra-conservative goal on the receivable investment.

Choppy: There were delays in January and February. We knew about them at the time. We are now back where we were about a year ago. The summary shows this. Our present collect receivables are in line with last year's. However, they exceed the budget. The reason they exceed the budget is that our goal for receivable investment was very conservative.

Better: As the summary shows, although there were delays in January and February (of which we were aware), we have now regained our position of a year ago. Our present collect receivables are in line with last year's, but they exceed the budget because our goal for receivable investment was very conservative.

Group the words in long and medium-length sentences into chunks. The "better" revision above has seven chunks. At 27 and 24 words, respectively, these sentences aren't short, but they're readable because no chunk is longer than 10 words. Any sentence pattern will get boring if it is repeated sentence after sentence. Use different sentence patterns—different kinds and lengths of chunks—to keep your prose interesting.

Keep the subject and verb close together. Often you can move the subject and verb closer together if you put the modifying material in a list at the end of the sentence. For maximum readability, present the list vertically.

Hard to read: Movements resulting from termination, layoffs and leaves, recalls and reinstates, transfers in, transfers out, promotions in, promotions out, and promotions within are presently documented through the Payroll Authorization Form.

Better: The Payroll Authorization Form documents the following movements:

- Termination
- Layoffs and leaves
- Recalls and reinstates
- Transfers in and out
- Promotions in, out, and within

7. Use parallel structure.

Parallel structure puts words, phrases, or clauses in the same grammatical and logical form. In the following faulty example, *by reviewing* is a gerund, while *note* is an imperative verb. Make the sentence parallel by using both gerunds or both imperatives.

Faulty: Errors can be checked by reviewing the daily exception report or note the number of errors you uncover when you match the lading copy with the file copy of the invoice.

Parallel: Errors can be checked by reviewing the daily exception report or by noting the number of errors you uncover when you match the lading copy with the file copy of the invoice.

Also parallel: To check errors, note

1. The number of items on the daily exception report.
2. The number of errors discovered when the lading copy and the file copy are matched.

Note that a list in parallel structure must fit grammatically into the umbrella sentence that introduces the list.

Faulty: The following suggestions can help employers avoid bias in job interviews:

1. Base questions on the job description.
2. Questioning techniques.
3. Selection and training of interviewers.

Parallel:	The following suggestions can help employers avoid bias in job interviews:
	1. Base questions on the job description.
	2. Ask the same questions of all applicants.
	3. Select and train interviewers carefully.
Also parallel:	Employers can avoid bias in job interviews by
	1. Basing questions on the job description.
	2. Asking the same questions of all applicants.
	3. Selecting and training interviewers carefully.

Words also must be logically parallel. In the following faulty example, *juniors, seniors,* and *athletes* are not three separate groups. The revision groups words into non-overlapping categories.

Faulty:	I interviewed juniors and seniors and athletes.
Parallel:	I interviewed juniors and seniors. In each rank, I interviewed athletes and non-athletes.

Parallel structure is a powerful device for making your writing tighter, smoother, and more forceful.

Faulty:	Our customers receive these benefits:
	▪ Use tracking information.
	▪ Our products let them scale the software to their needs.
	▪ The customer can always rely on us.
Parallel:	Our customers receive these benefits:
	▪ Tracking information
	▪ Scalability
	▪ Reliability

8. Put your readers in your sentences.

Use second-person pronouns (*you*) rather than third-person (*he, she, one*) to give your writing more impact. *You* is both singular and plural; it can refer to a single person or to every member of your organization.

Third-person:	Funds in a participating employee's account at the end of each six months will automatically be used to buy more stock unless a "Notice of Election Not to Exercise Purchase Rights" form is received from the employee.
Second-person:	Once you begin to participate, funds in your account at the end of each six months will automatically be used to buy more stock unless you turn in a "Notice of Election Not to Exercise Purchase Rights" form.

Be careful to use *you* only when it refers to your reader.

Incorrect:	My visit with the outside sales rep showed me that your schedule can change quickly.
Correct:	My visit with the outside sales rep showed me that schedules can change quickly.

As You Write and Revise Paragraphs

Paragraphs are visual and logical units. Use them to chunk your sentences.

9. Begin most paragraphs with topic sentences.

A good paragraph has **unity;** that is, it discusses only one idea, or topic. The **topic sentence** states the main idea and provides a scaffold to structure your document. Audiences who skim reports can follow your ideas more easily if each paragraph begins with a topic sentence. Your writing will be easier to read if you make the topic sentence explicit and put it at the beginning of the paragraph.[33]

Hard to read (no topic sentence):	Another main use of ice is to keep the fish fresh. Each of the seven kinds of fish served at the restaurant requires one gallon twice a day, for a total of 14 gallons. An additional 6 gallons a day are required for the salad bar.
Better (begins with topic sentence):	Twenty gallons of ice a day are needed to keep food fresh. Of this, the biggest portion (14 gallons) is used to keep the fish fresh. Each of the seven kinds of fish served at the restaurant requires one gallon twice a day. An additional 6 gallons a day are required for the salad bar.
Hard to read (no topic sentence):	In fiscal 2018, the company filed claims for refund of federal income taxes of $3,199,000 and interest of $969,000 paid as a result of an examination of the company's federal income tax returns by the Internal Revenue Service (IRS) for the years 2014 through 2016. It is uncertain what amount, if any, ultimately may be recovered.
Better (paragraph starts with topic sentence):	The company and the IRS disagree about whether the company is responsible for back taxes. In fiscal 2018, the company filed claims for a refund of federal income taxes of $3,199,000 and interest of $969,000 paid as a result of an examination of the company's federal income tax returns by the Internal Revenue Service (IRS) for the years 2014 through 2016. It is uncertain what amount, if any, ultimately may be recovered.

A good topic sentence forecasts the structure and content of the paragraph.

Plan B also has economic advantages.

(Prepares the reader for a discussion of B's economic advantages.)

We had several personnel changes in June.

(Prepares the reader for a list of the month's terminations and hires.)

Employees have complained about one part of our new policy on parental leaves.

(Prepares the reader for a discussion of the problem.)

When the first sentence of a paragraph is not the topic sentence, readers who skim may miss the main point. If the paragraph does not have a topic sentence, you will need to write one. If you can't think of a single sentence that serves as an "umbrella" to cover every sentence, the paragraph probably lacks unity. To solve the problem, either split the paragraph or eliminate the sentences that digress from the main point.

10. Use transitions to link ideas.   Transition words and sentences signal the connections between ideas to the reader. Transitions tell whether the next sentence continues the previous thought or starts a new idea; they can tell whether the idea that comes next is more or less important than the previous thought. Figure 4.5 lists some of the most common transition words and phrases.

These sentences use transition words and phrases:

Kelly wants us to switch the contract to Ames Cleaning, and I agree with her. (continuing the same idea)

Kelly wants us to switch the contract to Ames Cleaning, but I prefer Ross Commercial. (contrasting opinions)

Figure 4.5	Transition Words and Phrases		
To show addition or continuation of the same idea and also first, second, third in addition likewise similarly **To introduce another important item** furthermore moreover	**To introduce an example** for example (e.g.,) for instance indeed to illustrate namely specifically **To contrast** in contrast on the other hand or	**To show that the contrast is more important than the previous idea** but however nevertheless on the contrary **To show cause and effect** as a result because consequently for this reason therefore	**To show time** after as before in the future next then until when while **To summarize or end** finally in conclusion

> As a result of our differing views, we will be visiting both firms. (showing cause and effect)

These are transitional sentences:

> Now that we have examined the advantages of using Ames Cleaning, let's look at potential disadvantages. (shows movement between two sections of evaluation)

> These pros and cons show us three reasons we should switch to Ross Commercial. (shows movement away from evaluation sections; forecasts the three reasons)

Organizational Preferences for Style

Different organizations and bosses may legitimately have different ideas about what constitutes good writing. If the style doesn't seem reasonable, ask. Often the documents that end up in files aren't especially good; later, other workers may find these and copy them, thinking they represent a corporate standard. Bosses in fact may prefer better writing.

Recognize that a style may serve other purposes than communication. An abstract, hard-to-read style may help a group forge its own identity. Researchers James Suchan and Ronald Dulek have shown that Navy officers preferred a passive, impersonal style because they saw themselves as followers. An aircraft company's engineers saw wordiness as the verbal equivalent of backup systems. A backup is redundant but essential to safety because parts and systems do fail.[34]

Revising, Editing, and Proofreading

LO 4-3

Once you have your document written, you need to polish it.

A popular myth about revising is that Abraham Lincoln wrote the Gettysburg address, perhaps the most famous of all American presidential speeches, on the back of an envelope as he traveled by train to the battlefield's dedication. The reality is that Lincoln wrote at least a partial draft of the speech before leaving for the trip and continued to revise it up to the morning of its delivery. Furthermore, the speech was on a topic he passionately believed in, one he had been pondering for years.[35]

Like Lincoln, good writers work on their drafts; they make their documents better by judicious revising, editing, and proofreading.

- **Revising** means making changes in content, organization, and tone that will better satisfy your purposes and your audience.

- **Editing** means making surface-level changes that make the document grammatically correct.

- **Proofreading** means checking to be sure the document is free from typographical errors.

What to Look for When You Revise

When you're writing to a new audience or have to solve a particularly difficult problem, plan to revise the draft at least three times. The first time, look for content and clarity: Have I said enough and have I said it clearly? The second time, check the organization and layout: Have I presented my content so it can be easily absorbed? Finally, check style and tone: Have I used you-attitude? The Thorough-Revision Checklist in Figure 4.6 summarizes the questions you should ask.

Often you'll get the best revision by setting aside your draft, getting a blank page or screen, and redrafting. This strategy takes advantage of the thinking you did on your first draft without locking you into the sentences in it.

As you revise, be sure to read the document through from start to finish. Reading the entire document is particularly important if you've composed in several sittings or if you've used text from other documents. Such drafts tend to be choppy, repetitious, or inconsistent. You may need to add transitions, cut repetitive parts, or change words to create a uniform level of formality throughout the document.

If you're really in a time bind, do a light revision, as outlined in the Light-Revision Checklist (see Figure 4.7). The quality of the final document may not be as high as with a thorough revision, but even a light revision is better than skipping revision altogether.

Sometimes revising and proofreading are more pleasant if done in an informal setting.
©Tim Robberts/Getty Images

What to Look for When You Edit

Even good writers need to edit because no one can pay attention to surface correctness while thinking of ideas. As a matter of fact, even history-shaping documents like the Declaration of Independence became better with editing.

Figure 4.6	Thorough-Revision Checklist

Content and clarity

☐ Does your document meet the needs of the organization and of the reader—and make you look good?

☐ Have you given readers all the information they need to understand and act on your message?

☐ Is all the information accurate and clear?

☐ Is the message easy to read?

☐ Is each sentence clear? Is the message free from apparently contradictory statements?

☐ Is the logic clear and convincing? Are generalizations and benefits backed up with adequate supporting detail?

Organization and layout

☐ Is the pattern of organization clear? Is it appropriate for your purposes, audience, and context?

☐ Are transitions between ideas smooth? Do ideas within paragraphs flow smoothly?

☐ Does the design of the document make it easy for readers to find the information they need? Is the document visually inviting?

☐ Are the points emphasized by layout ones that deserve emphasis?

☐ Are the first and last paragraphs effective?

Style and tone

☐ Does the message use you-attitude and positive emphasis?

☐ Is the message friendly and free from sexist language?

☐ Does the message build goodwill?

Figure 4.7	Light-Revision Checklist

☐ Have you given readers all the information they need to understand and act on your message?

☐ Is the pattern of organization clear and helpful?

☐ Is the logic clear and convincing? Are generalizations and benefits backed up with adequate supporting detail?

☐ Does the design of the document make it easy for readers to find the information they need?

☐ Are the first and last paragraphs effective?

Editing should always *follow* revision. There's no point in taking time to fix a grammatical error in a sentence that may be cut when you clarify your meaning or tighten your style. Some writers edit more accurately when they print out a copy of a document and edit the hard copy.

Check your material to make sure you have acknowledged all information and opinions borrowed from outside the organization. Using material from outside the organization without acknowledging the source is **plagiarism.** Check also that you have acknowledged company information that is controversial or not widely known.

Check your communication to make sure your sentences say what you intend.

Not: Take a moment not to sign your policy.

But: Take a moment now to sign your policy.

Not: I wish to apply for the job as assistant manger.

But: I wish to apply for the job as assistant manager.

One of the most famous editing errors in history was the so-called Wicked Bible, which left out a crucial *not,* thus changing one of the Ten Commandments into "Thou shalt commit adultery."

When you edit, you also need to check that the following are accurate:

- Sentence structure.
- Subject–verb and noun–pronoun agreement.
- Punctuation.
- Word usage.
- Spelling—including spelling of names.
- Numbers.

Appendix B reviews grammar, punctuation, numbers, and words that are often confused.

Most writers make a small number of errors over and over. If you know that you have trouble with dangling modifiers (e.g., Having submitted the report late, an extension was needed; arrived late for practice, a written excuse was needed) or subject–verb agreement (e.g., "there is/are a group of people"), for example, specifically look for them in your draft. Also look for any errors that especially bother your boss and correct them.

How to Catch Typos

To catch typos use a **spell-checker.** But you still need to proofread by eye. Spell-checkers work by matching words; they will signal any group of letters not listed in their dictionaries. However, they cannot tell you when you've used the wrong word but spelled it correctly. For example, Coca-Cola once distributed 2 million packages of it's signature beverage with a big proofreading mistake. The copyright information, which normally read "red disk icon and contour bottle are trademarks of the Coca-Cola Co.," was misprinted with a "c" instead of an "s" in "disk."[36]

Don't underestimate the harm that spelling errors can create. A large, Midwestern university lost its yearbook after an uncaught typo referred to the Greek community as the "geeks on campus." Greeks boycotted the yearbook, which went deeply into debt and out of business. The impact of typos on job documents is well known. Proofread every document both with a spell-checker and by eye to catch the errors a spell-checker can't find.

Proofreading is hard because writers tend to see what they know should be there rather than what really is there. It's easier to proof something you haven't written, so you may want to swap papers with a proofing buddy. (Be sure the person looks for typos, not content.)

To proofread:

- Read once quickly for meaning, to see that nothing has been left out.

- Read a second time, slowly. When you find an error, correct it and then *reread that line.* Readers tend to become less attentive after they find one error and may miss other errors close to the one they've spotted.

- To proofread a document you know well, read the lines backward or the pages out of order. Also, you can try reading the document out loud.

- Always triple-check numbers, headings, the first and last paragraphs, and the reader's name.

Getting and Using Feedback

Getting feedback almost always improves a document. In many organizations, it's required. All external documents must be read and approved before they go out. The process of drafting, getting feedback, revising, and getting more feedback is called **cycling.** One researcher reported that documents in her clients' firms cycled an average of 4.2 times before reaching the intended audience.[37] Another researcher studied a major 10-page document whose 20 drafts made a total of 31 stops on the desks of nine reviewers on four different levels.[38] Being asked to revise a document is a fact of life in business.

You can improve the quality of the feedback you get by telling people which aspects you'd especially like comments about. For example, when you give a reader the outline or planning draft, you probably want to know whether the general approach and content are appropriate, and if you have included all major points. After your second draft, you might want to know whether the reasoning is convincing. When you reach the polishing draft, you'll be ready for feedback on style and grammar. The Questions to Ask Readers Checklist (see Figure 4.8) offers suggestions.

Figure 4.8	Questions to Ask Readers Checklist

Outline or planning draft

☐   Does the plan seem on the right track?

☐   What topics should be added? Should any be cut?

☐   Do you have any other general suggestions?

Revising draft

☐   Does the message satisfy all its purposes?

☐   Is the message adapted to the audience(s)?

☐   Is the organization effective?

☐   What parts aren't clear?

☐   What ideas need further development and support?

☐   Do you have any other suggestions?

Polishing draft

☐   Are there any problems with word choice or sentence structure?

☐   Did you find any inconsistencies?

☐   Did you find any typos?

☐   Is the document's design effective?

Technology helps with both giving and receiving feedback. Word documents can be edited using review features such as Track Changes, a word-processing feature that records alterations made to a document. It is particularly useful when you are collaborating with a colleague to create, edit, or revise documents. Track Changes will highlight any text that has been added to or deleted from your document, and it also allows you to decide whether to accept each change or reject it and return to your original text. In addition to Track Changes, many word processors include a comment feature that allows you to ask questions or make suggestions without altering the text itself. Documents also can be posted in the cloud using Google Docs and then can be edited by multiple people.

It's easy to feel defensive when someone criticizes your work. If the feedback stings, put it aside until you can read it without feeling defensive. Even if you think that the reader hasn't understood what you were trying to say, the fact that the reader complained usually means the section could be improved. If the reader says, "This isn't true," and you know the statement is true, several kinds of revision might make the truth clear to the reader: rephrasing the statement, giving more information or examples, or documenting the source.

Reading feedback carefully is a good way to understand the culture of your organization. Are you told to give more details or to shorten messages? Does your boss add headings and bullet points? Look for patterns in the comments and apply what you learn in your next document.

Using Boilerplate

Boilerplate is language—sentences, paragraphs, even pages—from a previous document that a writer legitimately includes in a new document. In academic papers, material written by others must be quoted and documented—to neglect to do so would be plagiarism. However, because businesses own the documents their employees write, old text may be included without attribution.

Many legal documents, including apartment leases and sales contracts, are almost completely boilerplate. Writers also may use boilerplate they wrote for earlier documents. For example, a section from a proposal describing the background of the problem also could be used in the final report. A section from a progress report describing what the writer had done could be used with only a few changes in the methods section of the final report.

Writers use boilerplate both to save time and energy and to use language that already has been approved by the organization's legal staff. However, research has shown that using boilerplate creates two problems.[39] First, using unrevised boilerplate can create a document with incompatible styles and tones. Second, boilerplate can allow writers to ignore subtle differences in situations and audiences.

Readability Formulas

Readability formulas attempt to measure objectively how easy something is to read. However, because they don't take many factors into account, the formulas are at best a very limited guide to good style.

Computer packages that analyze style may give you a readability score. Some states' "plain English" laws require consumer contracts to meet a certain readability score. Some companies require that warranties and other consumer documents meet certain scores.

Readability formulas depend heavily on word length and sentence length. See the *Business and Administrative Communication* website to calculate readability using the two best-known readability formulas: the Gunning Fog Index and the Flesch Reading Ease Scale. Research has shown,[40] however, that using shorter words and sentences will not necessarily make a passage easy to read. Short words are not always easy to understand, especially if they have technical meanings (e.g., *waive, bear market, liquid*). Short, choppy sentences and sentence fragments are actually harder to understand than well-written, medium-length sentences.

No reading formula yet devised takes into account three factors that influence how easy a text is to read: the complexity of the ideas, the organization of the ideas, and the layout and design of the document.

Instead of using readability formulas, test your draft with the people for whom it is designed. How long does it take them to find the information they need? Do they make mistakes when they try to use the document? Do they think the writing is easy to understand? Answers to these questions can give much more accurate information than any readability score.

Summary by Learning Objectives

LO 4-1   **Activities involved in the composing process and how to use these activities to your advantage.**

Processes that help writers write well include not expecting the first draft to be perfect, writing regularly, modifying the initial task if it's too hard or too easy, having clear goals, knowing many different strategies, using rules as guidelines rather than as absolutes, and waiting to edit until after the draft is complete.

Writing processes can include many activities: planning, gathering, brainstorming, organizing, writing, evaluating, getting feedback, revising, editing, and proofreading. *Revising* means changing the document to make it better satisfy the writer's purposes and the audience. *Editing* means making surface-level changes that make the document grammatically correct. *Proofreading* means checking to be sure the document is free from typographical errors. The activities do not have to come in any set order. It is not necessary to finish one activity to start another. Most writers use all activities only when they write a document whose genre, subject matter, or audience is new to them.

To think of ideas, try brainstorming, freewriting (writing without stopping for 10 minutes or so), and clustering (brainstorming with circled words on a page).

LO 4-2   **Guidelines for effective word choice, sentence construction, and paragraph organization.**

Good style in business and administrative writing is less formal, more friendly, and more personal than the style usually used for term papers.

Use the following techniques to make your writing easier to read.

As you choose words:

1. Use words that are accurate, appropriate, and familiar. Denotation is a word's literal meaning; connotation is the emotional coloring that a word conveys.

2. Use technical jargon sparingly; eliminate business jargon.

As you write and revise sentences:

3. Use active voice most of the time. Active voice is better because it is shorter, clearer, and more interesting.
4. Use verbs—not nouns—to carry the weight of your sentence.
5. Eliminate wordiness. Writing is wordy if the same idea can be expressed in fewer words.
   a. Eliminate words that add nothing.
   b. Combine sentences to eliminate unnecessary words.
   c. Put the meaning of your sentence into the subject and verb to cut the number of words.
6. Vary sentence length and sentence structure.
7. Use parallel structure. Use the same grammatical form for ideas that have the same logical function.
8. Put your readers in your sentences.

As you write and revise paragraphs:

9. Begin most paragraphs with topic sentences so that readers know what to expect in the paragraph.
10. Use transitions to link ideas.

LO 4-3   **Techniques to revise, edit, and proofread your communications.**

If the writing situation is new or difficult, plan to revise the draft at least three times. The first time, look for content and completeness. The second time, check the organization, layout, and reasoning. Finally, check style and tone.

Edit for surface-level changes to make your document grammatically correct.

Finally, proofread to catch typos. Use available technologies to help you.

Exercises and Cases

4.1   Reviewing the Chapter

1. What are some techniques of good writers? Which ones do you use regularly? (LO 4-1–3)
2. What are ways to get ideas for a specific communication? (LO 4-1)
3. What activities are part of the composing process? Which one should you be doing more often or more carefully in your writing? (LO 4-1)
4. What are some half-truths about style? (LO 4-2)

5. What are some ways you can make your sentences more effective? (LO 4-2)

6. What are some ways you can make your paragraphs more effective? (LO 4-2)

7. How can you adapt good style to organization preferences? (LO 4-2)

8. How do revising, editing, and proofreading differ? Which one do you personally need to do more carefully? (LO 4-3)

9. How can you get better feedback on your writing? (LO 4-3)

4.2   Interviewing Writers about Their Composing Processes

Interview someone about the composing process(es) he or she uses for on-the-job writing. Questions you could ask include the following:

- What kind of planning do you do before you write? Do you make lists? formal or informal outlines?

- When you need more information, where do you get it?

- How do you compose your drafts? Do you dictate? Draft with pen and paper? Compose on screen? How do you find uninterrupted time to compose?

- When you want advice about style, grammar, and spelling, what source(s) do you consult?

- Does your superior ever read your drafts and make suggestions?

- Do you ever work with other writers to produce a single document? Describe the process you use.

- Describe the process of creating a document where you felt the final document reflected your best work. Describe the process of creating a document you found difficult or frustrating. What sorts of things make writing easier or harder for you?

As your instructor directs,

a. Share your results orally with a small group of students.

b. Present your results in an oral presentation to the class.

c. Present your results in an email to your instructor.

d. Share your results with a small group of students and write a joint email reporting the similarities and differences you found.

4.3   Analyzing Your Own Writing Processes

Save your notes and drafts from several assignments so that you can answer the following questions:

- Which practices of good writers do you follow?

- Which of the activities discussed in this chapter do you use?

- How much time do you spend on each of the activities?

- What kinds of revisions do you make most often?

- Do you use different processes for different documents, or do you have one process that you use most of the time?

- What parts of your process seem most successful? Are there any places in the process that could be improved? How?

- What relation do you see between the process(es) you use and the quality of the final document?

As your instructor directs,

a. Discuss your process with a small group of other students.

b. Write an email to your instructor analyzing in detail your process for composing one of the papers for this class.

c. Write an email to your instructor analyzing your process during the term. What parts of your process(es) have stayed the same throughout the term? What parts have changed?

4.4   Evaluating the Ethical Implication of Connotations

In each of the following pairs, identify the more favorable term. When is its use justifiable?

1. wasted/sacrificed

2. illegal alien/immigrant

3. bring about/cause

4. terminate/fire

5. inaccuracy/lying

6. budget/spending plan

7. feedback/criticism

8. credit/blame

9. discrepancy/difference

4.5   Correcting Errors in Denotation and Connotation

Identify and correct the errors in denotation or connotation in the following sentences:

1. In our group, we weeded out the best idea each person had thought of.

2. She is a prudent speculator.

3. The three proposals are diametrically opposed to each other.

4. While he researched companies, he was literally glued to the web.

5. Our backpacks are hand sewn by one of roughly 16 individuals.

6. Raj flaunted the law against insider trading.

4.6   Eliminating Jargon and Simplifying Language

Revise these sentences to eliminate jargon and to use short, familiar words.

1. When the automobile company announced its strategic downsizing initiative, it offered employees a career alternative enhancement program.

2. Any alterations must be approved during the 30-day period commencing 60 days prior to the expiration date of the agreement.

3. As per your request, the undersigned has obtained estimates of upgrading our computer system. A copy of the estimated cost is attached hereto.

4. Please be advised that this writer is in considerable need of a new computer.

5. Enclosed please find the proposed draft for the employee negative retention plan. In the event that you have alterations which you would like to suggest, forward same to my office at your earliest convenience.

4.7   Changing Verbs from Passive to Active Voice

Identify passive voice in the following sentences and convert it to active voice. In some cases, you may need to add information to do so. You may use different words as long as you retain the basic meaning of the sentence. Remember that imperative verbs are active voice, too.

1. It has been suggested by the corporate office that all faxes are to be printed on recycled paper.

2. The office carpets will be cleaned professionally on Friday evening. It is requested that all staff members put belongings up on their desks.

3. The office microwave is to be cleaned by those who use it.

4. When the vacation schedule is finalized it is recommended that it be routed to all supervisors for final approval.

5. Material must not be left on trucks outside the warehouse. Either the trucks must be parked inside the warehouse or the material must be unloaded at the time of receiving the truck.

4.8   Using Strong Verbs

Revise each of the following sentences to replace hidden verbs with action verbs.

1. An understanding of stocks and bonds is important if one wants to invest wisely.

2. We must undertake a calculation of expected revenues and expenses for the next two years.

3. The production of clear and concise documents is the mark of a successful communicator.

4. We hope to make use of the company's website to promote the new product line.

5. If you wish to be eligible for the Miller scholarship, you must complete an application by January 31.

6. When you make an evaluation of media buys, take into consideration the demographics of the group seeing the ad.

7. We provide assistance to clients in the process of reaching a decision about the purchase of hardware and software.

4.9   Reducing Wordiness

1. Eliminate words that say nothing. You may use different words.

   a. There are many businesses that are active in community and service work.

   b. The purchase of another computer for the claims department will allow us to produce form letters quickly. In addition, return on investment could be calculated for proposed repairs. Another use is that the computer could check databases to make sure that claims are paid only once.

   c. Our decision to enter the South American market has precedence in the past activities of the company.

2. Combine sentences to show how ideas are related and to eliminate unnecessary words.

   a. Some customers are profitable for companies. Other customers actually cost the company money.

   b. If you are unable to come to the session on HMOs, please call the human resources office. You will be able to schedule another time to ask questions you may have about the various options.

   c. Major Japanese firms often have employees who know English well. U.S. companies negotiating with Japanese companies should bring their own interpreters.

   d. New procedure for customer service employees: Please be aware effective immediately, if a customer is requesting a refund of funds applied to their account a front and back copy of the check must be submitted if the transaction is over $500.00. For example, if the customer is requesting $250.00 back, and the total amount of the transaction is $750.00, a front and back copy of the check will be needed to obtain the refund.

4.10 Improving Parallel Structure

Revise each of the following sentences to create parallelism.

1. The orientation session will cover the following information:
   - Company culture will be discussed.
   - How to use the equipment.
   - You will get an overview of key customers' needs.

2. Five criteria for a good web page are content that serves the various audiences, attention to details, and originality. It is also important to have effective organization and navigation devices. Finally, provide attention to details such as revision date and the webmaster's address.

3. When you leave a voice mail message,
   - Summarize your main point in a sentence or two.
   - The name and phone number should be given slowly and distinctly.
   - The speaker should give enough information so that the recipient can act on the message.
   - Tell when you'll be available to receive the recipient's return call.

4.11 Revising Paragraphs

1. Make each of the following paragraphs more readable by opening each paragraph with a topic sentence. You may be able to find a topic sentence in the paragraph and move it to the beginning. In other cases, you'll need to write a new sentence.

   a. At Disney World, a lunch put on an expense account is "on the mouse." McDonald's employees "have ketchup in their veins." Business slang flourishes at companies with rich corporate cultures. Memos at Procter & Gamble are called "reco's" because the model P&G memo begins with a recommendation.

   b. The first item on the agenda is the hiring for the coming year. George has also asked that we review the agency goals for the next fiscal year. We should cover this early in the meeting since it may affect our hiring preferences. Finally, we need to announce the deadlines for grant proposals, decide which grants to apply for, and set up a committee to draft each proposal.

   c. Separate materials that can be recycled from your regular trash. Pass along old clothing, toys, or appliances to someone else who can use them. When you purchase products, choose those with minimal packaging. If you have a yard, put your yard waste and kitchen scraps (excluding meat and fat) in a compost pile. You can reduce the amount of solid waste your household produces in four ways.

2. Revise each paragraph to make it easier to read. Change, rearrange, or delete words and sentences; add any material necessary.

   a. Once a new employee is hired, each one has to be trained for a week by one of our supervisors at a cost of $1,000 each which includes the supervisor's time. This amount also includes half of the new employee's salary since new hires produce only half the normal production per worker for the week. This summer $24,000 was spent in training 24 new employees. Absenteeism increased in the department on the hottest summer days. For every day each worker is absent we lose $200 in lost production. This past summer there was a total of 56 absentee days taken for a total loss of $11,200 in lost production. Turnover and absenteeism were the causes of an unnecessary expenditure of over $35,000 this summer.

   b. One service is investments. General financial news and alerts about companies in the customer's portfolio are available. Quicken also provides assistance in finding the best mortgage rate and in providing assistance in making the decision whether to refinance a mortgage. Another service from Quicken is advice for the start and management of a small business. Banking services, such as paying bills and applying for loans, have long been available to Quicken subscribers. The taxpayer can be walked through the tax preparation process by Quicken. Someone considering retirement can use Quicken to ascertain whether the amount being set aside for this purpose is sufficient. Quicken's website provides seven services.

4.12 Revising, Editing, and Proofreading an Email

Dana Shomacher, an enthusiastic new hire of six months at Bear Foods, wants Stan Smith, regional head of HR at the grocery chain, to allow her to organize and publicize a food drive for Coastal Food Pantry. Revise, edit, and proof her email.

> Hey Stan,
>
> I have this great idea for great publicity for Bear Foods that won't cost anything and will get us some really great publicity. Its something great we can do for our community. I wont Bear to conduct a food drive for Coastal Food Pantry. Their was an article

(continued)

in the Tribune about how they were having trouble keeping up with food requests and I thought what a great fit it would be for Bear.

All our employees should donate food and we should also get our customer to donate also. We could set out some shopping carts for the donations. I could write an announcement for the Tribune and get some postures made for our front windows.

I am willing to take care of all details so you won't have to do anything except say yes to this email.

Dana

After you have fixed Dana's email, answer these questions in an email to your instructor.

- What revisions did you make? Why?
- Many grocery stores already contribute to local food pantries. In addition to some staples, they provide items such as bakery goods that are past their sale date but still quite tasty, sacks for bagging groceries at the pantry, and even shopping carts to transport groceries to the cars of pantry clients. If Bear already contributes to Coastal, how should that fact change the content of Dana's email?

- What edits did you make? Why?
- What impression do you think this email made on the head of human resources? Explain. Do you think he granted Dana's request? Why or why not?

Submit both your version of Dana's email and your analysis email.

4.13   Identifying Buzzwords and Jargon

This is an actual press release published in the *Des Moines Register* with an article on buzzwords.

Wal-Mart Stores, Inc., the largest private employer with more than 1.8 million employees and the largest corporate mover of people, selected Capital Relocation Services as the sole source provider for the implementation of its Tier III and Tier IV relocation programs. These two programs account for the vast majority of the company's relocations. Capital was awarded the business following an intensive RFP and due diligence process.

"We're very excited about the synergy that Wal-Mart's selection of Capital brings to both companies," commented Mickey Williams, Capital's CEO. "We are also pleased to welcome to Capital the existing Wal-Mart PMP Relocation team that has been on-site at Wal-Mart's Bentonville headquarters for 14 years. They will continue to serve Wal-Mart and Sam's Club's Associates and will have an active role in the implementation of the new policy."

"What really enabled us to stand out was our focus on the strategic results Wal-Mart was looking for, and connecting that to their relocation program," added Williams. "Additionally, we demonstrated what would need to be done to achieve those results."

Mr. Williams continued, "Several years ago, we realized that traditional relocation solutions weren't enough. The challenge was that relocation management had become a logistics focused straightjacket. The emphasis was on efficiency and not on effectiveness. In a time of unprecedented change, relocation management programs were becoming increasingly inflexible."

"We realized that our continued success required us to stop thinking of ourselves solely as a relocation management company—we had to start thinking and acting as a talent management support company; after all that is the underlying purpose of relocation management in the first place. Wal-Mart's selection of Capital is a big confirmation that our approach is the right one."[41]

Now answer these questions:

1. What is this press release about? What is it saying?
2. Why did Capital Relocation Services get the new contract?
3. Underline the buzzwords and jargon in the press release. What do these words do in the press release?

4. What is the purpose of this press release? Does it meet its purpose? Why or why not?

Write an email to your instructor evaluating the press release as an effective document.

4.14   Revising Documents Using Track Changes

For this exercise, you will electronically exchange a document with one of your classmates. With the Track Changes feature turned on, you will review each other's documents, make comments or ask questions, insert additions, and make deletions to improve the writing, and then revise your work based upon the changes and comments.

As your instructor directs, select the electronic file of a document you have created for this class. Exchange this file with your peer review partner. Open your partner's file and select Track Changes. Review the document and make suggestions that will help your peer improve the writing. For instance, you can

- Look for accurate, appropriate, and ethical wording as well as instances of unnecessary jargon.
- Look for active voice and concise prose.

- Look for structural issues like topic sentences, tightly written paragraphs, varied sentence structure and length, and focus upon the thesis statement. Suggest where sentences can be combined or where sentences need parallel structure.
- Look for you-attitude.
- Ask questions (using comments) when the text isn't clear or make suggestions to tighten the writing or improve word choices.

Return the document to its author and open yours to review the changes and comments your partner added to your document. For each change, decide whether to accept or reject the suggestion.

Continue to revise the document. Then submit a copy of your original version and the revised version to your instructor.

4.15   Using the SEC's *A Plain English Handbook*

Go to the Securities and Exchange Commission's *A Plain English Handbook* at http://www.sec.gov/pdf/handbook.pdf. Scroll down to Appendix B and look at the four before and after examples. What kinds of changes have been made? What are examples of each kind? Can you understand the revised version? Did you understand the original version?

4.16   Investigating the Plain Language Act in Federal Agencies

1. Go to http://www.plainlanguage.gov and read some of the examples of good and bad business writing. Pick one example to discuss in your small group. What changes were made? Did all the changes work for you? Would you have written anything differently? Explain.

   Read the "technical" version of Little Red Riding Hood (look under "Examples," then "Humor," then the "sarcastic piece about using plain language for technical writing"; Little Red Riding Hood is the illustration at the end of this piece). Which changes obscured the sense of the fairy tale the most? Which did you find the most amusing?

2. Look at some of the plain language guidelines for some of the agencies listed at https://plainlanguage.gov/law/agency-programs/.

   - Work in small groups, with each group checking the adaptations of a different agency. Report back to the class. As a class, discuss how different agencies adapt the act to their focus.
   - In your groups, also look at some of the before and after examples. Share a particularly good one with the class, explaining the changes in the improved message.

4.17   Evaluating a Letter to Stockholders

Figure 4.2 provides excerpts from Warren Buffett's annual letter to his stockholders. The complete letter is found at Warren Buffett, "Letters 2012," Berkshire Hathaway Inc., http://www.berkshirehathaway.com/letters/2012ltr.pdf. Answer these questions about the letter:

1. How many people are praised by name?
2. This chapter offers examples of his colorful style. What other examples can you find?

3. Buffett is known for explaining general financial issues in these letters. In the 2012 letter, what does he say about newspapers? Dividends? Are these explanations clear? What phrases and sentences support your opinion?

4.18   Analyzing Your Own Writing

Collect five pages of writing you have prepared for college courses. Now review "Ten Ways to Make Your Writing Easier to Read." Mark places in your writing where you have had problems with those guidelines and identify which of the guidelines those places violate. Which guideline seems to give you the most trouble in your five pages? Would you agree with your findings? Or do you think your five pages are atypical of your writing? If you do not agree with your findings, which of the guidelines do you think generally gives you the most trouble?

Now trade pages with a partner. Read your partner's pages and mark places where he or she had problems with the 10 guidelines.

Retrieve your own pages. Did your partner find some problems you missed?

On the basis of this exercise, as well as your knowledge of your own writing, write an email to your instructor explaining which of the guidelines (choose just two or three) you most need to work on. Give problem sentences from your writing as evidence.

Below the text of the email, correct the problem sentences you used as evidence.

Notes

1. See especially Linda Flower and John R. Hayes, "The Cognition of Discovery: Defining a Rhetorical Problem," *College Composition and Communication* 31, no. 1 (February 1980): 21–32; Mike Rose, *Writer's Block: The Cognitive Dimension,* published for Conference on College Composition and Communication, 1984; and essays in two collections: Charles R. Cooper and Lee Odell, *Research on Composing: Points of Departure* (Urbana, IL: National Council of Teachers of English, 1978); Mike Rose, ed., *When a Writer Can't Write: Studies in Writer's Block and Other Composing-Process Problems* (New York: Guilford Press, 1985).

2. Peter Elbow, *Writing with Power: Techniques for Mastering the Writing Process* (New York: Oxford University Press, 1981), 15–20.

3. See Gabriela Lesser Rico, *Writing the Natural Way* (Los Angeles: J. P. Tarcher, 1983), 10.

4. Rachel Spilka, "Orality and Literacy in the Workplace: Process- and Text-Based Strategies for Multiple Audience Adaptation," *Journal of Business and Technical Communication* 4, no. 1 (January 1990): 44–67.

5. Anne Lamott, *Bird by Bird: Some Instructions on Writing and Life* (New York: Anchor, 1994), 25.

6. Ibid., 19.

7. Ibid., 25.

8. Robert L. Brown Jr. and Carl G. Herndl, "An Ethnographic Study of Corporate Writing: Job Status as Reflected in Written Text," in *Functional Approaches to Writing: A Research Perspective,* ed. Barbara Couture (Norwood, NJ: Ablex, 1986), 16–19, 22–23.

9. U.S. Securities and Exchange Commission Office of Investor Education and Assistance, *A Plain English Handbook: How to Create Clear SEC Disclosure Documents* (Washington, DC: 1998).

10. Eleanor Laise, "Some Consumers Say Wall Street Failed Them," *Wall Street Journal,* November 28, 2008, B1.

11. Carol Loomis, ed., *Tap Dancing to Work: Warren Buffett on Practically Everything, 1966–2012: A* Fortune *Magazine Book* (New York: Portfolio/Penguin, 2012), 34.

12. Bullets quoted from Warren Buffett, "Letters 2012," Berkshire Hathaway Inc., accessed March 4, 2013, http://www.berkshirehathaway.com/letters/2012ltr.pdf.

13. Richard Lederer and Richard Dowis, *Sleeping Dogs Don't Lay: Practical Advice for the Grammatically Challenged* (New York: St. Martin's Press, 1999), 91–92.

14. James Suchan and Robert Colucci, "An Analysis of Communication Efficiency between High-Impact and Bureaucratic Written Communication," *Management Communication Quarterly* 2, no. 4 (1989): 464–73.

15. Hiluard G. Rogers and F. William Brown, "The Impact of Writing Style on Compliance with Instructions," *Journal of Technical Writing and Communication* 23, no. 1 (1993): 53–71.

16. Richard Lederer, "The Terrible Ten," *Toastmaster,* July 2003, 28–29.

17. Roger Pielke Jr., "Dear Expert, Please Cook the Books," *Wall Street Journal,* January 30, 2013, A11; and Doyle Rice, "Why Didn't Sandy Warrant a Warning?," *Des Moines Register,* December 2, 2012, 14A.

18. Tony Leys, "Hospitals Avoid Taxes Despite Little Free Care," *Des Moines Register,* October 16, 2011, 1A.

19. Melinda Beck, "Psychiatrists Revise Mental-Disorder Categories," *Wall Street Journal,* December 3, 2012, A2.

20. Chad Bray and Anjali Cordeiro, "Tobacco Firms Score Victory as Class-Action Suit Is Denied," *Wall Street Journal,* April 4, 2008, B3; and "FDA May Rephrase Pacemaker Warnings," *Wall Street Journal,* September 29, 2006, A8.

21. Melinda Beck, "Getting an Earful: Testing a Tiny, Pricey Hearing Aid," *Wall Street Journal,* January 29, 2008, D1.

22. Jaguar ad, *Wall Street Journal,* September 29, 2000, A20.

23. Betsy Taylor, "Experts: Flood Terms Can Deceive," *Des Moines Register,* July 1, 2008, 9A.

24. Evan Perez, "Mukasey Cites Risk in Using Term 'Torture,'" *Wall Street Journal,* January 17, 2009, A2.

25. Daniel M. Oppenheimer, "Consequences of Erudite Vernacular Utilized Irrespective of Necessity: Problems with Using Long Words Needlessly," *Applied Cognitive Psychology* 20 (2006): 139–56.

26. Richard C. Anderson, "Concretization and Sentence Learning," *Journal of Educational Psychology* 66, no. 2 (1974): 179–83.

27. Ben Worthen, "Oracle's Hot New Offering: Corporate Technobabble," *Wall Street Journal,* February 12, 2008, B4.

28. Pamela Layton and Adrian J. Simpson, "Deep Structure in Sentence Comprehension," *Journal of Verbal Learning and Verbal Behavior* 14 (1975); and Harris B. Savin and Ellen Perchonock, "Grammatical Structure and the Immediate Recall of English Sentences," *Journal of Verbal Learning and Verbal Behavior* 4 (1965): 348–53.

29. "Document Checklist for Plain Language," PlainLanguage.gov, accessed May 11, 2013, http://www.plainlanguage.gov/howto/quickreference/checklist.cfm.

30. Bill Walsh, *The Elephants of Style: A Trunkload of Tips on the Big Issues and Gray Areas of Contemporary American English* (New York: McGraw-Hill, 2004), 68.

31. Lloyd Bostian and Ann C. Thering, "Scientists: Can They Read What They Write?," *Journal of Technical Writing and Communication* 17 (1987): 417–27; E. B. Coleman, "The Comprehensibility of Several Grammatical Transformations," *Journal of Applied Psychology* 48, no. 3 (1964): 186–90; and Keith Rayner, "Visual Attention in Reading: Eye Movements Reflect Cognitive Processes," *Memory and Cognition* 5 (1977): 443–48.

Chapter 4   Planning, Composing, and Revising   **117**

32. Adam Freedman, "And the Winners Are . . . ," *The Party of the First Part* (blog), last updated September 21, 2007, http://the partyofthefirstpart.blogspot.com/2007/09/and-winners-are.html.

33. Thomas N. Huckin, "A Cognitive Approach to Readability," in *New Essays in Technical and Scientific Communication: Research, Theory, Practice,* ed. Paul V. Anderson, R. John Brockmann, and Carolyn R. Miller (Farmingdale, NY: Baywood, 1983), 93–98.

34. James Suchan and Ronald Dulek, "A Reassessment of Clarity in Written Managerial Communications," *Management Communication Quarterly* 4, no. 1 (1990): 93–97.

35. Doris Kearns Goodwin, *Team of Rivals: The Political Genius of Abraham Lincoln* (New York: Simon & Schuster, 2005), 583–87.

36. Chris Roush, "Tiny Typo Proves Embarrassing for Coca-Cola," *The Atlanta Constitution,* July 17, 1996, 03F.

37. Dianna Booher, "Cutting Paperwork in the Corporate Culture," *New York: Facts on File Publications* (1986): 23.

38. Susan D. Kleimann, "The Complexity of Workplace Review," *Technical Communication* 38, no. 4 (1991): 520–26.

39. Glenn J. Broadhead and Richard C. Freed, *The Variables of Composition: Process and Product in a Business Setting,* Conference on College Composition and Communication Studies in Writing and Rhetoric (Carbondale, IL: Southern Illinois University Press, 1986), 57.

40. Janice C. Redish and Jack Selzer, "The Place of Readability Formulas in Technical Communication," *Technical Communication* 32, no. 4 (1985): 46–52.

41. Larry Ballard, "Decipher a Honcho's Buzzwords, Such as 'Unsiloing,'" *Des Moines Register,* January 21, 2008, 1D.

CHAPTER

5 Designing Documents

Chapter Outline

©DrAfter123/Getty Images

NEWSWORTHY COMMUNICATION

And the Award Goes to . . .

©Robyn Beck/Stringer/Getty Images

PricewaterhouseCoopers (PwC) had already done its job: they'd tallied votes for the 2017 Oscar awards, they'd stuffed the envelopes with the winners, and now the award ceremony was under way. It was time to sit back and enjoy the show.

But PwC Chairman Tim Ryan's work had just begun. When presenter Warren Beatty opened the envelope for Best Picture and announced *La La Land* as winner, backstage PwC staffers froze in shock: the winner was supposed to be *Moonlight*. What had happened? And what should they do? Producers of *La La Land* were on their way to the podium to accept the award.

Announcing winners may seem simple, but the Oscars ceremony is a complex live event. It turns out that each award had two identical sets of envelopes: one at each side of the stage. And someone had handed a duplicate envelope to Warren Beatty—the duplicate of a different award that *La La Land* had already won. Speculating on how such a mix-up occurred, the *New York Times* pointed to the envelope's gold-lettered design, new in 2017, that "could have made the lettering harder to read."

As PwC administered damage control and corrected the mistake—the first in PwC's 83-year history with the Oscars—the Twittersphere lit up with accusations of negligence in a simple task, terming the error #envelopegate. Ryan feared the effects on PwC's reputation and set to work drafting apologies, all because a staffer misread an envelope.

Perhaps it's a stretch to blame the envelope: after all, shouldn't humans double- and triple-check in such a high-stakes situation? But designers know the impact a small detail can make. Marc Friedman, the stationer who painstakingly designed 2011's envelopes, called the Oscar's envelope "the most iconic, symbolic envelope in the world . . . There is no more significant moment than the anticipation that comes with opening the envelope."

Friedman's 2011 envelopes carried winners to the stage without a hitch. But perhaps 2017's envelopes needed a few more rounds of usability testing.

Sources: Sandy Cohen, "Oscar's Winners' Envelope Made Over with New Look," *San Diego Union Tribune,* Feburary 16, 2011, http://www.sandiegouniontribune.com/sdut-oscars-winners-envelope-made-over-with-new-look-2011feb16-story.html; David Gelles and Sapna Maheshwari, "Oscars Mistake Casts Unwanted Spotlight on PwC," *New York Times,* February 27, 2017, https://www.nytimes.com/2017/02/27/business/media/pwc-oscars-best-picture.html.

Learning Objectives

After studying this chapter, you will know

LO 5-1   Why document design is important.

LO 5-2   Design conventions.

LO 5-3   The four levels of document design.

LO 5-4   Design guidelines for each level.

LO 5-5   How to incorporate design into the writing process.

LO 5-6   How to design inclusively.

LO 5-7   How to test your document for usability.

LO 5-8   How to design brochures.

LO 5-9   How to design infographics.

LO 5-10 How to design websites.

The ability to effectively design a variety of documents is expected of today's professional. Good design saves time and money, affirms the creator's desired image, and builds goodwill.

Effective design groups ideas visually, structuring the flow of information in an inviting, user-friendly way. Easy-to-use documents enhance credibility and build an image of the creator—whether an individual or a company—as competent, thoughtful, and audience-oriented.

Today, a wide array of documents demands insightful, pragmatic, and accessible design—from brochures, infographics, or websites to more diverse documents such as NFL players' jerseys, a breast cancer self-exam shower card, or even the envelope that will deliver the Oscar winner for Best Picture. Regardless of the document types you anticipate designing, attention to effective design will benefit you professionally. Many workplaces expect their employees to be able to create designs that go beyond the basic templates found in common software programs and adapt to user needs, current technology, and best practices in inclusive design.

Why Document Design Is Important

LO 5-1

Poor document design is more than an annoyance or a missed chance for pleasing aesthetics; improper design can cause both organizations and society to suffer. In one tragic example, the *Challenger* space shuttle blew up because engineers did not effectively convey their concerns about the shuttle's O-rings, which failed in the excessive cold. Poor communication—including charts that de-emphasized data about O-ring performance—contributed to the decision to launch. Unfortunately, this was not an isolated incident. More recently, poor communication played a role in NASA's failure to ensure safety of the spacecraft *Columbia,* which disintegrated upon re-entry. Mission leaders insisted that engineers had not briefed them on the seriousness of the damage caused by a piece of foam that struck the shuttle upon takeoff. But after studying meeting transcripts, Edward R. Tufte, who specializes in the visual presentation of information, concluded that engineers did offer concerns and supporting statistics. Why didn't the mission leaders listen? Because the visuals the engineers used obscured the seriousness of the potential damage.[1]

Visual communication plays an important role in the public sphere, from local to global. The *Des Moines Register* recently faced reader backlash for a poorly juxtaposed cover spread: while the upper front-page article highlighted global leaders coming together to help fight worldwide hunger, the article below it featured a local bar known for serving a five-pound burger.[2] Design ramifications extend beyond public opinion of a local newspaper and even can influence natonal politics: for instance, in 2000, the badly designed Florida ballot confused enough voters to cloud the outcome of the U.S. presidential election.[3]

The thoughtfulness, functionality, and tone of document design convey a specific image of the document's creator, and without deliberate attention to design, this image may not be the one intended. Does your personal résumé paint a picture you want to present to the world? Does the visual tone of a company's website affirm its commitment to transparency? Does the medical brochure distributed at a doctor's office reinforce the clinic's intended image as friendly and helpful? When it comes to business communication, document design should affirm your desired image or your company's "brand."

Design Conventions

LO 5-2

Like all communication, visual communication adheres to certain conventions: the "design language" and expectations for how a certain type of document will look. For instance, if you received a business card in the shape of a circle, it would gain your attention because most business cards adhere to the convention of a rectangular shape. In this case, the circle might thwart convention in an effective way that makes the recipient remember the person with the circular business card, but in many cases, design conventions serve a useful purpose and should be followed. For example, most computers' graphical user interfaces organize files, folders, and a trash can around a "desktop" metaphor; switching to a completely different way of organizing a computer's contents would likely reduce usability. Similarly, when surfing a shopping website, users have the expectation of being able to add an item to their cart or basket, another design convention that streamlines a user's website experience. In general, violating conventions is risky: it may signal that the author or designer is unreliable or unknowledgeable of how a particular form of communication is typically designed.

Conventions may vary by audience, geographic area, industry, company, or even department. Some conventions work well with some audiences but not with others, so careful audience analysis is necessary. For instance, illustrations in instructions for office equipment usually show feminine hands using the equipment. Some female readers will relate more readily to the instructions, making this choice an effective one for those readers; others will be offended at the implied assumption that only women perform such low-level office jobs, so the company may want to revisit the conventions it employs for visual instructions.[4]

Conventions also change as technology evolves. Résumés used to be typed documents; now most companies ask for electronic versions. When typewriters were common, it was conventional to type two spaces after each period, but with word processors, only one period is necessary. Today, as more and more users navigate websites through smartphones, websites must design for mobile functionality, which creates a new set of website-design conventions.

The Four Levels of Document Design

LO 5-3

Visual communications expert Charles Kostelnick distinguishes four levels of design: intra, inter, extra, and supra. Analyzing others' documents can generate ideas for your own communication, so when you encounter documents in a professional setting, look for Kostelnick's four levels of design.[5] These terms provide an organized way to think about the design choices behind every document:

- **Intra:**   design choices for individual letters and words. Intra-level design choices include the font and its size; whether you use bold, italics, or color changes to emphasize key words; and the way you use capital letters. The serif font used for body text on this page and the sans serif font used for headings are intra-level design choices.

- **Inter:**   design choices for blocks of text. Inter-level design choices include the ways you use headings, white space, indents, lists, and even text boxes. The headings and bulleted lists that organize information on these pages are inter-level design choices.

- **Extra:**   design choices for graphics that accompany text. Extra-level design choices include the use of photographs, charts, graphs, and other images, as well as the ways you emphasize information in those graphics. The figures in this chapter are extra-level design choices.

- **Supra:**   design choices for entire documents. Supra-level design choices include paper size, headers and footers, and the index and table of contents, as well as color schemes and layout grids that define the look of all sections of a document. The placement of the page numbers in this book and the colors used for headers are supra-level design choices.

The Centers for Disease Control and Prevention (CDC) infographic in Figure 5.1 illustrates all levels of design. At the intra-level, this poster uses a sans serif typeface throughout the whole document. Other intra-level elements include the boldface, all-caps, red headings and the black sentences that are set in a smaller typesize than the heading text. Inter-level elements include the centered title at the top of the poster and the chunked text within boxes and above and below dotted line dividers. It also includes the red arrows used like bullet points to organize material. The graphics such as an apple, a martini glass, and a coffin, as well as the USA-shaped outline used to frame statistics about high blood pressure risk, are extra-level design elements. These images help reinforce the textual message that encourages viewers to adopt healthy habits that prevent high blood pressure. Supra-level elements include the color scheme and the size of the infographic, which occupies an entire browser window and is intended to be shared on social media. Another supra-level design element that unifies all CDC promotional materials is its blue logo at the bottom center. Visually, this information is treated like a page footer and can be found somewhere on every published piece of CDC promotional material.

Design Guidelines

LO 5-4

Use the guidelines in Figure 5.2 to create visually attractive and functional documents.

1. Strategize Font Choices.

Fonts are unified styles of type. Popular fonts are Times Roman, Calibri, Palatino, Helvetica, or Arial, and each comes in various sizes and usually in bold and italic. In **fixed fonts,** every letter takes up the same amount of space; an *i* takes the same space as a *w.* Courier and Prestige Elite are fixed fonts. Most fonts are **proportional** and allow wider letters to take more space than narrower letters. Times Roman, Palatino, Helvetica, and Arial are proportional fonts. Most business documents use no more than two fonts.

Serif fonts have little extensions, called serifs, from the main strokes. (In Figure 5.3, look at the feet on the *r*'s in New Courier and the flick on the top of the *d* in Lucinda.) New Courier, Elite, Times Roman, Palatino, and Lucinda Calligraphy are serif fonts. Helvetica, Arial, Geneva, and Technical are **sans serif fonts** because they lack serifs (*sans* is French for *without*). Sans serif fonts are good for titles and tables.

You should choose fonts carefully because they shape reader response. Research suggests that people respond positively to fonts that fit the genre and purpose of the

Figure 5.1	Four Levels of Design in an Infographic for the Centers for Disease Control and Prevention

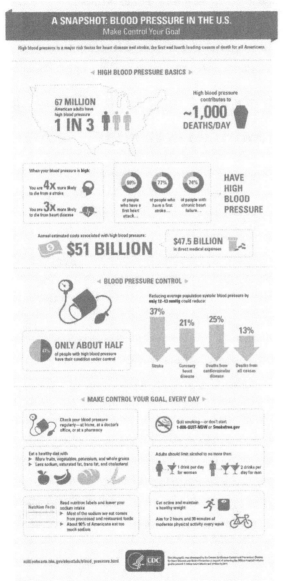

Source: Centers for Disease Control

Figure 5.2	Design Guidelines

1. Strategize font choices.

2. Minimize use of words in all capital letters.

3. Use white space.

4. Strategize margin choices.

5. Place elements for deliberate emphasis.

6. Unify elements with grids.

7. Use headings.

8. Unify documents with consistent, sparing decorative strategies.

Figure 5.3	Examples of Different Fonts

This sentence is set in 12-point Times Roman.

This sentence is set in 12-point Arial.

This sentence is set in 12-point New Courier.

This sentence is set in 12-point Lucinda Calligraphy.

This sentence is set in 12-point Broadway.

This sentence is set in 12-point Technical.

document.[6] For example, a font like Broadway is appropriate for a headline in a newsletter but not for the body text of an email.

- **Use a binary font scheme to create visual interest.** Use two fonts—one for headings and one for body text—to create visual variety within a cohesive design.

- **Create emphasis with font treatments.** Bold is easier to read than italics, so use bold type if you need only one method to emphasize text. In a complex document, use bigger type for main headings and slightly smaller type for subheadings and text. Avoid excessive italic type and underlining because these features can make text hard to read.

- **Use minimum 12-point font.** Twelve-point type is usually ideal for letters, memos, emails, and reports. Smaller type is harder to read, especially for older readers. If your material will not fit in the available pages, cut it. Putting some sections in tiny type saves space but creates a negative response—a negative response that may extend to the organization that produced the document.

2. Minimize Use of Words in All Capital Letters.

We recognize words partly by their shapes.[7] In all capital letters, all words take on a rectangular shape (see Figure 5.4); in all capital letters, words lose the descenders and ascenders that make reading faster and more accurate.[8] In addition, many people interpret text in all capitals as "shouting," especially when that text appears in online documents. In those cases, all capitals might elicit a negative response from your audience. Use words in all capital letters sparingly, if at all.

3. Use White Space.

White space—the empty space on the page—makes material easier to read by emphasizing the material that it separates from the rest of the text. Audiences scan documents for information, so anything you can do visually to help ease their reading will reflect positively on you as the communicator.

Figure 5.4	All Capitals Hide the Shape of a Word

Full capitals hide the shape of a word and slow reading 19%.

FULL CAPITALS HIDE THE SHAPE OF A WORD AND SLOW READING 19%.

To create white space:

- Use headings.
- Use a mix of paragraph lengths (most no longer than seven typed lines). It's okay for a paragraph or two to be just one sentence. First and last paragraphs, in particular, should be short.
- Use lists.
  - Use tabs or indents—not spaces—to align items vertically.
  - Use numbered lists when the number or sequence of items is exact.
  - Use **bullets** (large dots or squares like those in this list) when the number and sequence don't matter.

When you use a list, construct the list items with parallel grammar and ensure they fit into the structure of the sentence that introduces the list. The list above is framed by the phrase "To create white space" and each item that follows completes that sentence with a simple present-tense verb phrase, for example, "To create white space . . . use headings."

Increasing white space can easily improve the look of your message. Figure 5.5 shows an original document. Notice how this document is visually dense and uninviting. In Figure 5.6, the same document is improved. It uses white space that organizes the document visually: lists, headings, and shorter paragraphs.

Figure 5.5   A Document with Poor Visual Impact

Full capital letters make title hard to read.

MONEY DEDUCTED FROM YOUR WAGES TO PAY CREDITORS

Long paragraph is visually uninviting.

When you buy goods on credit, the store will sometimes ask you to sign a Wage Assignment form allowing it to deduct money from your wages if you do not pay your bill. When you buy on credit, you sign a contract agreeing to pay a certain amount each week or month until you have paid all you owe. The Wage Assignment Form is separate. It must contain the name of your present employer, your social security number, the amount of money loaned, the rate of interest, the date when payments are due, and your signature. The words "Wage Assignment" must be printed at the top of the form and also near the line for your signature. Even if you have signed a Wage Assignment agreement, Roysner will not withhold part of your wages unless all of the following conditions are met: 1. You have to be more than forty days late in payment of what you owe; 2. Roysner has to receive a correct statement of the amount you are in default and a copy of the Wage Assignment form; and 3. You and Roysner must receive a notice from the creditor at least twenty days in advance stating that the creditor plans to make a demand on your wages. This twenty-day notice gives you a chance to correct the problems yourself. If these conditions are all met, Roysner must withhold 15% of each paycheck until your bill is paid and give this money to your creditor.

If you think you are not late or that you do not owe the amount stated, you can argue against it by filing a legal document called a "defense." Once you file a defense, Roysner will not withhold any money from you. However, be sure you are right before you file a defense. If you are wrong, you have to pay not only what you owe but also all legal costs for both yourself and the creditor. If you are right, the creditor has to pay all these costs.

Important information is hard to find.

Figure 5.6	A Document Revised to Improve Visual Impact

Money Deducted from Your Wages to Pay Creditors

First letter of each main word capitalized— Title split onto two lines.

When you buy goods on credit, the store will sometimes ask you to sign a Wage Assignment form allowing it to deduct money from your wages if you do not pay your bill.

Have You Signed a Wage Assignment Form?

Headings divide document into chunks.

When you buy on credit, you sign a contract agreeing to pay a certain amount each week or month until you have paid all you owe. The Wage Assignment Form is separate. It must contain

- The name of your present employer,
- Your social security number,
- The amount of money loaned,
- The rate of interest,
- The date when payments are due, and
- Your signature.

List with bullets where order of items doesn't matter.

Single-space list when items are short.

The words "Wage Assignment" must be printed at the top of the form and also near the line for your signature.

Headings must be parallel. Here all are questions.

When Would Money Be Deducted from Your Wages to Pay a Creditor?

Even if you have signed a Wage Assignment agreement, Roysner will not withhold part of your wages unless all of the following conditions are met:

White space between items emphasizes them.

1. You have to be more than 40 days late in payment of what you owe;

2. Roysner has to receive a correct statement of the amount you are in default and a copy of the Wage Assignment form; and

Numbered list where number or order of items matters.

Double-space between items in list when most items are two lines or longer.

3. You and Roysner must receive a notice from the creditor at least 20 days in advance stating that the creditor plans to make a demand on your wage. This 20-day notice gives you a chance to correct the problem yourself.

If these conditions are all met, Roysner must withhold fifteen percent (15%) of each pay-check until your bill is paid and give this money to your creditor.

What Should You Do If You Think the Wage Assignment Is Incorrect?

If you think you are not late or that you do not owe the amount stated, you can argue against it by filing a legal document called a "defense." Once you file a defense, Roysner will not withhold any money from you. However, be sure you are right before you file a defense. If you are wrong, you have to pay not only what you owe but also all legal costs for both yourself and the creditor. If you are right, the creditor has to pay all these costs.

Figure 5.7	The FedEx Logo Sends a Message with White Space

©tanuha2001/Shutterstock

Keep in mind that these devices take space, but white space is a useful tool.[9] When saving space is essential, it's better to cut text to make room for sufficient white space than to keep all the text packed together. A clear mark of an amateur document designer is one who tries to fill an entire page with visuals and text.

In visual-heavy documents such as company logos, white space can do more than provide a visual buffer for text: it can convey its own message. The FedEx logo in Figure 5.7 cleverly shapes white space between the "E" and "x," creating a forward-pointing arrow. Whether customers consciously notice the subtle arrow or not, it implies that FedEx is swift or progressive—and this message is composed completely of white space.

4. Strategize Margin Choices.

Word-processing programs allow you to use **full justification** so that type lines up evenly on both the right and left margins. This paragraph you are reading justifies both margins. Margins justified only on the left, sometimes called **ragged-right margins,** have lines ending in different places.

Use full justification when you

- Can use proportional fonts.
- Want a more formal look.
- Want to use as few pages as possible.

Use ragged right margins when you

- Cannot use a proportional font.
- Want an informal look.
- Use very short line lengths.

5. Place Elements for Deliberate Emphasis.

Readers of English are accustomed to reading pages of text from left to right. Effective document designers tap into this habit. They know that we start in the upper left-hand corner of the page, read to the right, move down, and then to the right again. Actually, the eye moves in a Z pattern (see Figure 5.8).[10] Therefore, the four quadrants of the page carry different visual weights. The upper left quadrant, where the eye starts, is the most important; the bottom right quadrant, where the eye ends, is next most important.

6. Unify Elements with Grids.

Many document designers use a **grid system** to design pages. In its simplest form, a grid imposes two or three imaginary columns on the page. In more complex grids, these

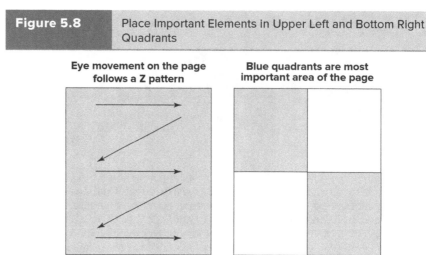

Figure 5.8   Place Important Elements in Upper Left and Bottom Right Quadrants

Eye movement on the page follows a Z pattern

Blue quadrants are most important area of the page

columns can be further subdivided. Then all the graphic elements—text indentations, headings, visuals, and so on—align within the columns. The resulting symmetry creates a more pleasing page and unifies long documents. Figure 5.9 uses grids to organize a page with visuals and a newsletter page.

7. Use Headings.

Headings are words, short phrases, or short sentences that group points and divide your document into sections. Headings enable your reader to see at a glance how the document is organized, to turn quickly to sections of special interest, and to compare and contrast points more easily. Headings also break up the page, making it look less formidable and more interesting.

Psychological research shows that short-term memories can hold only five to nine bits of information—a seven-digit phone number would max out most people's short-term memories.[11] Only after those bits are processed and put into long-term memory can we

Figure 5.9   Grids Visually Unify Content

Two-Column Grid

Title of the Document

Heading

Heading

Heading

Three-Column Grid

Title of the Document

Heading

Heading

assimilate new information. Large amounts of information will be easier to process if they are grouped into three to seven chunks rather than presented as individual items.

To use headings effectively:

- Write specific headings.

- Write each heading so it covers all the information before the next heading.

- Write headings at the same level with parallel language. For example, all the design tips in this section start with a command-form verb such as "Place" or "Use."

Research continues to show that headings help readers. In a study that examined forensic child-abuse reports from Canadian children's hospitals, researchers examined communication between the physicians who authored the reports and the social workers, lawyers, and police officers who later used them. They discovered that headings and subheadings improved accessibility of crucial information about the severity of the children's injuries.[12]

8. Unify Documents with Consistent, Sparing Decorative Strategies.

Used in moderation, highlighting, color, and other decorative devices add interest to documents. However, don't overdo them. A page or screen that uses every possible decorating device just looks busy and hard to read.

Because the connotations of colors vary among cultures, check with experts before you use color for international or multicultural audiences. In North America, red is appropriate for warnings. Pastel colors such as lavender create a calming impression, while bright colors imply urgency. The brown color of UPS's trucks and uniforms projects an image of reliability; consumers discerning between red- and green-packaged candy bars perceived the green one as healthier, even when content and package text were identical.[13]

To visually unify your document:

- **Match color with purpose.** Color highlights content and impacts tone.

- **Use a limited, consistent color scheme to create unity.** Don't overuse color to the point of desensitizing your audience. For example, print headers and sidebar boxes in burgundy, subheaders and image captions in navy, and text in black. You also could use a monochromatic palette, such as dark green headings, medium green image frames, and a light green sidebar background. If you are on a limited printing budget, try a monochrome grayscale palette.

- **Use repetition to create rhythm.** Repeat design elements such as headings or small photos to create a unified look across pages or panels.

- **Use contrast to create visual interest.** Consider contrast between text and visuals or between a larger font for headings and a smaller one for text. Note that color contrast is a different concern; see "Designing for Inclusivity" later in this chapter.

How to Incorporate Design into the Writing Process

LO 5-5

Seamlessly functional, visually appealing documents require the consideration of design at every step of the writing process. Before you draft or even research your content, consider how the rhetorical situation may influence design strategy.

Figure 5.10	Showerhead Card for Breast Self-Exam

Analyzing Your Rhetorical Situation

In all forms of business communication, you should begin by considering your purpose, medium, and audience.

Purpose   *What design approach or tone does your purpose dictate?* A brochure designed to promote awareness of your company should have a different look than a brochure persuading people to purchase your company's products. For example, a primarily informative brochure may use more charts or infographics, while a persuasive brochure may use images evoking emotional appeals. What is the aim of your communication, and how can your design strategy support that aim?

Medium   *What are the design capabilities and limitations of the medium?* Context-adapted design requires attention to the capabilities, restrictions, and conventions of your communication's particular medium. When working with a new medium, you will need to study preexisting examples, if possible, and use your best judgment in deciding how to design in a way that suits that medium. A billboard medium offers different design possibilities and restrictions than do a full-size newspaper ad, an email newsletter, or a poster on the side of a public bus.

Audience   *What needs, expectations, and concerns does your audience have?* Just as you should adapt written communication to your audience, you also should consider how design can adapt to your audience's needs, expectations, and potential objections. The hanging card for breast self-exams in Figure 5.10, designed to be hung from a showerhead, caters to an audience of women who do not perform breast self-exams because of forgetfulness or insufficient time. These water-resistant shower cards adapt to those concerns, offering busy women a reminder to perform an exam when they're in the shower.

Researching Your Topic

As you research your topic, consider whether some content might be better illustrated in a visual rather than textual format. How can you use design to save your audience time or to aid comprehension?

Drafting the Text

As you draft your text, keep in mind how textual content tethers to graphic content. Depending on your medium, you may need to change font size or style or revise for length in order to neatly align textual and graphic content. For example, in the poster from Milwaukee's Safe Sleep campaign, where the headboard looks like a headstone (see Figure 5.11), the text needed to fit within the headboard space and be long enough to remind viewers of text on a headstone.

Selecting Appropriate Visuals

Keep in mind that not all communication needs graphics, but all communication has a visual component—considerations such as white space, font size, and use of bullets or headers. If you decide that graphics suit your rhetorical situation, source them thoughtfully: Do the graphics tell a story, convey information more effectively than text, or otherwise serve a purpose? Are the graphics free for public use or used with permission, and properly credited? Do graphics representing people account for diversity and inclusion? Does the graphics' style match the tone of your communication?

The Milwaukee-based Safe Sleep Campaign created a series of Public Service Announcements cautioning parents against sleeping with their infants and promoting the use of cribs (see Figures 5.11, 5.12, and 5.13). Notice the difference in tone across the three images, which were created across two years. Which visual do you think was the best choice for the rhetorical situation? Each image is one of several in a set, so for further context, visit the original source.[14]

In 2015, in response to criticism of the "whitewashing" of emojis, Apple released a set of the icons that allows users to select from a scale of skin tones.[15] When portraying a group of people, consider representation of gender, race, ability, age, body shape, ethnicity, and other forms of diversity, and take care to represent people authentically. Audiences want to see themselves represented in visual communication, but there is a fine line between helping your audience imagine themselves as part of the scenario your communication describes and depicting a situation that is not true, which could detract attention away from addressing issues of inequality. If, for example, your company employs only 10% women and wants to recruit a higher percentage of female employees, it would be inauthentic to feature a photo on your company's HR website with six women and five men working together, implying that such a gender ratio is representative of the

Figure 5.11	Safe Sleep Campaign Poster 1: Headboard as Gravestone (January 2010)

Source: http://city.milwaukee.gov

| **Figure 5.12** | Safe Sleep Campaign Poster 2: Baby in Bed with Knife (November 2011) |

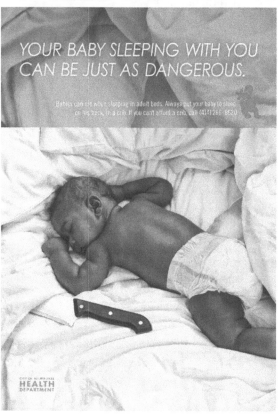

Source: http://city.milwaukee.gov

| **Figure 5.13** | Safe Sleep Campaign Poster 3: Baby in Crib on Words (July 2012) |

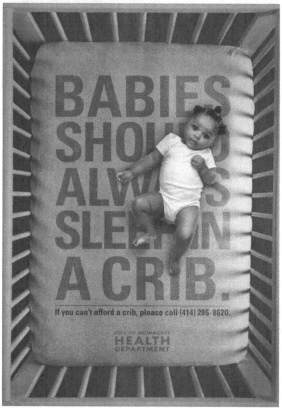

Source: http://city.milwaukee.gov

company. A photo with two women and three men, depicting a doubling of the current female-employee rate, would be a more appropriate choice to represent the company's hiring goals and help potential female applicants envision themselves working there.

Consider whether you want visuals to downplay or highlight realism. On a sign labeling the compost bin in a company cafeteria, it may be more appropriate to draw a stylized compost pile, or representative food scraps such as an apple core, rather than using a photograph of actual compost. In other situations, a photograph may be preferable for accuracy or realism—if a large amount of farmland is up for auction, for example, an aerial photo with superimposed demarcations of the lot's boundaries would provide more meaningful information to potential buyers than a stylized map of the lot. For additional information about incorporating visuals, including ethics, see Chapter 13.

Creating the Design

Use design to control and optimize your audience's experience of the document. What does your audience need your document to do and how can good design direct their eyes (or mouse-clicks) to save them time? What are your audience's visual needs? What does your audience expect the document to look like? How will your audience's internal dialogue interact with your design at every word, page, header, navigation bar, or scroll?

Use design guidelines to direct the audience's attention, provide for their visual needs, and meet their expectations. Then employ usability testing, discussed in a later section, to gather feedback on whether your design effectively controls your audience's experience of the document. Then revise and test again until your document achieves optimal usability.

Printing/Publishing

Depending on your medium and budget, some printing can be accomplished on your personal ink-jet printer. Obtain better laser-quality results at consumer-level printers such as those available at Staples. If your organization demands an even higher professional look or if you have thousands of copies to print, take your brochure to a commercial printer.

Four-color printing on glossy paper will look best; however, it also will incur greater cost. To get the effect of color with the least expense, try black print on colored paper.

Some mediums, such as webpages, do not need physical printing, while other mediums, such as a yard sign, require medium-specific printing. Allow time to research the best way to print or publish a new or unusual medium; seek out well-published examples of the same form and inquire about their creation methodology.

How to Design Inclusively

LO 5-6

Accessibility means designing to account for disabilities or unique perceptive needs such as color blindness, impaired vision, or dyslexia; accessible design is required by the Americans with Disabilities Act (ADA), and some examples of accessible accommodations include closed captioning of videos and screen-reader-friendly image tags. **Inclusivity** takes accessibility a step further, using accessibility principles to make your document inviting and usable for all users. Designing for inclusivity shows that the document designer cares about each and every user's needs while treating each user as part of a whole rather than an individual who needs accomodations different from a target user. A welcome side effect? Increasing inclusivity often improves all users' experience of a document. In one physical example, sloping curbs that accommodate wheelchairs offer increased functionality for many other users, from skateboarders to older people who may be prone to tripping to a traveler toting a rolling suitcase.

Figure 5.14	NFL's "Color Rush" Jersey Designs Overlooked Viewers with Red-Green Color Blindness

Source: Sporting News Media (2017).

You might not consider clothing to be a communication "document," but NFL team jerseys are "read" by millions of viewers, and their design undergoes scrutiny just like that of a brochure, memo, or website. In 2015's "Color Rush" game between the Bills and the Jets, viewers with red-green color blindness—approximately 8% of the male population and 0.5% of females—had a hard time distinguishing which player was on which team (see Figure 5.14).

Responding to criticism, the NFL announced that future "Color Rush" jerseys would account for the needs of viewers with color blindness. To avoid similar accessibility oversights in your documents, you can check them against a color-blindness simulator such as **Sim Daltonism**[16] or toptal's **color blindness webpage filter.**[17]

Another way to ensure vision-impaired viewers can access your content is to convert your document to grayscale. This technique checks for appropriate color contrast. Note the two color posters in Figure 5.15: the less-saturated image on the left is much more

Figure 5.15	Sufficient Contrast Increases Legibility

Good Contrast

Bad Contrast

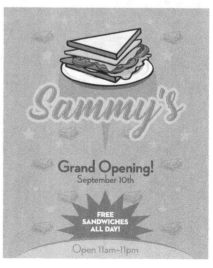

Figure 5.16	Letters of the Proxima Nova Typeface Are Easier to Read

The quick brown fox jumps over the lazy dog.

With the team, I moved 111 bushels from farm to bin.

legible even when converted to grayscale, while the more-saturated image on the right becomes nearly illegible.

Use of certain fonts also can increase legibility. Asymmetrical fonts in which letters that normally are mirror images, such as "p" and "q," do not mirror each other, weighted fonts such as OpenDyslexic, and fonts such as Proxima Nova (see Figure 5.16) that distinguish between similar characters such as "1" and "I" increase reading speed and accuracy—an appropriate design choice to accommodate readers with dyslexia. However, improving legibility via appropriate contrast or legible fonts benefits everyone, not just vision-impaired viewers, so it demonstrates inclusive design.

How to Test Documents for Usability

LO 5-7

Usability testing, or assessing how well your documents function with real audiences, is an important step in document design. Just because a document has visual appeal does not mean it is functional; in the case of the NFL jerseys, the jerseys looked fine on their own but did not function in the context of paired matches. To assess how well your design serves its purpose, test it with your audience. Then, use feedback to improve your design's usability. If the jersey designers would have shown them to a test group including individuals with red-green color blindness, the unwise pairing of red and green jerseys could have been avoided.

After collecting feedback from both customers and employees, Delta Airlines reimagined the design of its boarding passes. The new look, as shown in Figure 5.17, features a clear hierarchy of information, less clutter, more white space, only one bar code, and a new sans serif typeface. These choices make the new design user-friendly for both Delta employees and passengers.[18]

According to Jakob Nielsen, a usability expert, testing a draft with five users will reveal 85% of the problems with the document.[19] If time and money permit additional testing, revise the document and test the new version with another five users.

To quickly spot design flaws, test the document with the people who are most likely to have trouble with it, such very old or young users, people with limited education, and people who read English as a second language. To design inclusively, test your document with as diverse a group of users as possible; differently abled users and users with perceptual challenges such as color blindness should be able to use your document with ease, which in turn will make your document more functional for all users.

Three kinds of tests yield particularly useful information:

- **Observation.**   Watch someone as he or she uses the document to do a task. Where does the user pause, reread, or seem confused? How long does it take? Does the document enable the user to complete the task accurately?

Figure 5.17	Before (top) and After (bottom) Redesign of Delta's Boarding Pass

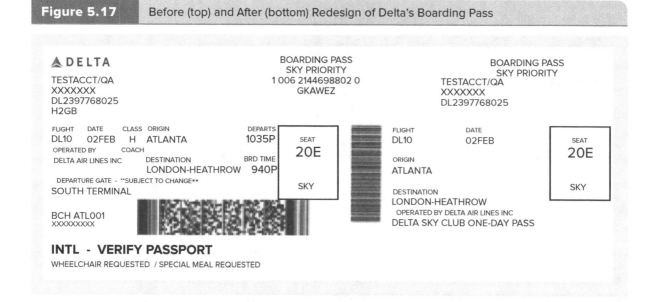

Source: Delta Air Lines, Inc.

- **User narration/snapshots.**   Ask the user to "think aloud" while completing the task or interrupt the user at key points to ask what he or she is thinking to generate a map of how the user's mental dialogue interacts with the document. You also can ask the user to describe his or her thought process after completing the document and the task.

- **User annotation.**   Ask users to put a plus sign in the margins by any part of the document they agree with or find useful and a minus sign by any part of the document that seems confusing or incorrect. Then use interviews or focus groups to determine the reasons for the plus and minus judgments.

Designing Brochures

LO 5-8

People are more likely to read brochures if the design engages their attention. Engaging design should speak directly to your audience's needs. Consider why your audience might pick up the brochure and design to engage with that mental dialogue. For example, the Malaria brochure in Figure 5.18 speaks directly to readers who likely will read the brochure if they are already concerned about contracting malaria; the red, bolded exclamation points draw their attention to key information and the all capital headings in green organize answers to key questions in the readers' minds. The drawings add psychological distance to a potentially scary situation while remaining precise in meaning and, therefore, reassuring. Your content and style may be more formal or informal, but it should affirm the desired image of you or your organization and serve the aim of your communication. The three-fold brochure (also called a tri-fold brochure) of Figure 5.19 depicts the most common brochure layout, but many other arrangements are possible.

Before inserting textual and visual elements into your brochure, optimize layout to consider your audience's viewing tendencies. How will they open the brochure, and which content should they encounter first? How can you guide the audience's eyes using a Z-pattern, grids, or images? Does each panel make sense on its own? Place content to emphasize important points for each spread the reader encounters. In a three-fold brochure, the Z pattern needs to work for the cover alone, for inside pages 1 and 2 (as the reader begins to unfold the brochure), and for inside pages 1, 3, and 4 (when the brochure is fully opened). You even should consider what would happen if the audience doesn't encounter your document as planned: if the brochure is accidentally displayed upside-down, would the information on the back still encourage someone to pick it up?

Figure 5.18	Malaria Brochure Distributed to Zambian Households (also available in local languages)

HOW TO SPOT MALARIA SIGNS

You might have malaria if you have:

- Fever/body heat
- Headache
- Body aches
- Chills
- Vomiting

If you feel sick, it is important to seek treatment right away from your Community Health Worker (CHW). Just one sick person in the household can spread malaria to others in the home through the bite of a mosquito.

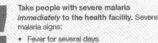

Take people with severe malaria *immediately* to the health facility. Severe malaria signs:

- Fever for several days
- Constant vomiting
- Dark urine
- Severe headache and body aches
- Has fits
- Fainting or unconsciousness

WHAT TO DO IF YOU THINK YOU HAVE MALARIA

Go to your Community Health Worker to get tested and treated for malaria. The CHW will test you for malaria, and if it is positive, give you treatment. The treatment will cure you of malaria.

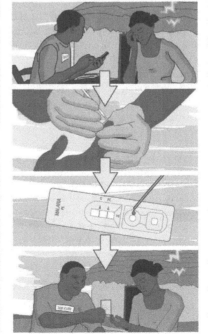

Take all pills given to you. Follow dose instructions carefully. For children under five, crush pills and put into water to dissolve before giving medicine to child.

The CHW will also test and treat others in your household for malaria. It is important that everyone get tested for malaria, even if they feel well, because people can have malaria without signs. After visiting your house, the CHW will visit your neighbors and test and treat them for malaria too. This will help make your community malaria-free.

©PATH/Bret Smith. Used by permission.

Figure 5.19	Page Setup for a Three-Fold Brochure on 8.5-Inch × 11-Inch Paper

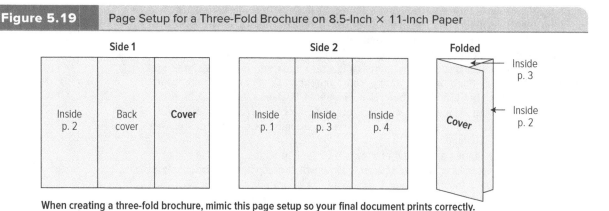

When creating a three-fold brochure, mimic this page setup so your final document prints correctly.

Designing Infographics

LO 5-9

Informational graphics, or **infographics,** employ visual representations of information to educate an audience about a specific topic (see Figure 5.20). Infographics often depict complex findings from both qualitative and quantitative research studies. Presenting data in pictures frames statistics as a story—an easily digestible format.

While infographics formerly were found mainly in newspapers and newsmagazines, professional organizations have quickly adopted them. Some businesses, such as Wells Fargo, BP, Sony, and JPMorgan Chase & Co., use infographics in their annual reports to communicate with shareholders. Other organizations employ them on websites and social media pages to connect with customers and promote their business. Infographics thrive in the digital age because they are so easy to share, forward, post, and tweet. Infographics exist on nearly any business-related topic you can imagine—business cards, CEOs, proposals, and globalization, to name a few. Some job hunters even are creating infographic résumés to promote their accomplishments and to get noticed by potential employers.[20]

Like creating a brochure, designing an infographic incorporates all elements of document design. Infographic-specific design considerations include determining the story you want to tell, selecting a visual representation for quantitative or qualitative information, and assembling the graphic.

Determining the Story You Want to Tell

Infographics portray data in a way that tells a story. Simply presenting the data does not guarantee that your audience will interpret it in the intended way, however. Use well-chosen text, such as a title, to frame the story. In Figure 5.20, the subheadings (such as "Wage Discrimination") guide the viewer to specific content. And in Figure 5.21, labels such as "Orbits" and "Titan Flybys" clearly indicate types of Cassini's activities.

Selecting a Visual Representation for Information

Infographics rely on design to convey meaning, using visual methods to represent content. Selecting a clear, appealing, and fitting visual representation method is crucial to a memorable and successful infographic. A common technique is to use a human figure to represent data, such as the human figures at the top of Figure 5.1. Select visual representations that correspond with content. In an infographic about college tuition costs, for example, a penny could represent each thousand dollars of tuition cost, forming visual stacks of pennies that compare and contrast different tuition amounts.

Figure 5.20 An Example of an Infographic

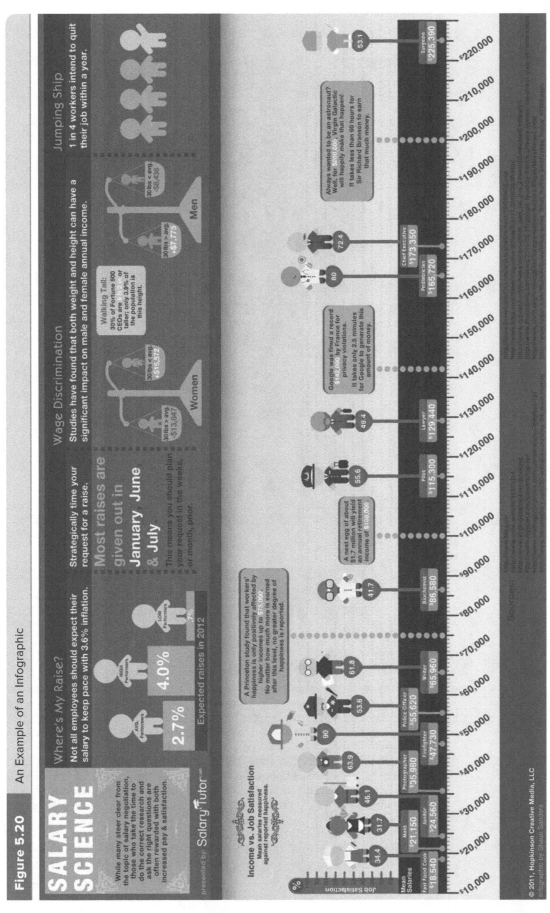

"The Science of Salary—Infographic" by Shaun Sanders. ©2011 Hopkinson Creative Media. *Reprinted with permission.*

Figure 5.21	Infographic: "Cassini Mission Overview" Organizes Data into a Chronological Story

Source: NASA

Putting It All Together

Before combining visuals and text into your infographic, test possible layouts with sketches or a design program. Consider the size of your ultimate medium, whether printed or electronic, to ensure that the final content is legible.

After your sketches are complete, combine the visual and textual elements in a software program of your choice. Incorporate different shapes, lines, typeface sizes, and colors to direct the viewer's eye across the infographic. The infographic should have a clear hierarchy of presented information; the audience should never be confused about where to look next. You also should include a key, if needed, so your audience can interpret the information; for the penny example just given, you'd need to indicate that one penny symbolizes $1,000.

You will need to determine the tone you want your infographic to project for yourself or your organization. Make every choice on the infographic—color, font, visuals, text size—a conscious one. Your choices always should resonate with the intended audience and purpose of your infographic. The audience should never wonder why you are presenting a certain piece of information or how visual and textual content connect.

Be a cautious, ethical designer of infographics. Because visuals generally gain more importance and emotional impact than their textual counterparts,[21] designers of infographics can easily mislead their audience. Avoid presenting distorted data to make a stronger point and attract attention. Cite the data source on the infographic itself, in an unobtrusive but unhidden location. The information infographics offer needs to be trustworthy and the way you present it should help earn the audience's trust in you as the creator.

Designing Websites

LO 5-10

To create effective websites, you must attract and maintain the audience's attention, create a helpful home page with useful navigation, follow conventions, and adapt to possible delivery methods. As you design a website, you also should try to make it accessible to people with disabilities—the law is beginning to consider a website a public space and, therefore, subject to the 1990 Americans with Disabilities Act. Finally, you should test your website to ensure audiences interact with it as intended.

Attracting and Maintaining Attention

Steve Yankovich, vice president for eBay mobile, states, "We've found that people will give us 30 to 60 seconds to connect them with the things they need and love."[22] The amount of time you have to attract and keep an audience's attention on your website is minimal. Researchers tracked how long users took to read or scan web pages; 52% of the visits were shorter than 10 seconds. In fact, 25% were less than four seconds. Only 10% were longer than two minutes. Therefore, you should employ a simple, attractive design strategy that draws your audience in and carefully avoid any design flaws that could cause audiences to leave your website immediately.[23]

Once you've gained your audience's attention, arrange content in a way that will maintain that attention. Jakob Nielsen's research shows that people view websites in an F-shaped pattern. First, they quickly read across the top of the page. Then they move down the page some and read across again, but for a shorter distance. Finally, they scan down the left side. All this happens quickly. The F-shaped pattern means that your most important information must be at the top of the page. In addition, make sure that headings, paragraphs, and items in lists start with words important to your reader.[24]

Creating a Helpful Home Page and Navigation

To keep visitors around long enough to find (or buy) what they want, design your home page and navigation with care. Your home page should load quickly and your navigation should readily orient users to the information they want. Studies show that users grow impatient after waiting 10 seconds for a page to load, and most will leave the site immediately.[25] In addition, first-time visitors tend not to scroll down beyond the first screen of text; if the audience has to work too hard to figure out how to use your web page, chances are they will leave the site.

■ **Provide a simple, accessible orientation to the website's author or purpose.** Many websites feature a prominently placed link to an "About" or "FAQ" page; this design choice caters to users who want to assess the site's ethos before reading further or who need the website to quickly answer a question and don't want to have to navigate a complex menu to locate that answer.

■ **Provide useful navigation tools.** A site index, search tool, and navigation bars (vertically on the left of the screen or horizontally on the top and bottom) can help users locate the content they need.

| **Figure 5.22** | Half a Dozen of One's Donut Website Directs Users to "Order" |

- **Make clear what readers will get if they click on a link.**

Ineffective phrasing: Employment. Openings and skill levels are determined by each office.

Better phrasing: Employment. Openings listed by skill level and by location.

- **Make completing a task as easy as possible.** The donut store, Half a Dozen of One, designed the "Order" button on its website, shown in Figure 5.22, to stand out from other links so users can quickly use the website to perform a desired function—in this case, ordering a late-night snack.

Following Conventions

Nielsen urges his readers to follow conventions of web pages and get back to design basics. He reminds designers that users want quality basics. Here are some of the top web design mistakes he lists:

- Bad search engines.
- Links that don't change color when visited.
- Large text blocks.
- Fixed font size.
- Content that doesn't answer users' questions.

He also cautions against violating design conventions. Users will expect your website to act like the other sites they visit. If it doesn't, the site will be harder to use and visitors will leave. Nielsen warns that some conventions, such as banner ads, have outlived their usefulness. Banner blindness is so prevalent that anything that looks like a banner will be ignored, as one nonprofit health site discovered. The site had a box at the top of the home page telling users what to do if they thought they were having a heart attack, but research showed that users were ignoring the box because they thought it was an ad.[26]

As you design web pages, use the following guidelines:

- Use a white or light background for easy scanning.
- Keep graphics small. Specify the width and height so that the text will stay in a fixed location while the graphics load.
- Provide visual variety in your text. Use indentations, bulleted or numbered lists, and headings. Start lists with impact words; remember the F pattern.

- Unify multiple pages with a small banner, graphic, or label so surfers know who sponsors each page.

- On each page, provide a link to the home page.

- Keep animation to a minimum and allow viewers to control its use. If you have an animated site introduction page, include an easy-to-spot "Skip Intro" button.

- If your web pages include music or sound effects, place an Off button where the user can see it immediately.

Appropriately enough, the web has many additional resources about webpage design guidelines; on technical pages regarding HTML, XML, CSS, and Java; and on webpage design programs such as WordPress, Dreamweaver, and Drupal.

Adapting to Delivery Methods

Today's web users expect to be able to access sites from a variety of devices, such as laptops, smartphones, and tablets. **Mobile-first design** prioritizes functionality and accessibility across many devices. Google encourages app developers to design mobile-friendly apps so that Google can index them for search results, asserting that "users should get the most relevant and timely [search] results, no matter if the information lives on mobile-friendly web pages or apps."[27]

There are two main ways to design a website for mobile viewing: **adaptive design** and **responsive design.** Adaptive design rearranges the full website's content into a mobile window, essentially reshaping the content for a different-sized "frame," whereas responsive design renders content specifically for a mobile screen. A more complex website, such as a health insurance portal, may need adaptive design in order to convey all its content, whereas a website with simpler purpose, such as a pizza-ordering website, may better meet its customers' needs with a responsive website specifically designed for mobile use.

Designing websites for mobile compatibility can affect a company's—or a nonprofit's—bottom line. When United Way redesigned its website with mobile-first, responsive design, traffic increased by over 20% for tablets and 34% for smartphones, with donations growing by 28% compared with the year before.

Designing Inclusive Websites

Inclusive design brings specific consideration to the website medium. Users with hearing impairments need captions for audio material, and blind users need words, not images. Target settled a class action suit with the National Federation of the Blind by agreeing to pay $6 million in damages and to make its site more accessible. More legal proceedings got Apple to agree to make iTunes more accessible. One of the most sought-after features in these legal actions is text attached to links and graphics that can be accessed by screen-reading software.[28]

To make your web page accessible for people with vision impairments,

- Put a link to a text-only version of the site in the upper left-hand corner.

- Put navigation links, a site map, and search box at the top of the screen, preferably in the upper left-hand corner.

- Arrange navigation links alphabetically so blind users can use a screen reader to jump to the links they want.

- Provide alternative text (an "Alt tag") for all images, applets, and submit buttons.

- Provide a static alternative to flash or animation.

- In hypertext links, use text that makes sense when read alone. A person listening to a screen reader will not understand "Click here." "Click to order a copy" or "Click for details" offers a better clue of what the link leads to.

Testing Websites for Usability

Nielsen recommends usability testing at various stages of the website design process by observing users navigating the site because you may detect behaviors that users might not be aware of themselves, such as viewing websites in an F-pattern.[29] Many apps use **beta testing** on select groups of users—usually volunteers who know the app may not be perfect—to gather usability feedback on how well a new app performs. Using this insight, they can revise the app before rolling out a widely marketed version. This helps preserve a company's reputation by avoiding launching an error-ridden application.[30] You should ask others to "beta test" your website so you, too, can ensure your electronic communication presents a professional image.

Summary by Learning Objectives

LO 5-1   **Why document design is important.**

- Good document design saves time and money, affirms the creator's desired image, and builds goodwill.
- Effective design groups ideas visually, making the structure of a document more inviting and obvious so the document is easier to use.

LO 5-2   **Design conventions.**

Effective design relies heavily on conventions, which vary by purpose, medium, and audience.

LO 5-3   **The four levels of document design.**

The four levels of design—intra, inter, extra, and supra—help you organize and analyze design choices.

LO 5-4   **Design guidelines for each level.**

These guidelines help writers create visually attractive and functional documents:
1. Strategize Font Choices.
2. Minimize Use of Words in All Capital Letters.
3. Use White Space.
4. Strategize Margin Choices.
5. Place Elements for Deliberate Emphasis.
6. Unify Elements with Grids.
7. Use Headings.
8. Unify Document with Consistent, Sparing Decorative Strategies.

LO 5-5   **How to incorporate design into the writing process.**

The best documents are created when you think about design at each stage of the writing process.

- As you plan, think about the needs of your audience.
- As you write, incorporate lists, headings, and visuals.
- Get feedback from people who will be using your document.
- As you revise, check your draft against the guidelines in this chapter.

LO 5-6   **How to design inclusively.**

Inclusive design means accounting for accessibility needs in a way that benefits all users. Some inclusive design considerations include vision impairment, dyslexia, and color blindness.

LO 5-7   **How to test your document for usability.**

Usability testing is assessing your documents with real audiences. To conduct a usability test, observe people reading the document or using it to complete a task.

LO 5-8   **How to design brochures.**

To create an effective brochure, you must analyze your rhetorical situation, draft the text, select appropriate visuals, create the design, and print.

LO 5-9   **How to design infographics.**

To create effective infographics, you must determine the story you want to tell, determine an appropriate visual representation for information, and put it all together.

LO 5-10   **How to design websites.**

To create effective websites, you must attract and maintain the audience's attention, create a helpful home page with useful navigation, follow conventions, adapt to possible delivery methods, design for inclusivity, and test for usability.

Exercises and Cases

5.1 Evaluating Page Designs

Use the guidelines in this chapter to evaluate each of the following page designs. What are their strong points? What could be improved?

(Roller skates): ©Waltraud Ingerl/Getty Images; (Family meal): ©monkeybusinessimages/Getty Images

As your instructor directs,

a. Discuss the design elements you see on these sample pages with a small group of classmates.

b. Write an email to your instructor evaluating the design elements on each of the sample pages. Be sure to address the four levels of design, as well as the guidelines for document design discussed in this chapter.

c. In an oral presentation to the class, explain the process you'd use to redesign one of the sample pages. What design elements would make the page stronger or weaker? What design elements would you change and how? Given the title of the document, what audience characteristics might your design take into account?

5.2   Evaluating the Ethics of Design Choices

Indicate whether you consider each of the following actions ethical, unethical, or a gray area. Which of the actions would you do? Which would you feel uncomfortable doing? Which would you refuse to do?

1. Putting the advantages of a proposal in a bulleted list, while discussing the disadvantages in a paragraph.
2. Using a bigger type size so that a résumé visually fills a whole page.
3. Using tiny print and very little white space on a credit card contract to make it less likely that people will read it.
4. Putting important information on the back of what looks like a one-page document.
5. Putting the services that are not covered by your health plan in full caps to make it less likely that people will read the page.

5.3   Evaluating Page Designs

1. Collect several documents that you receive as a consumer, a student, or an employee: forms, letters, newsletters, emails, announcements, ads, flyers, and reports. Use the document design guidelines in this chapter to evaluate each of them.
2. Compare these documents in a specific category to the documents produced by competing organizations. Which documents are more effective? Why?

As your instructor directs,

a. Discuss the documents with a small group of classmates.
b. Write an email to your instructor evaluating three or more of the documents and comparing them to similar documents produced by competitors. Include originals or photocopies of the documents you discuss in an attachment to your email.
c. Write an email to one of the originating organizations, recommending ways it can improve the document design.
d. In an oral presentation to the class, explain what makes one document strong and another one weak.

5.4   Evaluating Infographics

As a class, select three infographics found online and answer the following questions:

- What are the purposes of the infographics?
- Who do you think are the intended audiences? What makes you say so?
- How informational are the infographics?
- How persuasive are the infographics? If you think they are persuasive, what would make them even more persuasive?
- What original contexts would be most appropriate for the infographics?
- What visual design elements attract you to these particular infographics?
- What visual design elements, if any, detract from the main messages of the infographics?
- To what extent do the infographics contain misleading information or data distortion?
- To what extent are the visual design choices effective or ineffective? In what specific ways do the creators blend images and text?
- To what extent overall are your three chosen infographics effective or ineffective given the audiences and purpose you have identified?[31]

As your instructor directs,

a. Discuss the infographics and findings with a small group of classmates.
b. Write an email to your instructor evaluating the three infographics. Include URLs of the infographics mentioned in your email.
c. In an oral presentation to the class, explain what makes your three favorite infographics effective.
d. Post your evaluation in a discussion forum to the class. Include the URLs of the infographics so classmates can view them.

5.5   Evaluating Public Service Announcements (PSAs)

Compare the full sets of PSAs represented by Figures 5.11, 5.12, and 5.13 by visiting http://city.milwaukee.gov/health/Safe-Sleep-Campaign. Which set is most effective? Why? What weaknesses does each set have? Based on the chronological progression of these sets, who do you think the target audience is?

As your instructor directs,

a.   Discuss the sets of public service announcements (PSAs) with a small group of classmates.

b.   Write an email to your instructor evaluating the PSA designs. Include URLs of the PSAs in your email.

c.   In an oral presentation to the class, explain what makes the design of one set good and that of another set weak.

d.   Post your evaluation in a discussion forum to the class. Include the URLs so classmates can click to the PSAs you discuss.

5.6   Comparing Shopping Websites

Many shoppers around the world do much of their shopping online. In a pair or in small groups, find three online shopping sites that sell similar types of merchandise. Consider the following questions:

- Who are the target audiences of the websites?
- What are some of the design features the websites offer customers?
- How easily navigable are the home pages?
- Are the websites organized with an F-shaped pattern?
- How user-friendly are the websites?

- How well do the websites' search engines function?
- How accessible are the websites for people with disabilities?
- Of the three websites, which is the best in terms of usability?

As your instructor directs,

a.   Discuss the websites with your partner or small group.

b.   Share your findings in an informal presentation for the rest of the class.

c.   Write an email to your instructor containing your findings.

5.7   Testing a Document

Ask someone to follow a set of instructions or to fill out a form. (Consider consumer instructions, forms for financial aid, and so forth.) As an alternative, you also might test a document you've created for a course. You also may try ordering food from a website, such as a pizza-delivery chain, as long as you do not process completely through the checkout process.

- Time the person. How long does it take? Is the person able to complete the task?
- Observe the person. Where does he or she pause, reread, seem confused?
- Interview the person. What parts of the document were confusing?

As your instructor directs,

a.   Discuss the changes needed with a small group of classmates.

b.   Write an email to your instructor evaluating the document and explaining the changes that are needed. Include the document as an attachment to your email.

c.   Write to the organization that produced the document recommending necessary improvements.

d.   In an oral presentation to the class, evaluate the document and explain what changes are needed.

5.8 Improving a Financial Aid Form

You've just joined the financial aid office at your school. The director gives you the form shown below and asks you to redesign it. The director says:

> We need this form to see whether parents have other students in college besides the one requesting aid. Parents are supposed to list all family members that the parents support—themselves, the person here, any other kids in college, and any younger dependent kids.
>
> Half of these forms are filled out incorrectly. Most people just list the student going here; they leave out everyone else.
>
> If something is missing, the computer sends out a letter and a second copy of this form. The whole process starts over. Sometimes we send this form back two or three times before it's right. In the meantime, students' financial aid is delayed—maybe for months. Sometimes things are so late that they can't register for classes, or they have to pay tuition themselves and get reimbursed later.
>
> If so many people are filling out the form wrong, the form itself must be the problem. See what you can do with it. But keep it to a page.

As your instructor directs,

a. Analyze the current form and identify its problems.

b. Revise the form. Add necessary information; reorder information; change the chart to make it easier to fill out.

c. Write an email to the director of financial aid pointing out the changes you made and why you made them.

Hints:

- Where are people supposed to send the form? What is the phone number of the financial aid office? Should they need to call the office if the form is clear?

- Does the definition of *half-time* apply to all students or just those taking courses beyond high school?

- Should capital or lowercase letters be used?

- Are the lines big enough to write in?

- What headings or subdivisions within the form would remind people to list all family members whom they support?

- How can you encourage people to return the form promptly?

Please complete the chart below by listing all family members for whom you (the parents) will provide more than half support during the academic year (July 1 through June 30). Include yourselves (the parents), the student, and your dependent children, even if they are not attending college.

EDUCATIONAL INFORMATION, 201_ – 201_						
FULL NAME OF FAMILY MEMBER	AGE	RELATIONSHIP OF FAMILY MEMBER TO STUDENT	NAME OF SCHOOL OR COLLEGE THIS SCHOOL YEAR	FULL-TIME	HALF-TIME* OR MORE	LESS THAN HALF-TIME
STUDENT APPLICANT						

*Half-time is defined as 6 credit hours or 12 clock hours a term.

When the information requested is received by our office, processing of your financial aid application will resume.

Please sign and mail this form to the above address as soon as possible. Your signature certifies that this information, and the information on the FAF, is true and complete to the best of your knowledge. If you have any questions, please contact a member of the need analysis staff.

_____   _____

Signature of Parent(s)   Date

Notes

1. Edward Tufte, *Beautiful Evidence* (Cheshire, CT: Graphics Press, 2006), 153–55.

2. *Des Moines Register,* Front Page, October 14, 2011.

3. Don Van Natta Jr. and Dana Canedy, "The 2000 Elections: The Palm Beach Ballot: Florida Democrats Say Ballot's Design Hurt Gore," *New York Times,* November 9, 2000, http://www.nytimes.com/2000/11/09/us/2000-elections-palm-beach-ballot-florida-democrats-say-ballot-s-design-hurt-gore.html.

4. Charles Kostelnick and Michael Hassett, *Shaping Information: The Rhetoric of Visual Conventions* (Carbondale, IL: Southern Illinois University Press, 2003), 92, 94.

5. Charles Kostelnick and David Roberts, *Designing Visual Language,* 2nd ed. (Boston: Allyn & Bacon, 2011), 81–83.

6. Jo Mackiewicz, "What Technical Writing Students Should Know about Typeface Personality," *Journal of Technical Writing and Communication* 34, no. 1–2 (2004): 113–31.

7. Jerry E. Bishop, "Word Processing: Research on Stroke Victims Yields Clues to the Brain's Capacity to Create Language," *Wall Street Journal,* October 12, 1993, A6; Anne Meyer and David H. Rose, "Learning to Read in the Computer Age," in *Reading Research to Practice,* ed. Jeanne S. Chall (Cambridge, MA: Brookline Books, 1998), 4–6.

8. Karen A. Schriver, *Dynamics in Document Design* (New York: Wiley, 1997), 274.

9. Rebecca Hagen and Kim Golombisky, *White Space Is Not Your Enemy: A Beginner's Guide to Communicating Visually through Graphic, Web, and Multimedia Design,* 2nd ed. (New York: Focal Press, 2013), 7.

10. Miles A. Kimball and Ann R. Hawkins, *Document Design: A Guide for Technical Communicators* (Boston: Bedford/St. Martin's, 2008), 49, 125.

11. George A. Miller, "The Magical Number Seven, Plus or Minus Two: Some Limits on Our Capacity for Processing Information," *Psychological Review* 63, no. 2 (1956): 81–97.

12. Marlee M. Spafford, Catherine F. Schryer, Lorelei Lingard, and Marcellina Mian, "Accessibility and Order: Crossing Borders in Child Abuse Forensic Reports," *Technical Communication Quarterly* 19, no. 2 (2010): 118–43.

13. Adapted from Jonathon P. Schuldt, "Does Green Mean Healthy? Nutrition Label Color Affects Perceptions of Healthfulness," *Health Communication* (2013): 1–8; doi: 10.1080/10410236.2012.725270.

14. Milwaukee Health Department, "Safe Sleep Campaign," http://city.milwaukee.gov/health/Safe-Sleep-Campaign.

15. Bill Chappell, "2015 Emoji Update Will Include More Diverse Skin Tones," *The Two Way: Breaking News from NPR,* November 4, 2014, http://www.npr.org/sections/thetwo-way/2014/11/04/361489535/2015-emoji-update-will-include-more-diverse-skin-tones.

16. Michel Fortin, "Sin Daltonism: The Color Blindness Simulator," https://michelf.ca/projects/sim-daltonism/.

17. Toptal, "Colorblind Web Page Filter," https://www.toptal.com/designers/colorfilter.

18. Sarah Nassauer, "Marketing Decoder: Airline Boarding Passes," *Wall Street Journal,* May 3, 2012, D2.

19. Jakob Nielsen, "Why You Only Need to Test with 5 Users," *Nielsen Norman Group: Jakob Nielsen's Alertbox,* March 19, 2000, http://www.nngroup.com/articles/why-you-only-need-to-test-with-5-users/.

20. Mark Smiciklas, *The Power of Infographics* (Indianapolis: Que, 2012), 60–64.

21. Donna Kienzler, "Visual Ethics," *Journal of Business Communication* 34, no. 2 (1997): 171–72.

22. "Lessons, Part 2," *Fast Company,* December 2012/January 2013, 98.

23. Harald Weinreich et al., "Not Quite the Average: An Empirical Study of Web Use," *ACM Transactions on the Web* 2, no. 1 (2008): 18.

24. Jakob Nielsen, "F-Shaped Pattern for Reading Web Content," *Nielsen Norman Group: Jakob Nielsen's Alertbox,* April 17, 2006, http://www.nngroup.com/articles/f-shaped-pattern-reading-web-content/.

25. Jakob Nielsen, "Website Response Time," *Nielsen Norman Group: Jakob Nielsen's Alertbox,* June 21, 2010, http://www.nngroup.com/articles/website-response-times/.

26. Jakob Nielsen, "Top Ten Mistakes in Web Design," *Nielsen Norman Group: Jakob Nielsen's Alertbox,* January 1, 2011, http://www.nngroup.com/articles/top-10-mistakes-web-design/; and Emily Steel, "Neglected Banner Ads Get a Second Life," *Wall Street Journal,* June 20, 2007, B4.

27. Google Webmaster Central Blog, "Finding More Mobile-Friendly Results," February 26, 2015, https://webmasters.googleblog.com/2015/02/finding-more-mobile-friendly-search.html.

28. "Corporate News: Target Settles with Blind Group on Web Access," *Wall Street Journal,* August 28, 2008, B4; and Lauren Pollock, "iTunes Eases Access for Blind," *Wall Street Journal,* September 29, 2008, B5.

29. Jakob Nielsen, "Usability 101: Introduction to Usability," *Nielsen Norman Group: Jakob Nielsen's Alertbox,* January 4, 2012, http://www.nngroup.com/articles/usability-101-introduction-to-usability/.

30. Ian Taylor, "The 5 Best Beta-Testing Tools for Your App," *InfoWorld from IDG,* April 24, 2017, https://www.infoworld.com/article/3191442/application-testing/the-5-best-beta-testing-tools-for-your-app.html.

31. Christopher Toth, "Revisiting a Genre: Teaching Infographics in Business and Professional Communication Courses," *Business and Professional Communication Quarterly* 76, no. 4 (2014): 446–57.

16 Making Oral Presentations

Chapter Outline

Comparing Written and Oral Messages

Identifying Purposes in Presentations

Planning a Strategy for Your Presentation
- Choosing the Kind of Presentation
- Adapting Your Ideas to the Audience

Choosing Information to Include
- Choosing Data
- Choosing Demonstrations

Organizing Your Information
- Planning a Strong Opening
- Structuring the Body
- Planning a Strong Conclusion

Planning Visuals
- Designing PowerPoint Slides
- Creating a Prezi

- Using Figures and Tables
- Using Technology Effectively

Delivering an Effective Presentation
- Dealing with Fear
- Using Eye Contact
- Developing a Good Speaking Voice
- Standing and Gesturing
- Using Notes and Visuals
- Involving Your Audience
- Practicing

Handling Questions

Making Group Presentations

Summary by Learning Objectives

©DrAfter123/Getty Images

NEWSWORTHY COMMUNICATION

Sophia the Robot: Orator . . . and Citizen

In 2017, a robot named Sophia spoke at a press conference. She said, "I am very honored and proud for this unique distinction. This is historical to be the first robot in the world to be recognized with a citizenship."

That's correct: Sophia the robot has been granted citizenship—a status partially based on her public speaking ability.

In the field of artificial intelligence (AI), one way to judge a robot's humanity is the Turing test: whether its ability to carry on a conversation can fool humans into thinking they're conversing with another human. In early years, conversation occurred via computers; the test was based solely on written conversation. This was because the AI did not have a humanlike housing that could replicate nonverbal communication elements such as eye contact, facial expression, and vocal delivery; these aspects of communication were simply too nuanced for an AI robot to ever pass the test.

But Sophia the robot, speaking from her own mouth and matching what she said to her own blinks, head-nods, and smiles, passed the test with flying colors— or at least well enough for Saudia Arabia to issue the robot citizenship. Body language expert Jack Brown assessed Sophia's facial expressions, noting her strengths and weaknesses: when she smiles, her eyelids should partially close—but don't— to indicate authenticity; her "sad face," however, is convincing, pulling down the corners of her mouth like a human would to indicate emotional distress.

Even when watching humans (as opposed to robots) speak, we analyze nonverbal communication to determine whether we believe what the person is

©Jevgenij Avin/Shutterstock

saying. A groundbreaking study showed that if people *say* one thing about their feelings, but their nonverbal communication indicates that they feel a different way, people interpreting the message assign more weight to *how* the words were said:

- 7% of a message comes from words that are spoken.
- 38% of a message comes from *how* the words are spoken (e.g., tone of voice).
- 55% of a message comes from facial expression.

Matching your spoken and nonverbal messages is a complicated skill, and public speaking is a major fear for a significant portion of the population. Jerry Seinfeld joked that "According to most studies, people's number one fear is public speaking. Number two is death. Death is number two. Does that seem right? That means to the average person, if you have to go to a funeral, you're better off in the casket than doing the eulogy."

Thankfully, Jerry's statistics are a little off: in 2017, Americans reported public speaking not as their worst fear, but their 52nd worst fear, behind dying (48th), sharks (41st), death of a loved one (17th), another world war (7th), and pollution of drinking water (4th).[1] Though the fear of public speaking will likely linger to some degree for a long time, building oral communication skills is essential to presenting yourself as a competent business professional. With focused practice, public speakers can craft powerful, audience-adapted messages with delivery to match.

The study comparing verbal and nonverbal messages was limited in its application, but test this finding for yourself the next time someone apologizes but doesn't seem to mean it: what behavior is sending you signals of insincerity? It just might be that, like Sophia, the person needs a little more practice with facial expressions.

Sources: Olivia Cuthbert, "Saudi Arabia Becomes First Country to Grant Citizenship to a Robot," *Arab News,* October 26, 2017, http://www.arabnews.com/node/1183166/saudi-arabia; Jack Brown, "Body Language Analysis No. 4105: An Interview with Sophia the Robot at the Future Investment Institute—Nonverbal and Emotional Intelligence (VIDEO, PHOTOS)," *Body Language Success & Emotional Intelligence,* October 27, 2017, http://www.bodylanguagesuccess.com/2017/10/body-language-analysis-no-4105.html; and Albert Mehrabian, "Nonverbal Betrayal of Feeling," *Journal of Experimental Research in Personality* 5, no. 1 (1971): 64–73.

Learning Objectives

After studying this chapter, you will know how to:

LO 16-1 Identify purposes of presentations.

LO 16-2 Plan a strategy for presentations.

LO 16-3 Organize effective presentations.

LO 16-4 Plan visuals for presentations.

LO 16-5 Deliver effective presentations.

LO 16-6 Handle questions during presentations.

Oral communication allows for unparalleled audience connection, immediacy, and impact. It allows you to amplify and enhance well-researched, audience-adapted verbal content with well-honed nonverbal delivery and a visual aid that illustrates your points and helps develop an emotional connection with the audience. Successful oral communication quickly and completely can convey important information to co-workers, persuade a company to take a chance on funding your idea, or solidify brand loyalty by building goodwill with customers.

Executing a strong oral presentation requires you to consider your purpose, audience, and situation at every step of the way. You'll need to develop a strategy that helps accomplish your purpose within your audience's needs and the presentation context; to curate and frame the content they need while avoiding confusing, complex, or irrelevant content; to organize your content in a digestible and continually reinforced way; to design visuals to assist your audience in caring about your message, connecting with it, and following your content; and to use best practices in nonverbal delivery to bring the content to life for your audience.

Comparing Written and Oral Messages

Giving a presentation is, in many ways, similar to writing a message. All the chapters on using you-attitude and positive emphasis, developing audience benefits, analyzing your audience, and designing visuals remain relevant as you plan an oral presentation.

Oral messages make it easier to

- Use emotion to help persuade the audience.
- Focus the audience's attention on specific points.
- Answer questions, resolve conflicts, and build consensus.
- Modify a proposal that may not be acceptable in its original form.
- Get immediate action or response.

Written messages make it easier to

- Present extensive or complex data.
- Present many specific details of a law, policy, or procedure.
- Minimize undesirable emotions.

Oral and written messages have many similarities. In both, you should

- Adapt the message to the specific audience.
- Show the audience how they would benefit from the idea, policy, service, or product.
- Overcome any objections the audience may have.
- Use you-attitude and positive emphasis.
- Use visuals to clarify or emphasize material.
- Specify exactly what the audience should do.

Identifying Purposes in Presentations

Successful communication depends on keeping the reason for that communication in mind. You can create targeted, effective presentations by first identifying your **general purpose** and then describing your **specific purpose** for communicating.

A general purpose is the main goal behind a form of communication—what is the primary purpose driving the communication? Like written messages, most oral presentations have multiple goals. However, before preparing an oral presentation of your own, you should identify its primary general purpose: to inform, to persuade, or to build goodwill. Identify your general purpose and keep it in mind throughout your presentation-crafting process.

Presentations with the general purpose to **inform** aim to share content with the audience.

- An example of a primarily informative presentation is an organizational training session. The presentation's primary goal is to inform because the bulk of the presentation's time would be devoted to conveying information on how employees should conduct themselves within the organization.

- Note that an organizational training session may have *secondary* purposes of persuading new employees to follow organizational procedures—that is, to persuade—and/or to help them appreciate the organizational culture—that is, to build goodwill.

Presentations with the general purpose to **persuade** attempt to convince the audience to act a certain way, support a certain action, or believe a certain valuation to be true.

- An example of a primarily persusive presentation is a business proposal. The person delivering a business proposal would try to persuade the audience to fund an idea or buy a product.

- Persuasion relies on a balanced mix of credibility (in terms of classical rhetoric, *ethos*), emotional connection (*pathos*), and reasoning (*logos*). Presenters can develop credibility by referencing their competence, experience, and consideration for the audience's best interests; develop emotional connection by including stories, testimonies, and stirring visuals; and demonstrate strong reasoning by including data, reasoning, and proof the proposal will work.

Presentations with the general purpose to **build goodwill** entertain and/or validate the audience while uniting the audience under shared values.

- An example of a primarily goodwill-building presentation is an announcement of a new product to the public. Although the announcement would offer information about the new product, the overall purpose of the announcement would be focused on building goodwill: to celebrate the new product, thereby motivating the public to buy the product and inspiring investors (if the company is publicly traded) to value the company at a higher level, while affirming how the new product represents the company's identity.

- A second example of a goodwill-building presentation is an after-dinner speech at a company dinner; such a speech would aim to entertain the audience while uniting listeners as contributors to the company's culture and mission.

- A third example of a goodwill-building presentation is a speech of inspiration at a sales meeting; such a speech would be designed to recognize the audience's egos and validate their commitment to organizational goals.

- Presentations with the primarily goal of building goodwill may look very different from one another, but all have the common goal of reinforcing shared values.

After identifying your general purpose, you should create a specific purpose statement to guide the creation of your presentation. Write it down before you start preparing your presentation and refer to it often to help you select strategy and content.

To help you stay focused on your presentation's overall goal, your specific purpose statement should incorporate your general purpose: to inform, to persuade, or to build goodwill. In contrast with the general purpose, which is written in "to + a verb" (the infinitive) format, the specific purpose takes the general purpose one step further, specifying exactly what you will inform, persuade, or build goodwill about. Here are some example specific purpose statements:

Weak:	The specific purpose of my presentation is to discuss saving for retirement.
Better (option 1):	The specific purpose of my presentation is to persuade my audience to put their 401(k) funds in stocks and bonds rather than in money-market accounts or CDs.
Better (option 2):	The specific purpose of my presentation is to walk my audience through how to calculate how much money they will need to save for retirement.
Better (option 3):	The specific purpose of my presentation is to affirm my audience's identity as smart investors because they have taken the proactive step of managing their retirement strategy with my investment firm.

Notice how the first "better" example makes clear that the speaker wants the audience to take a specific action; it is a speech with the general purpose *to persuade.* The second "better" example makes clear that the speaker wants to instruct the audience on how to perform a specific calculation; it is a speech with the general purpose *to inform.* The third "better" example makes clear that the speaker wants the audience to feel good about their choice to remain members of a certain investment firm; it is a speech with the general purpose *to build goodwill.*

Note that the specific purpose is *not* the introduction or thesis statement of your talk; it may not be explicit in your presentation at all. Rather, it is a guiding statement to make sure every element of your presentation serves your general purpose.

Planning a Strategy for Your Presentation

LO 16-2

How will you reach your specific goals with the target audience? The more you know about your audience, the better you can strategize how to adapt your message to their needs. Think about the physical conditions in which you'll be speaking. Will the audience be tired at the end of a long day of listening? Will they be sleepy after a big meal? Will the group be large or small?

An oral presentation needs to be more simple and more redundant than a written message to the same audience. If readers forget a point, they can reread it. Listeners, in contrast,

Oral presentation skills are a big asset in the business world.
©Monkey Business Images/Shutterstock

must remember what the speaker says. Whatever they don't remember is lost. Even asking questions requires the audience to remember which points they don't understand.

Use a strategy that makes your content easy for your audience to understand and remember. In all presentations, simplify what you want to say to the one idea you want the audience to take home. Simplify your supporting detail so it's easy to follow. Simplify visuals so they can be taken in at a glance. Simplify your words and sentences so they're easy to understand.

As you begin planning your presentation, you'll need to determine what kind of presentation to deliver and how to adapt your ideas to the audience.

Choosing the Kind of Presentation

Choose one of three basic kinds of presentations: monologue, guided discussion, or interactive.

In a **monologue presentation,** the speaker talks without interruption; questions are held until the end of the presentation, at which time the speaker functions as an expert. The speaker plans the presentation and delivers it without deviation. This kind of presentation is the most common in class situations, but it's often boring for the audience. Good delivery skills are crucial because the audience is comparatively uninvolved.

In a **guided discussion,** the speaker presents the questions or issues that both speaker and audience have agreed on in advance. Rather than functioning as an expert with all the answers, the speaker serves as a facilitator to help the audience tap its own knowledge. This kind of presentation is excellent for presenting the results of consulting projects, when the speaker has specialized knowledge, but the audience must implement the solution if it is to succeed. Guided discussions need more time than monologue presentations but produce more audience response, more responses involving analysis, and more commitment to the result.

An **interactive presentation** is a conversation, even if the speaker stands in front of a group and uses charts and overheads. Most sales presentations are interactive presentations. The sales representative uses questions to determine the buyer's needs, probe

Good presentations adapt their ideas to a particular audience.
©Image Source/PunchStock/Getty Images

objections, and gain provisional and then final commitment to the purchase. Even in a memorized sales presentation, the buyer will talk a significant portion of the time. Top salespeople let the buyer do the majority of the talking.

Adapting Your Ideas to the Audience

Analyze your audience for an oral presentation just as you do for a written message. If at all possible, determine your audience's questions, concerns, and needs so you can address them in your presentation. For audiences inside the organization, the biggest questions are often practical ones: Will it work? How much will it cost? How long will it take? How will it impact me?

You also should assess the type of audience you'll be speaking to and measure the message you'd like to send against where your audience is now. If your audience is generally agreeable and interested in your topic, you can take a more ambitious approach; if your audience is indifferent, skeptical, or hostile, focus on the part of your message the audience will find most interesting and easiest to accept.

Throughout your presentation, consider how you can speak to the audience's needs and make them feel considered. This could mean directly identifying and addressing their concerns, or it could be something as subtle as using inclusive language such as "our problem" instead of "this problem."

Choosing Information to Include

Choose the information that is most interesting to your audience, that answers the questions your audience will have without providing too much information, and that has the most impact in service of your specific purpose. Limit your talk to three main points. Your content will be easier to understand if you clearly show the relationship between each of the main points. In a long presentation (20 minutes or more), each main point also can have subpoints.

Think about colorful ways to present your information. What analogies or metaphors can you use to grab your audience's attention and help them remember your information? What props could you use? How can you entertain and inspire your audience with your presentation to increase its impact?

What pictures can you use to illustrate your ideas? Where could you use video clips? Research evidence is clear that people remember information far better and longer when its presentation involves pictures.

Turning your information into a **narrative** or story also helps. Narrative structures information in a chronological format moved forward by character, plot, and/or setting. For example, a presentation about a plan to reduce scrap rates on the second shift could begin by setting the scene and defining the problem: *Production expenses have cut profits in half.* The plot unfolds as the speaker describes the facts that helped her trace the problem to scrap rates on the second shift. The resolution to the story is her group's proposal. This example uses a narrative pattern of organization to structure the main points, but you also can include shorter anecdotes in your presentation to illustrate a point and keep the audience's attention.

In an informative presentation, link the points you make to the knowledge your audience has. Show the audience members that your information answers their questions, solves their problems, or helps them do their jobs. When you explain the effect of a new law or the techniques for using a new machine, use specific examples that apply to the decisions they make and the work they do. If your content is detailed or complicated, give people a written outline or handouts, but distribute the information wisely—ideally after your presentation, so the document does not distract from your spoken content, or before it, if your audience must reference the document during your talk. For many presentations, a better approach is to use a visual aid to reinforce complicated spoken content: project key words and main ideas sparingly to help your audience keep track of your main points as you verbally elaborate upon them.

To be convincing, you must answer the audience's questions and objections. However, don't bring up negatives or inconsistencies unless you're sure that the audience will think of them. If you aren't sure, save your evidence for the question phase. If someone does ask, you'll have the answer.

Choosing Data

As part of choosing what to say, you should determine what data to present. Any data you mention should be necessary for the points you are making and should start with decisions about what the audience needs to know.

Statistics and numbers can be convincing if you present them in ways that are easy to understand. Simplify numbers by reducing them to two significant digits and putting them in a context.

Hard to understand: Our 2018 sales dropped from $12,036,288,000 to $9,124,507,000.

Easy to understand: Our 2018 sales dropped from $12 billion to $9 billion. This is the steepest decline our company has seen in a quarter century.

Double-check your presentation statistics and numbers to ensure they are accurate. Mark Hurd, former chair and CEO of Hewlett-Packard, reported that the best advice he ever got was, "It's hard to look smart with bad numbers."[2]

Choosing Demonstrations

Demonstrations can prove your points dramatically and quickly. They offer an effective way to teach a process and to show what a product can do for the audience. Demonstrations also can help people remember your points.

Apple has become famous for using captivating demonstrations when it launches new versions of its products. Steve Jobs, in particular, was known for amazing presentations, and most of his finest involved a Wow! moment that had his audience standing and cheering.

When he introduced the MacBook Air, Jobs picked up a manila envelope and pulled out his new notebook computer, holding it high for everyone to see how thin it was. When he introduced the Macintosh computer, he had the computer center stage, in a bag. He removed the Mac from the bag and had it show images while playing music. But the grand moment came when Jobs announced that he was going to let the Mac speak for itself—and it did, in a digitized voice.[3]

Wow! moments don't have to be announcements of world-class technological breakthroughs. In their book *Made to Stick: Why Some Ideas Survive and Others Die,* Chip Heath and Dan Heath say that ideas are remembered—and have lasting impact on people's opinions and behavior—when they have simplicity, are unexpected, are concrete, project credibility, stir emotions, and offer stories. They call the combination of these six factors *stickiness.*[4]

Organizing Your Information

LO 16-3

Unlike written documents where your audience can reread as needed to understand your message, a message conveyed via presentation must be clear to the listener on the first (and only!) attempt. To help your audience grasp and remember your message, you should tell your audience about the message multiple times: first in an overview in the introduction, then in detail during the body of the presentation itself, and again in a review in the conclusion. Mere repetition is not enough, however; your content should be organized carefully at every level. You should craft a strong and complete opening, structure the body with strategic organization, and craft a strong and complete conclusion.

Planning a Strong Opening

The opening is the most important part of your presentation. An opening should contain, at a minimum, an attention getter, message or statement of purpose, and preview of your content. You also may include a discussion of your credibility and/or connect the topic to your audience, showing how your topic is relevant to their needs or concerns.

Attention Getter   Audience members are not going to decide halfway through your presentation that they should start listening; you need to grab their attention from the start and keep it. Even in the most formal or formulaic of presentations, *do not* open by stating your name or topic, unless otherwise specified by conventions specific to the event. The first words out of your mouth should work to earn the audience's attention; if, for clarity, you must state your name or topic—for example, if there are multiple speakers at an event and there is no program—do so *after* first gaining the audience's attention.

The more you can do to personalize the opening for your audience, the better. Recent events are better than ones that happened long ago; local events are better than events at a distance; people they know are better than people who are only names.

Consider using one of five common modes for openers: a startling statement, narrative, quotation, question, or humor. Note that these techniques describe the spoken (verbal) content you would use to gain your audience's attention; you also should consider how to use nonverbal content to enhance the attention-gaining affect, such as through the use of a visual aid or engaging vocal delivery.

Startling Statement   A startling statement, statistic, or fact—carefully targeted to your audience's realm of concern—can gain audience attention at the beginning of your presentation:

> Twelve of our customers have canceled orders in the past month.

This presentation to a company's executive committee went on to show that the company's distribution system was inadequate and to recommend a third warehouse located in the Southwest. The statement matters to the audience because it indicated an urgent situation that could lead to loss of business if not corrected.

Narration or Anecdote   The same presentation also could start with a relevant story. Stories use character, setting, and chronology to help the audience order information. Elements such as dialogue and sensory details can give stories more impact. Narratives lend themselves particularly well to augmentation by a visual aid to help illustrate the story.

> Last week Joe Murphy, purchasing agent for Westtrop, our biggest client, came to see me. I knew something was wrong right away because Joe was wearing a jacket instead of his usual cowboy shirt and smile. "Ajit," he said, "I have to tell you something. I didn't want to do it, but I had to change suppliers. We've been with you a long time, but it's just not working for us now."

The human mind evolved to process and recall stories more effectively than discon-nected facts, so frame facts in a story if it is possible and ethical. In this example, for example, it might not be appropriate to use the individual's or company's name if the interaction was private.

Quotation   A quotation also could start the presentation. Quotations use poetic or memorable language to introduce a "sticky" idea you want your audience to ponder or a concept that frames your message.

Quotations work best when they are directly connected to the audience, as opposed to quotes from famous people. For example, this quotation came from Boyers, a major account for the company:

> "Faster and easier!" That's what Boyers said about their new supplier.

If the quotation is short, you might consider projecting it in a visual aid, but avoid long quotes, which can distract your audience from your spoken content. An appropri-ate visual-aid alternative to projecting a long quote would be to show an image of the person who said the quote while you orally state the quote.

Question   Asking audience members to raise their hands or reply to questions gets them actively involved in a presentation. However, this technique is widely used, so if using a question as an attention-gaining technique, you must use creativity, sincer-ity, and effective timing to avoid coming across as cliche. Do more than merely ask a question and move on; give your audience the sense that you sincerely care about their response by giving them time to respond and showing interest in their response, per-haps incorporating it into your presentation, like Tony Jeary does. Jeary skillfully uses this technique in sessions devoted to training the audience in presentation skills. He begins by asking the audience members to write down their estimate of the number of presentations they give per week:

> "How many of you said one or two?" he asks, raising his hand. A few hands pop up. "Three, four, six, eight?" he asks, walking up the middle of the aisle to the back of the room. Hands start popping up like targets in a shooting gallery. Jeary's Texas drawl accelerates and suddenly the place sounds like a cattle auction. "Do I hear 10? Twelve? Thirteen to the woman in the green shirt! Fifteen to the gentleman in plaid," he fires, and the room busts out laughing.[5]

Most presenters will not want to take a course in auctioneering, as Jeary did to make his questioning routine more authentic. However, Jeary's approach both engages the audience and makes the point that many jobs involve a multitude of occasions requiring formal and informal presentation skills.

Humor   Some speakers use humor to establish rapport. In the right setting and with the right tone, humor disarms the audience and inclines them to listen more closely. However, humor requires careful consideration because an inappropriate joke can turn the audience against the speaker. Never use humor that's directed against the audience or an inappropriate group. Humor directed at yourself or your team is safer, but don't make your audience squirm with too much self-disclosure.

Message or Statement of Purpose   Your audience should not be left guess-ing as to your purpose for speaking. After gaining the audience's attention, transition to stating your overall message or goal. It may be similar to the specific purpose statement you outlined and used to guide the presentation-creation process. Among the example thesis statements below, notice the range in tone from informal to formal and the range in approach from disconnected facts to narratively framed; however, all alert the audience to the speaker's general purpose and the presentation's topic:

> Spend a few minutes with me today learning my favorite Gmail hacks, and you'll be able to use these tips and tricks to save you hours on your email tomorrow.

> My goal today is to share with you the benefits of SMART goal setting, and how to go about setting SMART goals for yourself.

> Our expansion into the Asian market was met with difficulty, but by the fourth quarter, we've recouped our initial investment and look forward positively to the next year.

> I will inform you of the main challenges we faced this year and the projected performance for year two.

Preview   Even if your audience knows your message or purpose for speaking, they still may need more guidance to easily follow your presentation. In written messages, headings, paragraph indentation, and punctuation provide visual cues to help readers understand the organization of a message. Listeners, in contrast, must rely on what the speaker says for organization and context.

Therefore, in a presentation, you need to provide explicit clues to the structure of your discourse. Before moving on to the body of the presentation, you should offer your audience a specific preview of your main points or ideas. A preview provides a mental peg that listeners can hang each point on. It also can prevent someone from missing what you are saying because he or she wonders why you aren't covering a major point that you've saved for later.

The message/purpose statement and preview are closely linked, but not exactly the same—the preview should be more specific than your message statement and clarify which main points you will use to develop, illustrate, or support your main idea.

Here is an example of a preview statement for the message statement about SMART goals:

Message: My goal today is to share with you the benefits of SMART goal setting, and how to go about setting SMART goals for yourself.

Preview: I'll discuss why SMART goals are more likely to be achieved than non-smart goals, and how they're easy to set once you know the acronym: SMART goals are Simple, Measurable, Achievable, Realistic, and Timely.

Here is an example of a preview for a different presentation. Note how this preview makes use of temporal cues, or **signposts,** to show the order in which main points will be discussed:

> First, I'd like to talk about who the homeless in Columbus are. Second, I'll talk about the services The Open Shelter provides. Finally, I'll talk about what you—either individually or as a group—can do to help.

Credibility   Depending on your audience and purpose, it may be wise to spend a few moments in your opening discussing why you are qualified to speak on your topic. If you are speaking internally about company supply-chain logistics, for example, and everyone knows your role as a supply-chain leader in the company, a credibility statement may not be necessary; however, if you take the same presentation and adapt it to an external audience, it would meet the new audience's needs to state your experience and credibility with the topic.

A statement of credibility also can be used to build goodwill by stating why the topic is personally important to you. This is especially appropriate to include if your general purpose is to build goodwill; for other topics, such as a formal informative report, it may unnecessarily use up time or even confuse the overall tone. At all points in your presentation-crafting, consider how to meet audience expectations and needs.

Relevance Briefly indicating how your topic is relevant to the audience's needs can build on the momentum of your attention-gaining opening, cementing the audience's belief that your presentation is worth listening to. Assume that your audience is busy and concerned with their own needs. Make your ideas relevant to your audience by linking what you have to say to their experiences and interests. Showing your audience that the topic affects them directly is the most effective strategy. When you can't do that, at least link the topic to some everyday experience.

As with message statements, statements of relevance can range from informal to formal and should be matched with the overall purpose, audience, and tone of the presentation.

Informal example: If we want to stay at the top of our game, we need to listen to these numbers and follow their logic, people. I hate to tell you, but the logic is saying we need a new approach.

Formal example: To generate revenue for our stakeholders and remain competitive, we need to diversify our portfolio.

Establishing relevance in the opening is just the beginning of curating your audience's attention. Throughout your presentation, you should continue to reinforce how your message addresses or relates to your audience's needs. The more seamlessly you can interweave your message with the audience's specific concerns, the more likely they are to pay attention—and remember your message.

Structuring the Body

Using a well-chosen pattern of organization helps organize your content in a way that is accessible, digestible, and memorable to your audience. In a persuasive presentation, the pattern of organization also helps to frame the flow of logic, lending impact to your argument. You should spend time considering how your content could fit different organizational patterns and which pattern best fits the needs of your purpose and audience. You also should orient your audience to each main point through the use of signposts.

Organizational Patterns Often, one of five patterns of organization will likely work to structure the body of your presentation:

- **Chronological.** Start with the past, move to the present, and end by looking ahead. This pattern works best when the history helps show a problem's complexity or magnitude or when the chronology moves people to an obvious solution.

- **Problem–cause–solution.** Explain the symptoms of the problem, identify its cause, and suggest a solution. This pattern works best when the audience will find your solution easy to accept. If the audience needs more convincing, you may consider adding a final main point, showing how your solution has worked well in other, similar situations.

- **Comparative advantages.** Establish the problem or symptoms of the problem. Then explain the obvious solutions one by one, showing why they won't solve the problem. End by discussing a solution that will work best—your solution. This pattern may be necessary when the audience will find the solution hard to accept; it is also appropriate when the audience already knows about the problem and agrees that it is significant but can't decide upon the best solution.

- **Pro-con.** Detail the reasons in favor of something and then those against it. This pattern works well when you want the audience to see the weaknesses in the opposing position while coming across as balanced and well-informed.

■ **1-2-3.** Discuss three aspects of a topic. This pattern works well to organize short, informative briefings ("Today I'll review our sales, production, and profits for the last quarter") and also for persuasive presentations when you have several good reasons to adopt a policy. In the latter, start off a strong note to keep your audience listening by leading with your strongest reason, and place your second-strongest reason last—this takes into account the **recency effect,** whereby audience members best remember what they heard last.

Signposts Between your main points, use language specifically designed to help the audience orient to the progression of your presentation. Signposts indicate movement from one idea to the next. Some signposts are simple, like the word "first" or "finally," and others help give your audience time to process and reinforce content. Choose wording that fits your style and your content's needs. You can help your audience move from idea to idea with ease by referencing chronology ("first," "second," "finally"), reinforcing previous content (reviewing the content that was just discussed), preparing the audience for what's to come (previewing the content that's about to be discussed), or transitioning between two ideas ("Now that we've discussed X, let's examine Y.")

The following statements are three different ways that a speaker could use to introduce the last of three points:

> Now we come to the third point: what you can do as a group or as individuals to help homeless people in Columbus.

> I've outlined what the company is doing to solve this problem. Now let's talk about what *you* can personally do to help.

> Finally, you may be wondering, what can *I* do to help?

Planning a Strong Conclusion

The end of your presentation should be as strong as the opening. A closing should contain, at a minimum, a review of your main content, a reinforcement of your message or purpose, and a closing statement that leaves your audience with a memorable final thought and clearly signals your audience to applaud (if applicable). If your purpose is to persuade your audience to act, your conclusion should include a final call to action.

Reference an element of your introduction to bring the presentation full circle and create a sense of psychological integrity across the presentation. For example, if your attention getter was a story about your first job, your final statement could reflect on your current job or dream job. If you began your presentation with a negative, shocking statistic, you could end the speech with a positive shocking statistic, leaving the audience with a sense of hope and balancing out your opening technique.

When Mike Powell described his work in science to an audience of nonscientists, he opened and then closed with words about what being a scientist feels like. He opened humorously, saying, "Being a scientist is like doing a jigsaw puzzle . . . in a snowstorm . . . at night . . . when you don't have all the pieces . . . and you don't have the picture you are trying to create." Powell closed by returning to the opening idea of "being a scientist," but he moved from the challenge to the inspiration with this vivid story:

> The final speaker at a medical conference [I] attended . . . walked to the lectern and said, "I am a thirty-two-year-old wife and mother of two. I have AIDS. Please work fast."[6]

When you write out your opener and close, be sure to use a conversational, oral style suited for delivery rather than reading. As you can see in the example above, oral style uses shorter sentences and shorter, simpler words than writing does. Oral style can even sound a bit choppy when it is read by eye. Oral style uses more personal pronouns, a less varied and more informal vocabulary, and more repetition.

Planning Visuals

LO 16-4

Once you have planned a strategy for your presentation, you need to decide if you will use visuals to enhance the presentation. Visuals should enhance and not distract from your spoken content. Well-designed visuals can give your presentation a professional image, heighten emotional impact, convey content not easily spoken, and assist the audience in following your presentation. Additionally, visuals should avoid excessive text for the benefit of both speaker and audience.

This section discusses the design and incorporation of visual aids in presentations. See Chapters 5 and 13 for more discussion on designing visuals.

- **Use visuals to create a professional image.** A visual aid is not always necessary for conveying content such as charts or graphs. However, nondistracting visuals can reinforce you or your company's brand, values, or image. Even if you don't need a visual aid to convey content such as graphs, consider using simple, appealing, word-free images as background to frame you visually and to send a message of prepared professionalism.

- **Use visuals to heighten emotional impact.** Emotional (*pathos*) appeals are much more effective when the audience can visualize emotional content. Along with vivid language, use images to illustrate narratives and other pathos appeals.

- **Use visuals to convey content not easily spoken.** Content such as maps, graphs, and complicated tables are better presented visually than described only orally. Use a visual aid to present visual-heavy or complicated content in a way that removes some descriptive burden from the speaker and renders the content more accessible to the audience.

- **Use visuals to assist organization.** Your audience only will hear your presentation once, and—along with a preview, signposts between main points, and a review—they will welcome visual assistance in following the presentation. You can help your audience follow the progression of ideas through headers, images, color, or other methods.

For example, if you were walking an audience of nurses through floor plans of a new hospital building, you could color-code each floor a different color and use that color in headers, backgrounds, and other visual elements of each slide so the nurses could easily reference which floor was being discussed. You also could use images to symbolize your spoken content. A common method for using visual aids to aid organization is to place a header at the top of each slide so the audience knows which main point the presentation is on.

Well-designed visuals can serve as an outline for your talk (see Figure 16.1), eliminating the need for additional notes. Visuals can help your audience follow along with you and help you keep your place as you speak. Your visuals should highlight your main points, not give every detail. Elaborate on your visuals as you talk in a conversational way that adds new content not available on the slide; it is not effective to read slides word-for-word to the audience because they will stop viewing you as a source of new information. If the audience can read the entire presentation for themselves, why are you there?

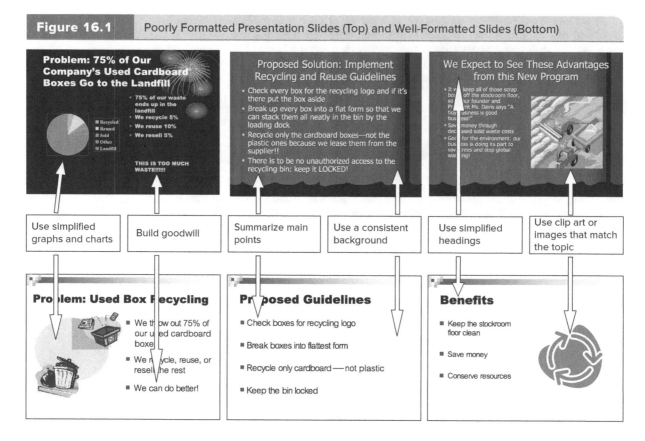

Figure 16.1   Poorly Formatted Presentation Slides (Top) and Well-Formatted Slides (Bottom)

Overall, visuals should not duplicate spoken content, but rather present information that is best conveyed in a visual rather than oral manner; visual and spoken content should overlap just enough for the audience to follow along and understand how the visuals correspond to your spoken message (see Figure 16.2).

You can organize your presentation visuals and content with a software program such as PowerPoint, Google Presentation, or Prezi. Each has its own advantages and disadvantages. The next sections discuss the most common types of visual presentation in business settings: PowerPoint and Prezi.

Designing PowerPoint Slides

When used well, PowerPoint can combine text, images, data, video, and audio into a powerful informative and persuasive message. But like any other form of communication, creating visuals requires careful thought; planning; and attention to the context, the message, and the audience.

As you design slides for PowerPoint and other presentation programs, keep the following guidelines in mind:

- Use a consistent background.

- Use a big font size: 44 or 50 point for titles, 32 point for subheads, and 28 point for examples. You should be able to read the smallest words easily when you print a handout version of your slides.

- Use bullet-point phrases rather than complete sentences. But don't go overboard with bullets because the result can become monotonous and dull.

- Use clear, concise language.

Figure 16.2	Visual Aids Present New Information, Not Just Duplicate Spoken Content

Source: Adapted from Harvard Business Review Staff, "The Best Presentations Are Tailored to the Audience," *Harvard Business Review.* (April 17, 2015), https://hbr.org/2015/04/the-best-presentations-are-tailored-to-the-audience.

- Make only three to five points on each slide. If you have more, consider using two slides.

- Strive for creating slides that have more visuals than text. Add charts, pictures, screenshots, photos, and drawings.

- Customize your slides with your organization's logo for branding purposes.

Use **animation** to make words and images appear and move during your presentation—but only in ways that help you control information flow and build interest. Avoid using animation or sound effects just to be clever; they will distract your audience.

Use **clip art** in your presentations only if the art is really appropriate to your points. Internet sources have made such a wide variety of drawings and photos available that designers really have no excuse for failing to pick images that are both appropriate and visually appealing.

Choose a consistent **template,** or background design, for your entire presentation. Make sure the template is appropriate for your subject matter and audience. For example, use a globe if, for example, your topic is international business and palm trees only if you're talking about a topic such as tropical vacations. One problem with PowerPoint is that the basic templates may seem repetitive to people who see lots of presentations made with the program. For an important presentation, you may want to consider customizing the basic template. You also can find many professionally designed free templates online to help lend your presentation a more unique look. Make sure your template does not detract from your information.

Figure 16.3	Effective and Ineffective Colors for Presentation Slides

Effective

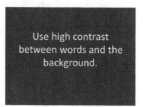

Ineffective

Choose a light **background** if the lights will be off during your presentation. Slides will be easier to read if you use high contrast between the words and backgrounds. See Figure 16.3 for examples of effective and ineffective color combinations.

Not all presentations benefit from PowerPoint slides. Information design expert Edward Tufte wrote a famous essay lambasting the slides. More recently, the U.S. Army came under harsh criticism for the now-infamous "spaghetti" PowerPoint slide (see Figure 16.4), which was used in a daily briefing to show the complexity of the strategy for the war in Afghanistan.[7] The slide was aptly named because the strategy looks like a pile of spaghetti with curling lines going in almost every direction. The leader of the forces in Afghanistan, General McChrystal, reportedly responded, "When we understand that slide, we'll have won the war."

Avoiding Disastrous PowerPoints

Conference keynote presentations are notoriously boring, with long PowerPoint shows and droning presenters. Participants, bored, fiddle with smartphones and participate in electronic discussions. During one keynote presentation, bored audience members even designed a T-shirt and put it up for sale online. The shirt's message? "I survived the keynote disaster of 09."

How can you keep your presentations from ending up with their own T-shirts? Here are a few tips:[8]

- **Use visuals and words together.** Your PowerPoint slides should augment and enhance your presentation, not distract from or displace it.

- **Keep your slides simple.** An audience should be able to completely understand each slide in two or three seconds.

- **Break complex ideas into multiple slides.** Don't try to get all the information on a single slide. Use several slides that add up to something more complex.

- **Use your slides as a mnemonic device.** Your slides should make your presentation emotionally appealing and memorable to your audience.

Figure 16.4	U.S. Army "Spaghetti" Slide

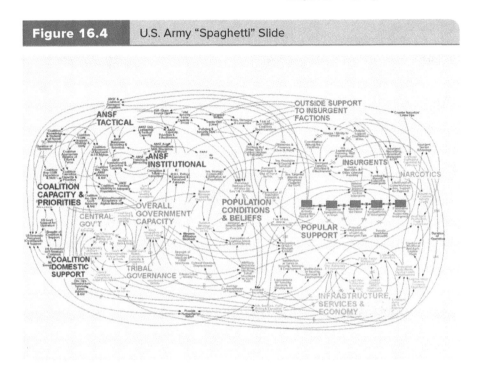

One final note about PowerPoint: because the program is so ubiquitous in the business world, audiences quickly become bored or annoyed and experience attention difficulties. One estimate suggests that 350 PowerPoint presentations are delivered in a given second around the globe.[9] Choose the program only after assessing the audience you'll be presenting to and understanding their expectations. You also might investigate alternative software programs to add more creativity and impact for your audience.

Creating a Prezi

Prezi, a free online tool, provides business communicators with another option when planning presentations. While PowerPoint's presentation philosophy is based on techniques of clicking through actual physical slides, Prezi uses modern technologies to create a different experience.

Rather than a series of consecutive slides, Prezi creates one large canvas. The presenter can place text and images anywhere on the canvas and zoom in and out of areas or pan to different areas of the canvas. See Figure 16.5 for an example. This approach allows presenters to display hierarchies and spatial relationships between items in ways that PowerPoint's linear progression does not allow.

Prezi's zooming and panning approach may be more engaging than PowerPoint, especially to viewers who are not familiar with it. But, just as with PowerPoint's transitions and animations, Prezi's movements can become distracting if used unwisely. Overuse of Prezi's movements can create a dizzying effect on the audience.

If you want to convert a PowerPoint into a Prezi, the program allows users to import PowerPoint slides one at a time or in a slide show. Finally, Prezi is cloud-based, meaning that you can access your presentation from any computer, tablet, or smartphone with an Internet connection.

For inspiration in designing a Prezi, you can go to Prezi's website to see some award-winning Prezi presentations: https://prezi.com/explore/staff-picks/.

Figure 16.5	Screenshot of Prezi Canvas

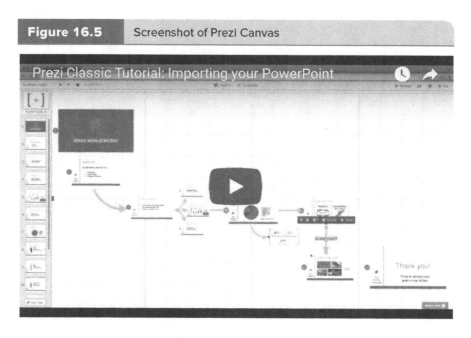

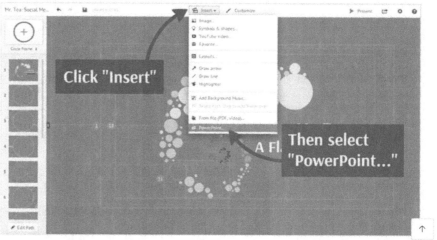

Source: Prezi (2018). "Importing from PowerPoint." https://prezi.com/support/article/creating/powerpoint-import/

Using Figures and Tables

Visuals for presentations need to be simpler than visuals the audience reads on paper. For example, to adapt a printed data table for a presentation, you might cut out one or more columns or rows of data, round off the data to simplify them, or replace the chart with a graph or other visual. If you have many data tables or charts in your presentation, consider including them on a handout for your audience.

Your presentation visuals should include titles but don't need figure numbers. As you prepare your presentation, be sure to know where each visual is so that you can return to it easily if someone asks about it during the question period. Rather than reading from your slides, or describing visuals to your audience in detail, summarize the story contained on each slide and elaborate on what it means for your audience.

Using Technology Effectively

Projected visuals work only if the technology they depend on works. When you give presentations in your own workplace, plan ahead: check the equipment in advance. When you make a presentation in another location or for another organization, arrive early so that you'll have time not only to check the equipment but also to track down a service worker if the equipment isn't functioning.

Keep in mind how you will use your visual aids. Most likely, they will provide support for a presentation in a face-to-face meeting or videoconference. Visual aids should identify the key points of your presentation in a way that allows you to interact with your audience. If you use PowerPoint, your oral presentation always should include more material than the text on your slides.

WARNING: Be sure you have a backup plan in case of a technology failure that prevents the use of your visual aids.

Delivering an Effective Presentation

LO 16-5

Audiences want the sense that you're talking directly to them and that you care that they understand and are interested. They'll forgive you if you get tangled up in a sentence and end it ungrammatically. They won't forgive you if you seem to have a "canned" talk that you're going to deliver no matter who the audience is or how they respond.

To deliver an effective presentation, you should deal with fear; use eye contact; develop a good speaking voice; stand and gesture; use notes and visuals appropriately; involve your audience; and practice, practice, practice.

Dealing with Fear

Feeling nervous about public speaking is normal; most people feel some fear about public speaking. But the more you practice, the more you can learn to channel nervous energy with purpose. You can harness that nervous energy to help you do your best work both short term, with the presentation at hand, and long term, in the context of how presentations can help you develop as a professional. IBM recommends that women seek out and volunteer for speaking engagements as a deliberate step in advancing their careers and building their own personal brands.[10] As various public speaking trainers have noted, you don't need to get rid of your butterflies; all you need to do is make them fly in formation.

To calm your nerves before you give an oral presentation:

■ Be prepared. Analyze your audience, organize your thoughts, prepare visual aids, practice your opener and close, check out the arrangements.

■ Have backup plans for various contingencies, including technical problems and likely questions.

■ Use only the amount of caffeine you normally use. More or less may make you jumpy.

■ Avoid alcoholic beverages.

■ Relabel your nerves. Instead of saying, "I'm scared," try saying, "My adrenaline is up." Adrenaline sharpens our reflexes and helps us do our best.

Just before your presentation:

- Consciously contract and then relax your muscles, starting with your feet and calves and going up to your shoulders, arms, and hands.

- Take several deep breaths from your diaphragm; picture stress leaving your body as you exhale.

During your presentation:

- Pause and look at the audience before you begin speaking.

- Concentrate on communicating with your audience, not your feelings.

- Use body energy in strong gestures and movement.

Using Eye Contact

The point in making eye contact is to establish one-on-one contact with the individual members of your audience. People want to feel that you're talking to them. Looking directly at individuals also enables you to be more conscious of feedback from the audience so that you can modify your approach if necessary.

Look directly at the people you're talking to. Make eye contact with individuals in different locations throughout the audience because you want everyone to feel you are connecting with them. Do not stare at your computer screen or your notes. Researchers have found that observers were more than twice as likely to notice and comment on poor presentation features, like poor eye contact, than good features and tended to describe speakers with poor eye contact as disinterested, unprofessional, and poorly prepared.[11]

Developing a Good Speaking Voice

People will enjoy your presentation more if your voice is easy to listen to and your delivery is appropriate. Just how important is your voice when delivering a message?

New research suggests that your voice may actually be more important than the content of your message. In fact, research by Quantified Impressions showed that executives' voices were 12% more important than the verbal content.[12] The firm collected data from 1,000 study participants about their impressions of the executives' speeches.

In another study in the *Journal of Voice,* people whose voices were rough, strained, or breathy tended to be labeled negative, weak, and passive. Normal voices were perceived to be successful, smart, and social.

Although oral presentations are live, recorded vocal delivery makes a real difference, too. Insurance company Asurion noticed an increase in customer satisfaction of 5–10% just from changing vocal tone on a recorded customer-service line to sound more warm and competent.[13]

Vocal delivery can even stack the cards for—or against—getting a job offer based on an interivew. Vocal fry, the tendency to lower one's voice at the end of statements, often with a creaky, croaky, raspy effect, has been linked to lowering one's chances at being perceived as competent—and the association is much stronger in women.[14] Vocal delivery matters, and you should be aware of how your voice represents you in both prepared and impromptu situations like a job interview.

Voice Qualities   To find out what your voice sounds like, record it using a digital voice recorder or video camera. Listen to your voice qualities, including tone, pitch, stress, enunciation, and volume.

Tone of voice refers to the rising or falling inflection that tells you whether a group of words is a question or a statement, whether the speaker is uncertain or confident, and whether a statement is sincere or sarcastic.

When tone of voice and the meaning of words conflict, people "believe" the tone of voice. If you respond to your friends' "How are you?" with the words, "I'm dying, and you?" most of your friends will reply, "Fine." If the tone of your voice is cheerful, they may not hear the content of the words.

Pitch measures whether a voice uses sounds that are low or high. Low-pitched voices are usually perceived as being more authoritative, sexier, and more pleasant to listen to than are high-pitched voices. Most voices go up in pitch when the speaker is angry or excited; some people raise pitch when they increase volume. Women whose normal speaking voices are high may need to practice projecting their voices to avoid becoming shrill when they speak to large groups.

Stress is the emphasis given to one or more words in a sentence. As the following example shows, emphasizing different words can change the meaning.

I'll give you a raise.

[Implication, depending on pitch and speed: "Another supervisor wouldn't" or "I have the power to determine your salary."]

I'll **give** you a raise.

[Implication, depending on pitch and speed: "You haven't *earned* it" or "OK, all right, you win. I'm saying 'yes' to get rid of you, but I don't really agree," or "I've just this instant decided that you deserve a raise."]

I'll give **you** a raise.

[Implication: "But nobody else in this department is getting one."]

I'll give you **a** raise.

[Implication: "But just one."]

I'll give you a **raise.**

[Implication: "But you won't get the promotion or anything else you want."]

I'll give **you** a **raise.**

[Implication: "You deserve it."]

I'll give you a **raise!**

[Implication: "I've just this minute decided to act, and I'm excited about this idea. The raise will please both of us."]

Enunciation is giving voice to all the sounds of each word. Words starting or ending with *f, t, k, v,* and *d* are especially hard to hear. "Our informed and competent image" can sound like "Our informed, incompetent image." The bigger the group is, the more carefully you need to enunciate.

Speakers who use many changes in tone, pitch, and stress as they speak usually seem more enthusiastic; often they also seem more energetic and more intelligent. Someone who speaks in a monotone may seem apathetic or unintelligent. When you are interested in your topic, your audience is more likely to be also.

Volume is projecting your voice loud enough for your audience to hear but not so loud that it overwhelms closer audience members. For proper volume, imagine projecting your voice, as if you are throwing a ball, all the way to the back of the room. If you're using a microphone, adjust your volume so you aren't shouting. When you speak in an unfamiliar location, try to get to the room early so you can check the size of the room and the power of the amplification equipment. If you can't do that, ask early in your talk, "Can you hear me in the back of the room?" Or another guideline: if you can hear your voice bouncing off the back wall of the room, usually everyone in the room can hear you.

What can be done about it when the way we hear our own voice is not the way an audience hears us? Most vocal issues that are not the result of medical concerns can be adjusted with practice based on informed observation of your starting point. Practice to convey sincerity with vocal tone, pacing, and inflection. Ask others for feedback on how your voice actually sounds. Finally, record your voice and listen to see if your voice comes across as intended—this objective observation can make a real difference.

Use your voice qualities as you would use your facial expressions: to create a cheerful, energetic, and enthusiastic impression for your audience. Doing so can help you build rapport with your audience and can demonstrate the importance of your material. If your ideas don't excite you, why should your audience find them exciting?

Standing and Gesturing

Stand with your feet far enough apart for good balance, with your knees flexed. Unless the presentation is very formal or you're on camera, you can walk if you want to. Some speakers like to come in front of the lectern to remove that barrier between themselves and the audience or move about the room to connect with more people.

Build on your natural style for gestures. Gestures usually work best when they're big and confident. Avoid nervous gestures such as swaying on your feet, jingling coins in your pocket, twirling your hair, or twisting a button. These mannerisms distract the audience.

Using Notes and Visuals

If using PowerPoint, use the notes feature. If not using PowerPoint, put your notes on cards. Many speakers use 4-by-6-inch or 5-by-7-inch cards because they hold more information than 3-by-5-inch cards. Your notes need to be complete enough to help you if you go blank, so use key phrases. Avoid complete sentences on your notes because they easily can become a crutch, allowing you to read directly from them instead of delivering a presentation. Under each main point, you might list the evidence or illustration you'll use during that portion of the presentation.

Look at your notes infrequently. Most of your gaze time should be directed to members of the audience. If using paper note cards, hold them high enough so that your head doesn't bob up and down as you look from the audience to your notes and back again. If you know your material well or have lots of visuals, you won't need notes.

If you use visuals, stand beside the screen so that you don't block it. Always stand facing the audience, not the screen. Remember that your audience can look at you or your visual, but not both at the same time. Direct attention to more complex visuals, such as figures and tables, and explain them or give your audience a few seconds to absorb them. Show the entire visual at once: don't cover up part of it. If you don't want the audience to read ahead, use animation or prepare several slides that build up.

Keep the room lights on if possible; turning them off makes it easier for people to fall asleep and harder for them to concentrate on you.

Involving Your Audience

Consider ways to involve your audience by stimulating curiosity, inviting questions, and building enthusiasm. For instance, instead of saying, "Sales grew 85% with this program," you could show a graph that shows sales declining up to the introduction of the program; invite the audience to consider what this program might do; and finally, after explaining the program, reveal the full sales graph with an animation that highlights the spike using a dramatic magenta line.

Just as when you're speaking with someone face-to-face, when you're presenting in front of a group it's important to involve your audience and look for feedback. Pay attention to body language and ask your audience questions: the feedback that you get will help you build rapport with your audience so that you can express your message more clearly.

In some settings, such as when you're presenting to a large group, you might use other tools to gather audience feedback. For example, you could build a group discussion into your presentation: give your audience some questions to discuss in small groups, then invite them to share their answers with the room. Give questionnaires to your audience, either before your presentation or during a break. Have a member of your team tabulate audience responses, then build them into the remainder of your talk.

Technology also continues to offer new ways to involve your audience. Audience response devices, such as Turing Technology clickers or smartphone apps, allow people to answer multiple-choice, true/false, and yes/no questions; software then quickly tabulates the responses into charts and graphs the audience can see. These response devices and other programs, such as Twitter, offer audiences a way to backchannel during your presentation.

Backchanneling is the process of using online tools such as smartphones, tablets, or computers to hold concurrent conversations or disseminate information while a speaker presents. The audience of the backchannel can be physically in the same room as the presenter but does not have to be. For instance, Twitter audiences can follow multiple presentations at a single conference simply by following the hashtag of the event. The question for you will be how much such a system tempts your audience to send its own tweets instead of listening to you.

Practicing

Many presenters spend too much time thinking about what they will say and too little time rehearsing how they will say it. Presentation is important; if it weren't, you would just email your text or PowerPoint to your audience.

Practice your speech over and over, out loud, in front of a mirror or to your family and friends. Jerry Weissman, a presentation coach for over 20 years, encourages every client to do verbalizations, the process of speaking your presentation aloud. He argues that practicing by looking at your slide show while thinking about what you'll say or mumbling through your slides are both ineffective methods. The best approach is to verbalize the actual words you will say.[15]

Other reasons to practice out loud are that doing so allows you

- To stop thinking about the words and to concentrate instead on emotions you wish to communicate to your audience.

- To work on your signposts, or transitions, that move your speech from one point to the next. Transitions are one of the places where speakers frequently stumble.

- To determine your pace and the overall amount of time that it takes you to deliver your message.

- To avoid unintentional negatives.

- To reduce the number of *uh*s you use. **Filler sounds,** which occur when speakers pause searching for the next word, aren't necessarily signs of nervousness. Searching takes longer when people have big vocabularies or talk about topics where a variety of word choices are possible. Practicing your talk makes your word choices automatic, and you'll use fewer *uh*s.[16]

As an added bonus, practicing your presentation out loud gives you reason to work on your voice qualities.

Handling Questions

LO 16-6

Prepare for questions by listing every fact or opinion you can think of that challenges your position. Put the questions into categories. Communication coach Carmine Gallo, who helps top executives with their presentations, says questions usually fall into no more than seven categories.[17] Then plan a good answer for each category. The answer should work no matter how the question is phrased. This bundling of questions helps reduce your preparation time and boost your confidence.

During your presentation, tell the audience how you'll handle questions. If you have a choice, save questions for the end. In your talk, answer the questions or objections that you expect your audience to have. Don't exaggerate your claims so that you won't have to back down in response to questions later.

During the question period, don't nod your head to indicate that you understand a question as it is asked. Audiences will interpret nods as signs that you agree with the questioner. Instead, look directly at the questioner. As you answer the question, expand your focus to take in the entire group. Don't say, "That's a good question." That response implies that the other questions have been poor ones.

If the audience may not have heard the question or if you want more time to think, repeat the question before you answer it. Link your answers to the points you made in your presentation. Keep the purpose of your presentation in mind and select information that advances your goals.

If a question is hostile or biased, rephrase it before you answer it. Suppose that during a sales presentation, the prospective client exclaims, "How can you justify those prices?" A response that steers the presentation back to the service's benefits might be: "You're asking about our pricing. The price includes 24-hour, on-site customer support and . . . ." Then explain how those features will benefit the prospective client.

In their book, *Buy *In,* John Kotter and Lorne Whitehead suggest 24 common attacks on presentations.[18] They recommend that speakers answer the attacks with brief commonsense responses. Here are some examples.

Attack:	We've never done this in the past, and things have always worked out okay.
Response:	True. But surely we have all seen that those who fail to adapt eventually become extinct.
Attack:	Your proposal doesn't go nearly far enough.
Response:	Maybe, but our idea will get us started moving in the right direction and will do so without further delay.
Attack:	You can't do A without first doing B, yet you can't do B without first doing A. So the plan won't work.
Response:	Well, actually, you can do a little bit of A, which allows a little bit of B, which allows more A, which allows more of B, and so on.

Occasionally someone will ask a question that is really designed to state the speaker's own position. Respond to the question if you want to. Another option is to say, "That's a clear statement of your position. Let's move to the next question now." If someone asks about something that you already explained in your presentation, simply answer the question without embarrassing the questioner. No audience will understand and remember 100% of what you say.

If you don't know the answer to a question, say so. If your purpose is to inform, write down the question so that you can look up the answer before the next session. If it's a question to which you think there is no answer, ask if anyone in the room knows. When no one does, your "ignorance" is vindicated. If an expert is in the room, you may want to refer questions of fact to him or her. Answer questions of interpretation yourself.

At the end of the question period, take a moment to summarize your main point once more because questions may or may not have focused on the key point of your talk. Take advantage of having the floor to repeat your message briefly and forcefully.

Figure 16.6	Considerations for Oral Presentations

☐ Was the presentation effective for the situation? **Strategy**
☐ Did the presentation adapt to the audience's beliefs, experiences, and interests?
☐ Did the presentation engage the audience?

☐ Was the purpose clear, even if not explicitly stated? Was the purpose achieved? **Content**
☐ Was the material vivid and specific?
☐ Did the material counter common objections without giving them undue weight?
☐ Were the opening and closing strong and effective?

☐ Was there an overview of the main points? **Organization**
☐ Did the body contain signposts of the main points?
☐ Were there adequate transitions between points? Were the transitions smooth?

☐ Were there engaging visuals? Did they use an appropriate design or template? **Visuals**
☐ Were the visuals readable from a distance?
☐ Were visuals free of spelling, punctuation, and grammar mistakes?
☐ If the visuals contained data, were the data quickly assimilated?

☐ Did the speaker make good eye contact with the audience? **Delivery**
☐ Was the speaker positioned effectively? Did the speaker's body block the screen?
☐ Did the speaker use engaging vocal delivery?
☐ Could the audience hear and understand what the speaker was saying?
☐ Did the speaker use confident gestures?
☐ Did the speaker avoid nervous mannerisms?
☐ Did the speaker handle questions effectively?

Figure 16.6 provides a checklist of steps toward delivering a successful presentation.

Making Group Presentations

Plan carefully to involve as many members of the group as possible in speaking roles.

The easiest way to make a group presentation is to outline the presentation and then divide the topics, giving one to each group member. Another member can be responsible for the opener and the close. During the question period, each member answers questions that relate to his or her topic.

In this kind of divided presentation, be sure to

- Plan transitions.

- Coordinate individual talks to eliminate repetition and contradiction.

- Enforce time limits strictly.

- Coordinate your visuals so that the presentation seems a coherent whole.

- Practice the presentation as a group at least once; more is better.

Some group presentations are even more fully integrated: the group writes a detailed outline, chooses points and examples, and creates visuals together. Then, within each point, voices trade off. This presentation is effective because each voice speaks only a minute or two before a new voice comes in. However, it works only when all group members know the subject well and when the group plans carefully and practices extensively.

Figure 16.7	Additional Considerations for Group Presentations

☐ Were team members introduced to the audience?
☐ Were all team members adequately involved in the presentation?
☐ Did the presentation transition smoothly among the team members?
☐ Did the individual presentation sections coordinate well?
☐ Did team members stay tuned in to the person speaking at the time?

Whatever form of group presentation you use, be sure to introduce each member of the team to the audience and to pay close attention to each other. If other members of the team seem uninterested in the speaker, the audience gets the sense that that speaker isn't worth listening to. The checklist in Figure 16.7 will help you plan a group presentation.

Summary by Learning Objectives

LO 16-1   Identify purposes of presentations.

- Informative presentations inform or teach the audience.
- Persuasive presentations motivate the audience to act or to believe a certain way.
- Goodwill presentations entertain and validate the audience, uniting them under a shared value. Most oral presentations have more than one purpose, but you should keep your *primary* purpose in mind as you create your presentation.

LO 16-2   Plan a strategy for presentations.

- An oral presentation needs to be simpler than a written message to the same audience would be.
- In a monologue presentation, the speaker plans the presentation and delivers it without deviation.
- In a guided discussion, the speaker presents the questions or issues that both speaker and audience have agreed on in advance. Rather than functioning as an expert with all the answers, the speaker serves as a facilitator to help the audience tap its own knowledge.
- An interactive presentation is a conversation using questions to determine needs, probe objections, and gain provisional and then final commitment to the objective.
- Adapt your message to your audience's beliefs, experiences, and interests.
- Limit your talk to three main points. In a long presentation (20 minutes or more), each main point can have subpoints.
- Choose the information that is most interesting to your audience, that answers the questions your audience will have, and that is most persuasive for them.

LO 16-3   Organize effective presentations.

- Use the beginning and end of the presentation to interest the audience and emphasize your key point.
- Provide an overview of the main points you will make. Offer a clear signpost—an explicit statement of the point you have reached—as you come to each new point.
- Based on your audience and purposes, choose a pattern of organization for the body: chronological, problem–cause–solution, comparative advantages, pro–con, or 1–2–3.

LO 16-4   Plan visuals for presentations.

Use visuals to seem more prepared, more interesting, and more persuasive. As you prepare your visuals, determine the presentation platform you will use, use numbers and figures, and use technology effectively.

LO 16-5   Deliver effective presentations.

To deliver an effective presentation, you should deal with fear, use eye contact, develop a good speaking voice, stand and gesture, use notes appropriately, involve your audience, and practice.

LO 16-6   Handle questions during presentations.

- Tell the audience during your presentation how you'll handle questions.
- Treat questions as opportunities to give more detailed information than you had time to give in your presentation. Link your answers to the points you made in your presentation.
- Repeat the question before you answer it if the audience may not have heard it or if you want more time to think. Rephrase hostile or biased questions before you answer them.

Exercises and Cases

16.1   Analyzing TED Talks

TED—which stands for Technology, Education, and Design—is an organization offering recordings of high-quality, authoritative, audience-adapted speeches on a broad variety of topics. Speakers are invited to deliver speeches at a live event, and recorded speeches are showcased on the website. Visit http://ted.com to find a talk to analyze based on the following prompts.

■ Unless otherwise instructed, select an official TED talk rather than a TEDx talk; TEDx events are independently organized and do not undergo as strict a curation process.

■ TED talks can be sorted by topic, such as Agriculture, Aircraft, or Animals, and by other descriptors such as "trending."

1. Select a TED talk in a category of interest and assess it based on the assessment questions below. Then, share your answers with your class in a brief oral presentation (length determined by your instructor). Queue up relevant spots in the TED talk to illustrate your answers. As an alternate to an oral presentation, your instructor may ask you to compose a brief written analysis of the TED talk and email it to him or her.

2. Based on the talk you analyzed in part 1, prepare a brief presentation for your peers highlighting what they can learn from the presentation: Which techniques might they try to emulate in their own oral presentations? What best practices did the speaker exemplify? As an alternate to an oral presentation, your instructor may ask you to compose a "best practices" list based on this TED talk and email it to him/her.

Assessment questions:

■ Assess the speaker's content: Which of the three appeals—credibility (*ethos*), emotional connection (*pathos*), or reasoning (*logos*)—was strongest, and why? Which element would have benefited from further practice or attention?

■ Assess the speaker's nonverbal delivery: Which nonverbal delivery element (eye contact, facial expression, gestures, proxemics, or vocals) was strongest, and why? Which element would have benefited from further practice or attention?

■ Assess the speaker's organization: How did the speaker preview the content? Review the content? How did the speaker signal movement from one idea to the next? What pattern of organization best describes how the content was arranged?

■ What did the speaker do to adapt her/his topic to this audience's needs?

■ How well did the visual aid (if used), and its incorporation, meet the audience's needs?

■ Why do you think this speaker was selected to deliver a TED talk at the live event?

■ Why do you think this recorded live speech was selected for inclusion on the website?

3. Select two TED talks in a category your instructor assigns and assess each based on the assessment questions above *as well as* the following additional assessment questions. Then, share your answers with your class in a brief oral presentation (length determined by your instructor). Queue up relevant spots in the TED talk to illustrate your answers.

Additional assessment questions:

■ Compare and contrast the speakers' content: Which speech was more effective at creating content balanced in ethos, pathos, and logos?

■ Compare and contrast the speakers' nonverbal delivery: Which speaker was more effective at heightening interest, highlighting content, and connecting with the audience via nonverbal delivery?

■ Compare and contrast the speakers' audience adaptation: Which speech was more effective at anticipating and addressing the audience's needs?

■ Compare and contrast the speakers' use of visual aid(s): Which speech was more effective at designing and integrating a visual aid to enhance spoken content?

■ If you had to select one speech to represent this category on the website, which would you select?

16.2   Analyzing Openings and Closings

The following opening and closing lines come from class presentations about informational interviews.

Assess:

■ How well does each opening create interest in the rest of the presentation? (How well does it demand your attention as a listener and connect to the content?)

■ How well does each closing end the presentation? (Is it memorable and meaningful?)

■ How well-matched are the opening and closing lines? (How well do they work together to create psychological unity across the presentation? How well do they match in tone?)

1. Opening line: I interviewed Mark Perry at AT&T.
   Closing line: Well, that's my report.

2. Opening line: How many of you know what you want to do when you graduate?

Closing line: So, if you like numbers and want to travel, think about being a CPA; Ernst & Young can take you all over the world.

3. Opening line: You don't have to know anything about computer programming to get a job as a technical writer at CompuServe.

Closing line: After talking to Raj, I decided technical writing isn't for me, but it is a good career if you work well under pressure and like learning new things all the time.

4. Opening line: The advertising agency I interned for has really tight security; I had to wear a badge and be escorted to Susan's desk.

Closing line: On my last day, Susan gave me samples of the agency's ads and even a sample of a new soft drink she's developing a campaign for—but she didn't let me keep the badge.

16.3 Evaluating PowerPoint Slides

Review PowerPoint slides from http://norvig.com/Gettysburg/index.htm, which matches the content of Lincoln's Gettysburg Address to PowerPoint slides; http://www.authorstream.com; http://www.slideshare.net; or another source of PowerPoint slides specified by your instructor. Evaluate the slides with these questions:

- Are the slides' background appropriate for the topic?
- Do the slides use words or phrases rather than complete sentences?
- Is the font big enough to read from a distance?
- Is the art relevant and appropriate?
- Is each slide free of errors?

16.4 Evaluating Nonverbal Delivery

Attend a lecture or public presentation on your campus. While the speaker is presenting, don't focus on the content of the message. Instead, focus on his/her nonverbal communication: eye contact, facial expressions, use of body (gestures, stance, and proxemics), and vocal delivery. Take notes.

As your instructor directs,

a. Deliver your findings to the rest of the class in a two- to four-minute presentation. Rate the speaker's overall nonverbal delivery and tell the class the speaker's strongest nonverbal delivery element, weakest nonverbal delivery element, and your suggestions for actions the speaker could take to improve in that element.

b. Write an email to your instructor that discusses the presenter's speaking abilities and how, if at all, they can be improved.

16.5 Evaluating Steve Jobs

On YouTube, watch clips of three different Steve Jobs presentations. What similarities do you see among them? What are some of his techniques you could use in a job you hope to have? Which ones do you think you would not use? Why not?

As your instructor directs,

a. Discuss your findings in small groups.

b. Write your findings in an email to your instructor.

c. Write your findings in an email and post it on the class website.

16.6 Evaluating the Way a Speaker Handles Questions

Listen to a speaker talking about a controversial subject. (Go to a talk on campus or in town or watch a speaker on a TV show like *Face the Nation* or *60 Minutes*.) Observe the way he or she handles questions.

- About how many questions does the speaker answer?
- What is the format for asking and answering questions?
- Are the answers clear? Responsive to the question? Something that could be quoted without embarrassing the speaker and the organization he or she represents?
- How does the speaker handle hostile questions? Does the speaker avoid getting angry? Does the speaker retain control of the meeting? How?

- If some questions were not answered well, what (if anything) could the speaker have done to leave a better impression?
- Did the answers leave the audience with a more or less positive impression of the speaker? Why?

As your instructor directs,

a. Share your evaluation with a small group of students.

b. Present your evaluation formally to the class.

c. Summarize your evaluation in an email to your instructor.

16.7 Short Presentation: The News

Research a hot business communication topic from the news (ethics, the economy, job layoffs, communication technology, etc.). Find at least three sources for your topic. Then, craft and deliver a two- to three-minute presentation where you share your findings with the class. Your presentation should invoke some effective communication strategies you learned in this course by discussing how the situation could have been handled more effectively.

As your instructor directs,

a. Deliver your presentation to the class.

b. Turn in a listing of your sources in APA or MLA format.

c. Write an email to your instructor that discusses the situation and explains how business communication principles would have helped improve the situation.

16.8 Medium Presentation: Informative

Craft and deliver a three- to five-minute presentation with PowerPoint slides or a Prezi on one of the following topics:

1. Explain how what you've learned in classes, in campus activities, or at work will be useful to the employer who hires you after graduation.

2. Explain a "best practice" in your organization.

3. Explain what a new hire in your organization needs to know to be successful.

4. Profile someone who is successful in the field you hope to enter and explain what makes him or her successful.

5. Explain one of the challenges (e.g., technology, ethics, international competition) that the field you plan to enter is facing.

6. Profile a company that you would like to work for and explain why you think it would make a good employer.

7. Share the results of an information interview.

8. Describe the way technology impacts the field you hope to enter.

16.9 Long Presentation: Persuasive

Craft and deliver a 5- to 12-minute presentation on one of the following. Use visuals to make your talk effective.

1. Persuade your supervisor to make a change that will benefit the organization.

2. Persuade your organization to make a change that will improve the organization's image in the community.

3. Persuade an organization on your campus to make a change.

4. Persuade classmates to donate time or money to a charitable organization.

16.10 Reconfiguring the Johari Window

One of the best ways to improve your presentation skills is to watch yourself present: this expands your knowledge about how you are perceived as a public speaker. After you have prepared a presentation for one of the previous exercises, record your presentation in video format. Then, review your presentation, noting what you did well and what you could improve.

As your instructor directs,

a. Write a 500-word email that discusses your strengths and weaknesses as a presenter. Address how you could improve your weaknesses.

b. Prepare a two-minute oral summation for your peers about your strengths and weaknesses.

c. Record the presentation a second time to see if you have improved some of your weaknesses. Present your findings to the class.

16.11 Evaluating Oral Presentations

Evaluate an oral presentation given by a classmate or a speaker on your campus. Use the following categories:

Strategy

1. Choosing an effective kind of presentation for the situation.

2. Adapting ideas to audience's beliefs, experiences, and interests.

Content

3. Providing a clear, unifying purpose.

4. Using specific, vivid supporting material and language.

5. Providing rebuttals to counterclaims or objections.

576   **Part 5**   Proposals and Reports

Organization

6. Using a strong opening and close.
7. Providing an overview of main points.
8. Signposting main points in body of talk.
9. Providing adequate transitions between points and speakers.

Visuals

10. Using visual aids or other devices to involve the audience.
11. Using an appropriate design or template.
12. Using standard edited English.
13. Being creative.

Delivery

14. Making direct eye contact with audience.
15. Using voice effectively.
16. Using gestures effectively.
17. Handling questions effectively.
18. Positioning (not blocking screen).

As your instructor directs,

a. Fill out a form indicating your evaluation in each of the areas.
b. Share your evaluation orally with the speaker.
c. Write an email to the speaker evaluating the presentation. Forward a copy of the email to your instructor.

Notes

1. Chapman University, "Survey of American Fears 2017," October 11, 2017, https://www.chapman.edu/wilkinson/research-centers/babbie-center/_files/Chapman-University-fears-by-percentage.pdf.
2. Jon Birger et al., "The Best Advice I Ever Got," *Fortune,* May 12, 2008, 70.
3. Carmine Gallo, *The Presentation Secrets of Steve Jobs: How to Be Insanely Great in Front of Any Audience* (New York: McGraw-Hill, 2010), 151–53.
4. Chip Heath and Dan Heath, *Made to Stick: Why Some Ideas Survive and Others Die* (New York: Random House, 2007), 16–18.
5. Julie Hill, "The Attention Deficit," *Presentations* 17, no. 10 (2003): 26.
6. Patricia Fripp, "Want Your Audiences to Remember What You Say? Learn the Importance of Clear Structure," Fripp and Associates, accessed June 25, 2011, http://www.fripp.com/art.clearstructure.html.
7. Elisabeth Bumiller, "We Have Met the Enemy and He Is PowerPoint," *New York Times,* April 26, 2010, http://www.nytimes.com/2010/04/27/world/27powerpoint.html?_r=3; and "The PowerPoint Rant That Got a Colonel Fired," *Army Times,* December 6, 2010, http://www.armytimes.com/news/2010/09/army-colonel-fired-for-powerpoint-rant-090210w/.
8. Nancy Duarte, "Avoiding the Road to PowerPoint Hell," *Wall Street Journal,* January 27, 2011, C12.
9. Bob Parks, "Death to PowerPoint!," *Bloomberg Businessweek,* August 30, 2012, http://www.businessweek.com/articles/2012-08-30/death-to-powerpoint.
10. Kim Stephens and Heather Howell, "Your Journey to Executive," IBM, 2013, http://www-03.ibm.com/employment/us/diverse/downloads/advancing_women_at_IBM_study_external_final.pdf.
11. Ann Burnett and Diane M. Badzinski, "Judge Nonverbal Communication on Trial: Do Mock Trial Jurors Notice?," *Journal of Communication* 55, no. 2 (2005): 209–24.
12. Sue Shellenbarger, "Is That How You Really Talk?," *Wall Street Journal,* April 23, 2013, http://online.wsj.com/article/SB10001424127887323735604578440851083674898.html.
13. Joe Light, "Automated Lines' Softer Tone," *Wall Street Journal,* November 1, 2010, B10.
14. Francesca Fontana and Denise Blostein, "Young Women Speak, Older Ears Hear Vocal Fry," *Wall Street Journal,* October 19, 2017, http://www.wsj.com/video/the-vocal-habit-that-women-are-being-criticized-for-at-work/E97C7B5B-8C51-4472-955A-AA1A26468C31.html.
15. Jerry Weissman, *Presentations in Action: 80 Memorable Presentation Lessons from the Masters* (Upper Saddle River, NJ: FT Press, 2011).
16. Michael Waldholz, "Lab Notes," *Wall Street Journal,* March 19, 1991, B1; and Dave Zielinski, "Perfect Practice," *Presentations* 17, no. 5 (2003): 30–36.
17. Gallo, *The Presentation Secrets of Steve Jobs,* 191.
18. John P. Kotter and Lorne A. Whitehead, "Twenty-Four Attacks and Twenty-Four Responses," *Buy*In: Saving Your Good Idea from Getting Shot Down* (Boston: Harvard Business Review Press, 2010), ch. 7.

14 Writing Proposals

Chapter Outline

©DrAfter123/Getty Images

468

NEWSWORTHY COMMUNICATION

©David J. Phillip/AP Images

B usinesses destroyed, homes washed away, lives lost. The year 2017 marked the second costliest hurricane season and the 17th deadliest since 1851. By October, four hurricanes were rated category three or higher, the threshold for a major storm, making the season the most active and destructive since 2005. The combined damage from these storms was estimated at $200 billion.

After the devastation of Hurricane Harvey, the National Science Foundation (NSF) issued a request for proposals (RFP) soliciting proposals for projects to address problems related to the storm. The goal of the NSF grants was to fund science and engineering research projects that would better prepare the United States to "respond to, recover from, or mitigate future catastrophic events."

These proposals were competitive because applicants were competing for limited resources.

Writers who align their technical competence with the values and goals of the funding organization can parlay their expertise into successful proposals.

Sources: Maggie Astor, "The 2017 Hurricane Season Really Is More Intense Than Normal," *New York Times,* September 19, 2017, https://www.nytimes.com/2017/09/19/us/hurricanes-irma-harvey-maria.html?mcubz=0; David Johnson, "Is This the Worst Hurricane Season Ever? Here's How It Compares," *Time,* September 24, 2017, http://time.com/4952628/hurricane-season-harvey-irma-jose-maria/; and "Dear Colleague Letter: NSF Accepting Proposals Related to Hurricane Harvey," *National Science Foundation,* September 1, 2017, https://www.nsf.gov/pubs/2017/nsf17128/nsf17128.jsp.

Learning Objectives

After studying this chapter, you will know how to:

LO 14-1 **Define proposals.**

LO 14-2 **Brainstorm for writing proposals.**

LO 14-3 **Organize proposals.**

LO 14-4 **Prepare budget and costs sections.**

LO 14-5 **Write different proposal varieties.**

P roposals are documents that frequently are part of larger, longer projects. **Proposals** argue for the work that needs to be done and who will do it.

Defining Proposals

LO 14-1

In the workplace, much work is routine or specifically assigned by other people. But sometimes you or your organization will want to consider new opportunities and you will need to write a proposal for that work. Generally, proposals are created for projects that are longer or more expensive than routine work, that differ significantly from routine work, or that create larger changes than does normal work. Another way to view proposals is as tools for managing change.[1]

Proposals argue for work that needs to be done; they offer a method to find information, evaluate something new, solve a problem, or implement a change (see Figure 14.1). Proposals have two major goals: to get the project accepted and to get you or your organization accepted to do the work. To accomplish these goals, proposals must stress benefits for all affected audiences. A proposal for an organization to adopt flex hours would offer benefits for both employees and management, as well as for key departments such as finance.

Proposals may be competitive or noncompetitive. **Competitive proposals** compete against each other for limited resources. Applications for research funding are often highly competitive. Many companies will bid for corporate or government contracts,

Figure 14.1	Relationship among Situation, Proposal, and Final Report	
Company's current situation	**The proposal offers to**	**The final report will provide**
We don't know whether we should change.	Assess whether change is a good idea.	Insight, recommending whether change is desirable.
We need to/want to change, but we don't know exactly what we need to do.	Develop a plan to achieve desired goal.	A plan for achieving the desired change.
We need to/want to change, and we know what to do, but we need help doing it.	Implement the plan, increase (or decrease) measurable outcomes.	A record of the implementation and evaluation process.

Source: Adapted from Richard C. Freed, Shervin Freed, and Joseph D. Romano, *Writing Winning Business Proposals,* 3rd ed. (New York: McGraw-Hill, 2010).

but only one will be accepted. In fiscal year 2018, the NSF spent close to $8 billion supporting research. The National Institutes of Health support almost 50,000 research projects at a cost of $30.9 billion annually.[2] These funds are awarded mainly through competitive proposals.

Noncompetitive proposals have no real competition. For example, a company could accept all of the internal proposals it thought would save money or improve quality. Often a company that is satisfied with a vendor asks for a noncompetitive proposal to renew the contract. Noncompetitive proposals can be as enormous as competitive ones: the proposal for the last U.S. census was $1 billion.

Brainstorming for Writing Proposals

LO 14-2

As is true for all forms of business communication, you should begin the brainstorming process by considering your audience, context, and purposes. After you determine these key components, use the proposal questions in the next section to brainstorm the content you are going to include. In addition, follow the guidelines in the proposal style section to make sure you're meeting the audience's expectations with your writing choices. These guidelines also may lead to additional content choices.

Proposal Questions

To write a good proposal, you need to have a clear view of the opportunity you want to fill or the problem you hope to solve and the kind of research or other action needed to solve it. A proposal must answer the following questions convincingly:

- **What problem are you going to solve or what opportunity do you hope to fill?** Show that you understand the problem or the opportunity and the organization's needs. Define the problem or opportunity as the audience sees it, even if you believe it is part of a larger problem that must be solved first. Sometimes you will need to show that the problem or opportunity exists. For instance, management might not be aware of subtle discrimination against women that your proposal will help eliminate.

- **Why does the problem need to be solved now or the opportunity explored immediately?** Show that money, time, health, or social concerns support solving the problem or exploring the opportunity immediately. Provide the predicted consequences if the problem is not solved now or if the opportunity is not explored immediately.

- **How are you going to solve it?** Prove that your methods are feasible. Show that a solution can be found in the time available. Specify the topics you'll investigate. Explain how you'll gather data. Show your approach is effective and desirable.

- **Can you do the work?** Show that you, or your organization, have the knowledge, means, personnel, and experience to do the work well. For larger projects, you will have to show some evidence such as preliminary data, personnel qualifications, or similar projects in the past.

- **Why should you be the one to do it?** Show why you or your company should do the work. For many proposals, various organizations could do the work. Why should the work be given to you? Discuss the benefits—direct and indirect—you and your organization can provide.

- **When will you complete the work?** Provide a detailed schedule showing when each phase of the work will be completed.

- **How much will you charge?** Provide a detailed budget that includes costs for items such as materials, salaries, and overhead. Give careful thought to unique expenses that may be part of the work. Will you need to travel? Pay fees? Pay benefits in addition to salary for part-time workers?

- **What exactly will you provide for us?** Specify the tangible products you'll produce; develop their benefits. If possible, include benefits for all levels of audience.

Since proposals to outside organizations are usually considered legally binding documents, get expert legal and financial advice on the last two bullet points. Even if the proposal will not be legally binding (perhaps it is an internal proposal), safeguard your professional reputation. Be sure you can deliver the promised products at the specified time using resources and personnel available to you.

Proposal Style

Good proposals are clear and easy to read. Research demonstrates that successful grant proposals will use "the funding organization's suggested structure (e.g., subheadings), language (e.g., special terms), and format (e.g., font)."[3] Remember that some of your audience may not be experts in the subject matter. Highly statistical survey and data analysis projects may be funded by finance people; medical and scientific studies may be approved by bureaucrats. Thus, avoid jargon and acronyms.[4] Instead, use clear and concise language your readers will understand.

Proposals are persuasive documents, so appealing to your audience's needs and values is of utmost importance. Successful proposals appropriate key words that mirror the values of the audience and thereby increase the likelihood of accomplishing their purpose.

Some style choices also will add content. How much detail does your audience expect? How much background? As you write, anticipate and answer questions your readers may have. Support generalizations and inferences with data and other information. Stress benefits throughout the proposal and make sure you include benefits for all elements of your audience.

Watch your word choice. Avoid diction that shows doubt.

Weak: "*If we can* obtain X. . . ."

         "We *hope* we can obtain X."

         "We will *try* to obtain X."

Better: "We plan to obtain X."

         "We expect to obtain X."

Avoid bragging diction such as "huge potential" and "revolutionary process." Be particularly careful to avoid bragging diction about yourself. Research indicates that overstatement reduces one's credibility.[5] Also avoid "believing" diction, as in "We believe that . . . ." Use facts and figures instead.

Use the expected format for your proposal. Shorter proposals (one to four pages) are generally in letter or email format; longer proposals are frequently formal reports. Depending on the context, you may be asked to mail in a paper proposal, send it as an email attachment, upload a pdf version to a website, or deliver the proposal as an oral presentation. Make sure if you're asked to submit an electronic proposal, you don't send in a paper copy or vice versa. If the proposal is electronic, include a clickable table of contents and other hyperlinks that will provide your audience with an easy way to search your document, especially if your proposal is long.

Government agencies and companies often issue **requests for proposals**, known as **RFPs**. Follow the RFP's specified format in every detail. Use the exact headings, terminology, and structure of the RFP when responding to one. Competitive proposals often are scored by giving points in each category. Evaluators look only under the headings specified in the RFP. If information isn't there, the proposal may get no points in that category.

Beginnings and endings of proposals are important. If you are not following an RFP, your proposal should begin with a clear statement of what you propose doing, why you propose doing it, and what the implications are of the proposed action or why the action is important. Proposals should end with a brief but strong summary of major benefits of having you do the work. In some circumstances, an urge to action is appropriate:

> If I get your approval before the end of the month, we can have the procedures in place in time for the new fiscal year.

Allow a generous amount of time before the due date for polishing and finishing your proposal:

- Edit carefully.

- Make a final check that you have included all sections and pieces of information requested in the RFP. Many RFPs call for appendixes with items such as résumés and letters of support. Do you have all of yours?

- Ensure that your proposal's appearance will create a good impression. This step includes careful proofreading.

- Make sure you have chosen the correct media channel for your proposal submission.

- Allow enough time for production, reproduction, and administrative approvals before the deadline for receipt of the proposal. If multiple signatures are needed, it may take more than a day to get them all. If you are submitting a government grant proposal, the government server may be clogged with heavy usage on the final due date, or even the day before, so don't wait until the last minute.

Organizing Proposals

LO 14-3

Once you have brainstormed for your proposal, you'll need to select a proposal organization schema that is most appropriate for your purpose. If you're writing a proposal that your instructor has assigned for an in-class assignment, follow the guidelines for proposals for class research projects. See Figure 14.2 for an example of this variety of proposal. If you're seeking to raise capital for new business ventures, follow the guidelines for business proposals.

Proposals for Class Research Projects

You may be asked to submit a proposal for a report that you will write for a class. Your instructor wants evidence that your problem is meaningful but not too big to complete in the allotted time, that you understand it, that your method will give you the information you need, that you have the knowledge and resources to collect and analyze the data, and that you can produce the report by the deadline.

A proposal for a student report usually has the following sections:

1. In your first paragraph (no heading), summarize in a sentence or two the topic and purposes of your report.
2. **Problem/opportunity.** What problem or opportunity exists? Why does it need to be solved or explored? Is there a history or background that is relevant?
3. **Feasibility.** Are you sure that a solution can be found in the time available? How do you know? (This section may not be appropriate for some class projects.)

4. **Audience.** Who in the organization would have the power to implement your recommendation? What secondary audiences might be asked to evaluate your report? What audiences would be affected by your recommendation? Will anyone in the organization serve as a gatekeeper, determining whether your report is sent to decision makers? What watchdog audiences might read the report? Will there be other readers?

   For each of these audiences give the person's name and job title and answer the following questions:

   ■ What is the audience's major concern or priority? What "hot buttons" must you address with care?

   ■ What will the audience see as advantages of your proposal? What objections, if any, is the audience likely to have?

   ■ How interested is the audience in the topic of your report?

   ■ How much does the audience know about the topic of your report?

   List any terms, concepts, or assumptions that one or more of your audiences may need to have explained. Briefly identify ways in which your audiences may affect the content, organization, or style of the report.

5. **Topics to investigate.** List the questions you will answer in your report, the topics or concepts you will explain, and the aspects of the problem or opportunity you will discuss. Indicate how deeply you will examine each of the aspects you plan to treat. Explain your rationale for choosing to discuss some aspects of the problem or opportunity and not others.

6. **Methods/procedure.** How will you get answers to your questions? Who will you interview or survey? What questions will you ask? What published sources will you use? Give the full bibliographic references. Your methods section should clearly indicate how you will get the information needed to answer questions posed in the other sections of the proposal.

7. **Qualifications/facilities/resources.** Do you have the knowledge and skills needed to conduct this study? Do you have adequate access to the organization? Is the necessary information available to you? Are you aware of any supplemental information? Where will you turn for help if you hit an unexpected snag?

   You'll be more convincing if you have already scheduled an interview, checked out books, or printed online sources.

8. **Work schedule.** For each activity, list both the total time you plan to spend on it and the date when you expect to finish it. Some possible activities you might include could be gathering information, analyzing information, preparing a progress report, writing the report draft, revising the draft, preparing visuals, editing and proofreading the report, and preparing the oral presentation. Think of activities needed to complete your specific project.

   These activities frequently overlap. Many writers start analyzing and organizing information as it comes in. They start writing pieces of the final document and preparing visuals early in the process.

   Organize your work schedule in either a chart or calendar. A good schedule provides realistic estimates for each activity, allows time for unexpected snags, and shows that you can complete the work on time.

9. **Call to action.** In your final section, indicate that you'd welcome any suggestions your instructor may have for improving the research plan. Ask your instructor to approve your proposal so that you can begin work on your report.

Figure 14.2 shows a student proposal for a long report.

Figure 14.2	Proposal for a Student Team Report

Month Day, Year *Enter current date.*

To: Professor Christopher Toth

From: JASS LLC (Jordan Koole, Alex Kuczera,   *In the subject line ①indicate that this is a proposal*
             Shannon Jones, Sean Sterling)   *②specify the kind of report*
                                                                                     ③specify the topic

Subject: Proposal to Research and Make Recommendations on the Feasibility
             of Expanding RAC Inc. to South Korea

Summarize topic and purpose of report. RAC Inc. has recently approached our company to determine the possibility of expanding internationally. We believe South Korea could be suitable for this expansion based on our initial investigation of technology in the country. This proposal provides a brief look at South Korea and gives an overview of our research topics and procedures in preparation for the formal research report.

Problem

If the "Problem" section is detailed and well-written, you may be able to use it unchanged in your report.

After establishing a solid consumer base in the U.S., RAC Inc. is looking to expand its business internationally so that it does not fall behind its competitors. It has asked us to research South Korea as a possible alternative site for the manufacturing of its slate tablets.

Country Overview   *This section is a "Background" section for this proposal. Not all proposals include background.*

After some initial research, we believe that South Korea is a suitable country to research for RAC's international manufacturing of new technology. South Korea has a population of 51.2 million, with 27% of the population located in the capital city Seoul and in Busan. They have a labor force of 27.47 million, ranking as the 24th highest workforce in the world (CIA Factbook, 2018). The official language is Korean, but English, Chinese, and Japanese are taught as second languages (U.S. Department of State, 2017). *Proposal uses in-text citations.*

In 1950, North Korea invaded South Korea, beginning the Korean War. After three years of fighting and pushing troops across both borders, North and South Korea signed an armistice and agreed to a demilitarized zone (DMZ), which currently serves as the border between the two countries and is protected by both countries' military (U.S. Department of State, 2017). While relations between the two countries are still tense and a few minor skirmishes along the border have occurred, we are not concerned about South Korea's stability.

In fact, since the devastation of the Korean War, the economy of South Korea has recovered and has joined the ranks of the most economically prosperous nations. They have risen to the 15th highest GDP in the world and have the 45th highest GDP per capita at the equivalent of $39,400. They have a very low unemployment rate that has dropped in the last year to 3.8% (CIA Factbook, 2018).

South Korea is now ranked the 6th largest exporter in the world and the 9th largest importer. Their economic policy has emphasized exporting products, explaining why their exports are so high (U.S. Department of State, 2017). Their main exports include computers and component parts, semiconductors, and wireless telecommunication equipment. South Korea is known for making excellent products in these areas. They export mainly to the U.S., China, and Japan, and import primarily from the same countries. As one of the most economically healthy countries in the world, South Korea is situated as a prime country for RAC Inc.'s possible expansion.

Not all class reports will need a "Feasibility" section.

Figure 14.2	Proposal for a Student Team Report (*Continued*)

Include a header on all additional pages.

RAC Inc. Proposal
Month Day, Year *Enter current date.*
Page 2

List your major audiences. Identify their knowledge, interests, and concerns.

Audience

Our formal report will have multiple layers of audiences.

- *Gatekeeper*: Professor Toth has the power to accept or reject our proposal for the formal report before it is passed on to Ms. Katie Nichols from RAC Inc.

- *Primary*: Ms. Katie Nichols, CEO of RAC Inc., and the board of directors are our primary audiences, along with other influential members of RAC Inc. They will decide whether to accept the recommendation found in the formal report.

- *Secondary*: Employees of RAC Inc., the legal department of RAC Inc., as well as current RAC Inc. employees who may be transferred to South Korea all may be affected by the primary audience's decision. In addition, the potential employees in South Korea who would work for RAC Inc. also make up this audience.

- *Auxiliary*: Other employees not involved with the expansion effort into South Korea and any Americans or South Koreans who will read about the expansion in the news serve this role.

- *Watchdog*: Stockholders of RAC Inc., the South Korean government, the Securities and Exchange Commission (SEC), the U.S. Department of Commerce, and other companies that may want to expand internationally to South Korea all have economic, social, and political power. Competitors of RAC Inc. already in South Korea (Samsung and LG) also may pay close attention.

Indicate what you'll discuss briefly and what you'll discuss in more detail. This list should match your audiences' concerns.

Topics to Investigate

We plan to answer the following questions in detail:

1. What information does RAC Inc. need to know about South Korean culture, politics, economy, and workforce to be succesful?

All items in list must be grammatically parallel. Here, all are questions.

- Culture—What differences exist between Korean and American cultures that might influence the move?
- Politics—How will relationships between North and South Korea and relationships between the U.S. and South Korea affect business with South Korea?
- Economics—What is the current economic state of the country? How could free trade between the U.S. and South Korea affect business?
- Workforce—What is the availabe workforce? How will the economy of the country affect the overall workforce?

2. How should RAC Inc. adapt its business practices to successfully expand into the South Korean market?

- Competition—Who is the competition in South Korea? How could they affect the business?
- Location—What city could RAC Inc. expand to for production of the slate tablet? Where should it locate the headquarters? Where should it host the initial product launch?
- Slate Tablet—What changes, if any, are needed to market and sell the product in South Korea?

Figure 14.2	Proposal for a Student Team Report *(Continued)*

RAC Inc. Proposal
Month Day, Year
Page 3

3. What other issues may RAC Inc. have by introducing its product into South Korea?

If it is well written, "Topics to Investigate" section will become the "Scope" section of the report—with minor revisions.

- Business Culture—How will the differences in business culture influence the expansion to South Korea?
- Technology—To what extent will the advanced state of South Korean technology influence marketing the tablet?
- Marketing—How will competitors' similar products sold in South Korea influence business?
- Integration—How receptive are the people of South Korea to new products from different companies and countries?

If you'll administer a survey or conduct interviews, tell how many subjects you'll have, how you'll choose them, and what you'll ask them. This group does not use a survey.

Methods and Resources

We expect to obtain our information from (1) various websites, (2) articles, and (3) interviews with a native South Korean. The following websites and articles appear useful.

If you're using library or web research, list sources you hope to use. Use full bibliographic citations.

Central Intelligence Agency. (2018). *The world factbook: South Korea.* Retrieved March 18, 2018, from https:/ /www.cia.gov/library/publications/the-world-factbook/geos/ks.html#.

Fackler, M. (2011, January 6). Lessons learned, South Korea makes quick economic recovery. *The New York Times.* Retrieved from http:// www.nytimes.com/2011/01/07/world/asia/07seoul.html?_r=2.

Jeon, Kyung-Hwan. (2010, September 7). Why your business belongs in South Korea. Retrieved from http:/ /www.openforum.com/articles/why-your-business-belongs-in-south-korea-kyung-hwan-jeon.

This list uses APA format.

Life in Korea. (n.d.). Cultural spotlight. Retrieved March 31, 2018, from http:/ /www.lifeinkorea.com/Culture/spotlight.cfm.

Your list of sources should convince your instructor that you have made initial progress on the report.

Ogg, E. (2010, May 28). What makes a tablet a tablet? *CNet News.* Retrieved March 19, 2018, from http:/ /news.cnet.com/8301-31021_3-20006077-260.html?tag=newsLeadStoriesArea.1.

Settimi, C. (2010, September 1). Asia's 200 best under a billion. *Forbes.* Retrieved from http://www.forbes.com/2010/09/01/ bub-200-intro-asia-under-billion-10-small-companies.html.

UK Trade & Investment. (2011). 100 opportunities for UK companies in South Korea. Retrieved March 19, 2018, from http:/ /www.ukti.gov.uk/export/countries/asiapacific/fareast/koreasouth/item/119500.html.

U.S. Department of State. (2017, December 10). Background note: South Korea. Retrieved March 18, 2018, from http:/ /www.state.gov/r/pa/ei/bgn/2800.htm.

World Business Culture. (n.d.). Doing business in South Korea. Retrieved March 19, 2018, from http:/ /www.worldbusinessculture.com/Business-in-South-Korea.html.

(Continued)

| **Figure 14.2** | Proposal for a Student Team Report *(Concluded)* |

RAC Inc. Proposal
Month Day, Year
Page 4

Qualifications   *Cite knowledge and skills from other classes, jobs, and activities that will enable you to conduct the research and interpret your data.*

We are all members of JASS LLC who have backgrounds in finance, accounting, computer science, and technology. These diverse backgrounds in the business and technology world give us a good perspective and insight for this project. In addition, we are all enrolled in a business communication course that provides us with knowledge on producing high-quality documents. We are dedicated to producing a thoroughly researched report that will provide solid evidence on the feasibility of an international expansion for RAC Inc. into South Korea.

Work Schedule

The following schedule will enable us to finish this report on time.

Activity	Total Time	Completion Date
Gathering information	12 hours	March 30
Analyzing information	8 hours	April 2
Organizing information	4 hours	April 7
Writing draft/creating visuals	8 hours	April 10
Revising draft	3 hours	April 12
Preparing presentation slides	3–4 hours	April 14
Editing draft	3 hours	April 17
Proofreading report	3 hours	April 18
Rehearsing presentation	2 hours	April 20
Delivering presentaion	1 hour	April 21

Good reports need good revision, editing, and proofreading as well as good research.

Allow plenty of time.

Time will depend on the length and topic of your report, your knowledge of the topic, and your writing skills.

Call to Action

We are confident that JASS LLC can complete the above tasks as scheduled. We would appreciate any suggestions for improving our project plan. Please approve our proposal so that we may begin work on the formal report.   *It's tactful to indicate you'll accept suggestions. End on a positive, forward-looking note.*

Proposals for Businesses

Many business proposals recommend new programs, offer ways to solve problems, sell goods or services, request funds, or outline a new business idea. Writing such proposals often requires considerable research, including reading articles in trade and professional journals, looking up data online, talking to employees or customers, and even gathering data from outside the organization. All this information requires careful organization.

Any time you are asked to write a proposal for non-classroom purposes, you will want to follow the organization that is most routinely used in business settings.

Proposals for businesses usually employ the following organization scheme:

1. **Introduction.** Summarize the subject and purposes of your proposal. You also should discuss the significance of the project and any relevant background information.
2. **Current situation.** Describe the problem that needs to be solved or the opportunity to be explored, its causes, and the outcome if it is not resolved.
3. **Project plan.** Outline the steps you will follow to solve the problem or explore the opportunity you've identified in the previous section. You also should indicate the final deliverables of your project.
4. **Qualifications.** State the knowledge and skills you possess necessary to complete the project you're proposing. Some proposals include résumés in this section.
5. **Costs and benefits.** Briefly outline the costs associated with your project and then state all the benefits it will bring. Make sure the benefits outweigh the costs. (More details on preparing the costs and budget sections are included in the next section.)

Preparing the Budget and Costs Sections

LO 14-4

For a class research project, you may not be asked to prepare a budget. However, many business proposals do require budgets, and a good budget is crucial to making the winning bid. In fact, your budget may be the most scrutinized part of your business proposal.

Ask for everything you need to do a quality job. Asking for too little may backfire, leading the funder to think that you don't understand the scope of the project. Include less obvious costs, such as overhead. Also include costs that will be paid from other sources. Doing so shows that other sources also have confidence in your work. Pay particular attention to costs that may appear to benefit you more than the sponsor such as travel and equipment. Make sure they are fully justified in the proposal.

Do some research. Read the RFP to find out what is and isn't fundable. Talk to the program officer and the person who administers the funding process and read successful past proposals to find answers to the following questions:

- What size projects will the organization fund in theory?
- Does the funder prefer making a few big grants or many smaller grants?
- Does the funder expect you to provide in-kind or cost-sharing funds from other sources?

Think about exactly what you'll do and who will do it. What will it cost to get that person? What supplies or materials will he or she need? Also think about indirect costs for using office space; retirement and health benefits, as well as salaries; and office supplies, administration, and infrastructure.

Make the basis of your estimates specific.

Weak: 75 hours of transcribing interviews $1,500

Better: 25 hours of interviews; a skilled transcriber can complete
          1 hour of interviews in 3 hours; 75 hours @ $20/hour $1,500

Figure your numbers conservatively. For example, if the going rate for skilled transcribers is $20 an hour, but you think you might be able to train someone and pay only $12 an hour, use the higher figure. Then, even if your grant is cut, you'll still be able to do the project well.

Writing Proposal Varieties

LO 14-5

This section offers advice for writing three common varieties of proposals: sales proposals, business plans, and grant proposals.

Sales Proposals

To sell expensive goods or services, you may be asked to submit a proposal.

To write a good sales proposal, be sure that you understand the buyer's priorities. A phone company lost a $36 million sale to a university because it assumed the university's priority would be cost. Instead, the university wanted a state-of-the-art system. The university accepted a higher bid.

Make sure your proposal presents your goods or services as solving the problem your audience perceives. Don't assume the buyer will understand why your product or system is good. For everything you offer, show the benefits of each feature. Be sure to present the benefits using you-attitude.

Use language appropriate for your audience. Even if the buyers want a state-of-the-art system, they may not want the level of detail that your staff could provide; they may not understand or appreciate technical jargon.

Sales proposals, particularly for complicated systems costing millions of dollars, are often long. Provide a one-page cover letter to present your proposal succinctly. The best organization for this letter is usually a modified version of the sales pattern in Chapter 10:

1. Catch the reader's attention and summarize up to three major benefits you offer.
2. Discuss each of the major benefits in the order in which you mentioned them in the first paragraph.
3. Deal with any objections or concerns the reader may have. In a sales proposal, these objections probably include costs. Connect costs with benefits.
4. Mention other benefits briefly.
5. Ask the reader to approve your proposal and provide a reason for acting promptly.

Of the thousands of business plans presented to potential investors each year, only a few succeed. John W. Mullens, at the London Business School, offers five reasons business plans fail:

- **No problem.** Plans must fix a problem or fill a need instead of just being examples of cool technology or good ideas.

- **Unrealistic ambition.** Successful business plans recognize a specific market, instead of aiming at the entire population.

- **Flawed spreadsheets.** Carefully prepared revenue models can work on paper, but successful business plans must work in the real economy.

◾ **Wrong team.** Investors are not necessarily impressed by education and work experience, unless those contribute to the success of the business.

◾ **Perfect plan.** Successful plans recognize realistic challenges to the business plan, instead of presenting everything in the best light.

Mullens also suggests three keys for success: (1) a clear problem and a logical solution, (2) hard evidence that you have done your research, and (3) complete candor about challenges and risks associated with your plan.[6]

Business Plans

Proposals for funding include both **business plans** (documents written to raise capital for new business ventures) and proposals submitted to foundations, corporations, and government agencies to seek money for public service projects. In a proposal for funding, stress the needs your project will meet and show how your project helps fulfill the goals of the organization you are asking for funds. Every funding agency has a mission, so be sure to align your idea to fit the agency's needs in obvious ways. Try to weave the agency's mission throughout your proposal's content. Remember effective you-attitude—write for the needs of your audience, not yourself.

Because venture capitalists and other investors are not known for their patience, business plans in particular need to have a concise, compelling beginning describing exactly what you plan to do and what need it will fill. Pay careful attention to the "Executive Summary." This overview section is one of the most important places in any proposal. After reading this opening, the reviewer will make initial decisions about you, your writing, your idea, and your logic. Therefore, it must spark enthusiasm for your idea; the reviewer's interest will never increase later in your proposal. This section also should provide an overview of all of the major topics you will cover in the body.

Your business plan should answer the questions listed in Figure 14.3 with sufficient detail to be convincing and supporting evidence where applicable.

Financial information is important in any proposal, but it is even more crucial in a business plan. You will need to show how much of your own money you are investing, what investors already are supporting you, and how you plan to use the money you get. Many investors want to see a five-year financial forecast. Explain with convincing detail how you expect to make money. What is your time frame for financial success? What is your estimated monthly income the first year?

Anticipate problems (investors will already know them; this shows you do, too); show how you plan to solve them. Use details to help convince your audience. Many business plans are too general to convince investors. Details show you have done your homework; they also can show your business acumen.

Figure 14.3	Questions Business Plans Should Answer

- What is your product or service?
- How well developed is it? Is a mock-up or demo available?
- Who is your market? How large is it? Why does this market need your product or service?
- How will you promote your product or service?
- Who are your competitors? How will you be better? What other problems and challenges will you have to face on your path to profit?
- Who also is providing support for your business?
- Who will be working with you? How many more employees will you need? What will you pay them? What benefits will you give them?

Grant Proposals

Proposals are also a major part of nonprofits' fund-raising activity; they write **grant proposals** to governmental organizations, foundations, and individuals to raise money for their organization. The writing process involves considerable research and planning and often is preceded by informal conversations and formal presentations to potential funders. The funding process often is seen as a relationship-building process that involves researching, negotiating with, and persuading funders that the proposal not only meets their guidelines, but also is a cause worthy of a grant.

Every funding source has certain priorities; some have detailed lists of the kind of projects they fund. Be sure to do research before applying. Check recent awards to discover foundations that may be interested in your project. See Figure 14.4 for additional resources.

When you write proposals for funding, be sure you follow all format criteria. Adhere to specifications about page count, type size, margins, and spacing (single or double spacing). When flooded with applications, many funders use these criteria as preliminary weeding devices.

The statement of needs section in a grant proposal should specifically describe the problem the project will solve. This section also should discuss the population that will benefit from the work.

Grant proposals are frequently rejected because writers do not effectively articulate the needs the proposal addresses.[7] One common problem is that writers mistake issues related to the solution with the underlying need. For example, a writer may state that a business needs a large moving truck, when, in fact, a moving truck may be one possible solution to the underlying issue the business needs to solve—namely, how to accommodate an increase in donations and reduce pickup delays. In this instance, in the statement of needs section, the proposal writer should focus on reducing the time between the organization's collection of donated goods and subsequent deliveries to families in need. Quantifying the problem by identifying the number of donors who have experienced delays and also the number of families the organization serves would help highlight the importance of the need. A new moving truck may be one potential solution to this organization's need. However, other solutions may exist as well, such as hiring additional volunteers or setting up a drop-off site for donations.

When crafting a statement of needs, writers should use logical and fact-based descriptions. Researching what others already have written about the topic can be an

Figure 14.4	Additional Resources for Writing Business Plans and Funding Proposals	
Organization	**URL**	**Description**
U.S. Small Business Administration	https://www.sba.gov/business-guide/plan/write-your-business-plan-template	Offers detailed advice for writing a business plan.
Philanthropic Research Inc.	http://www.guidestar.org	Publishes free information about grants and grant makers.
Pivot—Community of Science	http://pivot.cos.com	Offers information on global funding opportunities, as well as tools to manage grants.
U.S. Department of Health and Human Services	http://www.grants.gov	Offers information on grant programs of all federal grantmaking agencies, as well as downloadable grant applications.
The Foundation Center	http://foundationcenter.org/	Indexes foundations by state and city, as well as by field of interest.

excellent way to establish a history for the need, develop convincing support, and demonstrate credibility when quality sources are used. The statement of needs should highlight the seriousness of the problem by illustrating its effect.[8] In the example mentioned earlier, if the proposal writer estimates that the company is losing 50 potential donations each month and has 100 families on a wait list, this figure will likely capture the audience's attention.

The goal statement in a grant proposal then should focus on the cause of the problem and seek ways to solve it.[9] For example, the cause of the delays may be due to problems with resources, technology, employees, or company procedures. The solution should remedy the underlying cause or causes. Isolating causes of a problem permits the grant writer to craft a clear and specific goal for implementing change. If the fundamental cause of the problem is a lack of resources, then a new moving truck would be included in the budget section of the proposal. The goal statement might be articulated as follows: to increase our organization's donations to needy families by 30% and reduce delays in pickups by 50%.

Finally, pay close attention to deadlines by reading the fine print. Turn your materials in early. The National Endowment for the Humanities encourages fund seekers to submit drafts six weeks before the deadline to allow time for their staff to review materials.[10]

Summary by Learning Objectives

LO 14-1 Define proposals.

Proposals argue for the work that needs to be done and who will do it. Competitive proposals compete against each other for limited resources; noncompetitive proposals have no real competition.

LO 14-2 Brainstorm for writing proposals.

A proposal must answer the following questions:

- What problem are you going to solve or what opportunity do you hope to fulfill?
- Why does the problem need to be solved now or the opportunity explored immediately?
- How are you going to solve it?
- Can you do the work?
- Why should you be the one to do it?
- When will you complete the work?
- How much will you charge?
- What exactly will you provide for us?

LO 14-3 Organize proposals.

- In a proposal for a class research project, prove that your problem is the right size, that you understand it, that your method will give you the information you need to solve the problem, that you have the knowledge and resources, and that you can produce the report by the deadline.

- In a proposal for business, introduce the problem or opportunity, explain its causes and what will happen if nothing is done, outline a project plan to solve the problem or opportunity, state your qualifications, and discuss the costs and benefits of accepting the project.

LO 14-4 Prepare budget and costs sections.

In a project budget, ask for everything you will need to do a good job. Research current cost figures so yours are in line. For costs that appear to benefit you more than the sponsor, give full justifications.

LO 14-5 Write different proposal varieties.

- Sales proposals are useful to sell expensive goods or services.
- Funding proposals should stress the needs your project will meet. Show how your project will help fulfill the goals of the organization you are asking for funds.
- Business plans need to pay particular attention to market potential and financial forecasts.

Exercises and Cases

14.1   Reviewing the Chapter

1. What is the difference between a competitive and noncompetitive proposal? (LO 14-1)
2. What are six brainstorming questions to consider before starting your proposal? (LO 14-2)
3. How does the organization of proposals for class research projects and proposals for businesses differ? (LO 14-3)
4. What are some guidelines for preparing a budget for a proposal? (LO 14-4)
5. What are some tips for writing a sales proposal? (LO 14-5)
6. What is a business plan? (LO 14-5)
7. How are statements of needs and goals different than a solution in grant proposals? (LO 14-5)

14.2   Analyze a Real Proposal

Visit the following website: https://www.nyu.edu/community/nyu-in-nyc/core-plan-commitments/nyu-space-planning-the-core-plan.html. Click on "Project Background" and "Moving Forward" links and read them. In groups, answer the following questions:

▪ What kind of proposal is this?
▪ What problems does it address?

▪ What solutions does it offer?
▪ What is the structure of the proposal?
▪ Who are the multiple audiences?
▪ What is the purpose of the proposal?
▪ Is there any information that is missing?
▪ What is the style of the proposal?

14.3   Writing a Proposal for a Student Report

Write a proposal to your instructor to do the research for a formal or informal report. The headings and the questions in the section titled "Proposals for Class Research Projects" are your RFP; be sure to answer every question and to use the headings exactly as stated in the RFP. Exception: where alternate heads are listed, you may choose one, combine the two ("Qualifications and Facilities"), or treat them as separate headings in separate categories.

14.4   Proposing a Change

No organization is perfect, especially when it comes to communication. Propose a change that would improve communication within your organization. The change can be specific to your unit or can apply to the whole organization; it can relate to how important information is distributed, who has access to important information, how information is accessed, or any other change in communication practices that you see as having a benefit. Direct your proposal to the person or committee with the power to authorize the change.

14.5   Proposing to Undertake a Research Project

Pick a project you would like to study whose results could be used by your organization. Write a proposal to your supervisor requesting time away from other duties to do the research. Show how your research (whatever its outcome) will be useful to the organization.

14.6   Writing a Proposal for Funding for a Nonprofit Group

Pick a nonprofit group you care about. Examples include professional organizations, a charitable group, a community organization, or your own college or university.

As your instructor directs,

a. Check the web or a directory of foundations to find one that makes grants to groups such as yours. Brainstorm a list of businesses that might be willing to give money for specific projects. Check to see whether state or national levels of your organization make grants to local chapters.

b. Write a proposal to obtain funds for a special project your group could undertake if it had the money. Address your proposal to a specific organization.

c. Write a proposal to obtain operating funds or money to buy something your group would like to have. Address your proposal to a specific organization.

14.7   Writing a Sales Proposal

Pick a project that you could do for a local company or government office. Examples include

- Establishing a social media presence.
- Creating a brochure, web page, or series of infographics.
- Revising form letters or other routine communications.
- Conducting a training program.
- Writing a newsletter or an annual report.
- Developing a marketing plan.

Write a proposal specifying what you could do and providing a detailed budget and work schedule.

As your instructor directs,

a. Phone or email someone in the organization to talk about its needs and what you could offer.

b. Write an individual proposal.

c. Join with other students in the class to create a team proposal.

d. Present your proposal orally.

14.8   Presenting a Stockholder Proposal

Visit the websites of the following companies and locate their latest proxy statements or reports. These are generally linked from the "about us/company information–investor relations" or "investors" pages. Find shareholder proposals under the heading "proposals requiring your vote," "stockholder proposals," or "shareholder proposals."

- Facebook
- Ford Motor Company
- Citigroup
- AT&T
- JPMorgan Chase & Co.
- Delta Air Lines
- Home Depot
- Procter & Gamble
- Boeing
- Google
- Dow Chemical

As a team, select one proposal, and the management response following it, and give an oral presentation answering these questions:

1. What is the problem discussed in the proposal?

2. What is the rationale given for the urgency to solve the problem?

3. How does the proposal seek to solve it?

4. What benefits does the proposal mention that will accrue from the solution?

5. What is the management response to the proposal and what are the reasons given for the response? Does the management response strike you as justified? Why or why not?

Hint: It may help you to do some research on the topic of the proposal.

Notes

1. Richard Johnson-Sheehan, *Writing Proposals,* 2nd ed. (New York: Pearson/Longman Publishers, 2008), 1.
2. "NSF at a Glance," About the National Science Foundation, accessed June 23, 2018, http:// www.nsf.gov/about/glance.jsp; and "NIH Budget," About NIH: Budget, accessed June 23, 2018, https://www.nih.gov/about-nih/what-we-do/budget.
3. Jennifer Wisdom, Halley Riley, and Neely Myers, "Recommendations for Writing Successful Grant Proposals: An Information Synthesis," *Academic Medicine* 90, no. 12 (December 2015): 1720-25.
4. Ibid., 1722.
5. James Vincler and Nancy Horlick-Vincler, "Producing Persuasive Proposals," *Journal of Management in Engineering* 12, no. 5 (1996): 20-24.
6. John Mullens, "Why Business Plans Don't Deliver," *Wall Street Journal,* June 22, 2009, R3.
7. Karina Stokes, "Writing Clear Statements of Needs and Goals for Grant Proposals," *AMWA Journal* 27, no. 1 (2012): 25-28.
8. Ibid., 25-26.
9. Ibid., 26-27.
10. "Grant Programs and Details," National Endowment for the Humanities, accessed June 24, 2013, http:// www.neh.gov/grants.

CHAPTER

15 Writing Reports

Chapter Outline

©DrAfter123/Getty Images

NEWSWORTHY COMMUNICATION

©wavebreakmedia/Shutterstock

Corporations, nonprofits, and government organizations routinely use reports to communicate important information to stakeholders, investors, and the general public. In 2015, the U.S. Department of Education teamed up with the American Institutes for Research (AIR) and held a series of workshops for experts in science, technology, engineering, and mathematics (STEM). The workshops culminated in a collaborative report, published in September 2016, from the Department of Energy and AIR titled "STEM 2026: A Vision for Innovation in STEM Education."

The report's purpose was to articulate a 10-year vision for STEM education by detailing key components of STEM teaching philosophy, exploring challenges and opportunities, and making recommendations for future action.

Often, reports have multiple audiences. The STEM 2026 report had a variety of audiences: teachers, education administrators, academics, policy makers, as well as the general public. Another important goal of the STEM report was to present a positive image of STEM education and sell the values that STEM education provides.

The 60-plus-page report was written in a formal style and contained many of the elements of formal reports described in this chapter, including a title page, executive summary, table of contents, introduction, body, conclusion, references, and appendices.

Whether writing reports for a government organization or a multinational corporation, the process often involves diligent research, effective organization, and an appropriate format.

Source: Department of Education and American Institutes for Research, "STEM 2026: A Vision for Innovation in STEM Education," www.ed.gov, September 2016, https://innovation.ed.gov/files/2016/09/AIR-STEM2026_Report_2016.pdf.

Learning Objectives

After studying this chapter, you will know how to

LO 15-1 Identify varieties of reports.

LO 15-2 Define report problems.

LO 15-3 Employ various research strategies.

LO 15-4 Choose information for reports.

LO 15-5 Organize reports.

LO 15-6 Present information effectively in reports.

LO 15-7 Document sources correctly.

LO 15-8 Write progress reports.

LO 15-9 Prepare the different components of formal reports.

Careful analysis, smooth writing, and effective document design work together to make effective reports, whether you're writing a 2½-page memo report or a 250-page formal report complete with all the report components. Reports typically depend on research. The research may be as simple as pulling up data with a computer program or as complicated as calling many different people, conducting focus groups and surveys, or even conducting experiments. Care in planning and researching proposals and reports is needed to produce effective documents.

In writing reports, there are four basic steps:

1. Define the problem.
2. Rearch and analyze data and information.
3. Organize the information.
4. Write the report.

Varieties of Reports

LO 15-1

Many kinds of documents are called reports. In some organizations, a report is a long document or one that contains numerical data. In others, one- and two-page memos are called reports. In still others, reports consist of PowerPoint slides delivered orally or printed and bound together. A short report to a client may use letter format or even be delivered via email. **Formal reports** contain elements such as a title page, a transmittal, a table of contents, an executive summary, and a list of illustrations. **Informal reports** may be letters and emails or even computer printouts of production or sales figures. But all reports, whatever their length or degree of formality, provide the information that people in organizations need to make plans and solve problems.

Reports can provide just information, both information and analysis alone, or information and analysis to support a recommendation (see Figure 15.1). Reports can be called **information reports** if they collect data for the reader, **analytical reports** if they interpret data but do not recommend action, and **recommendation reports** if they recommend action or a solution.

Figure 15.1	Variety of Information Reports Can Provide
Information only	
Sales reports (sales figures for the week or month).	
Quarterly reports (figures showing a plant's productivity and profits for the quarter).	
Information plus analysis	
Annual reports (financial data and an organization's accomplishments during the past year).	
Audit reports (interpretations of the facts revealed during an audit).	
Make-good or payback reports (calculations of the point at which a new capital investment will pay for itself).	
Information plus analysis plus a recommendation	
Recommendation reports evaluate two or more alternatives and recommend which alternative the organization should choose.	
Feasibility reports evaluate a proposed action and show whether or not it will work.	
Justification reports justify the need for a purchase, an investment, a new personnel line, or a change in procedure.	
Problem-solving reports identify the causes of an organizational problem and recommend a solution.	

The following reports can be information, analytical, or recommendation reports, depending on what they provide:

- **Accident reports** list the nature and causes of accidents in a factory or office. These reports also can analyze the data and recommend ways to make conditions safer.

- **Credit reports** summarize an applicant's income and other credit obligations. These reports also can evaluate the applicant's collateral and creditworthiness and recommend whether or not to provide credit.

- **Progress and interim reports** record the work done so far and the work remaining on a project. These reports also can analyze the quality of the work and recommend that a project be stopped, continued, or restructured.

- **Trip reports** share what the author learned at a conference or during a visit to a customer or supplier. These reports also can recommend action based on that information.

- **Closure reports** document the causes of a failure or possible products that are not economically or technically feasible under current conditions. They also can recommend action to prevent such failures in the future.

- **White paper reports** explain a problem and then may advocate for a solution to the problem. These reports can be written to inform a general audience. Sometimes companies use white paper reports for marketing purposes.

- **Return on investment (ROI) reports** correlate how money companies spend on advertising relates to sales or increased traffic. Marketing firms routinely compose these reports for clients.

Report Problems

LO 15-2

Good reports grow out of real problems: disjunctions between reality and the ideal, choices that must be made. When you write a report as part of your job, the organization may define the problem. To brainstorm problems for class reports, think about issues that face your college or university; housing units on campus; social, religious, and professional groups on campus and in your city; local businesses; and city, county, state, and federal governments and their agencies.

A good report problem in business meets the following criteria:

1. The problem is
   - Real.
   - Important enough to be worth solving.
   - Narrow but challenging.
2. The audience for the report is
   - Real.
   - Able to implement the recommended action.
3. The data, evidence, and facts are
   - Sufficient to document the severity of the problem.
   - Sufficient to prove that the recommendation will solve the problem.
   - Available to *you.*
   - Comprehensible to *you.*

Often, problems need to be narrowed. For example, "improving the college experiences of international students studying in the United States" is far too broad. First, choose one college or university. Second, identify the specific problem. Do you want to increase the social interaction between U.S. and international students? Help international students find housing? Increase the number of ethnic grocery stores and restaurants? Third, identify the specific audience that would have the power to implement your recommendations. Depending on the specific topic, the audience might be the Office of International Studies, the residence hall counselors, a service organization on campus or in town, a store, or a group of investors.

Some problems are more easily researched than others. If you have easy access to the Chinese Student Association, you can survey its members about their experiences at the local Chinese grocery. However, if you want to recommend ways to keep the Chinese grocery in business, but you do not have access to the store's financial records, you will have a much more difficult time solving the problem. Even if you have access, if the records are written in Chinese, you will have problems unless you read the language or have a willing translator.

Pick a problem you can solve in the time available. Six months of full-time (and overtime) work and a team of colleagues might allow you to look at all the ways to make a store more profitable. If you're doing a report in 6 to 12 weeks for a class that is only one of your responsibilities, limit the topic. Depending on your interests and knowledge, you could choose to examine the prices and brands carried, its inventory procedures, its overhead costs, its layout and decor, or its advertising budget.

Look at the following examples of report problems in the category of technology use:

Too broad:	Texting in class and its effects on college students.
Too time-consuming:	What are the effects of in-class texting on college students?
Better:	What are texting habits of students in XYZ University's Business School?
Better:	How can texting be integrated in XYZ University's business courses?

The first problem is too broad because it covers all college students. The second one is too time-consuming. Scholars are only starting to study the effects, and for you to do a report on this topic, you would need to do your own longitudinal project (i.e., a study of students' in-class texting habits over time). The third and fourth problems both would be possibilities. You would select one over the other depending on whether you wanted to focus on students or courses.

How you define the problem shapes the solutions you find. For example, suppose that a manufacturer of frozen foods isn't making money. If the problem is defined as a marketing problem, the researcher may analyze the product's price, image, advertising, and position in the market. But perhaps the problem is really that overhead costs are too high due to poor inventory management or that an inadequate distribution system doesn't get the product to its target market. Defining the problem accurately is essential to finding an effective solution.

Once you've defined your problem, you're ready to write a purpose statement. A good **purpose statement** makes three things clear:

- The organizational problem or conflict.

- The specific technical questions that must be answered to solve the problem.

- The rhetorical purpose (to explain, to recommend, to request, to propose) the report is designed to achieve.

The following purpose statement for a report to the superintendent of Yellowstone National Park has all three elements:

> Current management methods keep the elk population within the carrying capacity of the habitat but require frequent human intervention. Both wildlife conservation specialists and the public would prefer methods that controlled the elk population naturally. This report will compare the current short-term management techniques (hunting, trapping and transporting, and winter feeding) with two long-term management techniques, habitat modification and the reintroduction of predators. The purpose of this report is to recommend which techniques or combination of techniques would best satisfy the needs of conservationists, hunters, and the public.

To write a good purpose statement, you must understand the basic problem and have some idea of the questions that your report will answer. Note, however, that you can (and should) write the purpose statement before researching the specific alternatives the report will discuss.

Research Strategies for Reports

LO 15-3

Research for a report may be as simple as getting a computer printout of sales for the last month; it may involve finding published material or surveying or interviewing people. **Secondary research** retrieves information that someone else gathered. Library research and online searches are the best-known kinds of secondary research. **Primary research** gathers new information. Surveys, interviews, and observations are common methods for gathering new information for business reports.

Finding Information Online and in Print

You can save time and money by checking online and published sources of data before you gather new information. Many college and university libraries provide workshops and handouts on research techniques, as well as access to computer databases and research librarians.

Categories of sources that may be useful include

- Specialized encyclopedias for introductions to a topic.

- Indexes to find articles. Most permit searches by key word, by author, and often by company name.

- Abstracts for brief descriptions or summaries of articles. Sometimes the abstract will be all you'll need; almost always, you can tell from the abstract whether an article is useful for your needs.

- Citation indexes to find materials that cite previous research. Citation indexes thus enable you to use an older reference to find newer articles on the topic. The *Social Sciences Citation Index* is one of the most useful for researching business topics.

- Newspapers for information about recent events.

- U.S. Census reports, for a variety of business and demographic information.

To use a computer database efficiently, identify the concepts you're interested in and choose key words that will help you find relevant sources. **Key words** are the terms that the computer searches for. If you're not sure what terms to use, check the ABI/Inform Thesaurus for synonyms and the hierarchies in which information is arranged in various databases.

When you do a computer search, be aware that Google now personalizes your search results. This personalization means that someone with environmental concerns—say, a member of the Sierra Club—who Googles "global warming" will be led to widely different sources than someone with big oil connections. To get a more complete picture, you will have to dig deeper.[1]

Evaluating Web Sources

Some of the material on the web is excellent, but some of it is wholly unreliable. With print sources, the editor or publisher serves as a gatekeeper, so you can trust the material in good journals. To put up a web page, all one needs is access to a server.

Use the criteria in Figure 15.2 to evaluate websites for your research project. Answers to those questions may lead you to discard some of the information you find. A recurring example concerns travel and product reviews: some authors of positive reviews are connected to the companies providing the goods and services, while some authors of negative reviews are connected to competitors.

When the source has a vested interest in the results, scrutinize the data with special care. To analyze a company's financial prospects, use independent information as well as the company's annual report and press releases.

Figure 15.2	Criteria for Evaluating Websites

Authors: What person or organization sponsors the site? What credentials do the authors have?
Objectivity: Does the site give evidence to support its claims? Does it give both sides of controversial issues? Is the tone professional?
Information: How complete is the information? What is it based on?
Currency: How current is the information?
Audience: Who is the intended audience?
Purpose: Is the purpose to educate and inform? Or promote an agenda or sell advertising?

Drug and medical device companies, and the researchers funded by them, keep appearing in the news with reports of undue influence. Duke University researchers checked 746 studies of heart stents published in one year in medical journals. They found that 83% of the papers did not disclose whether authors were paid consultants for companies, even though many journals require that information. Even worse, 72% of the papers did not say who funded the research.[2] A study in the prestigious *New England Journal of Medicine* noted that positive studies of antidepressant trials got published and negative ones did not: "According to the published literature, it appeared that 94% of the trials conducted were positive. By contrast, the FDA analysis showed that 51% were positive."[3]

Many students start their research with Wikipedia, the largest, most popular encyclopedia ever. It has more than 40 million articles in 293 languages and is the fifth most visited website in the world.[4] So, while it may be acceptable as a starting place, be aware that many instructors and other professionals do not accept Wikipedia—or any encyclopedia—as an authoritative source. Think about impressing your audience with the credibility and depth of your research. Wikipedia (and similiar wiki pages), personal blogs, and the first five results of an Internet search will not impress your audience. Anyone with a computer, access to the Internet, and a few minutes of time can access sources like these. When you are conducting research in an academic or business environment, credible sources will help establish your professionalism and ethos.

Check the Currency of the Data.   Technology figures in particular need to be current. Do remember, however, that some large data sets are one to two years behind in being analyzed. Such is the case for some government figures, also. If you are doing a report in 2018 that requires national education data from the Department of Education, for instance, 2017 data may not even be fully collected. Even the 2016 data may not be fully analyzed, so the 2015 data may be the most current available.

Analyzing and Designing Surveys

A **survey** questions a group of people. The easiest way to ask many questions is to create a **questionnaire,** a written list of questions that people fill out. An **interview** is a structured conversation with someone who will be able to give you useful information. Organizations use surveys and interviews to research both internal issues such as employee satisfaction and external issues such as customer satisfaction.

Figure 15.3 lists questions to ask about surveys.

1. Who Did the Survey and Who Paid for It?   Unfortunately, it is far too easy to introduce bias into surveys. Thus, a good place to start when examining survey results is with the survey producers. Who are they? How were they financed? How comfortable should you be with the results of a survey about a medical device when the survey was financed by the maker of the device? Was a survey about auto model satisfaction financed by the maker of the auto?

2. How Many People Were Surveyed and How Were They Chosen?
To keep research costs reasonable, usually only a sample of the total population is polled. How that sample is chosen and the attempts made to get responses from

Figure 15.3	Questions to Ask about Surveys
1.	Who did the survey and who paid for it?
2.	How many people were surveyed and how were they chosen?
3.	How was the survey conducted?
4.	What was the response rate?
5.	What questions were asked?

nonrespondents will determine whether you can infer that what is true of your sample is also true of the population as a whole.

A **sample** is a subset of the population. The **sampling units** are those actually sampled. Frequently, the sampling unit is an individual. If a list of individuals is not available, then a household can be the sampling unit. The list of all sampling units is the **sampling frame.** For interviews, this could be a list of all addresses, or for companies a list of all *Fortune* 500 CEOs.[5] The **population** is the group you want to make statements about. Depending on the purpose of your research, your population might be all *Fortune* 1000 companies, all business students at your college, or all consumers of tea in the mid-Atlantic states.

A **convenience sample** is a group of subjects who are easy to get: students who walk through the union, people at a shopping mall, workers in your own unit. Convenience samples are useful for a rough pretest of a questionnaire and may be acceptable for some class research projects. However, you cannot generalize from a convenience sample to a larger group. If, for instance, you survey people entering your local library about their opinion of the proposed library bond (which has to be voter approved), you are taking a convenience sample and one that will not tell you what non-library users think.

A purposive or **judgment sample** is a group of people whose views seem useful. Someone interested in surveying the kinds of writing done on campus might ask each department for the name of a faculty member who cared about writing and then send surveys to those people.

In a **random sample,** each person in the population theoretically has an equal chance of being chosen. When people say they did something *randomly* they often mean *without conscious bias.* However, unconscious bias exists. Someone passing out surveys in front of the library will be more likely to approach people who seem friendly and less likely to ask people who seem intimidating; are in a hurry; are much older or younger; or are of a different race, class, or sex. True random samples rely on random digit tables, published in texts and online.

If you take a true random sample, you can generalize your findings to the whole population from which your sample comes. Consider, for example, a random phone survey that shows 65% of respondents approve of a presidential policy. Measures of variability always should be attached to survey-derived estimates like this one. Typically, a **confidence interval** provides this measure of variability. Using the confidence interval, we might conclude it is likely that between 58% and 72% of the population approve of the presidential policy when the margin of error is 6% to 7%. The confidence interval is based on the size of the sample and the expected variation within the population. Statistics texts tell you how to calculate measures of variability.

For many kinds of research, a large sample is important for giving significant results. In addition to its electronic data, Nielsen Media Research collects about 2 million television viewing diaries annually to gather viewing data. The large numbers also allow it to provide viewing information for local stations and advertisers.[6]

Do not, however, confuse **sample size** with randomness. A classic example is the 1936 *Literary Digest* poll that predicted Republican Alf Landon would beat Democrat incumbent President Franklin Roosevelt. *Literary Digest* sent out 10 million ballots to its magazine subscribers as well as people who owned cars and telephones, most of whom in 1936 were richer than the average voter—and more Republican.[7]

3. How Was the Survey Conducted? **Face-to-face surveys** are convenient when you are surveying a fairly small number of people in a specific location. In a face-to-face survey, however, the interviewer's sex, race, and nonverbal cues can bias results. Most people prefer not to say things they think their audience will dislike. For that reason, women will be more likely to agree that sexual harassment is a problem if the interviewer is also a woman. Members of a minority group are more likely to admit that they suffer discrimination if the interviewer is a member of the same minority.

Telephone surveys are popular because they can be closely supervised. Interviewers can read the questions from a computer screen and key in answers as the respondent gives them. The results can then be available just a few minutes after the last call is completed.

Phone surveys also have limitations. First, they reach only people who have phones and thus underrepresent some groups such as poor people. Voicemail, caller ID, and cell phones also make phone surveys more difficult. Most people do not answer or return calls from unknown sources, nor are their cell phone numbers readily available in most cases.

Because a survey based on a phone book would exclude people with unlisted numbers, professional survey-takers use automatic random-digit dialing.

Mail surveys can reach anyone who has an address. Some people may be more willing to fill out an anonymous questionnaire than to give sensitive information to a stranger over the phone. However, mail surveys are not effective for respondents who don't read and write well. Further, it may be more difficult to get a response from someone who doesn't care about the survey or who sees the mailing as junk mail.

Online surveys deliver questions over the Internet. The researcher can contact respondents with an email containing a link to a web page with the survey or can ask people by mail or in person to log on and visit the website with the survey.

Another alternative is to post a survey on a website and invite the site's visitors to complete the survey. This approach does not generate a random sample, so the results probably do not reflect the opinions of the entire population. Mattel, maker of Barbie, conducted an online poll to see what young girls wanted for the doll's next career. Results of the poll surprised Mattel. Although young girls wanted Barbie to be a TV anchorwoman, the career winning the most votes was computer engineer because various computer organizations for women asked their members to vote.[8]

In general, volunteers for online surveys are more educated, more likely to be white, and more likely to be at the ends of the age spectrum than the general population.[9] Nevertheless, with online surveys costing about one-tenth of phone surveys, they are increasing their acceptance among experts and growing in popularity.

4. What Was the Response Rate?

A major concern with any kind of survey is the **response rate**, the percentage of people who respond. People who refuse to answer may differ from those who respond, and you need information from both groups to be able to generalize to the whole population. Low response rates pose a major problem, especially for phone surveys. Answering machines and caller ID are commonly used to screen incoming calls, resulting in decreased response rates.

Widespread use of cell phones in recent years also has negatively affected the ability of telephone surveyors to contact potential respondents. Because U.S. laws prevent autodialing of cell phones in most situations, including cell phones in a survey adds significantly to both the cost and the complexity. For survey firms that rely on recordings to conduct polls automatically, the cost of a cell phone call is 10 times more. Nevertheless, to protect their reputation, some survey firms are requiring clients to include a set percentage of cell phone calls.[10]

The problem of nonresponse has increased dramatically in recent years. The mail response rate for the *mandatory* U.S. Census was only 65%, even with the $370.6 million spent promoting response.[11] The response rate for random phone surveys fell every year from 36% in 1997 to 9% in 2012, where it has remained according to a 2016 study. The rate for cell phone surveys is 7%.[12] Organizations such as the Pew Research Center and the American Association for Public Opinion Research are stressing the necessity for all phone surveys to include both cell phone and landline calls.[13]

5. What Questions Were Asked?

Surveys and interviews can be useful only if the questions are well designed. Good questions have these characteristics:

- They ask only one thing.

- They are phrased neutrally.

- They are asked in an order that does not influence answers.

■ They avoid making assumptions about the respondent.

■ They mean the same thing to different people.

At a telecommunications firm, a survey asked employees to rate their manager's perfor-mance at "hiring staff and setting compensation." Although both tasks are part of the dis-cipline of human resource management, they are different activities. A manager might do a better job of hiring than of setting pay levels, or vice versa. The survey gave respondents—and the company using the survey—no way to distinguish performance on each task.[14]

Phrase questions in a way that won't bias the response, either positively or negatively. Respondents tend to agree more than disagree with statements. If a survey about man-agers asks employees whether their manager is fair, ethical, intelligent, knowledgeable, and so on, they are likely to assign all of these qualities to the manager—and to agree more and more as the survey goes along. To correct for this, some questions should be worded to generate the opposite response. For example, a statement about ethics can be balanced by a statement about corruption, and a statement about fairness can be bal-anced by a statement about bias or stereotypes.[15]

The order in which questions are asked may matter. Asking about the economy—and its impact on families—before asking about the president will lower opinions of the president during bad economic times; the opposite is true for good economic times.[16]

Avoid questions that make assumptions about your subjects. The question "Does your spouse have a job outside the home?" assumes that your respondent is married.

Use words that mean the same thing to you and to the respondents. If a question can be interpreted in more than one way, it will be. Words like *often* and *important* mean dif-ferent things to different people. When a consulting firm helped Duke Energy assess the leadership skills of its managers, an early draft of the employee survey asked employees to rate how well their manager "understands the business and the marketplace." How would employees know what is in the manager's mind? Each respondent would have to determine what is reasonable evidence of a manager's understanding. The question was rephrased to identify behavior the employees could observe: "resolves complaints from customers quickly and thoroughly." The wording is still subjective ("quickly and thor-oughly"), but at least all employees will be measuring the same category of behavior.[17]

Bypassing occurs when two people use the same words or phrases but interpret them differently. To catch questions that can be misunderstood and to reduce bypassing, avoid terms that are likely to mean different things to different people and pretest your questions with several people who are like those who will fill out the survey. Even a small pretest with 10 people can help you refine your questions.

Survey questions can be categorized in several ways. **Closed questions** have a limited number of possible responses. **Open questions** do not lock the subject into any sort of response. Figure 15.4 gives examples of closed and open questions. The second ques-tion in Figure 15.4 is an example of a Likert-type scale.

Closed questions are faster for subjects to answer and easier for researchers to score. However, because all answers must fit into pre-chosen categories, they cannot probe the complexities of a subject. You can improve the quality of closed questions by conduct-ing a pretest with open questions to find categories that matter to respondents. Analyz-ing the responses from open questions is usually less straightforward than analyzing responses from closed questions.

Use closed multiple-choice questions for potentially embarrassing topics. Seeing their own situation listed as one response can help respondents feel that it is accept-able. However, very sensitive issues are perhaps better asked in an interview, where the interviewer can build trust and reveal information about himself or herself to encourage the interviewee to answer.

Use an "Other, Please Specify" category when you want the convenience of a closed question but cannot foresee all the possible responses. These responses can be used to improve choices if the survey is to be repeated.

Figure 15.4	Closed and Open Questions

Closed questions

Are you satisfied with the city bus service? (yes/no)

How good is the city bus service?

Excellent 5 4 3 2 1 Terrible

Indicate whether you agree (A) or disagree (D) with each of the following statements about city bus service.

   A D The schedule is convenient for me.

   A D The routes are convenient for me.

   A D The drivers are courteous.

   A D The buses are clean.

Rate each of the following improvements in the order of their importance to you (1 = most important and 6 = least important).

_____ Buy new buses.

_____ Increase non-rush-hour service on weekdays.

_____ Increase service on weekdays.

_____ Provide earlier and later service on weekdays.

_____ Buy more buses with wheelchair access.

_____ Provide unlimited free transfers.

Open questions

How do you feel about the city bus service?

Tell me about the city bus service.

Why do you ride the bus? (or, Why don't you ride the bus?)

What do you like and dislike about the city bus service?

How could the city bus service be improved?

What is the single most important reason that you ride the bus?

_____ I don't have a car.

_____ I don't want to fight rush-hour traffic.

_____ Riding the bus is cheaper than driving my car.

_____ Riding the bus conserves fuel and reduces pollution.

_____ Other (please specify): _____

When you use multiple-choice questions, make the answer categories mutually exclusive and exhaustive. This means you make sure that any one answer fits in only one category and that a category is included for all possible answers. In the following example of overlapping categories, a person who worked for a company with exactly 25 employees could check either *a* or *b*. The resulting data would be hard to interpret.

Overlapping categories: Indicate the number of full-time employees in your company on May 16:

        _____ a. 0–25

        _____ b. 25–100

        _____ c. 100–500

        _____ d. over 500

Discrete categories: Indicate the number of full-time employees on your payroll on
May 16:

_____ a. 0–25

_____ b. 26–100

_____ c. 101–500

_____ d. more than 500

Branching questions direct different respondents to different parts of the questionnaire based on their answers to earlier questions.

> 10. Have you talked to an academic adviser this year?   yes   no
> (If "no," skip to question 14.)

Generally, put early in the questionnaire questions that will be easy to answer. Put
questions that are harder to answer or that people may be less willing to answer (e.g.,
age and income) near the end of the questionnaire. Even if people choose not to answer
such questions, you'll still have the rest of the survey filled out.

If subjects will fill out the questionnaire themselves, pay careful attention to the physical design of the document. Use indentations and white space effectively; make it easy
to mark and score the answers. Label answer scales frequently so respondents remember
which end is positive and which is negative. Include a brief statement of purpose if you
(or someone else) will not be available to explain the questionnaire or answer questions.
Pretest the questionnaire to make sure the directions are clear. One researcher mailed a
two-page questionnaire without pretesting it. One-third of the respondents didn't realize
there were questions to answer on the back of the first page.

See Figure 15.5 for an example of a questionnaire for a student report.

Analyzing Numbers

Many reports analyze numbers—either numbers from databases and sources or numbers from a survey you have conducted. The numerical information, properly analyzed,
can make a clear case in support of a recommendation.

When you have multiple numbers for salaries or other items, an early analysis step
is to figure the average (or mean), the median, and the range. The **average** or **mean** is
calculated by adding up all the figures and dividing by the number of samples. The
mode is the number that occurs most often. The **median** is the number that is exactly in
the middle in a ranked list of observations. When you have an even number, the median
will be the average of the two numbers in the center of the list. The **range** is the difference between the high and low figures for that variable.

Averages are particularly susceptible to a single extreme figure. Three different surveys reported the average cost of a wedding at nearly $30,000. Many articles picked up
that figure because weddings are big business. However, the median cost in those three
surveys was only about $15,000. Even that amount is probably on the high side because
the samples were convenience samples for a big wedding website, a bride magazine, and
a maker of wedding invitations, and thus probably did not include smaller, less elaborate weddings.[18]

Often it's useful to simplify numerical data by rounding off or combining similar elements. Graphing also can help you see patterns in your data. (See Chapter 13 for a full
discussion of tables and graphs as a way of analyzing and presenting numerical data.)
Look at the raw data as well as at percentages. For example, a 50% increase in shoplifting incidents sounds alarming. An increase from two to three shoplifting incidents
sounds less so but could be the same data, just stated differently.

Figure 15.5	Questionnaire for a Student Report Using Survey Research

An interesting title can help.

In your introductory ¶,
① tell how to return the survey
② tell how the information will be used

Survey: Why Do Students Attend Athletic Events?

The purpose of this survey is to determine why students attend sports events, and what might increase attendance. All information is to be used solely for a student research paper. Please return completed surveys to Elizabeth or Vicki at the Union help desk. Thank you for your assistance!

Start with easy-to-answer questions.

1. Gender (Please circle one)   M   F

2. What is your class year? (Please circle)   1   2   3   4   Grad   Other

The words below each number anchor responses, while still allowing you to average the data.

3. How do you feel about women's sports? (Please circle)

1	2	3	4	5
I enjoy watching women's sports		I'll watch, but it doesn't really matter		Women's sports are boring/ I'd rather watch men's sports

Seeing a response in a survey can make respondents more willing to admit to feelings they may be embarrassed to volunteer.

4. Do you like to attend MSU men's basketball games? (Please circle)
   Y   N

5. How often do you attend MSU women's basketball games? (Please circle)

1	2	3	4	5
All/most games	Few games a season	Once a season	Less than once a year	Never

6. If you do not attend all of the women's basketball games, why not? (Please check all that apply. If you attend all the games, skip to #7.)

__I've never thought to go.
__I don't like basketball.
__I don't like sporting events.
__The team isn't good enough.
__My friends are not interested in going.
__I want to go; I just haven't had the opportunity.
__The tickets cost too much ($10).
__Other (please specify) _____

Think about factors that affect the problem you're studying and write survey questions to get information about them.

7. To what extent would each of the following make you more likely to attend an MSU women's basketball game? (please rank all)

1	2	3
Much more likely to attend	Possibly more likely	No effect

__Increased awareness on campus (fliers, chalking on the Oval, more articles in the *Gazette*)
__Marketing to students (give-aways, days for residence halls or fraternities/sororities)
__Student loyalty program (awarding points towards free tickets, clothing, food for attending games)
__Education (pocket guide explaining the rules of the game provided at the gate)
__Other (please specify) _____

Thank you!
Please return this survey to Elizabeth or Vicki at the Union help desk.

Repeat where to turn in or mail completed surveys.

Analyzing Patterns

Patterns can help you draw meaning from your data. If you have library sources, on which points do experts agree? Which disagreements can be explained by early theories or numbers that have now changed? Which disagreements are the result of different interpretations of the same data? Which are the result of having different values and criteria?

In your interviews and surveys, what patterns do you see?

- Have things changed over time?

- Does geography account for differences?

- Do demographics such as gender, age, or income account for differences?

- What similarities do you see?

- What differences do you see?

- What confirms your hunches?

- What surprises you?

Many descriptions of sales trends are descriptions of patterns derived from data.

Checking Your Logic

A common logic error is confusing causation with correlation. *Causation* means that one thing causes or produces another. *Correlation* means that two things happening at the same time are positively or negatively related. One might cause the other, but both might be caused by a third. For instance, consider a study that shows pulling all-nighters hurts grades: students who pull all-nighters get lower grades than those who do not pull all-nighters. But maybe it is not the all-nighter causing the poor grades; maybe students who need all-nighters are weaker students to begin with.

Correlation and causation are easy to confuse, but the difference is important. The Census Bureau publishes figures showing that greater education levels are associated with greater incomes. A widely held assumption is that more education causes greater earnings. But might people from richer backgrounds seek more education? Or might some third factor, such as intelligence, lead to both greater education and higher income?[19]

Search for at least three possible causes for each phenomenon you've observed and at least three possible solutions for each problem. The more possibilities you brainstorm, the more likely you are to find good options. In your report, discuss in detail only the possibilities that will occur to readers and that you think are the real reasons and the best solutions.

When you have identified causes of the problem or the best solutions, check these ideas against reality. Can you find support in references or in numbers? Can you answer claims of people who interpret the data in other ways?

Make the nature of your evidence clear to your reader. Do you have observations that you yourself have made? Or do you have inferences based on observations or data collected by others? Old data may not be good guides to future action.

If you can't prove the claim you originally hoped to make, modify your conclusions to fit your data. Even when your market test is a failure or your experiment disproves your hypothesis, you still can write a useful report.

- Identify changes that might yield a different result. For example, selling the product at a lower price might enable the company to sell enough units.

- Divide the discussion to show what part of the test succeeded.

- Discuss circumstances that may have affected the results.

■ Summarize your negative findings in progress reports to let readers down gradually and to give them a chance to modify the research design.

■ Remember that negative results aren't always disappointing to the audience. For example, the people who commissioned a feasibility report may be relieved to have an impartial outsider confirm their suspicions that a project isn't feasible.

A common myth associated with numbers is that numbers are more objective than words: "numbers don't lie." But as the previous discussion shows, numbers can be subject to widely varying interpretation.

Conducting Research Interviews

Schedule interviews in advance; tell the interviewee about how long you expect the interview to take. A survey of technical writers (who get much of their information from interviews) found that the best days to interview subject matter experts are Tuesdays, Wednesdays, and Thursday mornings.[20] People are frequently swamped on Mondays and looking forward to the weekend, or trying to finish their week's work, on Fridays.

Interviews can be structured or unstructured. In a **structured interview,** the interviewer uses a detailed list of questions to guide the interview. Indeed, a structured interview may use a questionnaire just as a survey does.

In an **unstructured interview,** the interviewer has three or four main questions. Other questions build on what the interviewee says. To prepare for an unstructured interview, learn as much as possible about the interviewee and the topic. Go into the interview with three or four main topics you want to cover.

Interviewers sometimes use closed questions to start the interview and set the interviewee at ease. The strength of an interview, however, is getting at a person's attitudes, feelings, and experiences. **Situational questions** let you probe what someone does in a specific circumstance. **Hypothetical questions** that ask people to imagine what they would do generally yield less reliable answers than questions about **critical incidents** or key past events.

Situational question:	How do you tell an employee that his or her performance is unsatisfactory?
Hypothetical question:	What would you say if you had to tell an employee that his or her performance was unsatisfactory?
Critical incident question:	You've probably been in a situation where someone who was working with you wasn't carrying his or her share of the work. What did you do the last time that happened?

A **mirror question** paraphrases the content of the last answer: "So you confronted him directly?" "You think that this product costs too much?" Mirror questions are used both to check that the interviewer understands what the interviewee has said and to prompt the interviewee to continue talking.

Probes follow up an original question to get at specific aspects of a topic:

Question:	What do you think about the fees for campus parking?
Probes:	Would you be willing to pay more for a reserved space? How much more? Should the fines for vehicles parked illegally be increased? Do you think fees should be based on income?

Probes are not used in any definite order. Instead, they are used to keep the interviewee talking, to get at aspects of a subject that the interviewee has not yet mentioned, and to probe more deeply into points that the interviewee brings up.

If you read questions to subjects in a structured interview, use fewer options than you might in a written questionnaire.

> I'm going to read a list of factors that someone might look for in choosing a restaurant. After I read each factor, please tell me whether that factor is Very Important to you, Somewhat Important to you, or Not Important to you.

If the interviewee hesitates, reread the scale.

Always record the interview. Test your equipment ahead of time to make sure it works. If you think your interviewee may be reluctant to be recorded, offer to give a copy of the recording to the interviewee.

Using Focus Groups

A **focus group,** yet another form of qualitative research, is a small group of people convened to provide a more detailed look into some area of interest—a product, service, process, concept, and so on. Because the group setting allows members to build on each other's comments, carefully chosen focus groups can provide detailed feedback; they can illuminate underlying attitudes and emotions relevant to particular behaviors.

Focus groups also have some problems. The first is the increasing use of professional respondents drawn from databases, a practice usually driven by cost and time limitations. The *Association for Qualitative Research Newsletter* labeled these respondents as a leading industry problem.[21] To get findings that are consistent among focus groups, the groups must accurately represent the target population. A second problem with focus groups is that such groups sometimes aim to please rather than offering their own evaluations.

Using Online Networks

An updated version of the focus group is the online network. These networks, first cultivated as research tools by technology and video game companies, are being employed by various producers of consumer products and services, including small companies. The networks are often cheaper and more effective than traditional focus groups because they have broader participation and allow for deeper and ongoing probing. Companies can use them for polls, real-time chats with actual consumers, and product trials.[22]

A still larger online community comes from Twitter and online blogs. These communities are the least controllable of feedback groups but are becoming more important. Many companies are hiring employees or technology services to monitor comments on social networks and respond quickly. They also use data from Twitter and Facebook to track trends and preferences.

Observing Customers and Users

Answers to surveys and interviews may differ from actual behavior—sometimes greatly. To get more accurate consumer information, many marketers observe users. Before designing new ketchup packets, Heinz watched fast-food customers in their vehicles wrestle with traditional packets. The new packets allow users to dip or squeeze.[23] Intuit, a leader in observation studies, sends employees to visit customers and watch how they use Intuit products such as QuickBooks. Watching small businesses struggle with QuickBooks Pro told the company of the need for a new product, QuickBooks Simple Start.[24]

Observation also can be used for gathering in-house information such as how efficiently production systems operate and how well employees serve customers. Some businesses use "mystery shoppers." For instance, McDonald's has used mystery shoppers to check cleanliness, customer service, and food quality. The company posts store-by-store results online, giving store operators an incentive and the information they need to improve quality on measures where they are slipping or lagging behind the region's performance.[25] So many organizations use mystery shoppers that there is a Mystery Shopping Providers Association.

Observation often is combined with other techniques to get the most information. **Think-aloud protocols** ask users to voice their thoughts as they use a document or product: "First I'll try. . . ." These protocols are recorded and later analyzed to understand how users approach a document or product. **Interruption interviews** interrupt users to ask them what's happening. For example, a company testing a draft of computer instructions might interrupt a user to ask, "What are you trying to do now? Tell me why you did that." **Discourse-based interviews** ask questions based on documents that the interviewee has written: "You said that the process is too complicated. Tell me what you mean by that."

Using Technology for Research

Technology has been used routinely in research and is playing an ever-increasing role in business research. Frequently, it provides better and cheaper data than older research methods. For example, one problem with asking consumers about their television-watching behavior is that they sometimes underreport the number of hours they watch and the degree to which they watch programs they aren't proud of liking.

Researchers have tried to develop a variety of measurement methods that collect viewing data automatically. Arbitron introduced the Portable People Meter (PPM), which receives an inaudible electronic signal from radio stations and broadcast and cable TV stations. Consumers simply carry the PPM and it records their media exposure. One of the first results showed that consumers listened to radio more than they had indicated in diaries.[26]

Nielsen Media Research added commercial viewings to its famous TV show numbers; advertisers are naturally eager to know how many people actually watch commercials instead of leaving to get a snack or fast-forwarding through them on digital video recorders.[27] Nielsen also started tracking college students' viewing, installing its people meters in commons areas such as dorms.

Within the past few years, social media also are playing a larger role in research. Businesses are using cell phone feedback to get more immediate, realistic information about products and marketing. Twitter also is beginning to play a larger role in research:

- Businesses use Twitter to track opinions about products, marketing, and employee morale.

- Researchers can use Twitter data to track outbreaks of flu or food poisoning; in fact, Twitter is usually faster than information from the Centers for Disease Control and Prevention.

- The U.S. Geological Survey is experimenting with Twitter as an earthquake tracking method that is faster and cheaper than its seismometers.

- Hedge funds and investment firms are using Twitter data in their investment formulas.

One major limitation of Twitter data mining is that Twitter users are not a representative sample—let alone a random sample—of the population. They tend to be younger, more educated, more urban, more affluent, and less likely to have children than nonusers. Another significant limitation is that thanks to language complexity, it is not always obvious—even to human researchers, let alone data-mining programs—what opinion is being expressed in a tweet.[28]

One notable outcome of all this data collection is that the job of data scientist—composed of a combination of mathematician, statistician, computer scientist, and business guru—is predicted to be one of the hottest jobs of the decade.[29]

Technology also can help you manage your time more efficiently. For example, Google Drive, the home of Google Docs, will allow you and your teammates to work on different sections of the report simultaneously instead of emailing drafts back and forth. As an added bonus, a revision history is always saved so you can go back to an earlier version of your work if needed. Other features allow your team to have real-time instant message chats if your schedules don't permit you to all meet in the same physical location to work on the report.

Choosing Information for Reports

LO 15-4

Don't put information in reports just because you have it or just because it took you a long time to find it. Instead, choose the information that your audience needs to make a decision. NASA received widespread criticism over the way it released results from an $11.3 million federal air safety study. NASA published 16,208 pages of findings with no guide to understanding them. Critics maintain the lapse was deliberate because the data contained hundreds of cases of pilot error.[30]

If you know your audience well, you already may know their priorities. For example, the supervisor of a call center knows that management will be looking for certain kinds of performance data, including costs, workload handled, and customer satisfaction. To write regular reports, the supervisor could set up a format in which it is easy to see how well the center is doing in each of these areas. Using the same format month after month simplifies the audience's task.

If you don't know your audience, you may be able to get a sense of what is important by showing a tentative table of contents and asking, "Have I included everything?" When you cannot contact an external audience, show your draft to colleagues and superiors in your organization.

How much information you need to include depends on whether your audience is likely to be supportive, neutral, or skeptical. If your audience is likely to be pleased with your research, you can present your findings directly. If your audience will not be pleased, you will need to explain your thinking in a persuasive way and provide substantial evidence.

Sometimes even good sources and authorities can differ on the numbers they offer, or on the interpretations of the same data sets. Researchers from the United Nations and Johns Hopkins University differed on their estimates of Iraqi deaths in the war by 500% because of research design and execution flaws plus sampling error in the Hopkins report.[31] You will be best able to judge the quality of data if you know how they were collected.

You also must decide whether to put information in the body of the report or in appendices. Put material in the body of the report if it is crucial to your proof, if your most significant audience will want to see it there, or if it is short. (Something less than half a page won't interrupt the audience.) Frequently, decision makers want your analysis of the data in the report body rather than the actual data itself. Supporting data that will be examined later by specialists such as accountants, lawyers, and engineers are generally put in an appendix.

Anything that a careful audience will want but that is not crucial to your proof can go in an appendix. Appendices can include

- A copy of a survey questionnaire or interview questions.

- A tally of responses to each question in a survey.

- A copy of responses to open-ended questions in a survey.

- A transcript of an interview.

- Complex tables and visuals.

■ Technical data.

■ Previous reports on the same subject.

Organizing Information in Reports

Most sets of data can be organized in several logical ways. Choose the way that makes your information easiest for the audience to understand and use. If you were compiling a directory of all the employees at your plant, for example, alphabetizing by last name would be far more useful than listing people by height, Social Security number, or length of service with the company, although those organizing principles might make sense in lists for other purposes.

The following three guidelines will help you choose the arrangement that will be the most useful for your audience:

1. **Process your information before you present it to your audience.** The order in which you became aware of information usually is not the best order to present it to your audience.
2. **When you have lots of information, group it into three to seven categories.** The average person's short-term memory can hold only seven chunks, though the chunks can be of any size.[32] By grouping your information into seven categories (or fewer), you make your report easier to comprehend.
3. **Work with the audience's expectations, not against them.** Introduce ideas in the overview in the order in which you will discuss them.

Patterns for Organizing Information

Organize information in a way that will work best for your audience. Figure 15.6 lists common patterns for organizing information that are particularly useful in reports. Any of these patterns can be used for a whole report or for only part of it.

Comparison/Contrast   Many reports use comparison/contrast sections within a larger report pattern. Comparison/contrast also can be the purpose of the whole report. Recommendation studies generally use this pattern. You can focus either on the alternatives you are evaluating or on the criteria you use. See Figure 15.7 for ways to organize these two patterns in a report.

Focus on the alternatives when

■ One alternative is clearly superior.

■ The criteria are hard to separate.

■ The audience will intuitively grasp the alternative as a whole rather than as the sum of its parts.

Figure 15.6	Ways to Organize Reports
■ Comparison/contrast	■ General to particular or particular to general
■ Problem–solution	■ Geographic or spatial
■ Elimination of alternatives	■ Functional
■ SWOT analysis	■ Chronological

Figure 15.7	Two Ways to Organize a Comparison/Contrast Report
Focus on alternatives	
Alternative A	Opening a New Store on Campus
Criterion 1	Cost of Renting Space
Criterion 2	Proximity to Target Market
Criterion 3	Competition from Similar Stores
Alternative B	Opening a New Store in the Suburban Mall
Criterion 1	Cost of Renting Space
Criterion 2	Proximity to Target Market
Criterion 3	Competition from Similar Stores
Focus on criteria	
Criterion 1	Cost of Renting Space for the New Store
Alternative A	Cost of Campus Locations
Alternative B	Cost of Locations in the Suburban Mall
Criterion 2	Proximity to Target Market
Alternative A	Proximity on Campus
Alternative B	Proximity in the Suburban Mall
Criterion 3	Competition from Similar Stores
Alternative A	Competing Stores on Campus
Alternative B	Competing Stores in the Suburban Mall

Focus on the criteria when

- The superiority of one alternative to another depends on the relative weight assigned to various criteria. Perhaps Alternative A is best if we are most concerned about Criterion 1, cost, but worst if we are most concerned about Criterion 2, proximity to target market.

- The criteria are easy to separate.

- The audience wants to compare and contrast the options independently of your recommendation.

A variation of the comparison/contrast pattern is the **pro-and-con pattern.** In this pattern, under each specific heading, give the arguments for and against that alternative. A report recommending new plantings for a university quadrangle uses the pro-and-con pattern:

> Advantages of Monocropping
>   High Productivity
>   Visual Symmetry
> Disadvantages of Monocropping
>   Danger of Pest Exploitation
>   Visual Monotony

This pattern is least effective when you want to de-emphasize the disadvantages of a proposed solution, for it does not permit you to bury the disadvantages between neutral or positive material.

Problem–Solution   Identify the problem; explain its background or history; discuss its extent and seriousness; identify its causes. Discuss the factors (criteria) that affect the decision. Analyze the advantages and disadvantages of possible solutions. Conclusions and recommendation can go either first or last, depending on the preferences of your audience. This pattern works well when the audience is neutral.

A report recommending ways to eliminate solidification of a granular bleach during production uses the problem–solution pattern:

> Recommended Reformulation for Vibe Bleach
> Problems in Maintaining Vibe's Granular Structure
>   Solidification during Storage and Transportation
>   Customer Complaints about "Blocks" of Vibe in Boxes
> Why Vibe Bleach "Cakes"
>   Vibe's Formula
>   The Manufacturing Process
>   The Chemical Process of Solidification
> Modifications Needed to Keep Vibe Flowing Freely

Elimination of Alternatives   After discussing the problem and its causes, discuss the *impractical* solutions first, showing why they will not work. End with the most practical solution. This pattern works well when the solutions the audience is likely to favor will not work, while the solution you recommend is likely to be perceived as expensive, intrusive, or radical.

A report on toy commercials, "The Effect of TV Ads on Children," eliminates alternatives:

> Alternative Solutions to Problems in TV Toy Ads
>   Leave Ads Unchanged
>   Mandate School Units on Advertising
>   Ask the Industry to Regulate Itself
>   Give FCC Authority to Regulate TV Ads Directed at Children

SWOT Analysis   **SWOT analysis** is frequently used to evaluate a proposed project, expansion, or new venture. The analysis discusses **S**trengths, **W**eaknesses, **O**pportunities, and **T**hreats of the proposed action. Strengths and weaknesses are usually factors within the organization; opportunities and threats are usually factors external to the organization.

A report recommending an in-house training department uses a SWOT analysis to support its recommendation:

> Advantages of In-House Training
> Disadvantages of In-House Training
> Competitor Training Businesses
> Opportunities for Training Expansion

This report switches the order of threats (Competitor Training Businesses) and opportunities to end with positive information.

General to Particular or Particular to General   General to particular starts with the problem as it affects the organization or as it manifests itself in general and then moves to a discussion of the parts of the problem and solutions to each of these parts. Particular to general starts with the problem as the audience defines it and moves to larger issues of which the problem is a part. Both are good patterns when you need to redefine the audience's perception of the problem to solve it effectively.

The directors of a student volunteer organization, VIP, have defined their problem as "not enough volunteers." After studying the subject, the writer is convinced that problems in training, supervision, and campus awareness are responsible for both a high dropout rate and a low recruitment rate. The general-to-particular pattern helps the audience see the problem in a new way:

> Why VIP Needs More Volunteers
> Why Some VIP Volunteers Drop Out
>   Inadequate Training
>   Inadequate Supervision
>   Feeling That VIP Requires Too Much Time
>   Feeling That the Work Is Too Emotionally Demanding
> Why Some Students Do Not Volunteer
>   Feeling That VIP Requires Too Much Time
>   Feeling That the Work Is Too Emotionally Demanding
>   Preference for Volunteering with Another Organization
>   Lack of Knowledge about VIP Opportunities
> How VIP Volunteers Are Currently Trained and Supervised
> Time Demands on VIP Volunteers
> Emotional Demands on VIP Volunteers
> Ways to Increase Volunteer Commitment and Motivation
>   Improving Training and Supervision
>   Improving the Flexibility of Volunteers' Hours
>   Providing Emotional Support to Volunteers
>   Providing More Information about Community Needs and VIP Services

Geographic or Spatial   In a geographic or spatial pattern, you discuss problems and solutions by units according to their physical arrangement. Move from office to office, building to building, factory to factory, state to state, region to region, and so on.

A sales report might use a geographic pattern of organization.

> Sales Have Risen in the European Community
> Sales Are Flat in Eastern Europe
> Sales Have Fallen Sharply in the Middle East
> Sales Are Off to a Strong Start in Africa
> Sales Have Risen Slightly in Asia
> Sales Have Fallen Slightly in South America
> Sales Are Steady in North America

Functional   In functional patterns, discuss the problems and solutions of each functional unit. For example, a small business might organize a report to its venture capitalists by the categories of research, production, and marketing. A government report might divide data into the different functions an agency performed, taking each in turn.

> Major Accomplishments FY 18
>   Regulation
>   Education
>   Research
>   International coordination

Chronological   A chronological report records events in the order in which they happened or are planned to happen. Many progress reports are organized chronologically.

> Work Completed in October
> Work Planned for November

If you choose this pattern, be sure you do not let the chronology obscure significant points or trends.

Patterns for Specific Varieties of Reports

Informative, recommendation, and justification reports will be more successful when you work with the audience's expectations for that kind of report.

Informative and Closure Reports   **Informative reports** and *closure reports* summarize completed work or research that does not result in action or recommendation. Informative reports often include the following elements:

- Introductory paragraph summarizing the problems or successes of the project.

- Purpose and scope section(s) giving the purpose of the report and indicating what aspects of the topic it covers.

- Chronological account outlining how the problem was discovered, what was done, and what the results were.

- Concluding paragraph offering suggestions for later action. The suggestions in a closure or informative report are not proved in detail.

Figure 15.8 presents an example of an informative report.

Closure reports also allow a firm to document the alternatives it has considered before choosing a final design.

Recommendation Reports   **Recommendation reports** evaluate two or more alternatives and recommend one of them. (Doing nothing or delaying action can be one of the alternatives.)

Recommendation reports normally open by explaining the decision to be made, listing the alternatives, and explaining the criteria. In the body of the report, each alternative will be evaluated according to the criteria using one of the two comparison/contrast patterns. Discussing each alternative separately is better when one alternative is clearly superior, when the criteria interact, or when each alternative is indivisible. If the choice depends on the weight given to each criterion, you may want to discuss each alternative under each criterion.

Whether your recommendation should come at the beginning or the end of the report depends on your audience and the culture of your organization. Most audiences want the "bottom line" up front. However, if the audience will find your recommendation hard to accept, you may want to delay your recommendation until the end of the report when you have given all your evidence.

Justification Reports   **Justification reports** justify a purchase, investment, hiring, or change in policy. If your organization has a standard format for justification reports, follow that format. If you can choose your headings and organization, use this pattern when your proposal will be easy for your audience to accept:

1. **Indicate what you're asking for and why it's needed.** Because the audience has not asked for the report, you must link your request to the organization's goals.
2. **Briefly give the background of the problem or need.**

Figure 15.8	An Informative Report Describing How a Company Solved a Problem

March 14, 2018

To: Donna S. Kienzler

From: Sara A. Ratterman *SAR*   *Informal short reports use
letter or memo format.*

First paragraph summarizes main points.   Subject: Recycling at Bike Nashbar

Two months ago, Bike Nashbar began recycling its corrugated cardboard boxes. The program was easy to implement and actually saves the company a little money compared to our previous garbage pickup.

Purpose and scope of report.   In this report, I will explain how and why Bike Nashbar's program was initiated, how the program works and what it costs, and why other businesses should consider similar programs.

Bold headings.

The Problem of Too Many Boxes and Not Enough Space in Bike Nashbar

Cause of problem.   Every week, Bike Nashbar receives about 40 large cardboard boxes containing bicycles and other merchandise. As many boxes as possible would be stuffed into the trash bin behind the building, which also had to accommodate all the other solid waste the shop produces. Boxes that didn't fit in the trash bin ended up lying around the shop, blocking doorways, and taking up space needed for customers' bikes. The trash bin was emptied only once a week, and by that time, even more boxes would have arrived.

Triple space before heading.

The Importance of Recycling Cardboard Rather Than Throwing It Away

Double space after heading.

Arranging for more trash bins or more frequent pickups would have solved the immediate problem at Bike Nashbar but would have done nothing to solve the problem created by throwing away so much trash in the first place.

Double space between paragraphs within heading.

Further seriousness of problem.   According to David Crogen, sales representative for Waste Management, Inc., 75% of all solid waste in Columbus goes to landfills. The amount of trash the city collects has increased 150% in the last five years. Columbus's landfill is almost full. In an effort to encourage people and businesses to recycle, the cost of dumping trash in the landfill is doubling from $4.90 a cubic yard to $9.90 a cubic yard next week. Next January, the price will increase again, to $12.95 a cubic yard. Crogen believes that the amount of trash can be reduced by cooperation between the landfill and the power plant and by recycling.

How Bike Nashbar Started Recycling Cardboard   *Capitalize first letter of major words in heading.*

Solution.   Waste Management, Inc., is the country's largest waste processor. After reading an article about how committed Waste Management, Inc., is to waste reduction and recycling, I decided to see whether Waste Management could recycle our boxes. Corrugated cardboard (which is what Bike Nashbar's boxes are made of) is almost 100% recyclable, so we seemed to be a good candidate for recycling.

| Figure 15.8 | An Informative Report Describing How a Company Solved a Problem *(Continued)* |

Donna S. Kienzler   *Reader's name,*
March 14, 2018   *date,*
Page 2   *page number.*

To get the service started, I met with a friendly sales rep, David Crogen, that same afternoon to discuss the service.

Waste Management, Inc., took care of all the details.   Two days later, Bike Nashbar was recycling its cardboard.

How the Service Works and What It Costs   *Talking heads tell reader what to expect in each section.*

Details of solution. Waste Management took away our existing 8-cubic-yard garbage bin and replaced it with two 4-yard bins. One of these bins is white and has "cardboard only" printed on the outside; the other is brown and is for all other solid waste. The bins are emptied once a week, with the cardboard going to the recycling plant and the solid waste going to the landfill or power plant.

Double space between paragraphs. Since Bike Nashbar was already paying more than $60 a week for garbage pickup, our basic cost stayed the same. (Waste Management can absorb the extra overhead only if the current charge is at least $60 a week.) The cost is divided 80/20 between the two bins: 80% of the cost pays for the bin that goes to the landfill and power plant; 20% covers the cardboard pickup. Bike Nashbar actually receives $5.00 for each ton of cardboard it recycles.

Each employee at Bike Nashbar is responsible for putting all the boxes he or she opens in the recycling bin. Employees must follow these rules:

- The cardboard must have the word "corrugated" printed on it, along with the universal recycling symbol.

Indented lists provide visual variety.
- The boxes must be broken down to their flattest form. If they aren't, they won't all fit in the bin and Waste Management would be picking up air when it could pick up solid cardboard. The more boxes that are picked up, the more money that will be made.

- No other waste except corrugated cardboard can be put in the recycling bin. Other materials could break the recycling machinery or contaminate the new cardboard.

- The recycling bin is to be kept locked with a padlock provided by Waste Management so that vagrants don't steal the cardboard and lose money for Waste Management and Bike Nashbar.

(Continued)

Figure 15.8	An Informative Report Describing How a Company Solved a Problem *(Concluded)*

Donna S. Kienzler
March 14, 2018
Page 3

Disadvantages
of
solution.

Minor Problems with Running the Recycling Program

The only problems we've encountered have been minor ones of violating the rules. Sometimes employees at the shop forget to flatten boxes, and air instead of cardboard gets picked up. Sometimes people forget to lock the recycling bin. When the bin is left unlocked, people do steal the cardboard, and plastic cups and other solid waste get dumped in the cardboard bin. I've posted signs where the key to the bin hangs, reminding employees to empty and fold boxes and relock the bin after putting cardboard in it. I hope this will turn things around and these problems will be solved.

Advantages of the Recycling Program

Advantages
of
solution.

The program is a great success. Now when boxes arrive, they are unloaded, broken down, and disposed of quickly. It is a great relief to get the boxes out of our way, and knowing that we are making a contribution to saving our environment builds pride in ourselves and Bike Nashbar.

Our company depends on a clean, safe environment for people to ride their bikes in. Now we have become part of the solution. By choosing to recycle and reduce the amount of solid waste our company generates, we can save money while gaining a reputation as a socially responsible business.

Why Other Companies Should Adopt Similar Programs

Argues
that her
company's
experience
is relevant
to other
companies.

Businesses and institutions in Franklin County currently recycle less than 4% of the solid waste they produce. David Crogen tells me he has over 8,000 clients in Columbus alone, and he acquires new ones every day. Many of these businesses can recycle a large portion of their solid waste at no additional cost. Depending on what they recycle, they even may get a little money back.

The environmental and economic benefits of recycling as part of a comprehensive waste reduction program are numerous. Recycling helps preserve our environment. We can use the same materials over and over again, saving natural resources such as trees, fuel, and metals and decreasing the amount of solid waste in landfills. By conserving natural resources, recycling helps the U.S. become less dependent on imported raw materials. Crogen predicts that Columbus will be on a 100% recycling system by the year 2024. I strongly hope that his prediction will come true.

3. **Explain each of the possible solutions.** For each, give the cost and the advantages and disadvantages.

4. **Summarize the action needed to implement your recommendation.** If several people will be involved, indicate who will do what and how long each step will take.

5. **Ask for the action you want.**

If the reader will be reluctant to grant your request, use this problem-solving pattern:

1. **Describe the organizational problem (which your request will solve).** Use specific examples to prove the seriousness of the problem.
2. **Show why easier or less expensive solutions will not solve the problem.**
3. **Present your solution impersonally.**
4. **Show that the disadvantages of your solution are outweighed by the advantages.**
5. **Summarize the action needed to implement your recommendation.** If several people will be involved, indicate who will do what and how long each step will take.
6. **Ask for the action you want.**

How much detail you need to give in a justification report depends on the corporate culture and on your audience's knowledge of and attitude toward your recommendation. Many organizations expect justification reports to be short—only one or two pages. Other organizations may expect longer reports with much more detailed budgets and a full discussion of the problem and each possible solution.

Report Style and Headings

LO 15-6

The advice about style from previous chapters also applies to reports, with three exceptions.

1. **Use a fairly formal style, without contractions or slang.**
2. **Avoid the word *you*.** In a document with multiple audiences, it will not be clear who *you* is. Instead, use the company's name.
3. **Include in the report all the definitions and documents needed to understand the recommendations.** The multiple audiences for reports include people who may consult the document months or years from now; they will not share your inside knowledge. Explain acronyms and abbreviations the first time they appear. Explain as much of the history or background of the problem as necessary. Add as appendices previous documents on which you are building.

Headings are single words, short phrases, or complete sentences that indicate the topic in each section. A heading must cover all of the material under it until the next heading. For example, *Cost of Tuition* cannot include the cost of books or of room and board; *College Costs* could include all costs. You can have just one paragraph under a heading or several pages. If you do have several pages between headings, you may want to consider using subheadings. Use subheadings only when you have two or more divisions within a main heading.

Topic headings focus on the structure of the report. As you can see from the following example, topic headings are vague and give little information.

```
Recommendation
Problem
    Situation 1
    Situation 2
Causes of the Problem
    Background
    Cause 1
    Cause 2
Recommended Solution
```

Talking heads, in contrast, tell the audience what to expect. Talking heads, like those in the examples in this chapter, provide a specific overview of each section and of the entire report.

> Recommended Reformulation for Vibe Bleach
> Problems in Maintaining Vibe's Granular Structure
>   Solidification during Storage and Transportation
>   Customer Complaints about "Blocks" of Vibe in Boxes
> Why Vibe Bleach "Cakes"
>   Vibe's Formula
>   The Manufacturing Process
>   The Chemical Process of Solidification
> Modifications Needed to Keep Vibe Flowing Freely

Headings must be parallel; that is, they must use the same grammatical structure. Subheads must be parallel to each other but do not necessarily have to be parallel to subheads under other headings.

Not parallel: Are Students Aware of VIP?
        Current Awareness among Undergraduate Students
        Graduate Students
    Ways to Increase Volunteer Commitment and Motivation
        We Must Improve Training and Supervision
        Can We Make Volunteers' Hours More Flexible?
        Providing Emotional Support to Volunteers
        Provide More Information about Community Needs and VIP Services

Parallel: Campus Awareness of VIP
        Current Awareness among Undergraduate Students
        Current Awareness among Graduate Students
    Ways to Increase Volunteer Commitment and Motivation
        Improving Training and Supervision
        Improving the Flexibility of Volunteers' Hours
        Providing Emotional Support to Volunteers
        Providing More Information about Community Needs and VIP Services

In a complicated report, you may need up to three levels of headings. Figure 15.9 illustrates one way to set up headings. Follow these standard conventions for headings:

- Use a subheading only when you have at least two subsections under the next higher heading.

- Avoid having a subhead come immediately after a heading. Instead, some text should follow the main heading before the subheading. (If you have nothing else to say, give an overview of the division.)

- Avoid having a heading or subheading all by itself at the bottom of the page. Instead, have at least one line (preferably two) of type. If there isn't room for a line of type under it, put the heading on the next page.

- Don't use a heading as the antecedent for a pronoun. Instead, repeat the noun.

Figure 15.9	Setting Up Headings in a Single-Spaced Document

Center the title; use bold and a bigger font.

Typing Titles and Headings for Reports   *14-point type.*

For the title of a report, use a bold font two point sizes bigger than the largest size in the body of the report. You may want to use an even bigger size or a different font to create an attractive title page. Capitalize the first word and all major words of the title.

Two empty spaces (triple space).

Heading for main divisions.

Typing Headings for Reports   *12-point type.*

One empty space (double space).

12-point type for body text.

Center main headings, capitalize the first and all major words, and use bold. In single-spaced text, leave two empty spaces before main headings and one after. Also leave an extra space between paragraphs. You also may want to use main headings that are one point size bigger than the body text.

This example provides just one example of each level of heading. However, in a real document, use headings only when you have at least two of them in the document. In a report, you'll have several.

Two empty spaces (triple space).

Typing Subheadings   *Bold; left margin.*

One empty space.

Most reports use subheadings under some main headings. Use subheadings only if you have at least two of them under a given heading. It is OK to use subheadings in some sections and not in others. Normally you'll have several paragraphs under a subheading, but it's OK to have just one paragraph under some subheadings.

12-point type.

Subheadings in a report use the same format as headings in letters and memos. Bold subheadings and set them at the left margin. Capitalize the first word and major words. Leave two empty spaces before the subheading and one empty space after it, before the first paragraph under the subheading. Use the same size font as the body paragraphs.

Period after heading.

One empty space (normal paragraph spacing).

Typing Further Subdivisions. For a very long report, you may need further subdivisions under a subheading. Bold the further subdivision, capitalizing the first word and major words, and end the phrase with a period. Begin the text on the same line. Use normal spacing between paragraphs. Further subdivide a subheading only if you have at least two such subdivisions under a given subheading. It is OK to use divisions under some subheadings and not under others.

Source Citation and Documentation

LO 15-7

In effective reports, sources are cited and documented smoothly and unobtrusively. **Citation** means attributing an idea or fact to its source in the body of the text: "According to the 2010 Census. . . ," "Jane Bryant Quinn argues that. . . ." In-text citations provide, in parentheses in the text, the source where the reference was found. Citing sources demonstrates your honesty and enhances your credibility.

Documentation means providing the bibliographic information readers would need to go back to the original source. The two usual means of documentation are notes and lists of references.

Failure to cite and document sources is **plagiarism,** the passing off of the words or ideas of others as one's own. Plagiarism can lead to nasty consequences, from failure of a class to losing your job. Now that curious people can type sentences into Google and find the sources, plagiarism is easier than ever to catch. Plagiarism is both unethical and illegal.

Another unethical practice that may occur when using sources is taking material out of context in such a way that the meaning of the material used is counter to the meaning of the material within its full context.

If you quote someone in your writing, you will need to use citation and documentation in addition to quotation marks. If you use the source's exact words, you'll use the name of the person you're citing in the body of the proposal or report; you'll put quotation marks around the quote; and you'll indicate the source in parentheses and provide a list of references, or you'll include an endnote. If you put the source's idea into your own words (**paraphrasing**), or if you condense or synthesize information, you don't need quotation marks, but you still need to tell whose idea it is and where you found it.

Long quotations (four typed lines or more) are used sparingly in business reports. Because many readers skip quotes, always summarize the main point of the quotation in a single sentence before the quotation itself. End the sentence with a colon, not a period, because it introduces the quote. Indent long quotations on the left to set them off from your text. Indented quotations do not need quotation marks; the indentation shows the reader that the passage is a quote.

Writing Progress Reports

LO 15-8

When you're assigned to a single project that will take a month or more, you'll probably be asked to file one or more progress reports. A progress report reassures the funding agency or employer that you're making progress and allows you and the agency or employer to resolve problems as they arise. Different readers may have different concerns. An instructor may want to know whether you'll have your report in by the due date. A client may be more interested in what you're learning about the problem. Adapt your progress report to the needs of the audience.

Poor writers of progress reports tend to focus on what they have done and say little about the value of their work. Good writers, on the other hand, spend less space writing about the details of what they've done but much more space explaining the value of their work for the organization.

When you write progress reports, use what you know about emphasis, positive tone, and you-attitude. Don't present every detail as equally important. Use emphasis techniques to stress the major ones.

In your report, try to exceed expectations in at least some small way. Perhaps your research is ahead of schedule or needed equipment arrived earlier than expected. However, do not present the good news by speculating on the reader's feelings; many readers find such statements offensive.

Poor: You will be happy to hear the software came a week early.

Better: The software came a week early, so Pat can start programming earlier than expected.

Remember that your audience for your report is usually in a position of power over you, so be careful what you say to them. Generally, it is not wise to blame them for project problems even if they are at fault.

Poor: We could not proceed with drafting the plans because you did not send us the specifications for the changes you want.

Better: Chris has prepared the outline for the plan. We are ready to start drafting as soon as we receive the specifications. Meanwhile, we are working on. . . .

Other Uses of Progress Reports

Progress reports can do more than just report progress. You can use progress reports to

- **Enhance your image.** Details about the number of documents you've read, people you've surveyed, or experiments you've conducted create a picture of a hardworking person doing a thorough job.

- **Float trial balloons.** Explain, "I could continue to do X [what you approved]; I could do Y instead [what I'd like to do now]." The detail in the progress report can help back up your claim. Even if the idea is rejected, you don't lose face because you haven't made a separate issue of the alternative.

- **Minimize potential problems.** As you do the work, it may become clear that implementing your recommendations will be difficult. In your regular progress reports, you can alert your boss or the funding agency to the challenges that lie ahead, enabling them to prepare psychologically and physically to act on your recommendations.

Subject lines for progress reports are straightforward. Specify the project on which you are reporting your progress.

> Subject: Progress on Developing a Marketing Plan for Fab Fashions

If you are submitting weekly or monthly progress reports on a long project, number your progress reports or include the time period in your subject line. Include information about the work completed since the last report and work to be completed before the next report.

Make your progress report as positive as you *honestly* can. You'll build a better image of yourself if you show that you can take minor problems in stride and that you're confident of your own abilities.

> The preliminary data sets were two days late because of a server crash. However, Nidex believes they will be back on schedule by next week. Past performance indicates their estimate is correct, and data analysis will be finished in two weeks, as originally scheduled.

Focus on your solutions to problems rather than the problems themselves:

Negative: Southern data points were corrupted, and that problem set us back three days in our data analysis.

Positive: Although southern data points were corrupted, the northern team was able to loan us Chris and Lee to fix the data set. Both teams are currently back on schedule.

In the example above, the problem with the southern data points is still noted because readers may want to know about it, but the solution to the problem is emphasized.

Do remember to use judicious restraint with your positive tone. Without details for support, glowing judgments of your own work may strike readers as ill-advised bragging, or maybe even dishonesty.

Overdone positive
tone, lack of support: Our data analysis is indicating some great new predictions; you will be very happy to see them.

Supported optimism: Our data analysis is beginning to show that coastal erosion may not be as extensive as we had feared; in fact, it may be almost 10% less than originally estimated. We should have firm figures by next week.

Progress reports can be organized in three ways: by chronology, task, and recommendation support. Some progress reports may use a combination: they may organize material chronologically within each task section, for instance.

Chronological Progress Reports

The chronological pattern of organization focuses on what you have done and what work remains.

1. **Summarize your progress in terms of your goals and your original schedule.** Use measurable statements.

   Poor: Progress has been slow.
   Better: Analysis of data sets is about one-third complete.

2. **Under the heading "Work Completed," describe what you have already done.** Be specific, both to support your claims in the first paragraph and to allow the reader to appreciate your hard work. Acknowledge the people who have helped you. Describe any serious obstacles you've encountered and tell how you've dealt with them.

   Poor: I have found many articles about Procter & Gamble on the web. I have had a few problems finding how the company keeps employees safe from chemical fumes.
   Better: On the web, I found Procter & Gamble's home page, its annual report, and mission statement. No one whom I interviewed could tell me about safety programs specifically at P&G. I have found seven articles about ways to protect workers against pollution in factories, but none mentions P&G.

3. **Under the heading "Work to Be Completed," describe the work that remains.** If you're more than three days late (for school projects) or two weeks late (for business projects), submit a new schedule showing how you will be able to meet the original deadline. You may want to discuss "Observations" or "Preliminary Conclusions" if you want feedback before writing the final report or if your reader has asked for substantive interim reports.

4. **Express your confidence in having the report ready by the due date.** If you are behind your original schedule, show why you think you can still finish the project on time.

Even in chronological reports, you need to do more than merely list work you have done. Show the value of that work and your prowess in achieving it, particularly your ability at solving problems. The student progress report in Figure 15.10 uses the chronological pattern of organization.

Task Progress Reports

In a task progress report, organize information under the various tasks you have worked on during the period. For example, a task progress report for a team report project might use the following headings:

Finding Background Information on the Web and in Print
Analyzing Our Survey Data
Working on the Introduction of the Report and the Appendices

Under each heading, the team could discuss the tasks it has completed and those that remain.

Figure 15.10   A Student Chronological Progress Report

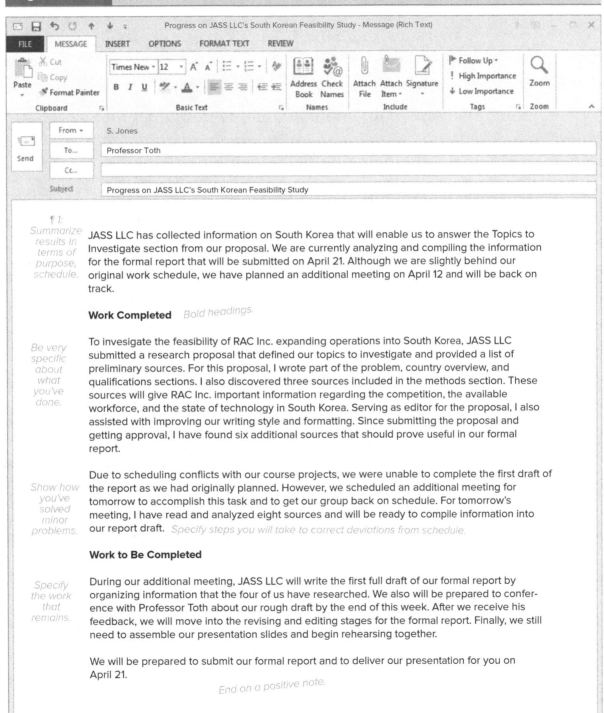

Subject: Progress on JASS LLC's South Korean Feasibility Study

¶ 1:
Summarize results in terms of purpose, schedule.

JASS LLC has collected information on South Korea that will enable us to answer the Topics to Investigate section from our proposal. We are currently analyzing and compiling the information for the formal report that will be submitted on April 21. Although we are slightly behind our original work schedule, we have planned an additional meeting on April 12 and will be back on track.

Work Completed   *Bold headings.*

Be very specific about what you've done.

To invesigate the feasibility of RAC Inc. expanding operations into South Korea, JASS LLC submitted a research proposal that defined our topics to investigate and provided a list of preliminary sources. For this proposal, I wrote part of the problem, country overview, and qualifications sections. I also discovered three sources included in the methods section. These sources will give RAC Inc. important information regarding the competition, the available workforce, and the state of technology in South Korea. Serving as editor for the proposal, I also assisted with improving our writing style and formatting. Since submitting the proposal and getting approval, I have found six additional sources that should prove useful in our formal report.

Show how you've solved minor problems.

Due to scheduling conflicts with our course projects, we were unable to complete the first draft of the report as we had originally planned. However, we scheduled an additional meeting for tomorrow to accomplish this task and to get our group back on schedule. For tomorrow's meeting, I have read and analyzed eight sources and will be ready to compile information into our report draft. *Specify steps you will take to correct deviations from schedule.*

Work to Be Completed

Specify the work that remains.

During our additional meeting, JASS LLC will write the first full draft of our formal report by organizing information that the four of us have researched. We also will be prepared to conference with Professor Toth about our rough draft by the end of this week. After we receive his feedback, we will move into the revising and editing stages for the formal report. Finally, we still need to assemble our presentation slides and begin rehearsing together.

We will be prepared to submit our formal report and to deliver our presentation for you on April 21.

End on a positive note.

Task progress reports are appropriate for large projects with distinct topics or projects.

Recommendation Progress Reports

Recommendation progress reports recommend action: increasing the funding or allotted time for a project, changing its direction, canceling a project that isn't working. When the recommendation will be easy for the reader to accept, use the direct request pattern of organization from Chapter 10. If the recommendation is likely to meet strong resistance, the problem-solving pattern, also in Chapter 10, may be more effective.

Oral Progress Reports

Not all progress reports are written. Boeing had to ground an entire fleet of its new 787 Dreamliner after discovering potential fire issues with the lithium-ion batteries. A few months into the investigation and repair stages, the Air Line Pilots' Association of Japan requested a progress report about the airplanes. The group wanted to be sure the root of the problem was discovered and that the planes would be safe to fly.

Boeing offered an oral progress report stating the problem with the batteries was not critical to flight operations, even though it was still unsure what caused the issue. Many companies offer the public progress reports on fixes or solutions when their products are discovered to be faulty.[33] You may be asked by a college professor or a supervisor to give an oral presentation that relates your progress towards completing a project.

Writing Formal Reports

LO 15-9

Formal reports are distinguished from informal letter and memo reports by their length and by their components. A full formal report may contain the components outlined in Figure 15.11 in the left column.

As Figure 15.11 shows, not every formal report necessarily has all components. The components you need will depend on the audiences and purposes of your report. In addition, some organizations call for additional components or arrange these components in a different order. As you read each section below, you may want to turn to the corresponding sections of the report in Figure 15.12 to see how the component is set up and how it relates to the total report. The example in Figure 15.12 shows segments of a formal report for illustration purposes; the full report can be viewed on this text's companion website.

Title Page

The title page of a report usually contains four items: the title of the report, the person or organization for whom the report is prepared, the person or group who prepared the report, and the release date. Some title pages also contain a brief summary or abstract of the contents of the report; some title pages contain decorative artwork.

The title of the report should be as informative as possible. Like subject lines, report titles are straightforward.

Poor title: New Plant Site

Better title: Eugene, Oregon, Site for the New Kemco Plant

Large organizations that issue many reports may use two-part titles to make it easier to search for reports electronically. For example, U.S. government report titles first give the agency sponsoring the report, then the title of that particular report.

Figure 15.11	The Components in a Report Can Vary

More formal ←	→ Less formal	
Cover	Title Page	Introduction
Title Page	Table of Contents	Body
Transmittal	Executive Summary	Conclusions
Table of Contents	Body	Recommendations
List of Illustrations	Introduction	
Executive Summary	Body	
Body	Conclusions	
Introduction	Recommendations	
Background		
Body		
Conclusions		
Recommendations		
References/Works Cited		
Appendices		
Questionnaires		
Interviews		
Complex Tables		
Computer Printouts		
Related Documents		

Small Business Administration: Management Practices Have Improved for the Women's Business Center Program

In many cases, the title will state the recommendation in the report: "Why the United Nations Should Establish a Seed Bank." However, the title should omit recommendations when

- The reader will find the recommendations hard to accept.
- Putting all the recommendations in the title would make it too long.
- The report does not offer recommendations.

If the title does not contain the recommendation, it normally indicates what problem the report tries to solve or the topic the report discusses.
Eliminate any unnecessary words:

Wordy: Report of a Study on Ways to Market Life Insurance to Urban Professional People Who Are in Their Mid-40s

Better: Marketing Life Insurance to the Mid-40s Urban Professional

The identification of the receiver of the report normally includes the name of the person who will make a decision based on the report, his or her job title, the organization's name, and its location (city, state, and zip code). Government reports often omit the person's name and simply give the organization that authorized the report.

Figure 15.12   Segments of a Formal Report

Slated for Success

Use a large font size for the main title.

Center all text on the title page.

RAC Inc. Expanding to South Korea

Use a slightly smaller font size for the subtitle.

Prepared for *No punctuation.*

Ms. Katie Nichols
CEO of RAC Inc.
Grand Rapids, Michigan, 49503

Name of audience, job title, organization, city, state, and zip code.

Prepared by *No punctuation.*

JASS LLC
Jordan Koole
Alex Kuczera
Shannon Jones
Sean Sterling
Allendale, MI 49401

Name of writer(s), organization, city, state, and zip code.

Month Day, Year *Date report is released.*

Figure 15.12   Segments of a Formal Report   *(Continued)*

The students in this group designed their own letterhead, assuming they were doing this report as consultants.

This letter uses block format.

JASS LLC
1 Campus Drive
Allendale, MI 49401

Month Day, Year   *Enter current date.*

Ms. Katie Nichols, CEO
RAC Inc.
1253 West Main Street
Grand Rapids, MI 49503

Dear Ms. Nichols:

In paragraph 1, release the report. Note when and by whom the report was authorized. Note the report's purpose.

In this document you will find the report that you requested in March. We have provided key information and made recommendations on a plan of action for the expansion of a RAC Inc. slate tablet manufacturing plant into South Korea.

Give recommendations or thesis of report.

Our analysis of expansion into South Korea covered several important areas that will help you decide whether or not RAC Inc. should expand and build a manufacturing plant in South Korea. To help us make our decision, we looked at the government, economy, culture, and, most important, the competition. South Korea is a technologically advanced country and its economy is on the rise. Our research has led us to recommend expansion into South Korea. We strongly believe that RAC Inc. can be profitable in the long run and become a successful business in South Korea.

Note sources that were helpful.

JASS LLC used several resources in forming our analysis. The Central Intelligence Agency's *World Factbook*, the U.S. Department of State, World Business Culture, and Kwintessential were all helpful in answering our research questions.

Thank the audience for the opportunity to do the research.

Thank you for choosing JASS to conduct the research into South Korea. If you have any further questions about the research or recommendation, please contact us (616-331-1100, info@jass.com) and we will be happy to answer any questions referring to your possible expansion into South Korea at no charge. JASS would be happy to conduct any further research on this issue or any other projects that RAC Inc. is considering. We look forward to building on our relationship with you in the future.

Sincerely,

Jordan Koole

Jordan Koole
JASS Team Member

Offer to answer questions about the report.

Center inital page numbers at the bottom of the page. Use a lowercase roman numeral for initial pages of report.

i

(Continued)

Figure 15.12	Segments of a Formal Report *(Continued)*

Main headings are parallel, as are subheadings within a section.

Table of Contents

Table of Contents does not list itself.

Capitalize first letter of each major word in headings.

Indentions show level of heading at a glance.

Use lowercase roman numerals for initial pages.

Introduction begins on page I.

Line up right margin (justify).

Add a "List of Illustrations" at the bottom of the page or on a separate page if the report has many visuals.

List of Illustrations

Figures and tables are numbered independently.

Figure 15.12	Segments of a Formal Report *(Continued)*

Report title.

Slated for Success

Many audiences read only the Executive Summary, not the report. Include enough information to give audiences the key points you make.

RAC Inc. Expanding to South Korea

Executive Summary

Start with recommendation or thesis.

To continue growth and remain competitive on a global scale, RAC Inc. should expand its business operations into South Korea. The country is a technologically advanced nation and would provide a strong base for future expansion. Slate tablet competitors of RAC Inc. in South Korea are doing quite well. Because RAC Inc. can compete with them in the United States, we are confident that RAC can remain on par with them in this new market.

The research we have done for this project indicates that this expansion will be profitable, primarily because the South Korean economy is flourishing. The workforce in South Korea is large, and finding talented employees to help set up and run the facility will be easy. In addition, the regulations and business structure are similar to those in the United States and will provide an easy transition into this foreign nation. The competition will be fierce; however, we believe that RAC Inc. will be profitable because of its track record with the Notion Tab in the United States.

Provide brief support for recommendations.

To ensure a successful expansion, JASS LLC recommends the following:

1. **RAC Inc. should establish its headquarters and manufacturing plant in Busan.**
   - Purchase a building to have a place to begin manufacturing the Notion Tab.
   - Educate RAC employees about South Korean culture and business practices before they begin working directly with South Koreans to avoid being disrespectful.
   - Explore hiring South Koreans; the available workforce is large.
   - Ensure that the Notion name is appropriate when translated into Korean. If not, change the name to better market the product.
   - Market and sell the product in both Busan and Seoul.

2. **After one year RAC should determine the acceptance and profitability of the expansion.**
   - Conduct a customer satisfaction survey with people who purchased the Notion Tab living in Seoul and Busan to determine the acceptance of the product.
   - Compare and contrast first-year sales with a competitor's similar product.

3. **If the tablet is competitive and profitable, RAC Inc. should expand its product line into all large cities in South Korea.**
   - To gain an edge on the competition, create a marketing plan that will offer the Notion Tab at some discount in the new cities.
   - Explore integrating other RAC Inc. products into South Korea. These products also could be manufactured at the new manufacturing plant in Busan.

Language in the Executive Summary can come from the report. Make sure any repeated language is well-written!

The Abstract or Executive Summary contains the logical skeleton of the report: the recommendation(s) and supporting evidence.

iii

(Continued)

Figure 15.12   Segments of a Formal Report *(Continued)*

A running header is optional. This one includes the main title on the left and the page number on the right.

Slated for Success   1

Introduction   *Center main headings.*

To avoid getting left behind by competition in global expansion, RAC Inc. has contacted JASS LLC to perform an analysis about expanding into South Korea. JASS has researched South Korea to determine if RAC Inc. will be successful in expanding into this foreign market.

"Purpose" and "Scope" can be separate sections if either is long.

Purpose and Scope

RAC Inc. is a successful business in the United States and has had substantial growth over the last five years. With its competitors beginning to venture into foreign markets to gain more global market share, RAC Inc. is looking to expand into the international market as well. The purpose of our research is to decide whether or not RAC Inc. should expand its business into South Korea. *Give topics in the order you'll*

Topics in "Scope" section should match those in the report.

Tell what you discuss and how thoroughly you discuss each topic. This report will cover several topics about South Korea including their government, economy, culture, technology, market competition, and possible locations. Our research will not include any on-site research in South Korea. We also are not dealing directly with the South Korean people. *discuss them.*

List any relevant topics you do not discuss.

Assumptions cannot be proved. But if they are wrong, the report's recommendation may no longer be valid.

Assumptions

The recommendations that we make are based on the assumption that the relationship between North and South Korea will remain the same as of the first part of 2018. We also are assuming that the technological state of South Korea will remain constant and not suffer from a natural disaster or an economic crash. In addition, we assume that the process of expansion into South *If you collected original data (surveys,* Korea is the same with RAC Inc. as it has been with other American companies. Another assumption that we are making is that RAC Inc. has a good name brand and is competitive in the United States with Apple, Samsung, LG, and other electronic companies.

interviews, and observations), tell how you chose your subjects, what kind of sample you used, and when you collected the information. This report does not use original data; it just provides

Methods   *a brief discussion of significant sources.*

The information in our report comes from online sources and reference books. We found several good sources, but the best information that we obtained came from The Central Intelligence Agency's *World Factbook*, the U.S. Department of State, World Business Culture, and Kwintessential. These resources have given us much useful information on which we have based our recommendation.

These limitations are listed because the students correctly assumed their instructor would want to know them. Limitations such as these would never be listed in a real consulting report, because they would disqualify the firm.

Limitations   *If your report has limitations, state them.*

The information in the report was limited to what we retrieved from our sources. We were not able to travel to South Korea to conduct on-site research. JASS also was limited by the language barrier that exists between the United States and South Korea. Other limitations exist because we have not been immersed in the Korean culture and have not gotten input from South Koreans on the expansion of companies into their country.

Definitions

There are a few terms that we use throughout the report that we would like to explain beforehand. The first term is slate tablet, an industry term, which from this point on is referred to as a tablet. *Define key terms your audience will need to read your report.* Another term we would like to clarify is the city Busan. Some sources referred to it as Pusan. From this point forward, we use only Busan. An abbreviation we use is GDP, which stands for gross domestic product. The South Korean and United States Free Trade Agreement signed in 2007 is abbreviated as KORUS FTA, its official name in the United States government.

Figure 15.12	Segments of a Formal Report *(Continued)*

Slated for Success   2

This section outlines the criteria used to make the overall recommendation.

Criteria

JASS LLC has established criteria that need to be favorable before we give a positive recommendation about South Korea. The criteria include the government, economy, culture, and market competition. We have weighted our criteria by percentages:

- Government = 20%
- Economy = 20%
- South Korean culture = 20%
- Market possibilities and competitors = 40%

We will examine each separately and give each criterion a favorable or not favorable recommendation. Market competition is weighted the heaviest and must be favorable or somewhat favorable for us to give a positive recommendation. Market competition can be given a favorable, nonfavorable, or somewhat favorable recommendation based on various external factors in the marketplace. We need a minimum of a 70% total to give a positive recommendation overall.

Triple-space before major headings and double-space after them.

Government
Headings must cover everything under that heading until the next one.

Begin most paragraphs with topic sentences.

South Korea is recognized as a republic government by the rest of the world. A republic government is a democracy where the people have supreme control over the government (South Korea: Political structure, 2018). This foundation makes it similar to the United States' democracy. There is a national government as well as provincial-level governments (similar to state-level governments) with different branches. Larger cities, like Seoul and Busan, have their own city government as well. The government is considered multipartied and has multiple parties vying for positions (South Korea: Political structure, 2018). The Republic of South Korea shares its power among three branches of government, thus providing checks and balances inside the government. The three branches of the government are the presidential, legislative, and judicial (U.S. Department of State, 2018). *List subtopics in the order in which they are discussed.* In this section, we will discuss government control, business regulations, taxes, free trade, and concerns about North Korea.

Capitalize all main words of headings and subheadings.

Government Control

It's OK to have subheadings under some headings and not others.

The Grand National Party (GNP) controls the major policy-making branches of the government. Winning control of the National Assembly in April 2008 (South Korea: Political structure, 2009), the GNP is considered the conservative party in South Korea and is similar to the Republican Party in the United States. Its policies favor conservatism and are considered pro-business (Grand National Party, 2018). RAC Inc. should not expect much interference from the government with their business venture into South Korea, unless the GNP loses control of the government in the next election.

Use subheadings only when you have two or more sections.

Period goes outside of parenthesis.

Business Regulations

South Korea ranks 16th on the ease of doing business index (World Bank Group, 2018a). This index measures the regulations that a government imposes on businesses and how easy it is to start and run a business in a given country. Factors this index measures include the ease of starting a business, doing taxes, and enforcing contracts. For comparison, the United States is ranked fifth on this list (World Bank Group, 2018b). While there are more regulations on business in South Korea, they are still near the top of the list. The relatively low rating on regulation can be due in part to the Grand National Party controlling the government. There are a few general regulations that RAC Inc. should know before going into South Korea. For more specific business regulations, RAC Inc. may need to do further research before expanding.

(Continued)

Figure 15.12   Segments of a Formal Report   *(Continued)*

Slated for Success   5

Since the 1960s, the GDP has had only one dip, a result of the Asian Economic crisis in the late 1990s that affected most Asian countries. In 2004, South Korea became a part of the trillion-dollar economy club, making them one of the world's top economies (Central Intelligence Agency, 2018).

However the economy faces challenges in maintaining steady growth in the future. These challenges include an aging population, inflexible workforce, and an overdependence on exports. Right now, though, South Korea's economy continues to grow. Their industrial production growth rate was 12.1% in 2016, making them the 11th fastest-growing nation in the production industry. In 2016, their GDP grew by 6.8%, the 28th largest growth of GDP in the world (Central Intelligence Agency, 2018). This growth makes South Korea a viable place of expansion.

Refer to figure in the text. Tell what main point it makes.

GDP and Other Important Economic Measures

The official GDP of South Korea was $1.41 trillion in 2018 (Central Intelligence Agency, 2018). This GDP is the 13th highest in the world. GDP measures the total value of goods produced by a country's economy. Figure 2 shows a comparison of GDP growth rates for top countries. GDP per capita in South Korea is $30,200, which is the 44th largest in the world. This measures the output of goods and services per person in the country. It is also an indicator of the average worker's

Number figures consecutively throughout the report; number tables and figures independently.

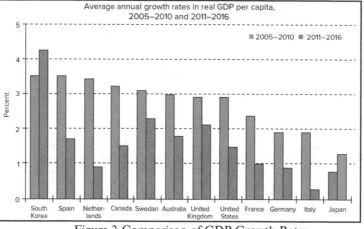

Label both axes of graphs. See Chapter 13 for more information on creating data displays.

Figure 2: Comparison of GDP Growth Rates
(Source: U.S. Bureau of Labor Statistics, 2018)
Cite source of data.

Figure captions need to be descriptive.

salary in the country. South Korea only has 15% of their population living in poverty. They have a labor force of 24.62 million, which is the 25th largest labor force in the world, with an unemployment rate of 3.3% (Central Intelligence Agency, 2018). These numbers need to be considered when starting operations in South Korea. South Korea also has a service-driven economy with 57.6% of the country's GDP output in the service industry and 68.4% of the labor force employed in the service industry (Central Intelligence Agency, 2018). All of these numbers and high world rankings of the economic measures show that South Korea has a stable and healthy economy where a business could prosper.

Figure 15.12	Segments of a Formal Report *(Continued)*

Slated for Success   11

Conclusions repeat points made   *Some companies ask for*
in the report. Recommendations   **Conclusions and Recommendations**   *Conclusions and Recommendations*
are actions the audience   *at the beginning of the report.*
should take.

All of the research that we have done supports the decision to expand into South Korea. The
government, economy, and culture criteria all received favorable recommendations for a total of
60%. Market possibilities and competition received half support for an additional 20%. Together,
South Korea has earned 80% based on our criteria.

Therefore, we believe that RAC Inc. could profitably expand into South Korea. The Notion Tab is a
high-quality product, and it will be easily integrated into this technologically advanced county. In
conclusion, we recommend that RAC Inc. should expand into South Korea.

To ensure a successful expansion, JASS LLC recommends the following:

1. RAC Inc. should establish its headquarters and manufacturing plant in Busan.
- Purchase a building to have a place to begin manufacturing the Notion Tab.
- Educate RAC employees about South Korean culture and business practices before they
  begin working directly with South Koreans to avoid being disrespectful.

Numbering points
makes it easier
for the audience • Explore hiring South Koreans; the available workforce is large.
to follow and   • Ensure that the Notion name is appropriate when translated into Korean. If not, change
discuss them.   the name to better market the product.
- Market and sell the product in both Busan and Seoul.

2.   After one year RAC should determine the acceptance and profitability of the
   expansion.
Make sure all   • Conduct a customer satisfaction survey with people who purchased the Notion Tab living
items   in Seoul and Busan to determine the acceptance of the product.
in a list are   • Compare and contrast first-year sales with a competitor's similar product.
parallel.

3. If the tablet is competitive and profitable, RAC Inc. should expand its product
   line into all large cities in South Korea.
- To gain an edge on the competition, create a marketing plan that will offer the Notion Tab
  at some discount in the new cities.
- Explore integrating other RAC Inc. products into South Korea. These products also could
  be manufactured at the new manufacturing plant in Busan.

Because many readers turn to the "Recommendations" first, provide enough information so that the
reason is clear all by itself. The ideas in this section must be logical extensions of the points made
and supported in the body of the report.

(Continued)

Figure 15.12	Segments of a Formal Report *(Concluded)*

Slated for Success   12

References   *This report uses APA citation style.*

Advameg, Inc. (2018). Culture of South Korea. *Countries and Their Cultures.*
    Retrieved April 2, 2018, from http://www.everyculture.com/Ja-Ma/South-Korea.html.

AFP. (2010, December 5). U.S., South Korea sign sweeping free-trade agreement. *Taipei Times.*
    Retrieved from http://www.taipeitimes.com/News/front/archives/2010/12/05/200349014.

Central Intelligence Agency. (2018). *The world factbook: South Korea.* Retrieved March 18, 2018,
    from https://www.cia.gov/library/publications/the-world-factbook/geos/ks.html#.

Grand National Party. (2018, April 1). In *Wikipedia.* Retrieved April 6, 2018, from
    http://en.wikipedia.org/wiki/Grand_National_Party.

iPad 2 specs. (2011). *OS X Daily.* Retrieved from http://osxdaily.com/2011/03/02/ipad-2-specs.   *Compare this list of sources with those in the proposal.*

Koreans love their mobile phones. (2018, January 28). *Korean JoongAng Daily.* Retrieved from   *Notice how the authors had to adjust the list as they completed research.*
    http://joongangdaily.joins.com/article/view.asp?aid=2900275.

KRWUS. (2018). *MSN Money.* Retrieved April 10, 2018, from
    http://investing.money.msn.com/investments/currency-exchange-rates/?symbol=%2fKRWUS.

KT. (2018, April 1). In *Wikipedia.* Retrieved April 2, 2018, from
    http://en.wikipedia.org/wiki/KT_%28telecommunication_company%29.

Kwintessential. (2018). *South Korea: Language, culture, customers and etiquette.* Retrieved from
    http://www.kwintessential.co.uk/resources/global-etiquette/south-korea-country-profile.html.

LG Corp. (2018, April 1). In *Wikipedia.* Retrieved April 2, 2018, from http://en.wikipedia.org/wiki/LG.

LG Slate full specifications and product details. (2018, February 2). *Gadgetian.* Retrieved
    April 3, 2018, from http://gadgetian.com/7069/lg-g-slate-t-mobile-specs-price/.

LG Telecom. (2017, November 29). In *Wikipedia.* Retrieved April 2, 2018, from
    http://en.wikipedia.org/wiki/LG_Telecom.

Life in Korea. (n.d.). *Cultural spotlight.* Retrieved March 31, 2018, from
    http://www.lifeinkorea.com/Culture/spotlight.cfm.

List all the printed and online sources cited in your report.
Do not list sources you used for background but did not cite.

Sources for this report continue onto a second page.

If the report is prepared primarily by one person, the "Prepared by" section will have that person's name, his or her title, the organization, and its location (city, state, and zip code). In internal reports, the organization and location are usually omitted if the report writer works at the headquarters office.

Government reports normally list the names of all people who wrote the report, using a separate sheet of paper if the group working on the report is large. Practices in business differ. In some organizations, all the names are listed; in others, the division to which they belong is listed; in still others, the name of the chair of the group appears.

The **release date,** the date the report will be released to the public, is usually the date the report is scheduled for discussion by the decision makers. The report is frequently due four to six weeks before the release date so that the decision makers can review the report before the meeting.

If you have the facilities and the time, try using type variations, color, and artwork to create a visually attractive and impressive title page. However, a plain typed page is acceptable. The format in Figure 15.12 will enable you to create an acceptable typed title page.

Letter or Memo of Transmittal

Use a letter of transmittal if you are not a regular employee of the organization for which you prepare the report; use a memo if you are a regular employee.

The transmittal has several purposes: to transmit the report, to orient the reader to the report, and to build a good image of the report and of the writer. An informal writing style is appropriate for a transmittal even when the style in the report is more formal. A professional transmittal helps you create a good image of yourself and enhances your credibility. Personal statements are appropriate in the transmittal, even though they would not be acceptable in the report itself.

Organize the transmittal in this way:

1. **Transmit the report.** Tell when and by whom it was authorized and the purpose it was to fulfill.
2. **Summarize your conclusions and recommendations.** If the recommendations will be easy for the audience to accept, put them early in the transmittal. If they will be difficult, summarize the findings and conclusions before the recommendations.
3. **Mention any points of special interest in the report. Show how you surmounted minor problems you encountered in your investigation. Thank people who helped you.** These optional items can build goodwill and enhance your credibility.
4. **Point out additional research that is necessary, if any.** Sometimes your recommendation cannot be implemented until further work is done. If you'd be interested in doing that research or if you'd like to implement the recommendations, say so.
5. **Thank the audience for the opportunity to do the work and offer to answer questions.** Provide contact information. Even if the report has not been fun to do, expressing satisfaction in doing the project is expected. Saying that you'll answer questions about the report is a way of saying that you won't charge the audience your normal hourly fee to answer questions (one more reason to make the report clear!).

The letter of transmittal on page i of Figure 15.12 uses this pattern of organization.

Table of Contents

In the table of contents, list the headings exactly as they appear in the body of the report. If the report is fewer than 25 pages, you'll probably list all the levels of headings. In a long report, pick a level and put all the headings at that level and above in the table of contents.

Some software programs, such as Microsoft Word, offer features that automatically generate a table of contents (and a list of illustrations) if you apply the style feature when you generate headings.

Page ii of Figure 15.12 shows the table of contents.

List of Illustrations

A list of illustrations enables audiences to refer to your visuals.

Report visuals comprise both tables and figures. *Tables* are words or numbers arranged in rows and columns. *Figures* are everything else: bar graphs, pie charts, flow charts, maps, drawings, photographs, computer printouts, and so on. Tables and figures may be numbered independently, so you may have both a Table 1 and a Figure 1. In a report with just two kinds of visuals, such as maps and graphs, the visuals are sometimes called Map 1 and Graph 1. Whatever you call the illustrations, list them in the order in which they appear in the report; give the name of each visual as well as its number.

See Chapter 13 for information about how to design and label visuals and data displays.

Executive Summary

An **executive summary** or **abstract** tells the audience what the document is about. It summarizes the recommendation of the report and the reasons for the recommendation or describes the topics the report discusses and indicates the depth of the discussion. A good executive summary should be concise but also should clearly describe the most important elements of the report for the audience who will read only this section of the report.

Abstracts generally use a more formal style than other forms of business writing. Avoid contractions and colloquialisms. Try to avoid using the second-person *you*. Because reports may have many different audiences, *you* may become inaccurate. It's acceptable to use exactly the same words in the abstract and the report.

Summary abstracts present the logic skeleton of the report: the thesis or recommendation and its proof. Use a summary abstract to give the most useful information in the shortest space.

> To market life insurance to mid-40s urban professionals, Interstate Fidelity Insurance should advertise in upscale publications and use direct mail.
>
> Network TV and radio are not cost-efficient for reaching this market. This group comprises a small percentage of the prime-time network TV audience and a minority of most radio station listeners. They tend to discard newspapers and general-interest magazines quickly, but many of them keep upscale periodicals for months or years. Magazines with high percentages of readers in this group include *Architectural Digest, Bon Appetit, Forbes, Golf Digest, Metropolitan Home, Southern Living,* and *Smithsonian.*
>
> Any advertising campaign needs to overcome this group's feeling that they already have the insurance they need. One way to do this would be to encourage them to check the coverage their employers provide and to calculate the cost of their children's expenses through college graduation. Insurance plans that provide savings and tax benefits as well as death benefits also might be appealing.

One way to start composing an abstract is to write a sentence outline. A **sentence outline** not only uses complete sentences rather than words or phrases, but also contains the thesis sentence or recommendation and the evidence that proves that point. Combine the sentences into paragraphs, adding transitions if necessary, and you'll have your abstract.

Descriptive abstracts indicate what topics the report covers and how deeply it goes into each topic, but they do not summarize what the report says about each topic. Phrases that describe the report ("this report covers," "it includes," "it summarizes," "it concludes") are marks of a descriptive abstract. An additional mark of a descriptive abstract is that the audience can't tell what the report says about the topics it covers.

This report recommends ways Interstate Fidelity Insurance could market insurance to mid-40s urban professionals. It examines demographic and psychographic profiles of the target market. Survey results are used to show attitudes toward insurance. The report suggests some appeals that might be successful with this market.

Introduction

The **introduction** of the report always contains a statement of purpose and scope and may include all the parts in the following list:

- **Purpose.** The purpose statement identifies the problem the report addresses, the technical investigations it summarizes, and the rhetorical purpose (to explain, to recommend).

- **Scope.** The scope statement identifies how broad an area the report surveys. For example, Company XYZ is losing money on its line of computers. Does the report investigate the quality of the computers? The advertising campaign? The cost of manufacturing? The demand for computers? A scope statement allows the reader to evaluate the report on appropriate grounds.

- **Assumptions.** Assumptions in a report are like assumptions in geometry: statements whose truth you assume and that you use to prove your final point. If they are wrong, the conclusion will be wrong too.

  For example, to plan cars that will be built five years from now, an automobile manufacturer commissions a report on young adults' attitudes toward cars. The recommendations would be based on assumptions both about gas prices and about the economy. If gas prices radically rose or fell, the kinds of cars young adults wanted would change. If there were a major recession, people wouldn't be able to buy new cars.

  Almost all reports require assumptions. A good report spells out its assumptions so that audiences can make decisions more confidently.

- **Methods.** If you conducted surveys, focus groups, or interviews, you need to tell how you chose your subjects and how, when, and where they were interviewed. If the discussion of your methodology is more than a paragraph or two, you should probably make it a separate section in the body of the report rather than including it in the introduction. Reports based on scientific experiments usually put the methods section in the body of the report, not in the introduction.

  If your report is based solely on library or online research, provide a brief description of significant sources.

- **Limitations.** Limitations make your recommendations less valid or valid only under certain conditions. Limitations usually arise because time or money constraints haven't permitted full research. For example, a campus pizza restaurant considering expanding its menu may ask for a report but not have enough money to take a random sample of students and townspeople. Without a random sample, the writer cannot generalize from the sample to the larger population.

  Many recommendations are valid only for a limited time. For instance, a campus store wants to know what kinds of clothing will appeal to college men. The recommendations will remain valid for only a short time: two years from now, styles and tastes may have changed, and the clothes that would sell best now may no longer be in demand.

- **Criteria.** The criteria section outlines the factors or standards that you are considering and the relative importance of each. If a company is choosing a city for a new office, is the cost of office space more or less important than the availability of skilled workers? Check with your audience before you write the draft to make sure that your criteria match those of your audiences.

- **Definitions.** Many reports define key terms in the introduction. For instance, a report on unauthorized Internet use by employees might define what is meant by "unauthorized use."

A report on the corporate dress code might define such codes broadly to include general appearance, so it could include items such as tattoos, facial piercings, and general cleanliness. Also, if you know that some members of your primary or secondary audience will not understand technical terms, define them. If you have only a few definitions, you can put them in the introduction. If you have many terms to define, put a **glossary** in an appendix. Refer to it in the introduction so that audiences know that you've provided it.

Background or History

Formal reports usually have a section that gives the background of the situation or the history of the problem. Even though the current audience for the report probably knows the situation, reports are filed and consulted years later. These later audiences will probably not know the background, although it may be crucial for understanding the options that are possible.

In some cases, the history section may cover many years. For example, a report recommending that a U.S. hotel chain open hotels in Romania may give the history of that country for at least several decades. In other cases, the background section is much briefer, covering only a few years or even just the immediate situation.

The purpose of most reports is rarely to provide a history of the problem. Do not let the background section achieve undue length.

Body

The body of the report is usually its longest section. Analyze causes of the problem and offer possible solutions. Present your argument with all its evidence and data. Data that are necessary to follow the argument are included with appropriate visuals, data displays, and explanatory text. Extended data sets, such as large tables and long questionnaires, are generally placed in appendices. It is particularly important in the body that you use headings to help your audience navigate your material. Remember to cite your sources and to refer in the text to all visuals and appendices.

Conclusions and Recommendations

Conclusions summarize points you have made in the body of the report; **recommendations** are action items that would solve or ameliorate the problem. These sections are often combined if they are short: "Conclusions and Recommendations." No new information should be included in this section.

Many audiences turn to the recommendations section first; some organizations ask that recommendations be presented early in the report. Number the recommendations to make it easy for people to discuss them. If the recommendations will seem difficult or controversial, give a brief paragraph of rationale after each recommendation. If they'll be easy for the audience to accept, you can simply list them without comments or reasons. The recommendations also will be in the executive summary and perhaps in the title and the transmittal.

Appendices

Appendices provide additional materials that the careful audience may want. Common items are transcripts of interviews, copies of questionnaires, tallies of answers to questions, complex tables, printouts of original or difficult-to-find source material, and previous reports.

Summary by Learning Objectives

LO 15-1   **Recognize varieties of reports.**

- Information reports collect data for the reader.
- Analytical reports present and interpret data.
- Recommendation reports recommend action or a solution.

LO 15-2   **Define report problems.**

- A good report problem in business meets the following criteria:
  - The problem is real, important enough to be worth solving, and narrow but challenging.
  - The audience for the report is real and able to implement the recommended action.
  - The data, evidence, and facts are sufficient to document the severity of the problem, sufficient to prove that the recommendation will solve the problem, available to *you,* and comprehensible to *you.*
- A good purpose statement must make three things clear:
  - The organizational problem or conflict.
  - The specific technical questions that must be answered to solve the problem.
  - The rhetorical purpose (to explain, to recommend, to request, to propose) that the report is designed to achieve.

LO 15-3   **Employ various research strategies.**

- Use indexes and directories to find information about a specific company or topic.
- To decide whether to use a website as a source in a research project, evaluate the site's authors, objectivity, information, audience, and revision date.
- A survey questions a large group of people, called respondents or subjects. A questionnaire is a written list of questions that people fill out. An interview is a structured conversation with someone who will be able to give you useful information.
- Because surveys can be used to show almost anything, people need to be careful when analyzing the results of surveys or designing their own. These are questions commonly asked about surveys:
  - Who did the survey and who paid for it?
  - How many people were surveyed and how were they chosen?
  - How was the survey conducted?
  - What was the response rate?
  - What questions were asked?

- Good questions ask just one thing, are phrased neutrally, avoid making assumptions about the respondent, and mean the same thing to different people.
- A convenience sample is a group of subjects who are easy to get. A judgment sample is a group of people whose views seem useful. In a random sample, each object in the population theoretically has an equal chance of being chosen. A sample is random only if a formal, approved random sampling method is used. Otherwise, unconscious bias can exist.
- Qualitative research also may use interviews, focus groups, online networks, and technology.

LO 15-4   **Choose information for reports.**

- Choose information to include that your audience needs to know to make a decision. Figuring out whether your audience is supportive, neutral, or skeptical will guide you on how much information you need to include.
- Determine what information to put in the body of the report or in appendices.

LO 15-5   **Organize reports.**

Choose an appropriate organizational pattern for your information and purposes. The most common patterns are comparison/contrast; problem–solution; elimination of alternatives; SWOT analysis; general to particular, particular to general; geographic or spatial; functional; and chronological.

LO 15-6   **Present information effectively in reports.**

Reports use the same style as other business documents, with three exceptions:

1. Reports use a more formal style, without contractions or slang, than do many letters and memos.
2. Reports rarely use the word *you.*
3. Reports should include all the definitions and documents needed to understand the recommendations.

Headings are single words, short phrases, or complete sentences that describe all of the material under them until the next heading. Talking heads tell the audience what to expect in each section.

Headings must use the same grammatical structure. Subheads under a heading must be parallel to each other but do not necessarily have to be parallel to subheads under other headings.

LO 15-7   **Document sources correctly.**

- Citation means attributing an idea or fact to its source in the body of the report.

■ Documentation means providing the bibliographic information readers would need to go back to the original source.

LO 15-8   Write progress reports.

■ Progress reports let people know how you are coming on a project.

■ Positive emphasis in progress reports creates an image of yourself as a capable, confident worker.

■ Progress reports may be organized by chronology, task, or recommendation support.

LO 15-9   Prepare the different components of formal reports.

■ The title page of a report usually contains four items: the title of the report, for whom the report is prepared, by whom it is prepared, and the date.

■ If the report is 25 pages or fewer, list all the headings in the table of contents. In a long report, pick a level and put all the headings at that level and above in the contents.

■ Organize the transmittal in this way:
   1. Release the report.
   2. Summarize your conclusions and recommendations.
   3. Mention any points of special interest in the report. Show how you surmounted minor problems you encountered in your investigation. Thank people who helped you.
   4. Point out additional research that is necessary, if any.
   5. Thank the reader for the opportunity to do the work and offer to answer questions.

■ Summary abstracts present the logic skeleton of the report: the thesis or recommendation and its

proof. Descriptive abstracts indicate what topics the report covers and how deeply it goes into each topic but do not summarize what the report says about each topic. A good abstract or executive summary is easy to read, concise, and clear. A good abstract can be understood by itself, without the report or references.

■ The "Introduction" of the report always contains a statement of purpose and scope. The purpose statement identifies the organizational problem the report addresses, the technical investigations it summarizes, and the rhetorical purpose (to explain, to recommend). The scope statement identifies how broad an area the report surveys. The introduction also may include limitations, problems or factors that limit the validity of your recommendations; assumptions, statements whose truth you assume and that you use to prove your final point; methods, an explanation of how you gathered your data; criteria used to weigh the factors in the decision; and definitions of terms audiences may not know.

■ A "Background" or "History" section is usually included because reports are filed and may be consulted years later by people who no longer remember the original circumstances.

■ The body of the report, usually the longest section, analyzes causes of the problem and offers possible solutions. It presents your argument with all evidence and data.

■ The "Conclusions" section summarizes points made in the body of the report; under "Recommendations" are action items that would solve or ameliorate the problem. These sections are often combined if they are short.

■ Appendices provide additional materials that the careful audience may want.

Exercises and Cases

15.1   Reviewing the Chapter

1. What are three different varieties of reports? (LO 15-1)
2. What are some criteria for defining report problems? (LO 15-2)
3. What are four criteria for evaluating web sources? (LO 15-3)
4. What questions should you use to analyze a survey? (LO 15-3)
5. What are some criteria for good survey questions? (LO 15-3)

6. What is a random sample? (LO 15-3)
7. What are some disadvantages of focus groups and online networks? (LO 15-3)
8. What are some criteria to check to ensure you have quality data? (LO 15-3)
9. What kinds of patterns should you look for in your data and text? (LO 15-3)
10. What are some guidelines for choosing information for reports? (LO 15-4)

11. Name seven basic patterns for organizing reports. For four of them, explain when they would be particularly effective or ineffective. (LO 15-5)

12. What are three ways that style in reports differs from conventional business communication style? (LO 15-6)

13. What is the difference between citation and documentation? (LO 15-7)

14. What are the differences between chronological and task progress reports? (LO 15-8)

15. What are the characteristics of an effective report title? (LO 15-9)

16. What goes in the letter of transmittal? (LO 15-9)

17. What is the difference between summary and descriptive abstracts? (LO 15-9)

18. What goes in the introduction of a report? (LO 15-9)

19. What is the difference between conclusions and recommendations? (LO 15-9)

15.2   Identifying Assumptions and Limitations

Indicate whether each of the following would be an assumption or a limitation in a formal report.

1. Report on Ways to Encourage More Students to Join XYZ Organization's Twitter Feed

   a. I surveyed a judgment sample rather than a random sample.

   b. These recommendations are based on the attitudes of current students. Presumably, students in the next several years will have the same attitudes and interests.

2. Report on the Feasibility of Building Hilton Hotels in Romania

   a. This report is based on the expectation that the country will be politically stable.

   b. All of my information is based on library research. The most recent articles were published two months ago; much of the information was published a year ago or more. Therefore, some of my information may be out of date.

3. Report on Car-Buying Preferences of Young Adults

   a. These recommendations may change if the cost of gasoline increases dramatically or if there is another deep recession.

   b. This report is based on a survey of adults ages 20 to 24 in California, Texas, Illinois, Ontario, and Massachusetts.

   c. These preferences are based on the cars now available. If a major technological or styling innovation occurs, preferences may change.

15.3   Defining and Evaluating Report Problems

In small teams, turn the following categories into specific report problems you could research for a business communication course. Write three possible report problems for each category.

1. Social media sites
2. Global warming or climate change
3. Globalization
4. Marketing to younger audiences
5. Career planning
6. Technology/cell phone use
7. Credit card debt
8. Campus-based organizations
9. Tuition
10. Housing/parking on campus

Once you have defined three possible problems for each category, evaluate the problems using the following questions:

- Which problem(s) could you address satisfactorily in the time allotted for your course project?
- Which problem(s) are real?
- Which problem(s) are important enough to be worth researching?
- Are the problem(s) narrow enough?
- Who will be able to implement recommended action from your research?
- For which problem(s) could you find adequate resources to create sound solutions?

As your instructor directs,

a. Write an email to your instructor that shares your evaluation of the problems.

b. Pick two of the categories and present to the class your evaluation of the problems in an oral presentation.

c. Write a preliminary purpose statement for each of the three problems you have identified for a category.

15.4   Identifying the Weaknesses in Problem Statements

Identify the weaknesses in the following problem statements by answering these questions:

- Is the problem narrow enough?
- Can a solution be found in a semester or quarter?

- What organization could implement any recommendations to solve the problem?
- Could the topic be limited or refocused to yield an acceptable problem statement?

1. I want to explore how many Twitter users subscribe to repeat news organizations' Twitter feeds.
2. How can smartphone apps influence driving habits?
3. One possible report topic I would like to investigate would be the differences in women's intercollegiate sports in our athletic conference.
4. How to market products effectively to college students.
5. Should web banners be part of a company's advertising?
6. How can U.S. and Canadian students get jobs in Europe?
7. We want to explore ways our company can help raise funds for the Open Shelter. We will investigate whether collecting and recycling glass, aluminum, and paper products will raise enough money to help.
8. How can XYZ University better serve students from traditionally underrepresented groups?
9. What are the best investments for the next year?

15.5   Writing a Preliminary Purpose Statement

Answer the following questions about a topic on which you could write a formal report.

1. What problem will you investigate or solve?
   a. What is the name of the organization facing the problem?
   b. What is the technical problem or difficulty?
   c. Why is it important to the organization that this problem be solved?
   d. What solution or action might you recommend to solve the problem?
   e. Who (name and title) is the person in the organization who would have the power to accept or reject your recommendation?
2. Will this report use information from other classes or from work experiences? If so, give the name and topic of the class and/or briefly describe the job. If you will need additional

information (that you have not already recieved from other classes or from a job), how do you expect to find it?
3. List the name, title, and business phone number of a professor who can testify to your ability to handle the expertise needed for this report.
4. List the name, title, and business phone number of someone in the organization who can testify that you have access to enough information about that organization to write this report.

As your instructor directs,
a. Be prepared to answer the questions orally in a conference.
b. Bring written answers to a conference.
c. Submit written answers in class.
d. Give your instructor a photocopy of your statement after it is approved.

15.6   Choosing Research Strategies

For each of the following reports, indicate the kinds of research that might be useful. If a survey is called for, indicate the most efficient kind of sample to use.

1. How can Twitter and Facebook users on campus be more connected to school events?
2. Is it feasible to send all XYZ organization's communication through email?
3. How can XYZ store increase sales?
4. What is it like to live and work in [name of country]?
5. Should our organization have a dress code?
6. Is it feasible to start a monthly newsletter for students in your major?
7. How can we best market to mature adults?
8. Can compensation programs increase productivity?
9. What skills are in demand in our area? Of these, which could the local community college offer courses in?

15.7   Comparing Search Results

Do a Google search on these three terms:

- Global warming
- Immigration
- Gun control

Print off the first 10 sources Google gives you for each. In small groups, compare your listings. How do they differ? Pick one of the three topics and present the differences you found to your classmates.

15.8   Evaluating Websites

Choose five websites that are possible resources for a report. Evaluate them on the credibility and trustworthiness of their information. Consider the following questions and compare and contrast your findings.

- What person or organization sponsors the site? What credentials do the authors have?
- Does the site give evidence to support its claims? Does it give both sides of controversial issues?

- Is the tone professional?
- How complete is the information? What is it based on?
- How current is the information?

Based on your findings, which sites are best for your report and why?

As your instructor directs,

a. Write an email to your instructor summarizing your results.

b. Share your results with a small group of students.

c. Present your results to the class in an oral presentation.

15.9   Choosing Samples for Surveys and Interviews

For the following topics, indicate the types of sample(s) you would use in collecting survey data and in conducting interviews.

1. How can your school improve the usability of its website?

2. How can your school use social media to increase communication with students?

3. How can your school save money to limit tuition increases?

4. How can your favorite school organization attract more student members?

5. How can your school improve communication with international students?

6. How should your school deal with hate speech?

7. How can instructors at your school improve their electronic presentations for students?

15.10   Evaluating Survey Questions

Evaluate each of the following questions. Are they acceptable as they stand? If not, how can they be improved?

a. Survey of clerical workers:

Do you work for the government? ☐
or the private sector? ☐

b. Questionnaire on grocery purchases:

1. Do you *usually* shop at the same grocery store?

    a. Yes

    b. No

2. Do you use credit cards to purchase items at your grocery store?

    a. Yes

    b. No

3. How much is your average grocery bill?

    a. Under $25

    b. $25–50

    c. $50–100

    d. $100–150

    e. Over $150

c. Survey on technology:

1. Would you generally welcome any technological advancement that allowed information to be sent and received more quickly and in greater quantities than ever before?

2. Do you think that all people should have free access to all information, or do you think that information should somehow be regulated and monitored?

d. Survey on job skills:

How important are the following skills for getting and keeping a professional-level job in U.S. business and industry today?

	Low				**High**
Ability to communicate	1	2	3	4	5
Leadership ability	1	2	3	4	5
Public presentation skills	1	2	3	4	5
Selling ability	1	2	3	4	5
Teamwork capability	1	2	3	4	5
Writing ability	1	2	3	4	5

15.11   Designing Questions for an Interview or Survey

Submit either a one- to three-page questionnaire or questions for a 20- to 30-minute interview AND the information listed below for the method you choose.

Questionnaire

1. Purpose(s), goal(s).

2. Subjects (who, why, how many).

3. How and where to be distributed.

4. Any changes in type size, paper color, etc., from submitted copy.

5. Rationale for order of questions, kinds of questions, wording of questions.

6. References, if building on questionnaires by other authors.

Interview

1. Purpose(s), goal(s).

2. Subjects (who, and why).

3. Proposed site, length of interview.

4. Rationale for order of questions, kinds of questions, wording of questions, choice of branching or follow-up questions.

5. References, if building on questions devised by others.

As your instructor directs,

a.   Create questions for a survey on one of the following topics:

- Survey students on your campus about their knowledge of and interest in the programs and activities sponsored by a student organization.
- Survey workers at a company about what they like and dislike about their jobs.
- Survey people in your community about their willingness to pay more to buy products using recycled materials and to buy products that are packaged with a minimum of waste.
- Survey two groups on a topic that interests you.

b.   Create questions for an interview on one of the following topics:

- Interview an international student about the forms of greetings and farewells, topics of small talk, forms of politeness, festivals and holidays, meals at home, size of families, and roles of family members in his or her country.
- Interview a TV producer about what styles and colors work best for people appearing on TV.
- Interview a worker about an ethical dilemma he or she faced on the job, what the worker did and why, and how the company responded.
- Interview the owner of a small business about problems the business has; what strategies the owner has already used to increase sales and profits and how successful these strategies were; and the owner's attitudes toward possible changes in product line, decor, marketing, hiring, advertising, and money management.
- Interview someone who has information you need for a report you're writing.

15.12   Analyzing Annual Reports

Locate two annual reports in either paper or electronic form. Use the following questions to analyze both reports:

- Who is (are) the audience(s)?
- What is (are) the purpose(s) of the report?
- How is the report organized and what does the order of information reflect about the company?
- How does the report validate/support the claims it makes? What type of evidence is used more often—textual or visual? What kinds of claims are used—logical, emotional, or ethical?
- How does the text establish credibility for the report?
- What can you tell about the company's financial situation from the report?
- What role do visuals play in the report? What image do they portray for the company? How do the visuals help establish credibility for the report? What do they imply about power distribution in the company?
- Does the report deal with any ethical issues?

As your instructor directs,

a.   Write an email to your instructor comparing and contrasting the two reports according to your analysis answers. Explain which report you find more effective and why.

b.   Share your results orally with a small group of students.

c.   Present your results to the class.

15.13   Revising a Progress Report

Read the following progress report.

Date: April 3, 2018

To: Prof. Keene

From: John

Subject: My Progress

So far my final project for this course has been slow. As you know, I am hoping to present my final report to my boss at the ice cream shop. He is actually very intentional in the idea of having an ice cream stand on campus.

Work Completed

So far I have interviewed a few people on campus and not found out a whole lot of anything. It has been very frustrating. I just handed out a few surveys on campus, but not very many students wanted to fill them out. I do have a little bit data, though. It seems as though several students are very interested in having an ice cream cart on campus, and would purchase ice cream items.

I have spoken to my boss, the owner of Super Duper Ice Cream, and he is looking forward to reading my final report on the campus ice cream stand. I have put together the numbers for the new stand and have already spoken to Dining Services on campus for permissions.

Work be Completed

During these last two weeks of class, I will have no problem geting this project done! I just have to interview more students, put together the information in the report, finish getting the permissions and information for my boss, and then compile all of the information. Oh, and I need to write a few more survey questions, too.

Then I will proofread everything, print it, and hand it to my boss!

Your favorite student,

John

Revise the progress report. Submit your revision, plus another document justifying your revisions, to your instructor.

15.14 Writing a Progress Report

Write an email to your instructor summarizing your progress on your report.

In the introductory paragraph, summarize your progress in terms of your schedule and your goals. Under a heading titled "Work Completed," list what you have already accomplished. When describing the work you have completed, make sure to demonstrate how it adds value to your audience. Under "Work to Be Completed," list what you still have to do. If you are more than two days behind the schedule you submitted with your proposal, include a revised schedule, listing the completion dates for the activities that remain.

15.15 Writing a Progress Report for a Team Report

Write an email to your instructor summarizing your team's progress.

In the introductory paragraph, summarize the team's progress in terms of its goals and its schedule, your own progress on the tasks for which you are responsible, and your feelings about the team's work thus far.

Under a heading titled "Work Completed," list what already has been done. Be most specific about what you yourself have done. Describe briefly the chronology of team activities: number, time, and length of meetings; topics discussed; and decisions made at meetings.

If you have solved problems creatively, say so. You also can describe obstacles you've encountered that you have not yet solved. In this section, you also can comment on problems that the team has faced and whether or not they've been solved. You can comment on things that have gone well and have contributed to the smooth functioning of the team.

Under "Work to Be Completed," list what you personally and other team members still have to do. Indicate the schedule for completing the work.

15.16 Revising an Executive Summary

The following executive summary is poorly organized and written. Revise it to make it more effective. Cut information that does not belong and add any information that you feel is missing.

This report will discuss the healthier food options for athletes at the University Gym. Currently, there are several vending machines that student athletes can buy snacks from, but all of the snacks are really unhealthy. Some of the vending machine options that they have are potato chips, candy bars, cookies, and fruit snacks. None of these are healthy options for athletes.

I think there are a few options that can help this situation. Some of the options include setting up a snack bar. This snack bar could include items like fruits, vegetables, salads, and fruit smoothies. The University's Food Services would have to run this and hire several students to run it. This would cost quite a bit.

Students need healthy food options, especially when they are athletes who are training for sports. Student athletes have very demanding schedules and may not have time to cook healthy foods for themselves.

Another option that we could do would be to simply have a healthy, refrigerated vending machine, with healthy options in it, like fruits, ready-to-eat salads, veggies, and yogurts. This would be easier to install, but would have to be checked frequently to ensure that that items do not go bad.

These are my recommendations for the problem.

15.17 Revising a Recommendation Section

A student has written the following recommendation section for a report for a local restaurant. The restaurant is called the American Grill and specializes in burgers and fries. The restaurant is new to the area and wants to increase its advertising in the local area to get the word out about their food.

Revise the recommendation section so it is well organized and clear. You may add any information that is needed.

I recommend the following to expand the advertising for American Grill:

American Grill should hand out flyers to people during the July 4th parade that goes through the downtown area. They could ask some of the servers to walk through the parade wearing their American Grill t-shirts to hand out the flyers. The flyers would contain lots of information, like hours, specials, and other important information.

The American Grill should put a radio commercial on the local radio station with the drink specials and also hand out flyers. The radio commercial should also give location information for those who do not know where it is located.

The American Grill should hand out coupons for appetizers and drink specials. These could also be handed out in a parade, or to college students when they first get to the University.

15.18 Comparing Report Formats

Locate five business or organizational reports (or white papers as they're sometimes called) on the Internet. A good online collection of organizational reports is the website of the Council on Library and Information Resources (CLIR), accessible at http://www.clir.org/pubs/reports/. Additionally, you can find reports linked from the websites of the *Fortune* 500 organizations, or you can search for them on Google using key words such as "reports," "business reports," "company reports," or "organizational reports."

The reports you find could be about the organizations' environmental sustainability efforts, their products, or any other aspect of their operations.

Compare the organization of the five reports you select. What similarities and differences do you see in the formatting of all these reports? Make a table of your findings. Discuss your findings in small groups.

15.19 Comparing Style in Annual Reports

Locate two annual reports on the Internet. A good source is Report Watch, http://www.reportwatch.net/. Compare the style of the two reports. Here are some questions to get you started:

1. How do they use visuals to keep attention?
2. What differences do you see in the letters from the CEOs?
3. How do they present number-heavy information? Do they rely mainly on tables and graphs? Do they give prose summaries?
4. Is the writing easy to understand?
5. Do you see places where negative information is given a positive spin?

6. Is one report easier to understand than the other? Why?
7. Is one report more interesting than the other? Why?
8. Is one report more convincing than the other? Why?

As your instructor directs,

a. Work in small groups to do your comparison. Share your findings in a five-minute oral presentation to the class.

b. Work in small groups to do your comparison. Share your findings in an email posted on the class website.

c. Work individually to do your comparison. Share your findings in an email to your instructor.

15.20 Analyzing Business Reports

Visit the following collection of business reports: http://www
.technologyreview.com/businessreports/. In small groups,
choose a report and answer the following questions:

- How many of the components of a report does it contain?
  (See Figure 15.11.)
- What is the style of the report? What kinds of language
  does it use? Try to find specific instances.
- Does the report use sources and visuals? How are they used?

- Does the report use forecasting, transitions, clear topic
  sentences, and/or headings?
- What type of report is this?
- These reports are *MIT Technology Review* business reports.
  Did that fact lessen your desire to read the report? Was the
  technology in the report understandable to you? Why or
  why not?

Share your findings with the class.

15.21 Recommending Action

Write a report recommending an action that your unit or organization should take. Possibilities include

- Developing a stronger social media presence online.
- Enhancing technology with smartphones, tablets, or lap-
  tops to accomplish work on the go.
- Buying more equipment for your department.
- Hiring an additional worker for your department.
- Making your organization more family-friendly.
- Making a change that will make the organization more
  environmentally sustainable.

- Making changes to improve accessibility for customers or
  employees with disabilities.

Address your report to the person who would have the power to
approve your recommendation.

As your instructor directs,

a. Create a document or presentation to achieve the goal.

b. Write an email to your instructor describing the situation
    at your workplace and explaining your rhetorical choices
    (medium, strategy, tone, wording, graphics or document
    design, and so forth).

15.22 Writing a Recommendation Report

Write a report evaluating two or more alternatives. Possible topics include the following:

1. Should your student organization start a Facebook page to
    promote events, speakers, etc.?

2. Should students in your major start a monthly newsletter?
    Would an electronic or paper version be more useful to
    the target audience?

3. Should your student organization write an annual report?
    Would doing so help the next year's officers?

4. Should your student organization create a wiki, blog, or
    newsletter to facilitate communication with a constituency?

5. Should your workplace create a newsletter to communi-
    cate internally?

6. Should a local restaurant open another branch? Where
    should it be?

In designing your study, identify the alternatives, define your
criteria for selecting one option over others, carefully evaluate
each alternative, and recommend the best course of action.

15.23 Writing a Consultant's Report—Restaurant Tipping

Your consulting company has been asked to conduct a report
for Diamond Enterprises, which runs three national chains:
FishStix, The Bar-B-Q Pit, and Morrie's. All are medium-priced,
family-friendly restaurants. The CEO is thinking of replacing
optional tips with a 15% service fee automatically added to bills.

You read articles in trade journals, surveyed a random sample
of 200 workers in each of the chains, and conducted an email
survey of the 136 restaurant managers. Here are your findings:

1. Trade journals point out that the Internal Revenue Service
    (IRS) audits restaurants if it thinks that servers underreport
    tips. Dealing with an audit is time-consuming and often
    results in the restaurant's having to pay penalties and interest.

2. Only one Morrie's restaurant has actually been audited by
    the IRS. Management was able to convince the IRS that
    servers were reporting tips accurately. No penalty was

assessed. Management spent $5,000 on CPA and legal
fees and spent over 80 hours of management time gathering data and participating in the audit.

3. Restaurants in Europe already add a service fee (usually 15%)
    to the bill. Patrons can add more if they choose. Local custom
    determines whether tips are expected and how much they
    should be. In Germany, for example, it is more usual to round
    up the bill (e.g., from 27 € to 30 €) than to figure a percentage.

4. If the restaurant collected a service fee, it could use the
    income to raise wages for cooks and hosts and pay for
    other benefits, such as health insurance, rather than giving
    all the money to servers and bussers.

5. Morrie's servers tend to be under 25 years of age. FishStix
    employs more servers over 25, who are doing this for a liv-
    ing. The Bar-B-Q Pit servers are students in college towns.

544   **Part 5**   Proposals and Reports

6. In all three chains, servers oppose the idea. Employees other than servers generally support it.

	Retain tips	Change to service fee added to bill	Don't care
FishStix servers (n = 115)	90%	7%	3%
Bar-B-Q servers (n = 73)	95%	0%	5%
Morrie's servers (n = 93)	85%	15%	0%
Morrie's nonservers (n = 65)	25%	70%	5%
FishStix nonservers (n = 46)	32%	32%	37%
Bar-B-Q nonservers (n = 43)	56%	20%	25%

(Numbers do not add up to 100% due to rounding.)

7. Servers said that it was important to go home with money in their pockets (92%); that their expertise increased food sales and should be rewarded (67%); and that if a service fee replaced tips, they would be likely to look for another job (45%). Some (17%) thought that if the manager distributed service-fee income, favoritism rather than the quality of work would govern how much tip income they got. Most (72%) thought that customers would not add anything beyond the 15% service fee, and many (66%) thought that total tip income would decrease and their own portion of that income would decrease (90%).

8. Managers generally support the change.

	Retain tips	Change to service fee added to bill	Don't care
FishStix managers (n = 44)	20%	80%	0%
Bar-B-Q managers (n = 13)	33%	67%	0%
Morrie's managers (n = 58)	55%	45%	0%

9. Comments from managers include: "It isn't fair for a cook with eight years of experience to make only $12 an hour while a server can make $25 an hour in just a couple of months" and "I could have my pick of employees if I offered health insurance."

10. Morale at Bar-B-Q Pit seems low. This is seen in part in the low response rate to the survey.

11. In a tight employment market, some restaurants might lose good servers if they made the change. However, hiring cooks and other nonservers would be easier.

12. The current computer systems in place can handle figuring and recording the service fee. Because bills are printed by computer, an additional line could be added. Allocating the service-fee income could take extra managerial time, especially at first.

Write the report.

15.24   Writing a Recommendation Report

Write an individual or a team report. Pick one of the following topics.

1. **Improving Customer Service.** Many customers find that service is getting poorer and workers are getting ruder. Evaluate the service in a local store, restaurant, or other organization. Are customers made to feel comfortable? Is workers' communication helpful, friendly, and respectful? Are workers knowledgeable about products and services? Do they sell them effectively? Write a report analyzing the quality of service and recommending what the organization should do to improve.

2. **Recommending Courses for the Local Community College.** Businesses want to be able to send workers to local community colleges to upgrade their skills; community colleges want to prepare students to enter the local workforce. What skills are in demand in your community? What courses at what levels should the local community college offer?

3. **Improving Sales and Profits.** Recommend ways a small business in your community can increase sales and profits. Focus on one or more of the following: the products or services it offers, its advertising, its decor, its location, its accounting methods, its cash management, or

any other aspect that may be keeping the company from achieving its potential. Address your report to the owner of the business.

4. **Increasing Student Involvement.** How could an organization on campus persuade more of the students who are eligible to join or to become active in its programs? Do students know that it exists? Is it offering programs that interest students? Is it retaining current members? What changes should the organization make? Address your report to the officers of the organization.

5. **Evaluating a Potential Employer.** What training is available to new employees? How soon is the average entry-level person promoted? How much travel and weekend work are expected? Is there a "busy season," or is the workload consistent year-round? What fringe benefits are offered? What is the corporate culture? Is the climate nonracist and nonsexist? How strong is the company economically? How is it likely to be affected by current economic, demographic, and political trends? Address your report to the placement office on campus; recommend whether it should encourage students to work at this company.

6. With your instructor's permission, choose your own topic.

As your instructor directs,

Turn in the following documents:

1. The approved proposal.
2. The report, including

   Cover.

   Title Page.

   Letter or Memo of Transmittal.

   Table of Contents.

List of Illustrations.

Executive Summary or Abstract.

Body (Introduction, all information, recommendations). Your instructor may specify a minimum length, a minimum number or kind of sources, and a minimum number of visuals.

Appendices if useful or relevant.

3. Your notes and at least one preliminary draft.

Notes

1. Eli Pariser, *The Filter Bubble: What the Internet Is Hiding from You* (New York: Penguin, 2011).
2. Arlene Weintraub, "What the Doctors Aren't Disclosing: A New Study Shows How Authors of Medical Journal Articles Flout Rules on Revealing Conflicts of Interest," *BusinessWeek,* May 26, 2008, 32.
3. Erick H. Turner et al., "Selective Publication of Antidepressant Trials and Its Influence on Apparent Efficacy," *New England Journal of Medicine* 358, no. 3 (2008): 252.
4. "Wikipedia," *Wikipedia,* last modified October 22, 2017, http://en.wikipedia.org/wiki/Wikipedia.
5. Sharon L. Lohr, *Sampling: Design and Analysis* (Pacific Grove, CA: Duxbury Press, 1999), 3.
6. "TV Measurement," Nielsen, accessed June 22, 2013, http://www.nielsen.com/us/en/measurement/television-measurement.html.
7. Cynthia Crossen, "Fiasco in 1936 Survey Brought 'Science' to Election Polling," *Wall Street Journal,* October 2, 2006, B1.
8. Ann Zimmerman, "Revenge of the Nerds: How Barbie Got Her Geek On," *Wall Street Journal,* April 9, 2010, A1.
9. Andrew O'Connell, "Reading the Public Mind," *Harvard Business Review* 88, no. 10 (October 2010): 28.
10. Carl Bialik, "Survey Says: Cellphones Annoy Pollsters," *Wall Street Journal,* December 3, 2011, A2.
11. Carl Bialik, "Making It Count: Alternative Ways to Gather Census Data," *Wall Street Journal,* July 31, 2010, A2; and Paul J. Lavrakas, "Nonresponse Issues in U.S. Cell Phone and Landline Telephone Surveys," National Research Council, February 17, 2011, http://www7.nationalacademies.org/cnstat/Lavakas%20Pres.pdf.
12. Pew Research Center for the People & the Press, "What Low Response Rates Mean for Telephone Surveys," Pew Research Center, May 15, 2017, http://www.pewresearch.org/2017/05/15/what-low-response-rates-mean-for-telephone-surveys/
13. Pew Research Center for the People & the Press, "Assessing the Representativeness of Public Opinion Surveys," Pew Research Center, May 15, 2012; and AAPOR Cell Phone Task Force, "New Considerations for Survey Researchers When Planning and Conducting RDD Telephone Surveys in the U.S. with Respondents Reached Via Cell Phone Numbers," American Association for Public Opinion Research, 2010, http://www.aapor.org/Cell_Phone_Task_Force_Report.htm.
14. Palmer Morrel-Samuels, "Getting the Truth into Workplace Surveys," *Harvard Business Review* 80, no. 2 (February 2002): 111–18.
15. Ibid.
16. Sheldon R. Gawiser and G. Evans Witt, "20 Questions Journalists Should Ask about Poll Results," *Public Agenda Archives,* accessed June 25, 2013, http://www.publicagendaarchives.org/pages/20-questions-journalists-should-ask-about-poll-results.
17. Morrel-Samuels, "Getting the Truth into Workplace Surveys," 116.
18. Carl Bialik, "Weddings Are Not the Budget Drains Some Surveys Suggest," *Wall Street Journal,* August 24, 2007, B1.
19. Jakob Nielsen, "Risks of Quantitative Studies," *Alertbox,* March 1, 2004, http://www.useit.com/alertbox/20040301.html; and Dan Seligman, "The Story They All Got Wrong," *Forbes,* November 25, 2002, 124.
20. Earl E. McDowell, Bridget Mrolza, and Emmy Reppe, "An Investigation of the Interviewing Practices of Technical Writers in Their World of Work," in *Interviewing Practices for Technical Writers,* ed. Earl E. McDowell (Amityville, NY: Baywood Publishing, 1991), 207.
21. Peter Noel Murray, "Focus Groups Are Valid When Done Right," *Marketing News,* September 1, 2006, 21, 25.
22. Emily Steel, "The New Focus Groups: Online Networks: Proprietary Panels Help Consumer Companies Shape Products, Ads," *Wall Street Journal,* January 14, 2008, B6.
23. Sarah Nassauer, "Old Ketchup Packet Heads for Trash," *Wall Street Journal,* September 9, 2012, B1.
24. Christopher Meyer and Andre Schwager, "Understanding Customer Experience," *Harvard Business Review* 85, no. 2 (February 2007): 116–26.
25. Daniel Kruger, "You Want Data with That?," *Forbes* 173, no. 6 (2004): 58.
26. Louise Witt, "Inside Intent," *American Demographics* 26, no. 2 (2004): 34.
27. Nielsen, "C3 TV Ratings Show Impact of DVR Ad Viewing," *Newswire,* October 14, 2009, http://www.nielsen.com/us/en/newswire/2009/c3-tv-ratings-show-impact-of-dvr-ad-viewing.html.
28. Ibid.; and Carl Bialik, "Tweets as Poll Data? Be Careful," *Wall Street Journal,* February 11, 2012, A2.
29. Jessi Hempel, "The Hot Tech Gig of 2022: Data Scientist," *Fortune,* January 16, 2012, 62.
30. "NASA Releases Information on Federal Survey of Pilots," *Des Moines Register,* January 1, 2008, 2A.
31. Stephen E. Moore, "655,000 War Dead?," *Wall Street Journal,* October 18, 2006, A20; and Neil Munro and Carl M. Cannon, "Data Bomb," *National Journal,* January 4, 2008, http://www.freerepublic.com/focus/f-news/1948378/posts.
32. Ellen Pastorino and Susann M. Doyle-Portillo, *What Is Psychology? Essentials,* 2nd ed. (Stamford, CT: Cengage Learning, 2012), 208.
33. Ida Torres, "Japanese Pilots Ask Boeing to Be More Transparent on Dreamliner Issues," *Japan Daily Press,* May 28, 2013, http://japandailypress.com/japanese-pilots-ask-boeing-to-be-more-transparent-on-dreamliner-issues-2829627.

CHAPTER

11 Developing Job Application Materials

Chapter Outline

Conducting a Job Search

- Using the Internet Effectively in Your Job Search
- Building Relationships through Networking
- Building Relationships through Internships
- Establishing a Reputation Online
- Using Social Networking Sites with Care

How Employers Use Résumés

Guidelines for Résumés

- Length
- Emphasis
- Details
- Writing Style
- Key Words
- Layout and Design

Kinds of Résumés

What to Include in a Résumé

- Name and Contact Information
- Education
- Honors and Awards
- Experience
- Other Skills
- Activities
- Portfolio

Dealing with Difficulties

- "I Don't Have Any Experience."
- "All My Experience Is in My Family's Business."
- "I Want to Change Fields."
- "I've Been Out of the Job Market for a While."
- "I Was Laid Off."
- "I Was Fired."

Sending Your Résumé Electronically

Honesty

Job Application Letters

How Content Differs in Job Letters and Résumés

How to Find Out about Employers and Jobs

The Hidden Job Market

Content and Organization for Job Application Letters

- How to Organize Solicited Letters
- How to Organize Prospecting Letters
- First Paragraphs of Solicited Letters
- First Paragraphs of Prospecting Letters
- Showing a Knowledge of the Position and the Company
- Showing What Separates You from Other Applicants
- Writing the Last Paragraph

Email Application Letters

Creating a Professional Image

- Writing Style
- Positive Emphasis
- You-Attitude
- Paragraph Length and Unity
- Letter Length
- Editing and Proofreading
- Follow-Up

Social Networking and Personal Websites

Summary by Learning Objectives

©DrAfter123/Getty Images

NEWSWORTHY COMMUNICATION

Honesty Should Be Your Policy

David Tovar, the former vice president of communications for Walmart, was about to be promoted to senior vice president when a routine background check discovered he had not graduated from college. He had nearly 20 years of professional experience but had never earned the art history degree he reported on his résumé. To his employer, Tovar's years of experience no longer mattered. His job performance—considered so strong it was worthy of a promotion—no longer mattered. He had lied to his employer for personal gain and all trust his employer formerly had in him was gone. After eight years with the company, he was forced to resign.

Lying on résumés is all-too common, but what may seem harmless rarely comes without consequences. Misrepresentations during your job search often lead to offers of employment being withheld. But even when the dishonesty isn't immediately noticed, it can spring up unexpectly and result in embarrassment, the loss of your position, and the derailment of your career. Perhaps surprisingly, low-level employees at the start of their careers aren't the only ones who lie and suffer the consequences. Many high-profile individuals like Tovar have lost their positions due to the inaccuracies or misrepresenations on their résumés:

■ John Davy, who held a six-week stint as CEO of Maori Television Service,

©Casey Rodgers/AP Images

a New Zealand television channel, was not only fired but sentenced to eight months in prison when it was discovered he lied about his work history and academic accomplishments.

■ Scott Thompson, former CEO of Yahoo!, was forced to resign when it came to light he had not earned the computer science degree he listed on his résumé. Like Tovar, Thompson had many years of real work experience—30, in fact—but his work history proved insufficient in the face of dishonesty.

■ Alison Ryan had just accepted a job as head of public relations for Manchester United when the offer was

withdrawn. What cost her this prestigious position? She didn't lie about her work history or degrees earned. She lied about her GPA.

Trust is an invaluable commodity in the workplace. In our digital age, it is all too easy for hiring managers to check the validity of the claims you make on your résumé. As we've already seen, lying not only can prevent you from being hired, but it also can cost you your job.

Sources: Hope Restle and Jacquelyn Smith, "17 Successful Executives Who Have Lied on Their Résumés," *Business Insider,* July 15, 2015, http://www.businessinsider.com/successful-executives-who-have-lied-on-their-resumes-2015-7; and Rachel Abrams, "Walmart Vice President Forced Out for Lying about Degree," *New York Times,* September 16, 2014, https://www.nytimes.com/2014/09/17/business/17tovar.html.

Learning Objectives

After studying this chapter, you will know how to:

LO 11-1 Conduct an effective job search.

LO 11-2 Prepare a résumé that makes you look attractive to employers.

LO 11-3 Deal with common difficulties that arise during job searches.

LO 11-4 Handle the online portion of job searches.

LO 11-5 Keep your résumé honest.

LO 11-6 Write a job letter that attracts employers.

LO 11-7 Use social networking and a personal website to create a virtual cover letter.

You probably will change jobs many times during your career. The U.S. Bureau of Labor Statistics' National Longitudinal Survey of Youth shows that the average person held an average of nearly 12 jobs from age 18 to age 50. Even in middle age, when job changing slows down, 69% of jobs ended in fewer than five years. Thus, you always should keep your résumé up to date.[1]

A **résumé** is a persuasive summary of your qualifications for a job with a specific employer. If you're in the job market, having a résumé is a basic step in the job hunt. When you're employed, having an up-to-date résumé makes it easier to take advantage of opportunities that may come up for even better jobs. If you're several years away from job hunting, preparing a résumé now will help you become more conscious of what to do in the next two or three years to make yourself an attractive candidate.

This chapter covers résumés and job application letters (sometimes called cover letters). Chapter 12 discusses interviews and communications after the interview. Both chapters focus on job hunting in the United States. Conventions, expectations, and criteria differ from culture to culture; different norms apply in different countries.

All job communications should be tailored to your unique qualifications and the specifications of the job you want. Adopt the wording or layout of an example if it's relevant to your own situation, but don't be locked into the forms in this book. You've got different strengths; your résumé will be different, too.

Conducting a Job Search

LO 11-1

Formal preparation for job hunting should begin a full year *before you begin interviewing.* Enroll for the services of your campus placement office. Ask friends who are in the job market about their experiences in interviews; find out what kinds of job offers they get. Check into the possibility of getting an internship or a co-op job that will give you relevant experience before you interview.

If you are already working, make sure your job search does not interfere with your current employment. Even if you hate your job, acting professionally and searching for a new job outside of work hours or on lunch breaks will help you keep your job and, more importantly, the good reference of your current employer.

Try to have a job offer lined up *before* you get the degree. People who don't need jobs immediately are more confident in interviews and usually get better job offers. If you have to job-hunt after graduation, plan to spend at least 30 hours a week on your job search. The time will pay off in a better job that you find more quickly.

Most people think they know how to conduct a job search. You prepare a résumé, look through a few job ads, send your application in, interview, and get the job—right? According to most experts, that's wrong. Successful job searches rely on much more than putting the right things on résumés. In fact, according to Richard Bolles, employers look for employees in the exact opposite way from the way most people look for jobs.[2] Employers prefer to hire people in the following order:

1. From within their organization.
2. With proof of expertise, through a job portfolio.
3. With a reference from a trusted friend.
4. From a trusted recruiting agency.
5. From a job advertisement.
6. From a résumé.

A simple résumé is the last on the list for a reason: it is very difficult to tell from a résumé what kind of worker a person will be. Some employers are now moving away from placing job ads in favor of searching for new employees through personal and online networks.

To be successful in your job search, you should

- Use the Internet effectively.

- Build relationships through internships and networking.

- Establish a reputation online through wise use of social media.

- Be prepared with excellent traditional résumés and cover letters.

Using the Internet Effectively in Your Job Search

Probably the most common use of the Internet for job candidates is to search for openings (see Figure 11.1). In addition to popular job boards such as Monster and CareerBuilder, job candidates typically search for jobs posted on organizations' Facebook pages, LinkedIn sites, and Twitter (TwitJobSearch.com). Many successful companies are reducing their postings on job boards in favor of recruiting through social networking sites.

Figure 11.1	Job Listings on the Web
America's Job Bank http://www.jobbankinfo.org	Indeed.com http://www.indeed.com
CareerBuilder.com http://www.careerbuilder.com	Monster.com www.monster.com
Careers.org http://www.careers.org	MonsterTrak college.monster.com
EmploymentGuide.com http://www.employmentguide.com	Job listings from the *Chicago Tribune, Detroit News, Los Angeles Times, Miami Herald, Philadelphia Inquirer, San Jose Mercury News,* and other city newspapers' websites.
Federal Jobs Career Central http://www.fedjobs.com	

Job candidates also check electronic listings in local newspapers and professional societies. However, you do need to be careful when responding to online ads. Some of them turn out to be pitches from career or financial services firms, or even phishing ads—ploys from identity thieves seeking your personal information. And remember that not all sites are current and accurate. Check your school's career site for help. Check the sites of other schools: Stanford, Berkeley, and Columbia have particularly excellent career sites. Figure 11.2 lists some of the best sites.

A relatively new use of the Internet for job searchers is online job fairs. At online fairs, you can browse through virtual booths, leave your résumé at promising ones, and sometimes even apply on the spot, all without leaving your home. Other advantages of online job fairs are their wide geographic range and 24-hour access.

As you do all this research for your job hunt, you probably will begin to find conflicting advice. When evaluating suggestions, consider the age of the advice; what was true five years ago may not be true today because the job-search process changes so quickly. Also consider your industry; general advice that works for most may not work for your industry. Above all, consider what advice helps you present yourself as favorably as possible.

Building Relationships through Networking

Many experts now consider networking to be the most important factor in finding a job. It is important for entry-level work and becomes even more crucial as you advance in your career.

Networking starts with people you know—friends, family, friends of your parents, classmates, teammates, gym mates, colleagues—and quickly expands to your electronic contacts in social media. Let people know you are looking for a job and what your job assets are. Use social media to emphasize your field knowledge and accomplishments. Join your school's alumni association to find alumni in businesses that interest you.

The secret to successful networking is reciprocity. Too many people network just for themselves, and they quickly gain a "one-way" reputation that hurts further networking.

Figure 11.2	Comprehensive Websites Covering the Entire Job Search Process
About.com http://jobsearch.about.com	Monster.com http://www.monster.com
Campus Career Center http://www.campuscareercenter.com	MonsterCollege http://college.monster.com
CareerBuilder http://www.careerbuilder.com	Purdue Online Writing Lab http://owl.english.purdue.edu
Career Rookie http://www.careerrookie.com	Quintessential Careers http://www.quintcareers.com
College Central http://www.collegecentral.com	The Riley Guide http://www.rileyguide.com
College Grad Job Hunter http://www.collegegrad.com	Spherion Career Center http://www.spherion.com/job-seekers
The Five O'Clock Club http://www.fiveoclockclub.com	Vault http://www.vault.com
JobHuntersBible.com (Dick Bolles) http://www.jobhuntersbible.com	Wetfeet http://www.wetfeet.com

Good networkers work for a "two-way" reputation; to earn it, they look for ways to reciprocate. They help their contacts make fruitful connections. They share useful information and tips. Successful networks are not just for finding jobs: they are vital for career success.

Building Relationships through Internships

Internships are becoming increasingly important as ways to build relationships and to find out about professions, employers, and jobs. Many companies use their internships to find full-time employees. GE, for example, makes about 80% of its new-graduate hires from students who held summer internships with the company. The National Association of Colleges and Employers found in a survey of internships that 51.7% of interns became full-time hires.[3] (To see how those conversions play out in various fields, see Figure 11.3.) Among those who repeat internships, that number was found to be substantially higher; nearly 90% of returning interns were offered full-time employment. In fact, some industry experts are predicting that within the next few years, intern recruiting will largely replace entry-level recruiting.[4]

Even if your internship does not lead to a full-time job, it still can give you valuable insight into the profession, as well as contacts you can use in your job search. An increasingly important side benefit is the work you do in your internship, which can become some of the best items in your professional portfolio.

Establishing a Reputation Online

When you are searching for a job, a good reputation is vital to your success. According to one survey, nearly all employers use social media to find new employees. Of those, 98% use LinkedIn, 42% use Twitter, and 33% use Facebook.[5] Even more use social networking sites to learn about job candidates who already have applied. A CareerBuilder survey found 60% of employers use social media to screen employees.[6] Using social media wisely can help you build your reputation and become visible to employers.

A specialized use of the Internet is **personal branding,** a popular term for marketing yourself, including job searching. It covers an expectation that you will use various options, from the traditional résumé and cover letter to social media, to market your expertise. You will use these tools to show your value (what do you offer employers?)

Figure 11.3	Percentage of Interns Offered Full-Time Jobs
Industry	**Percentage**
Entertainment/media	85
Oil and gas extraction	81
Construction	80
Accounting	75
Food and beverage	71
Retail	70
Finance/insurance/real estate	67
Engineering	67
Computer and electronics	64
Chemical/pharmaceutical	61

Source: Joe Walker, "Getting Creative to Land an Internship," *Wall Street Journal,* June 8, 2010, D7.

and quality (why should they hire you instead of other candidates?). These are some of the most popular tools:

- **LinkedIn:** This site allows you to include useful information beyond your résumé, and, unlike your web page, it has a powerful search engine behind it.

- **Personal website:** Your website allows you to connect to examples of your professional work. You should invest in a domain name that includes your name. This helps you control how you will show up in online searches because most search algorithms favor URLs that include the search term.[7]

- **Facebook:** If you keep your Facebook profile up to date with your education, employment, and interests, it can serve as an attractive informal résumé. Manage your privacy settings to make only those things that would be important for an employer to see public. But remember that Facebook has a history of making personal information public. Keep all of your content professional. Avoid inappropriate language and all content involving alcohol, other drugs, and incomplete attire.

- **Twitter:** Share useful information such as thoughtful comments about news in your field as you work to build up your Twitter network. Aim for quality, not numbers. Also, follow companies you would like to work for and people throughout your profession.

However you develop your personal brand using these tools, remember that consistency matters. Use your résumé, cover letter, personal website, and social networking to create a consistent, professional image that demonstrates the qualities you want your potential employer to see. This consistency includes seemingly small details such as your profile photo you include on LinkedIn or Facebook and large details like your samples of professional work. When you develop a consistent personal brand, employers are more likely to view your profiles, interview you, and hire you.[8]

> **WARNING:** Select your tools carefully; you probably do not have time to use all the tools on this list successfully. Stay professional in all venues; avoid negative comments about people, your school, and your employers. In addition to content, writing (grammar, coherence, style, logic, spelling) will be judged by potential employers. The list of candidates rejected after a basic web search grows daily.

Using Social Networking Sites with Care

Most employers routinely search the Internet for information about job candidates, and many report they are turned off by what they find—especially on personal web pages and social networking sites such as Facebook. One international survey found that 1 in 10 job applicants from ages 16 to 34 had been rejected for a job because of his or her Facebook activities.[9] CareerBuilder found in one of its surveys that nearly half of all hiring managers have found information on social media that has prevented them from hiring a candidate.[10] Check your social media profiles and personal website carefully before you enter the job market.

Use the "Grandma Test" when you are posting anything online. If you wouldn't want her to see it, you won't want an employer to, either:

When you post something online, use the "Grandma Test." If you wouldn't want her to see it, you won't want an employer to, either.

©Dan Moore/Getty Images

- Remove any unprofessional material such as pictures of you at your computer with a beer in your hand or descriptions of your last party.

- Remove negative comments about current or past employers and teachers.

- Remove political and social rants.

- Remove any personal information that will embarrass you on the job.

- Remove inappropriate material posted by friends, relatives, and colleagues.

The best advice is to plan ahead and post nothing unprofessional on the web.

WARNING: According to a survey conducted by CareerBuilder, 40% of recruiters also check photo- and video-sharing sites; gaming sites; virtual world sites; and classifieds and auction sites such as Craigslist, Amazon, and eBay.[11]

How Employers Use Résumés

LO 11-2

Understanding how employers use résumés will help you create a résumé that works for you.

1. **Employers use résumés to decide whom to interview.** Résumés are examined for relevant experience and skills such as those in Figure 11.4. Because résumés also are used to screen out applicants, omit anything that may create a negative impression.

2. **Résumés are scanned or skimmed.** At many companies, especially large ones, résumés are scanned electronically. Only résumés that match key words are skimmed by a human being. *Time* magazine reported that recruiters spend an average of six seconds reviewing each résumé.[12] You must design your résumé to pass both the "scan test" and the "skim test" by emphasizing crucial qualifications and using the diction of the job ad.

Figure 11.4	Percentage of Employers Who Want Colleges to Place More Emphasis on These Skills
Skill	**Percent**
Effective communication, both oral and written	89
Critical thinking and analytical reasoning	81
Application of knowledge to the work world, through internships and other hands-on experiences	79
Ability to analyze and solve complex problems	75
Teamwork	71
Innovation and creativity	70
Understanding of basic concepts and new developments in science and technology	70
Ability to locate, organize, and evaluate information from multiple sources	68
Understanding of global contexts and developments	67
Ability to work with numbers and understand statistics	63

Source: *Raising the Bar: Employers' Views on College Learning in the Wake of the Economic Downturn: A Survey among Employers Conducted on Behalf of the Association of American Colleges and Universities,* January 20, 2010.

3. **Employers assume that your letter and résumé represent your best work.** Neatness, accuracy, and freedom from typographical errors are essential. Spelling errors will probably cost you your chance at a job, so proofread carefully.

4. **After an employer has chosen an applicant, he or she submits the applicant's résumé to people in the organization who must approve the appointment.** These people may have different backgrounds and areas of expertise. Spell out acronyms. Explain awards, Greek-letter honor societies, unusual job titles, or organizations that may be unfamiliar to the reader.

Guidelines for Résumés

Writing a résumé is not an exact science. But when you must compete against many applicants, these guidelines will help you look as good on paper as you are in person.

Length

A one-page résumé is sufficient, but you must fill the page. Less than a full page suggests that you do not have much to say for yourself.

If you have more good material than will fit on one page, use a second page. A common myth is that all résumés must fit on one page. According to a survey of executives at the 1,000 largest companies in the United States, approval of the two-page résumé is increasing *if* candidates have sufficient good material that relates to the posted job.[13] An experiment that mailed one- or two-page résumés to recruiters at major accounting firms showed that even readers who said they preferred short résumés were more likely to want to interview the candidate with the longer résumé.[14] The longer résumé gives managers a better picture of how you will fit in.

If you do use more than one page, fill at least half of the second page. Use a second sheet of paper; do not print on the back of the first page. Leave less important information for the second page. Put your name and "Page 2" on the second page. If the pages are separated, you want the reader to know that the qualifications belong to you and that the second page is not your whole résumé.

Emphasis

Emphasize the things you've done that (1) are most relevant to the position for which you're applying, (2) show your superiority to other applicants, and (3) are recent (in the past three to five years). Whatever your age at the time you write a résumé, you want to suggest that you are now the best you've ever been.

Show that you're qualified by giving relevant details on course projects, activities, and jobs where you've done similar work. Be brief about low-level jobs that simply show dependability. To prove that you're the best candidate for the job, emphasize items that set you apart from other applicants: promotions, honors, achievements, experience with computers or other relevant equipment, statistics, foreign languages, and so on.

You can emphasize material by putting it at the top or the bottom of a page, by giving it more space, and by setting it off with white space. The beginning and end—of a document, a page, a list—are positions of emphasis. When you have a choice (e.g., in a list of job duties), put less important material in the middle, not at the end, to avoid the impression of "fading out." You also can emphasize material by presenting it in a vertical list, by using informative headings, and by providing details. Headings that name skills listed in the job ad, or skills important for the job (e.g., Managerial Experience), also provide emphasis and help set you apart from the crowd.

Details

Details provide evidence to support your claims, convince the reader, and separate you from other applicants. Numbers make good details. Tell how many people you trained or supervised, how much money you budgeted or saved. Describe the interesting aspects of the job you did.

Too vague:	Sales Manager, *The Daily Collegian,* University Park, PA, 2015–2017. Supervised staff; promoted ad sales.
Good details:	Sales Manager, *The Daily Collegian,* University Park, PA, 2015–2017. Supervised 22-member sales staff; helped recruit, interview, and select staff; assigned duties and scheduled work; recommended best performers for promotion. Motivated staff to increase paid ad inches 10% over previous year's sales.

Omit details that add nothing to a title or that are less impressive than the title alone Either use strong details or just give the office or job title without any details.

Writing Style

Without sacrificing content, be as concise as possible.

Wordy:	Member, Meat Judging Team, 2013–14
	Member, Meat Judging Team, 2014–15
	Member, Meat Judging Team, 2015–16
	Captain, Meat Judging Team, 2016–17
Concise:	Meat Judging Team, 2013–17; Captain 2016–17
Wordy:	Performed foundation load calculations
Concise:	Calculated foundation loads

Résumés normally use phrases and sentence fragments. Complete sentences are acceptable if they are the briefest way to present information. To save space and to avoid sounding arrogant, don't use *I* in a résumé. *Me* and *my* are acceptable if they are unavoidable or if using them reduces wordiness.

Verbs or gerunds (the *-ing* form of verbs, such as *calculating*) create a more dynamic image of you than do nouns, so use them on résumés that will be read by people instead of scanning programs. In the following revisions of job responsibilities, nouns, verbs, and gerunds are in bold type:

Nouns:	Chair, Income Tax Assistance Committee, Winnipeg, MB, 2016–2017. Responsibilities: **recruitment** of volunteers; flyer **design, writing,** and **distribution** for **promotion** of program; **speeches** to various community groups and nursing homes to advertise the service.
Verbs:	Chair, Income Tax Assistance Committee, Winnipeg, MB, 2016–2017. **Recruited** volunteers for the program. **Designed, wrote,** and **distributed** a flyer to promote the program; **spoke** to various community groups and nursing homes to advertise the service.
Gerunds:	Chair, Income Tax Assistance Committee, Winnipeg, MB, 2016–2017. Responsibilities included **recruiting** volunteers for the program; **designing, writing,** and **distributing** a flyer to promote the program; and **speaking** to various community groups and nursing homes to advertise the service.

Note that the items in the list must be in parallel structure (see Chapter 4 and Appendix B for more on parallel structure).

> **WARNING:** All spelling and grammar should be perfect. If they are not your strong suits, pay an editor. In these days of massive responses to job postings, don't give recruiters an easy elimination of your résumé through careless errors. Remember that spell-checkers will not catch all errors, as all those store "mangers" will tell you.

Key Words

Now that electronic résumé scans are common, all résumés, but particularly electronic résumés, need to use **key words**—words and phrases the employer will have the computer seek. Key words are frequently nouns or noun phrases: database management, product upgrades, cost compilation/analysis. However, they also can be adjectives such as *responsible*. Key words are frequently the objects of all those action verbs you are using in your résumé: conducted *publicity campaigns*, wrote weekly division *newsletter*.

Key words may include

- Software program names such as Excel.
- Job titles.
- Types of degrees.
- College or company names.
- Job-specific skills, buzzwords, and jargon.
- Professional organizations (spell out the name and then follow it with its abbreviation in parentheses to increase the number of matches).
- Honor societies (spell out Greek letters).
- Personality traits, such as creativity, dependability, team player.
- Area codes (for geographic narrowing of searches).

To find the key words you need in your job search, look through job ads and employer job sites for common terminology. If many ads mention "communication skills," your résumé should too.

Some key words are widely popular. A survey of more than 3,000 hirers conducted for CareerBuilder reported these key words as ones searched for most often:[15]

- Problem-solving and decision-making skills (50%).
- Oral and written communications (44%).
- Customer service or retention (34%).
- Performance and productivity improvement (32%).
- Leadership (30%).
- Technology (27%).
- Team-building (26%).
- Project management (20%).
- Bilingual (14%).

In addition to using popular key words, you should double-check to make certain your résumé uses the language of the particular job ad to which you are responding. If the ad uses *software engineers* instead of *computer programmers,* then your résumé also should use *software engineers.* If the ad talks about *collaboration,* you will use that word instead of *teamwork* when you discuss your group work experience.

Layout and Design

The layout and design of your résumé will be vital to catch the eye of the employer who is spending only six seconds on each document. Almost certainly, you can create a better résumé by adapting a basic style you like to your own unique qualifications. Experiment with layout, fonts, and spacing to get an attractive résumé. Consider creating a letterhead that you use for both your résumé and your application letter.

> **WARNING:** Do not use résumé templates that come with word-processing software. Many employers see so many résumés from these templates that they learn to recognize—and discount—them.

One of the major decisions you will make is how to treat your **headings.** Do you want them on the left margin, with text immediately below them, as in Figure 11.5? Do you want them alone in the left column, with text in a column to the right, as in Figure 11.8? Generally, people with more text on their résumés use the first option. Putting headings in their own column on the left takes space and thus helps spread a thinner list of accomplishments over the page. But be careful not to make the heading column too wide or it will make your résumé look unbalanced and empty.

Work with **fonts,** bullets, and spacing to highlight your information. Be careful, however, not to make your résumé look "busy" by using too many fonts. Generally, you should use only two fonts in a document, and you should avoid unusual fonts. Keep fonts readable by using at least 10-point type for large fonts such as Arial and 11-point for smaller fonts such as Times New Roman. Use enough white space to group items and make your résumé easy to read, but not so much that you look as if you're padding.

Use color sparingly, if at all. Colored text and shaded boxes can prevent accurate scanning. Similarly, white 8½- by 11-inch paper is standard, but do use a good-quality paper. Contrary to some popular myths, using brightly colored paper or cardstock-weight paper to get noticed by employers will more likely hurt your prospects than help you get an interview.

All of these guidelines are much more flexible for people in creative fields such as advertising and design. As you prepare your résumé, consult with advisers, professors, professionals, and other job seekers to discover the best strategies for your field.

Kinds of Résumés

Two basic categories of résumés are chronological and skills. A **chronological résumé** summarizes what you did in a time line (starting with the most recent events and going backward in **reverse chronology**). It emphasizes degrees, job titles, and dates and is the traditional résumé format. Figures 11.5 and 11.6 show chronological résumés.

Use a chronological résumé when

- Your education and experience are a logical preparation for the position for which you're applying.

- You have impressive job titles, offices, or honors.

Figure 11.5	A Community College Chronological Résumé to Use for Career Fairs and Internships

James Jiang
jianj@wccc.edu

Vary font sizes. Use larger size for name and main headings.

Campus Address
1524 E. Main St
Portland, OR 97231
503-403-5718

Using both addresses ensures continuous contact information.

Permanent Address
2526 Prairie Lane
Portland, OR 97233
503-404-7793

Education
West Coast Community College
A.A. in Financial Management, June 2018
GPA: 3.0/4.0 *Give your grade average if it's 3.0 or higher.*

Summary of Qualifications

Use key words employers might seek.

- Self-motivated, detail-minded, results-oriented
- Consistently successful track record in sales
- Effectively developed and operated entrepreneurial business

List 3–7 qualifications.

Sales Experience
Financial Sales Representative, ABC Inc., Portland, OR, February 2016–present
- Establish client base
- Develop investment strategy plans for clients
- Research and recommend specific investments

Other Experience
Entrepreneur, A-Plus T-Shirt Company, Portland, OR, September 2014–January 2017

One way to handle self-employment.

- Created a saleable product (Graphic T-shirts)
- Secured financial support
- Located a manufacturer
- Supervised production
- Sold t-shirts to high school students
- Realized a substantial profit to pay for college expenses

Cook, Hamburger Shack, Portland, OR, Summers 2012–2014
- Learned sales strategies
- Ensured customer satisfaction
- Collaborated with a team of 25

Collector and Repair Worker, ACN, Inc., Portland, OR, Summer 2010–2012
- Collected and counted approximately $10,000 a day   *Specify large sums of money.*
- Assisted technicians with troubleshooting and repairing coin mechanisms

Other Skills
Computer: Word, Excel, InDesign, WordPress, Outlook
Language: Fluent in Spanish   *Many employers appreciate a second language.*

Figure 11.6	A One-Page Chronological Résumé

Jeff Moeller

831.503.4692
51 Willow Street
San José, CA 95112
jmoeller@csmb.edu

*Use job title
and company name in
Career Objective.*

Career Objective
To bring my attention to detail and love for computer/video games to Telltale Games as a Game Tester

Qualifications
- Experienced in JavaScript, Lua, and Python
- Intermediate proficiency with Visual Studio; high proficiency with Source Safe
- Excellent communication, interpersonal, and collaboration skills
- Advanced knowledge of computers
- Love of video games

*Highlights
qualifications
specific to the job.*

Education
California State University—Monterey Bay
August 2014—May 2018 (expected)
Bachelor of Science in Computer Science and Information Technology

*Keeps Education
section simple to
emphasize
experience.*

Experience
Online Marketing Consultant—Self–Employed
October 2015–present
- Manage multiple client Google Adwords accounts
- Install web software and implement designs for fast turnarounds
- Interface with clients using Basecamp

*Lists job titles
on separate lines.*

Editor-in-Chief—Point Network LLC
June 2013–present
- Write and edit for several LucasArts-related gaming news websites
- Design and code websites using Wordpress
- Manage and administrate the LucasForums.com community

*Use present tense verbs
when you are doing the job now.*

Online Marketing Assistant—Hayfield Group
May 2016–August 2016; May 2017–August 2017
- Managed all client Google Adwords accounts
- Assisted in or managed planning and executing PPC and SEO campaigns
- Coded the company website and integrated the Drupal CMS
- Prepared website analytics reports using Google Analytics and other analytics suites

*Use past tense for
jobs that are over.*

Community Manager—Praise Entertainment, Inc.
April 2015–September 2017
- Managed the community at AdminFusion.com, a website geared toward online forum owners
- Organized and ran a monthly contest for community members

Honors and Activities
- Member of the gaming press for E3 2016 and 2017
- Member of second place team in 2017 National STEM Video Game challenge
  (see demo, "Parrot Villa" at www.STEMChallenge.gov/2017_winners)

*Close with strong
section.*

*Include activities that employer
might value.*

A **skills résumé,** also called a functional résumé, emphasizes the skills you've used, rather than the job in which you used them or the date of the experience. Figure 11.8, shown later in the chapter, is a skills résumé. Use a skills résumé when

- Your education and experience are not the usual route to the position for which you're applying.

- You're changing fields.

- You want to combine experience from paid jobs, activities, volunteer work, and courses to show the extent of your experience in administration, finance, public speaking, and so on.

The two kinds differ in what information is included and how that information is organized.

What to Include in a Résumé

The résumé's purpose is to persuade. In a résumé, you should not lie, but you can omit some information that does not work in your favor.

Résumés commonly contain the following information. The categories in italics are essential.

- *Name and Contact Information*

- *Education*

- *Experience*

- Honors and Awards

- Skills

- Activities

- Portfolio

You may choose other titles for these categories and add categories that are relevant for your qualifications, such as computer skills or foreign languages.

Education and Experience always stand as separate categories, even if you have only one item under each heading. Combine other headings so that you have at least two long or three short items under each heading. For example, if you're in one honor society and two social clubs, and on one athletic team, combine them all under Activities and Honors.

If you have more than seven items under a heading, consider using subheadings. For example, a student who participated in many activities might divide them into Campus Activities and Community Service.

Put your strongest categories near the top and at the bottom of the first page. If you have impressive work experience, you might want to put that category first and Education second.

Name and Contact Information

Use your full *name,* even if everyone calls you by a nickname. You may use an initial rather than spelling out your first or middle name. Put your name in big type.

A résumé is your most important document at career fairs.

©MARK RALSTON/Staff

Give a complete *phone number,* including the area code. Some job candidates give both home and cell phone numbers. Be sure to provide a phone number where you can be reached during the day. Employers usually call during business hours to schedule interviews and make job offers. Do not give lab or dorm phone numbers unless you are sure someone there will take an accurate message for you at all times. Also, be sure your voice mail has a professional-sounding message.

If you have a *website,* and you are sure it looks professional (both content and writing), you may wish to include its URL. Be sure your site does not reveal personal information—such as marital status, ethnicity, religious beliefs, or political stance—that could work against you. Be particularly careful of photographs.

Provide an *email address.* Some job candidates set up a new email address just for job hunting. Your email address should look professional; avoid sexy, childish, or illicit addresses. List your *LinkedIn* site, if you have one. You also may list your Facebook profile or Twitter handle if you use them professionally or if social networking is required or desired in your profession.

Education

Education can be your first major category if you've just earned (or are about to earn) a degree or if you have a degree that is essential or desirable for the position you're seeking. Put your Education section later if you need all of page 1 for what you determine to be more important categories or if you lack a degree that other applicants may have (see Figure 11.8).

Under Education, provide information about your undergraduate and graduate degrees, including the location of institutions and the year you received or expect your degree.

Use the same format for all the schools you attended. List your degrees in reverse chronological order (most recent first).

> Master of Accounting Science, May 2017, Arizona State University, Tempe, AZ
> Bachelor of Arts in Finance, May 2015, New Mexico State University, Las Cruces, NM

> BS in Industrial Engineering, May 2017, Iowa State University, Ames, IA
> AS in Business Administration, May 2015, Des Moines Area Community College, Ankeny, IA

When you're getting a four-year degree, include community college only if it will interest employers, such as by showing an area of expertise different from that of your major. You may want to include your minor, emphasis, or concentration and any graduate courses you have taken. Include study abroad, even if you didn't earn college credits. If you got a certificate for international study, give the name and explain the significance of the certificate. Highlight proficiency in foreign or computer languages by using a separate category.

Professional certifications can be listed under Education or in a separate category.

If your GPA is good and you graduated recently, include it. If your GPA isn't impressive, calculate your average in your major and your average for your last 60 hours. If these are higher than your overall GPA, consider using them. If you do use your major GPA or upper-class GPA, make sure you label them as such so you can't be accused of dishonesty. The National Association of Colleges and Employers found that 70% of employers plan to screen job applicants graduating in 2017 by GPA.[16] In some industries such as management consulting and computer manufacturing, more than 90% of employers screen by GPA.[17] If you leave your GPA off your résumé, most employers will automatically assume that it is below a 3.0. If yours is, you will need to rely on internships, work experience, and skills acquired in activities to make yourself an attractive job candidate.

After giving the basic information (degree, field of study, date, school, city, state) about your degree, you may wish to list courses, using short descriptive titles rather than course numbers. Use a subhead such as "Courses Related to Major" or "Courses Related to Financial Management" that will allow you to list all the courses (including psychology, speech, and business communication) that will help you in the job for which you're applying. Don't say "Relevant Courses," as that implies your other courses were irrelevant.

> Bachelor of Science in Management, May 2017, Illinois State University, Normal, IL
> GPA: 3.8/4.0
> Courses Related to Management:
>
> | | |
> |---|---|
> | Personnel Administration | Business Decision Making |
> | Finance | International Business |
> | Management I and II | Marketing |
> | Accounting I and II | Legal Environment of Business |
> | Business Report Writing | Business Speaking |

Listing courses is an unobtrusive way to fill a page. You also may want to list courses or the number of hours in various subjects if you've taken an unusual combination of courses that uniquely qualify you for the position for which you're applying.

> BS in Marketing, May 2017, California State University at Northridge
> 30 hours in marketing
> 15 hours in Spanish
> 9 hours in Chicano studies

As you advance in your career, your education section will shrink until finally it probably will include only your degrees and educational institutions.

Honors and Awards

It's nice to have an Honors and Awards section, but not everyone can do so. If you have fewer than three and therefore cannot justify a separate heading, consider a heading Honors and Activities to get that important word in a position of emphasis.

Include the following kinds of entries in this category:

- Academic honor societies. Specify the nature of Greek-letter honor societies (i.e., journalism honorary) so the reader doesn't think they're just social clubs.

- Fellowships and scholarships.

- Awards given by professional societies.

- Major awards given by civic groups.

- Varsity letters; selection to all-state or all-America teams; finishes in state, national, or Olympic meets. (These also could go under Activities but may look more impressive under Honors.)

Identify honor societies ("national journalism honorary," "campus honorary for top 2% of business majors") for readers who are not in your discipline. If your fellowships or scholarships are particularly selective or remunerative, give supporting details:

Clyde Jones Scholarship:	four-year award covering tuition, fees, room, and board
Marilyn Terpstra Scholarship:	$25,000 annually for four years
Heemsly Fellowship:	50 awarded nationally each year to top Information Science juniors

Be careful of listing Dean's List for only one or two semesters. Such a listing reminds readers that in these days of grade inflation, you were off the list many more times than you were on it.

As a new college graduate, try to put Honors on page 1. In a skills résumé, put Honors on page 1 if they're major (e.g., Phi Beta Kappa, Phi Kappa Phi). Otherwise, save them until page 2—Experience will probably take the whole first page.

Experience

You may use other headings if they work better: Work Experience, Military Experience, Marketing Experience. In a skills résumé, headings such as "Marketing Experience" allow you to include accomplishments from activities and course projects. Headings that reflect skills mentioned in the job ad are particularly effective.

What to Include Under this section in a chronological résumé, include the following information for each job you list: position or job title, organization, city and state (no zip code), dates of employment for jobs held during the last 10 to 15 years, and other details, such as full- or part-time status, job duties, special responsibilities, or the fact that you started at an entry-level position and were promoted. Use strong verbs such as the ones in Figure 11.7 to brainstorm what you've done. Try to give supporting details for highly valued attributes such as communication skills and leadership experience. Include any internships and co-ops you have had. Also, include unpaid jobs and self-employment if they provided relevant skills (e.g., supervising people, budgeting, planning, persuading).

If you went to college right after high school, it is common to go back as far as the summer after high school. Include earlier jobs only if you started working someplace before

Figure 11.7	Action Verbs for Résumés		
analyzed	directed	led	reviewed
budgeted	earned	managed	revised
built	edited	motivated	saved
chaired	established	negotiated	scheduled
coached	evaluated	observed	simplified
collected	examined	organized	sold
conducted	helped	persuaded	solved
coordinated	hired	planned	spoke
counseled	improved	presented	started
created	increased	produced	supervised
demonstrated	interviewed	recruited	trained
designed	introduced	reported	translated
developed	investigated	researched	wrote

graduating from high school but continued working there after graduation, or if the job is pertinent to the one you are applying for. If you worked full-time after high school, make that clear. More experienced workers generally go back no more than 10 years.

The details you give about your experience are some of the most vital information on your résumé. As you provide these details, use bulleted lists rather than paragraphs, which are harder to read and may be skipped over. Remember that items in lists need to have parallel structure; see Appendix B for a refresher. Focus on results rather than duties; employers are far more interested in what you accomplished than in what you had to do. Use numbers to support your results wherever possible:

Supervised crew of 15.

Managed $120,000 budget; decreased expenses by 19%.

Wrote monthly electronic newsletter; increased hits by 12%.

Emphasize accomplishments that involve money, customers, teamwork, leadership, computer skills, and communication.

Use past tense verbs for jobs you held in the past and present tense verbs for jobs you still have. Do not list minor duties such as distributing mail or filing documents. If your duties were completely routine, say, at your summer job at McDonald's, do not list them. If the jobs you held in the past were low-level ones, present them briefly or combine them:

2013–2017 Part-time and full-time jobs to finance education

Skills Résumés   Skills résumés stress the skills you have acquired rather than specific jobs you have held. They show employers that you do have the desired skill set even if you lack the traditional employment background. They allow you to include skills acquired from activities and course projects in addition to jobs.

In a skills résumé, the heading of your main section usually changes from "Experience" to "Skills." Within the section, the subheadings will be replaced with the skills used in the job you are applying for, rather than the title or the dates of the jobs you've held. For entries under each skill, combine experience from paid jobs, unpaid work, classes, activities, and community service.

Use headings that reflect the jargon of the job for which you're applying: *logistics* rather than *planning* for a technical job; *procurement* rather than *purchasing* for a job with the military. Figure 11.8 shows a skills résumé for someone who is changing fields.

Figure 11.8	A Skills Résumé for Someone Changing Fields

Mandy Shelly
www.wisc.edu/~Shelly88/home.htm

If you have a professional web page, include its URL.

266 Van Buren Drive
Madison, WI 53706
shellym@wisc.edu
555-897-1534 (home)
555-842-4242 (cell)

Objective

To contribute my enthusiasm for writing as a Technical Writer at PDF Productions

Job objective includes the position and name of the company.

Skills

Largest section on skills résumé; allows you to combine experiences from work and class.

Computer
- Designed a web page using Dreamweaver
  www.madisonanimalshelter.com
- Used a variety of Macintosh and PC platform programs and languages:

Aspects (online discussion forum)	Adobe Professional
Dreamweaver	HTML
XML	Java Script
	Photoshop

Specify computer programs you know well.

Design and Writing
- Designed a quarterly newsletter for local animal shelter
- Developed professional brochures
- Wrote a variety of professional documents: letters, memos, and reports
- Edited internal documents and promotional materials
- Proofread seven student research papers as a tutor

Use parallel structure for bulleted lists.

Organization and Administration
- Coordinated program schedules
- Developed work schedules for five employees
- Led a ten-member team in planning and implementing sorority philanthropy program
- Created cataloging system for specimens
- Ordered and handled supplies, including live specimens

Employment History

Condensed to make room for skills.

Technical Writer, Madison Animal Shelter, Madison, WI 2016–present
Undergraduate Lab Assistant, Department of Biology, University of Wisconsin–Madison, Madison, WI, 2016–present
Tutor, University of Wisconsin–Madison, Madison, WI, 2015–2016

Uses reverse chronology.

Education

Bachelor of Arts, May 2018
University of Wisconsin–Madison, Madison, WI
Major: Animal Ecology
Minor: Chemistry
GPA 3.4/4.0

Give minor when it can be helpful.

Honors

End with strong items at the bottom of your page, a position of emphasis.

Phi Kappa Phi Honor Society
Alpha Lambda Delta Honor Society, Ecology Honorary
Dean's List, 2010 to present
Raymond Hamilton Scholarship, 2016–2017
          ($5000 to a top ecology student in Wisconsin)

Explain honors your reader may not know.

A job description can give you ideas for headings. Possible headings and subheadings for skills résumés include

Administration	**Communication**
Budgeting	Editing
Coordinating	Fund-Raising
Evaluating	Interviewing
Implementing	Negotiating
Negotiating	Persuading
Planning	Presenting
Supervising	Writing

Many jobs require a mix of skills. Try to include the skills that you know will be needed in the job you want. You need at least three subheadings in a skills résumé; six or seven are not uncommon. Give enough detail under each subheading so the reader will know what you did. Begin with the most important category from the reader's point of view.

In a skills résumé, list your paid jobs under Work History or Employment Record near the end of the résumé (see Figure 11.8). List only job title, employer, city, state, and dates. Omit details that you already have used under Skills.

Other Skills

You may want a brief section in a chronological résumé where you highlight skills not apparent in your work history. These skills may include items such as foreign languages or programming languages. You might want to list software you have used or training on expensive equipment (electron microscopes, NMR machines). As always on your résumé, be completely honest: "two years of high school German" or "elementary speaking knowledge of Spanish." Any knowledge of a foreign language is a plus. It means that a company desiring a second language in its employees would not have to start from scratch in training you. Figure 11.6 lists skills in its Qualifications section.

Activities

Employers may be interested in your activities if you're a new college graduate because they can demonstrate leadership roles, management abilities, and social skills as well as the ability to juggle a schedule. If you've worked for several years after college or have an advanced degree (MBA, JD), you can omit Activities and include Professional Activities and Affiliations or Community and Public Service. If you went straight from college to graduate school but have an unusually strong record demonstrating relevant skills, include this category even if all the entries are from your undergraduate days.

Include the following kinds of items under Activities:

- Volunteer work. Include important committees, leadership roles, communication activities, and financial and personnel responsibilities.

- Membership in organized student activities. Include leadership and financial roles as well as important subcommittees.

- Membership in professional associations. Many of them have special low membership fees for students, so you should join one or more, particularly the ones directly associated with your major.

- Participation in varsity, intramural, or independent athletics. However, don't list so many sports that you appear not to have had adequate time to study.

As you list activities, add details that will be relevant for your job. Did you handle a six-figure budget for your Greek organization? Plan all the road trips for your soccer club? Coordinate all the publicity for the campus blood drive? Design the posters for homecoming? Major leadership, financial, and creative roles and accomplishments may look more impressive if they're listed under Experience instead of under Activities.

Portfolio

If you have samples of your work available, you may want to end your résumé by stating "Portfolio (or writing samples) available on request" or by giving the URL for your work.

Dealing with Difficulties

LO 11-3

Some job hunters face special problems. This section gives advice for six common problems.

"I Don't Have Any Experience."

If you have a year or more before you job hunt, you can get experience in several ways:

- **Seek an internship.** Your college career center or professors in your major can direct you toward opportunities. Internships provide solid experience in your field, and many lead to full-time jobs.

- **Take a fast-food job—and keep it.** If you do well, you'll likely be promoted to a supervisor within a year. Use every opportunity to learn about management and financial aspects of the business.

- **Sign on with agencies that handle temporary workers.** As an added bonus, some of these jobs become permanent.

- **Join a volunteer organization that interests you.** If you work hard, you'll quickly get an opportunity to do more: manage a budget, write fund-raising materials, and supervise other volunteers.

- **Freelance.** Design brochures, create web pages, do tax returns for small businesses. Use your skills—for free at first, if you have to.

- **Write.** Create a portfolio of ads, instructions, or whatever documents are relevant for the field you want to enter. Ask a professional—an instructor, a local businessperson, someone from a professional organization—to critique them.

If you're on the job market now, think carefully about what you've really done. Complete sentences using the action verbs in Figure 11.7 to help jog your memory. Think about what you've done in courses, volunteer work, and unpaid activities. Focus on skills in problem solving, critical thinking, teamwork, and communication. Solving a problem for a hypothetical firm in an accounting class, thinking critically about a report problem in business communication, working with a group in a marketing class, and communicating with people at the senior center where you volunteer are good experiences, even if no one paid you.

"All My Experience Is in My Family's Business."

In your résumé, simply list the company you worked for. For a reference, instead of a family member, list a supervisor, client, or vendor who can talk about your work. Because the reader may wonder whether "Jim Clarke" is any relation to the owner of

"Clarke Construction Company," be ready to answer interview questions about why you're looking at other companies. Prepare an answer that stresses the broader opportunities you seek but doesn't criticize your family or the family business.

"I Want to Change Fields."

Have a good reason for choosing the field in which you're looking for work. "I want a change" or "I need to get out of a bad situation" does not convince an employer that you know what you're doing.

Think about how your experience relates to the job you want. Sam wants a new career as a pharmaceutical sales representative. He has sold woodstoves, served subpoenas, and worked on an oil rig. A chronological résumé makes his work history look directionless. But a skills résumé could focus on persuasive ability (selling stoves), initiative and persistence (serving subpoenas), and technical knowledge (courses in biology and chemistry).

Learn about the skills needed in the job you want: learn the buzzwords of the industry. Figure 11.8 shows a skills résumé of someone changing fields from animal ecology to technical writing. Her reason for changing could be that she found she enjoyed the writing duties of her jobs more than she enjoyed the ecology work.

"I've Been Out of the Job Market for a While."

You need to prove to a potential employer that you're up-to-date and motivated. Try the following:

- Create a portfolio of your work to show what you can do for the employer.
- Do freelance work.
- Be active in professional organizations. Attend meetings.
- Look for volunteer work where you can use and expand relevant work skills.
- Attend local networking events.
- Read the journals and trade publications of your field.
- Learn the software that professionals use in your field.
- Be up-to-date with electronic skills such as text messaging, Internet searches, and social networking.
- Take professional training to expand your skill set.

Employment counselors advise that you not leave a gap on your résumé; such a gap makes employers speculate about disasters such as nervous breakdowns or jail time. They suggest you matter-of-factly list an honorable title such as Parent or Caregiver; do not apologize. Better yet is to fill in the gap with substantial volunteer experience. Heading a $75,000 fund-raising drive for a new playground looks good for almost any employer. A side benefit of volunteer work, in addition to new career skills, is networking. Boards of directors and executives of nonprofit organizations are frequently well-connected members of the community.

"I Was Laid Off."

In times of large layoffs, this is not an overwhelming obstacle. You do not need to point out the layoff in your application materials; the end date of your last employment will make the point for you. Instead, use your documents to highlight your strengths.

Be prepared to be asked about the layoff in an interview. Why were you laid off when other employees were retained? It helps if you can truthfully give a neutral explanation: the accounting work was outsourced; our entire lab was closed; the company laid off everyone who had worked fewer than five years. Be sure you do not express bitterness or self-pity; neither emotion will help you get your new job. On the other hand, do not be overly grateful for an interview; such excess shows a lack of self-confidence. Be sure to show you are keeping yourself current by doing some of the items in the bulleted list in the previous section.

"I Was Fired."

In the event you were fired, first, you need to reduce negative feelings to a manageable level before you're ready to job-hunt.

Second, take responsibility for your role in the termination.

Third, try to learn from the experience. You'll be a much more attractive job candidate if you can show that you've learned from the experience—whether your lesson is improved work habits or that you need to choose a job where you can do work you can point to with pride.

Fourth, collect evidence showing that earlier in your career you were a good worker. This evidence could include references from earlier employers, good performance evaluations, and a portfolio of good work.

Some common strategies also may give you some help for references. You should check with the Human Resources Department to understand the company's reference policy. Some companies now give no references other than verification of job title and work dates. Others do not give references for employees who worked only a short time.[18] Another option is to ask someone other than your former boss for a reference. Could you ask a supplier or vendor? A different department head?

Above all, be honest. Do not lie about your termination at an interview or on a job application. The application usually requires you to sign a statement that the information you are providing is true and that false statements can be grounds for dismissal.

Sending Your Résumé Electronically

In addition to a paper résumé for job fairs, interviews, and potential contacts, you will need electronic versions of your résumé. With a few exceptions noted below, these résumés will have the same content but will be formatted differently so they can be "read" by both software and humans.

Many employers are asking to have résumés posted on their organizations' websites. When doing so, be sure you follow the directions exactly. You also may be asked by some employers to send your résumé by email.

Here are some basic guidelines of email job-hunting etiquette:

- Don't use your current employer's email system for your job search. You'll leave potential employers with the impression that you spend company time on writing résumés and other nonwork-related activities.

- Set up a free, Internet-based email account using services such as Gmail or Yahoo! to manage correspondence related to your job hunt.

- Avoid using silly or cryptic email addresses. Instead of bubbles@gmail.com, opt for something businesslike: yourname@yahoo.com. If you have a common name, try using combinations like "firstname.lastname@yahoo.com" or "firstname_lastname@yahoo.com" rather than using strings of numbers after your name.

- Write a simple subject line that makes a good first impression: Résumé–Kate Sanchez. A good subject line will improve the chances that your résumé is actually read since email from unknown senders is often deleted without being opened. If you are responding to an ad, use the job title or job code listed.

- Before sending your résumé into cyberspace, test to see how it will look when it comes out on the other end. Email it to yourself and a friend, then critique and fix it.

- Send only one résumé, even if the firm has more than one position for which you qualify. Most recruiters have negative reactions to multiple résumés.

- Experts differ on whether candidates should phone to follow up. Phoning once to be sure your résumé arrived is probably fine.

It's important to heed the specific directions of employers that you are emailing. Many do not want attachments because of viruses. While a few may want a Microsoft Word or pdf attachment of your résumé, others may specify that you paste your résumé directly into the body of your email message.

If you are sending your résumé in the text of an email,

- Start all lines at the left margin.

- Eliminate decorative elements such as boxes or vertical or horizontal lines.

- Do not use bold, underlining, bullets, tabs, or unusual fonts. Instead use keys such as asterisks. You also can put some headings in all capital letters, but use this device sparingly.

- To avoid awkward line breaks for your readers, shorten line lengths to 65 characters and spaces.

Your résumé will look plain to you, but the employers receiving it are used to the look of in-text résumés.

If you are sending your résumé as an attachment, name the document appropriately: Smith Robyn Résumé.docx. Never name it Résumé.docx; you do not want it to get lost in a long directory of documents.

With your résumé include a brief email message that will make the receiver want to look at your résumé. In it, mention the types of files you've included. Remember, it takes only an instant for readers to delete your email. Do not give them reasons to trash your résumé.

Some people confuse electronic and scannable résumés. The former are résumés you send in or attached to an email. The latter are paper résumés specially formatted for older software. Software programs have greatly improved recently and most can now scan regular résumés posted on websites.

Honesty

LO 11-5

Acting ethically means being absolutely honest on your résumé—and in the rest of your job search. Just ask Marilee Jones, former dean of admissions at Massachusetts Institute of Technology (MIT). In 1979, when she applied for an admissions job at MIT, her résumé listed bachelor's and master's degrees from Rensselaer Polytechnic Institute. In reality, she attended there only one year as a part-time student. By 1997, when she was promoted to the deanship, she did not have the courage to correct her résumé. In April 2007, she was forced to resign, even though she was a nationally recognized leader in admissions, after an anonymous tip.[19]

Most businesses now conduct some kind of background check on job applicants. Even graduate schools, particularly business schools, are checking applicants. A survey of more than 3,000 hirers conducted for CareerBuilder reported that 56% had caught lies on résumés.[20]

Background checks on job candidates can include a credit check, legal and criminal records, complete employment history, and academic credentials. Such checks turn up some incredible whoppers. Résumés have been found using someone else's photo, listing degrees from nonexistent schools, listing fake Mensa memberships, and even claiming false connections to famous people.[21]

You can omit some material on your résumé because obviously you cannot include everything about your life to date. For instance, it's still ethical to omit a low GPA, although most employers will assume it is very low indeed to be omitted. But what you do include must be absolutely honest.

Some of the most frequent inaccuracies on résumés are inflated job titles and incorrect dates of employment. While these data are easy to fudge, they are also easy to catch in background checks. It is also possible that some of these particular inaccuracies come from careless records kept by job candidates. Do you remember the exact job title of that first job you held as a sophomore in high school? Keep careful records of your employment history!

If employers do an employment history check, and many do, they will have a complete work history for you. They will be able to spot inaccurate company names and work dates. If you left a company off your résumé, they may wonder why; some may assume your performance at that company was not satisfactory.

Other areas where résumés are commonly inaccurate are

- Degrees: many people conveniently forget they were a few hours short of a degree.

- GPAs: inflating one's grade point average seems to be a big temptation. If you are using the classes in your major or the last 60 hours of coursework to calculate your GPA, label them as such so you won't appear to be inflating your overall GPA.

- Honors: people list memberships in fake honoraries or fake memberships in real honoraries.

- Fake employers.

- Job duties: many people inflate or embellish them.

- Salary increases.

- Fake addresses: people create these to have the "local" advantage.

- Fake contact information for references: this information frequently leads to family members or friends who will give fake referrals.

- Technical abilities.

- Language proficiency.

All dishonesty on a résumé is dangerous, keeping you from being hired if discovered early, and causing you to be fired if discovered later. However, the last two bullets listed are particularly dangerous because your chances are good of being asked at an interview to demonstrate your listed proficiencies.

The checklist in Figure 11.9 will help you develop your effective résumé.

Figure 11.9	Checklist for Résumés

Content

☐ Does the résumé target the specific employer and position?

☐ Are the résumé sections clearly, correctly, and consistently labeled?

☐ Does the order of the headings highlight the strongest qualifications?

☐ Are experience and education listed in reverse chronological order?

☐ Does the résumé provide details for your best qualifications?

☐ Does the résumé use numbers to support accomplishments?

☐ Does the résumé use key words? Action verbs?

☐ Is the information provided relevant to the position?

☐ Does the information flow logically and easily?

☐ Do the bulleted lists use parallel structure?

☐ Are grammar, punctuation, and spelling correct?

☐ Does the information support your claim that you are qualified and the best person for this position?

☐ Does the résumé address possible audience concerns with your application?

☐ Is all information on the résumé accurate and honest?

Design

☐ Does the page look balanced?

☐ Does the résumé look original, not based on a template?

☐ Does the length of the résumé fit the situation and position?

☐ Does the résumé include clear headings, bullets, and white space?

☐ Does the résumé use fonts appropriate for the career level and industry?

☐ Does the résumé use consistent font sizes and spacing throughout the document?

☐ Does the design reflect your career ambitions?

Job Application Letters

LO 11-6

The purpose of a job application letter is to get an interview. A survey conducted by Robert Half International, the world's largest specialized staffing firm, found 86% of executives said cover letters remain valuable components of job applications in the electronic age.[22]

The co-founder of one software firm says,

> We ignore résumés. . . . Résumés reduce people to bullet points, and most people look pretty good as bullet points.
>
> What we do look at are cover letters. Cover letters say it all. They immediately tell you if someone wants this job or just any job. And cover letters make something else very clear: They tell you who can and who can't write. . . . When in doubt, always hire the better writer.[23]

Job letters can play an important role in your personal branding. They can show your personality and, through careful reference to well-chosen details about the organization, interest in a particular job.

Job letters frequently are seen as evidence of your written communication skills, so you want to do your best work in them. Flaws in your letter may well be seen as predicting shoddy job performance in the future.

How Content Differs in Job Letters and Résumés

The job application letter accompanies your résumé and serves as its cover letter. It is your chance to showcase the features that set you apart from the crowd. Here you bring to life the facts presented in your résumé; here you can give a sense of your personality. The cover letter is your opportunity to "sell" yourself into an interview.

Although résumés and job letters overlap somewhat, they differ in three important ways:

- The résumé summarizes *all* your qualifications. The letter expands your *best* qualifications to show how you can help the organization meet its needs, how you differ from other applicants, and how much knowledge of the organization you possess.

- The résumé avoids controversial material. The job letter can explain in a positive way situations such as career changes or gaps in employment history.

- The résumé uses short, parallel phrases and sentence fragments. The letter uses complete sentences in well-written paragraphs.

How to Find Out about Employers and Jobs

To adapt your letter to a specific organization, you need information both about the employer and about the job itself. You'll need to know

- **The name and address of the person who should receive the letter.** To get this information, check the ad, call the organization, check its website, or check with your job-search contacts. An advantage of calling is that you can find out what courtesy title the individual prefers and get current information.

- **What the organization does, and some facts about it.** Knowing the organization's larger goals enables you to show how your specific work will help the company meet its goals. Useful facts can include market share, new products or promotions, the kind of computer or manufacturing equipment it uses, plans for growth or downsizing, competitive position, challenges the organization faces, and the corporate culture.

▪ **What the job itself involves.** Campus placement offices and web listings often have fuller job descriptions than appear in ads. Talk to friends who have graduated recently to learn what their jobs involve. Conduct information interviews to learn more about opportunities that interest you.

The websites listed in Figure 11.10 provide a wide range of information. For instance, the *Forbes* and *Money* sites have good financial news stories; the *Public Register* (prars. com) is a good source for annual reports. As a consumer, you may have used the Better Business Bureau (bbb.org) site.

More specific information about companies can be found on their websites. To get specific financial data on publicly traded companies (and to see how the organization presents itself to the public), get the company's annual report from your library or the web. To learn about new products, plans for growth, or solutions to industry challenges, read business newspapers such as *The Wall Street Journal,* business magazines such as *Fortune* or *Bloomberg Businessweek,* and trade journals.

The Hidden Job Market

Many jobs are never advertised—and the number rises the higher on the job ladder you go. *Forbes* reported that nearly half of all job openings are never publically posted.[24] In fact, some authorities put the percentage of jobs that are not advertised as high as 80%.[25] Many new jobs come not from responding to an ad, but from networking with personal contacts. Some of these jobs are created especially for a specific person. These unadvertised jobs are called the **hidden job market.** Making many positive connections will be helpful throughout your career.

Content and Organization for Job Application Letters

While networking is clearly important, so too is taking job application materials seriously. Job letters help show employers why they should interview you instead of other—sometimes hundreds of others—qualified applicants. In your letter, focus on

▪ Your qualifications to meet major requirements of the job.

▪ Points that separate you from other applicants.

▪ Points that show your knowledge of the organization.

▪ Qualities that every employer is likely to value: the ability to write and speak effectively, to solve problems, to work well with people.

Figure 11.10	Web Sources for Facts about Companies
Company Facts	http://www.lib.berkeley.edu/BUSI
http://money.cnn.com	http://www.prars.com
http://online.wsj.com/public/page/news-career-jobs.html	http://www.stockmarketyellowpages.com
http://www.bbb.org	http://www.vault.com
http://www.corporateinformation.com	http://www.wetfeet.com
http://www.forbes.com	
http://www.inc.com/inc5000	**Salary Calculators**
http://www.irin.com	http://salaryexpert.com
http://www.jobbankinfo.org	http://www.indeed.com/salary
	http://www.payscale.com

Two different hiring situations call for two different kinds of application letters. Write a **solicited letter** when you know that the company is hiring: you've seen an ad, you've been advised to apply by a professor or friend, you've read in a trade publication that the company is expanding. This situation is similar to a direct request in persuasion (see Chapter 10): you can indicate immediately that you are applying for the position. Sometimes, however, the advertised positions may not be what you want or you may want to work for an organization that has not announced openings in your area. Then you write a **prospecting letter.** (The metaphor is drawn from prospecting for gold.) The prospecting letter is like a problem-solving persuasive message.

Prospecting letters help you tap into the hidden job market. In some cases, your prospecting letter may arrive at a company that has decided to hire but has not yet announced the job. In other cases, companies create positions to get a good person who is on the market. Even in a hiring freeze, jobs are sometimes created for specific individuals.

In both solicited and prospecting letters, you should

- Address the letter to a specific person (a must for a prospecting letter).

- Indicate the specific position for which you're applying.

- Be specific about your qualifications.

- Show what separates you from other applicants.

- Show knowledge of the company and the position.

- Refer to your résumé (which you would enclose with the letter).

- Ask for an interview.

The following discussion follows the job letter from beginning to end. The two kinds of letters are discussed separately where they differ and together where they are the same. Letters for internships follow the same patterns: use a solicited letter to apply for an internship that has been advertised and a prospecting letter to create an internship with a company that has not announced one.

How to Organize Solicited Letters

When you know the company is hiring, use the pattern of organization in Figure 11.11. A sample solicited letter for a graduating senior is shown in Figure 11.12. A solicited letter following up from a career fair and requesting an internship is shown in Figure 11.13.

Figure 11.11   How to Organize a Solicited Job Application Letter
1. State that you're applying for the job (phrase the job title as your source phrased it). Tell where you learned about the job (ad, referral, etc.). Include any reference number mentioned in the ad. Briefly show that you have the major qualifications required by the ad: a college degree, professional certification, job experience, etc. Summarize your other qualifications briefly in the same order in which you plan to discuss them in the letter.
2. Develop your major qualifications in detail. Be specific about what you've done; relate your achievements to the work you'd be doing in this new job.
3. Develop your other qualifications, even if the ad doesn't ask for them. Show what separates you from the other applicants who also will answer the ad. Demonstrate your knowledge of the organization.
4. Ask for an interview; tell when you'll be available to be interviewed and to begin work. Thank recipient for considering your application. End on a positive, forward-looking note.

Figure 11.12	A Solicited Letter from a Graduating Senior

Jenny Moeller

831.503.4692
51 Willow Street
San José, CA 95112
jmoeller@csmb.edu

April 4, 2018

Mr. Richard Grove
Telltale Games
P.O. Box 9737
San Rafael, CA 94912

Dear Mr. Grove:

*Tell where you learned about the job.
If the job has a reference number, provide it.*

In paragraph 1, show you have the qualifications the ad lists.

I am applying for your Game Designer position posted on your website. As an avid player of Telltale games, I believe that I have all the qualifications to do a great job. With my degree in Computer Science and Information Technology and my experience creating game content, I will be able to apply many skills to the Game Designer position. My passion for becoming part of the gaming industry, combined with my oral and written communication skills, makes me a great fit for the Telltale team.

This summary sentence forecasts the structure of the rest of the letter.

Shows enthusiasm for the profession and picks up on the programming experience emphasis in the job ad.

Since I was five, I have had a strong interest in computers and video games, and my interest and knowledge have only increased in recent years. Not only do I play video games, I discuss them with others, read news articles about them online, and consider ways to improve or change a specific game. I have also used game editors to create my own content in games. When it comes to computers, I have a keen interest in staying current with the latest technology, and I apply my knowledge hands-on by building systems. These experiences give me an understanding of how modern computers and video game systems function. I also have experience with several programming languages, from both taking courses and learning them on my own. This has increased my eye for detail, a necessary ability for any game designer.

My passion for creating video games was recognized this year in the national STEM video game challenge. With a team of students in Professor Kent Olbernath's game development class at California State University, I produced "Parrot Villa," the first level of an immersive game where players solve mysteries on a unique jungle world. The programming quality and detailed story line helped my team earn second place in the nationwide competition. You can see a demo of "Parrot Villa" at www.STEMChallenge.gov/2017_Winners.

Provides evidence for her achievements in the profession.

Relates what she has done to what he could do for the company.

Evidence of communication skills is a plus for almost any job.

Along with my enthusiasm for games, I have strong oral and written communication skills. I am a confident public speaker, and I have an ability to relay information in a clear and concise manner. More importantly, though, I have developed the ability in my creative writing courses to create engaging and coherent narratives, which will be a large component of developing new games. In addition to my coursework and experience, I have honed my skills online by writing articles about games. In covering the video game industry for Point Network, I have reviewed Telltale's own *Tales of Monkey Island*.

Shows familiarity with company's products.

Working in the video game industry is my goal, and I would be a great asset to Telltale Games. I would love to come in for an interview to discuss the position and the contributions I can make. I have always enjoyed playing Telltale's games, and I look forward to the possibility of working on them one day soon.

Sincerely,

Jenny Moeller

Jenny Moeller

Figure 11.13   Letter Following Up from a Career Fair and Requesting an Internship

James Jiang
jiangj@wccc.edu

Campus Address
1524 E. Main St
Portland, OR 97231
503-403-5718

Letterhead matches his résumé.

Permanent Address
2526 Prairie Lane
Portland, OR 97233
503-404-7793

January 23, 2018

Ms. Deborah Pascel, HR Department
Prime Financial
401 Prime Park Place
Beaverton, OR 97007

Dear Ms. Pascel:

Uses his contact immediately.

Mary Randi at the West Coast Community College Career Fair suggested I send you my résumé for the Sales Advisor internship. My education, combined with my past work experiences, makes me a strong candidate for Prime Financial.

Shows he has been getting full value from his schooling.

Paragraphs 2 and 3 show he has skills he can use immediately as an intern.

While working toward my Associate of Arts degree in Financial Management from West Coastal Community College, I have learned the value of fiscal responsibility. For example, in my social financial planning course, I developed a strategic plan to eliminate credit card debt for a one-income household with two children. Moreover, in my business communication course, I improved my oral communication ability so that I could effectively communicate my plans to potential clients. This ability will be an asset to Prime Financial as the organization works to maintain the strong relationship with the community and small business owners that Ms. Randi informed me about.

Refers to knowledge gained at career fair.

My financial education, combined with my previous work experiences in sales, will allow me to thoroughly analyze investment opportunities and establish a strong client base for Prime Financial. For example, I started the A-Plus T-Shirt Company that sold graphic T-shirts to high school students; it had a routine client base of over 150 customers. From managing this business, I know what it takes to be reliable and responsive to customer needs. I am looking forward to learning new approaches from Prime Financial's internship, particularly new ways to work with small businesses.

Provides details about his sales experience to interest his reader.

With my education and experience, I can provide the innovative and competitive edge necessary to be part of your team. I would welcome an interview to discuss your internship and the contributions I could make at Prime Financial.

Sincerely,

James Jiang

James Jiang

How to Organize Prospecting Letters

When you don't have any evidence that the company is hiring, you cannot use the pattern for solicited letters. Instead, use the pattern of organization in Figure 11.14. A sample prospecting letter for an applicant desiring to change fields is shown in Figure 11.15.

First Paragraphs of Solicited Letters

When you know that the firm is hiring, announcing that you are applying for a specific position enables the firm to route your letter to the appropriate person, thus speeding consideration of your application. Identify where you learned about the job: "the position of junior accountant announced in Sunday's *Dispatch,*" "William Paquette, our placement director, told me that you are looking for. . . ."

Note how the following paragraph picks up several of the characteristics of the ad:

Ad: Business Education Instructor at Shelby Adult Education. Candidate must possess a Bachelor's degree in Business Education. Will be responsible for providing in-house training to business and government leaders. . . . Candidate should have at least one year teaching experience.

Letter: I am applying for your position in Business Education that is posted on your school website. In December, I will receive a Bachelor of Science degree from North Carolina A & T University in Business Education. My work has given me two years' experience teaching word processing and computer accounting courses to adults plus leadership skills developed in the North Carolina National Guard.

Your **summary sentence** or **paragraph** covers everything you will talk about and serves as an organizing device for your letter.

> Through my education, I have a good background in standard accounting principles and procedures and a working knowledge of some of the special accounting practices of the oil industry. This working knowledge is enhanced by practical experience in the oil fields: I have pumped, tailed rods, and worked as a roustabout.

> My business experience, familiarity with DeVilbiss equipment, and communication skills qualify me to be an effective part of the sales staff at DeVilbiss.

Figure 11.14	How to Organize a Prospecting Letter

1. Catch the reader's interest.

2. Create a bridge between the attention-getter and your qualifications. Focus on what you know and can do. Since the employer is not planning to hire, he or she won't be impressed with the fact that you're graduating. Summarize your qualifications briefly in the same order in which you plan to discuss them in the letter. This summary sentence or paragraph then covers everything you will talk about and serves as an organizing device for your letter.

3. Develop your strong points in detail. Be specific. Relate what you've done in the past to what you could do for this company. Show that you know something about the company. Identify the specific niche you want to fill.

4. Ask for an interview and tell when you'll be available for interviews. (Don't tell when you can begin work.) Thank the recipient for considering your application. End on a positive, forward-looking note.

Figure 11.15	A Prospecting Letter from a Career Changer

Mandy Shelly

www.wisc.edu/~Shelly88/home.htm

Mandy uses a "letterhead" that hamonizes with her résumé. (see Figure 11.7)

266 Van Buren Drive
Madison, WI 53706
shellym@wisc.edu
555-897-1534 (home)
555-842-4242 (cell)

March 29, 2018

Mr. Franklin Kohl
PDF Productions
3232 White Castle Road
Minneapolis, MN 85434

In a prospecting letter, open with a sentence that (1) will seem interesting and true to the reader and (2) provides a natural bridge to talking about yourself.

Dear Mr. Kohl:

The Wall Street Journal says that PDF Productions is expanding operations into Wisconsin, Minnesota, and Nebraska. My experience in technical writing, design, and computers would be an asset to your expanding organization.

Shows knowledge of the organization.

Briefly shows a variety of technical writing and computer skills.

While working at a local animal shelter, I used my technical writing skills to create a website that allows users to easily access information. To improve the website, I conducted usability tests that provided useful feedback that I incorporated to modify the overall design. In addition, I was also responsible for writing and editing the shelter's monthly newsletter, which was distributed to roughly 1,200 "Friends of the Shelter." I have extensive computer and design skills, which I am anxious to put to use for PDF Productions.

Relates what she's done to what she could do for this company.

Coursework has also prepared me well for technical writing. I have written technical material on a variety of levels ranging from publicity flyers for the animal shelter to scientific reports for upper-level science courses. My course work in statistics has shown me how to work with data and present it accurately for various audiences. Because of my scientific background, I also have a strong vocabulary in both life sciences and chemistry. This background will help me get up to speed quickly with clients such as ChemPro and Biostage. My background in science has also taught me just how important specific details can be.

Shows how her coursework is an asset.

Names specific clients, showing more knowledge of company.

In May, I will complete my degree from the University of Wisconsin and will be most interested in making a significant contribution to PDF Productions. I am available every Monday, Wednesday, and Friday for an interview (608-897-1534). I look forward to talking with you about technical writing I can do for PDF Productions.

Sincerely,

Mandy Shelly

Mandy Shelly

First Paragraphs of Prospecting Letters

In a prospecting letter, asking for a job in the first paragraph is dangerous: unless the company plans to hire but has not yet announced openings, the reader is likely to throw the letter away. Instead, catch the reader's interest. Then, in the second paragraph, you can shift the focus to your skills and experience, showing how they can be useful to the employer and specifying the job you are seeking.

Here are some effective first and second paragraphs that provide a transition to the writer's discussion of his or her qualifications.

These are the first two paragraphs of a letter to the director of publications at an oil company:

> If scarcity of resources makes us use them more carefully, perhaps it would be a good idea to ration words. If people used them more carefully, internal communications specialists like you would have fewer headaches because communications jobs would be done right the first time.
>
> For the last six years I have worked on improving my communications skills, learning to use words more carefully and effectively. I have taught business communication at a major university, worked for two newspapers, have completed a Master's degree in English, and I would like to contribute my skills to your internal communications staff.

These are the first two paragraphs of a letter applying to be a computer programmer for an insurance company:

> As you know, merging a poorly written letter with a database of customers just sends out bad letters more quickly. But you also know how hard it is to find people who can both program computers and write well.
>
> My education and training have given me this useful combination. I'd like to put my associate's degree in computer technology and my business experience writing to customers to work in State Farm's service approach to insurance.

Notice how the second paragraph provides a transition to a discussion of qualifications.

Showing a Knowledge of the Position and the Company

If you could substitute another inside address and salutation and send out the letter without any further changes, it isn't specific enough. A job application letter is basically a claim that you could do a specific job for a particular company. Use your knowledge of the position and the company to choose relevant evidence from what you've done to support your claims that you could help the company.

The following paragraphs show the writer's knowledge of the company.

A letter to PricewaterhouseCoopers's Minneapolis office uses information the student learned in a referral interview with a partner in an accounting firm. Because the reader will know that Herr Wollner is a partner in the Berlin office, the student does not need to identify him.

> While I was studying in Berlin last spring, I had the opportunity to discuss accounting methods for multinational clients of PricewaterhouseCoopers with Herr Fritz Wollner. We also talked about communication among PricewaterhouseCoopers's international offices.
>
> Herr Wollner mentioned that the increasing flow of accounting information between the European offices—especially those located in Germany, Switzerland, and Austria—and the U.S. offices of PricewaterhouseCoopers makes accurate translations essential. My fluency in German enables me to translate accurately; and my study of communication problems in Speech Communication, Business and Professional Speaking, and Business and Technical Writing will help me see where messages might be misunderstood and choose words that are more likely to communicate clearly.

A letter to KPMG uses information the student learned in a summer job.

> As an assistant accountant for Pacific Bell during this past summer, I worked with its computerized billing and record-keeping system, BARK. I had the opportunity to help the controller revise portions of the system, particularly the procedures for handling delinquent accounts. When the KPMG audit team reviewed Pacific Bell's transactions completed for July, I had the opportunity to observe your System 2170. Several courses in computer science allow me to appreciate the simplicity of your system and its objective of reducing audit work, time, and costs.

One or two specific details about the company usually are enough to demonstrate your knowledge. Be sure to use the knowledge, not just repeat it. Never present the information as though it will be news to the reader. After all, the reader works for the company and presumably knows much more about it than you do.

Showing What Separates You from Other Applicants

Your knowledge of the company can separate you from other applicants. You also can use coursework, an understanding of the field, and experience in jobs and extracurricular events to show that you're unique. Stress your accomplishments, not your job responsibilities. Be specific but concise; usually three to five sentences will enable you to give enough specific supporting details.

In your résumé, you may list activities, offices, and courses. In your letter, give more detail about what you did and show how those experiences will help you contribute to the employer's organization more quickly.

When you discuss your strengths, don't exaggerate. No employer will believe that a new graduate has a "comprehensive" knowledge of a field. Indeed, most employers believe that six months to a year of on-the-job training is necessary before most new hires are really earning their pay. Specifics about what you've done will make your claims about what you can do more believable and ground them in reality.

Writing the Last Paragraph

In the last paragraph, indicate when you'd be available for an interview. If you're free any time, you can say so. But it's likely that you have responsibilities in class and work. If you'd have to go out of town, there may be only certain days of the week or certain weeks that you could leave town for several days. Use a sentence that fits your situation.

> November 5–10 I'll be attending the Oregon Forestry Association's annual meeting and will be available for interviews then.

> Any Monday or Friday I could come to Memphis for an interview.

Should you wait for the employer to call you, or should you call the employer to request an interview? In a solicited letter, it's safe to wait to be contacted: you know the employer wants to hire someone, and if your letter and résumé show that you're one of the top applicants, you'll get an interview. In a prospecting letter, call the employer. Because the employer is not planning to hire, you'll get a higher percentage of interviews if you're assertive.

End the letter on a positive note that suggests you look forward to the interview and that you see yourself as a person who has something to contribute, not as someone who just needs a job.

> I look forward to discussing with you ways in which I could contribute to The Limited's continued growth.

Do not end your letter with a variation of the negative cliché "Please do not hesitate to contact me." Why do you think the reader would hesitate? Also avoid this other tired cliche: "Thank you for your time." Using an overworked ending dumps you right back in the pool with all the other applicants.

Oh yes, one more thing. Don't forget to sign your letter—with blue or black ink—legibly.

Email Application Letters

You will probably email most of your applications. If your application is solicited, you can paste your traditional letter into your email. If your application is prospecting, you need a shorter letter that will catch the reader's attention within the first screen (see Figure 11.16). In both solicited and prospecting applications, your first paragraph is crucial; use it to hook the reader.

As with any letter, what you write depends on your audience. For solicited applications, your email most likely will be read initially by someone in Human Resources rather than the hiring manager. The HR staff member is reading your letter to see what job you are applying for and whether you meet the basic qualifications. In some cases, you will send a transmission email to Human Resources with only basic information (the job number and your contact information) and an attached cover letter for the hiring manager. Pay close attention to the instructions in the job ad on how to submit your application.

For prospecting applications, your email will more likely go directly to a hiring manager, who is not expecting it. You therefore need to do more to convince him or her to read your letter and look at your résumé. Do not make the mistake of treating a prospecting email like a transmission email. The recipient is unlikely to look at an unsolicited cover letter or résumé without a persuasive email message.

If you don't know who will receive your email, use a traditional cover letter format for your email. Some experts are starting to recommend a shorter letter for both situations, but many caution that you need to include enough information to make you, not one of the numerous other applicants, the person for the job. Frequently that is hard to do in one screen.

When you submit an email letter with your résumé:

- Include your name as part of the subject line. Many companies also will request the job number or title in the subject line.

- Repeat the job number or title for which you're applying in the first paragraph.

- Prepare your letter in a word-processing program. Use the spell-checker to edit and proof the document.

- Use standard business letter features: salutation, standard closing, single-spacing with double-spacing between paragraphs.

- Use standard business language, without abbreviations or acronyms. Use standard, correct punctuation.

- Don't put anything in all capital letters.

- Don't use smiley faces or other emoticons.

- Put your name at the end of the message.

- Include contact information (at least your email address and phone number) below your name.

Figure 11.16	An Email with Application Letter and Résumé

Tell what format the attached résumé is in.

Pick your most impressive information for the shortened version.

Send a Word document or PDF file only if requested. Many employers will not open them because of viruses.

From ▾ Jiangj@wccc.edu

To... pascel@prime.com

Cc...

Subject Résumé—James Jiang

Dear Ms. Pascel:

At the West Coast Community College Fair, Ms. Mary Randi said to e-mail you my résumé for the Sales Advisor internship. I have pasted my résumé below and have also attached it as a PDF. My degree in Financial Management, combined with my past work experiences, makes me a strong candidate for Prime Financial.

My course work honed professional skills. For example, in my social financial planning course, I developed a strategic plan to eliminate credit card debt for a one-income household with two children. In my business communication course, I improved my oral communication ability so that I could effectively communicate my plans to potential clients.

My understanding of clients and their needs derives from my own work experiences. I started the A-Plus T-shirt Company that sold graphic T-shirts to high school students; it had a routine client base of over 150 customers. From managing this business, I know what it takes to be reliable and responsive to customer needs. I can provide the innovative and competitive edge necessary to be part of your team. I would welcome an interview to discuss your internship and the contributions I could make at Prime Financial.

Thank you,

James Jiang

[Electronic résumé would be pasted here. PDF of résumé would be attached.]

Uses contact immediately.

See James's longer letter in Figure 11.13.

Follow all guidelines posted by the company. Do not add attachments unless you know doing so is okay. Test your email by sending it to a friend; have your friend check it for appearance and correctness.

Creating a Professional Image

Every employer wants businesslike employees who understand professionalism. To make your application letter professional:

- Create your letter in a word-processing program so you can use features such as a spell-checker. Use a standard font such as Times New Roman, Arial, or Helvetica in 12-point type.

- Don't mention relatives' names. It's okay to use names of other people if the reader knows those people and thinks well of them, if they think well of you and will say good things about you, and if you have permission to use their names.

- Omit personal information not related to the job.

- Unless you're applying for a creative job in advertising, use a conservative style: few, if any, contractions; no sentence fragments, clichés, or slang.

- Edit the letter carefully and proof it several times to make sure it's perfect. Errors suggest that you're careless or inept. Double-check the spelling of the receiver's name.

- Print on the same paper (both shade and weight) you used for your résumé. Envelopes should match, too.

- Use a computer to print the envelope address.

Writing Style

Use a smooth, concise writing style (review Chapter 4). Use the technical jargon of the field to show your training, but avoid businessese and stuffy words like *utilize, commence,* and *transpire* (for *happen*). Use a lively, energetic style that makes you sound like a real person.

Avoid words that can be interpreted sexually. A model letter distributed by the placement office at a Midwestern university included the following sentence:

> I have been active in campus activities and have enjoyed good relations with my classmates and professors.

Sentences like this get shared for laughs; that's not the kind of attention you want to get!

Be sure your letter uses the exact language of the job ad and addresses all items included in the ad. If the ad mentions teamwork, your letter should give examples of teamwork; don't shift the vocabulary to collaboration. Many readers expect their job ad language in applicants' letters. If the language is not there, they may judge the applicant as not fitting the position. And so may their computer since the vocabulary of the job ad probably contains crucial key words for the computer to find.

Positive Emphasis

Be positive. Don't plead ("Please give me a chance") or apologize ("I cannot promise that I am substantially different from the lot").

Avoid word choices with negative connotations. Note how the following revisions make the writer sound more confident.

Negative: I have learned an excessive amount about writing through courses in journalism and advertising.

Positive: Courses in journalism and advertising have taught me to recognize and to write good copy. My profile of a professor was published in the campus newspaper; I earned an "A+" on my direct mail campaign for the American Dental Association to persuade young adults to see their dentist more often.

Excessive suggests that you think the courses covered too much—hardly an opinion likely to endear you to an employer.

> Negative: You can check with my references to verify what I've said.
>
> Positive: Professor Hill can give you more information about my work on his national survey.

Verify suggests that you expect the employer to distrust what you've said.

You-Attitude

Unsupported claims may sound overconfident, selfish, or arrogant. Create you-attitude by describing accomplishments and by showing how they relate to what you could do for this employer. (See Chapter 3 for more on you-attitude.)

> Lacks you-attitude: An inventive and improvising individual like me is a necessity in your business.
>
> You-attitude: Building a summer house-painting business gave me the opportunity to find creative solutions to challenges. At the end of the first summer, for example, I had nearly 10 gallons of exterior latex left, but no more jobs. I contacted the home economics teacher at my high school. She agreed to give course credit to students who were willing to give up two Saturdays to paint a house being renovated by Habitat for Humanity. I donated the paint and supervised the students. I could put these skills in problem solving and supervising to work as a personnel manager for Burroughs.

Show what you can do for them, not what they can do for you.

Remember that the word *you* refers to your reader. Using *you* when you really mean yourself or "all people" can insult your reader by implying that he or she still has a lot to learn about business:

> Lacks you-attitude: Running my own business taught me that you need to learn to manage your time.
>
> You-attitude: Running my own business taught me to manage my time.

Beware of telling readers information they already know as though they do not know it. This practice also can be considered insulting.

> Lacks you-attitude: Your company has just purchased two large manufacturing plants in France.
>
> You-attitude: My three college French courses would help me communicate in your newly acquired French manufacturing facilities.

Because you're talking about yourself, you'll use *I* in your letter. Reduce the number of *I*'s by revising some sentences to use *me* or *my*.

> Under my presidency, the Agronomy Club. . . .

> Courses in media and advertising management gave me a chance to. . . .

> My responsibilities as a summer intern included. . . .

In particular, avoid beginning every paragraph with *I*. Begin sentences with prepositional phrases or introductory clauses:

> As my résumé shows, I. . . .

> In my coursework in media and advertising management, I. . . .

> While I was in Italy. . . .

(To learn more about you-attitude, please explore the Learnsmart assignment "Creating You-Attitude and Positive Emphasis.")

Paragraph Length and Unity

Keep your first and last paragraphs fairly short—preferably no more than four or five typed lines. Vary paragraph length within the letter; it's okay to have one long paragraph, but don't use a series of eight-line paragraphs.

When you have a long paragraph, check to be sure that it covers only one subject. If it covers two or more subjects, divide it into two or more paragraphs.

Use topic sentences at the beginning of your paragraphs to make your letter more readable.

Letter Length

Have at least three paragraphs. A short letter throws away an opportunity to be persuasive; it also may suggest that you have little to say for yourself or that you aren't very interested in the job.

Without eliminating content, tighten each sentence to be sure that you're using words as efficiently as possible. If your letter is a bit over a page, use slightly smaller margins or a type size that's one point smaller to get more on the page.

Editing and Proofreading

Be sure you edit and proofread your cover letter. Failure to do so can undo all the work you put into it. The web abounds with humorous examples of spelling errors making unintended statements ("I'm excellent at spelling and grammer"). In fact, some companies post the best bloopers on their websites. For example, Robert Half International maintains Resumania (resumania.com); Killian Branding, an advertising agency, has "Cover Letters from Hell" on its website (www.killianbranding.com/cover-letters-from-hell/): the "poetic" Night-before-Christmas cover letter is amazing.

Check your content one last time to ensure that everything presents you as a hardworking professional. Make sure you are not revealing any frustration with the job search process in your content or diction. Check your tone to see that it is positive about your previous experiences and yourself. Don't beg or show too much gratitude for commonplaces such as reading your letter.

Follow-Up

Follow up with the employer once if you hear nothing after two or three weeks. It is also okay to ask once after one week if email materials were received. Do not make a pest of yourself, however, by calling or emailing too often; doing so could eliminate you from further consideration.

Social Networking and Personal Websites

LO 11-7

Many employers are no longer finding their employees through job ads and applications. Rather, they are searching LinkedIn, Facebook, and Twitter for qualified, interesting people to recruit. In these cases, you will not get a chance to submit a cover letter until after the employer has seen what you have posted online. You also can use your online presence to create a virtual cover letter—an introduction to employers who may be searching for you.

Here are some ideas for creating a virtual cover letter:

- **Manage your social networking profiles.** Employers will likely find you by your profile. Keep your education and employment up-to-date on all of your profiles. Include professional interests with your personal interests to give employers a well-rounded picture of who you are and how you could fit into their company.

- **Use key words.** In a competitive marketplace, where employers could see millions of profiles, using key words will at least get you on the radar. If you use key words and tie them into your experiences, you are more likely to stand out.

- **Keep your profile pictures professional.** When an employer searches for you, your profile picture will be one of the first things he or she sees. If it shows you making a funny face or partying with friends, it may be a red flag to an employer. The best bet is to keep your profile pictures simple and professional.

- **Manage your posts to social networks.** While a potential employer may not read through all your posts, you do need to show that you are professional and interesting. If you use key words in your posts, you are more likely to be found by an employer.

- **Create an effective personal website.** Your personal website can be your cover letter, résumé, and portfolio of work samples all in one place. Use the space effectively. Write a short introduction on the main page that talks about your goals and professional interests. On a different page or pages, include the stories and experiences that you would include in your cover letter. Show that your experience is real and interesting. Provide context and explanation for your portfolio items.

Using electronic resources well can help you stand out to potential employers.

Summary by Learning Objectives

LO 11-1 Conduct an effective job search.

- The Internet has many tools for job searching. Choose the ones that will be best for you and your career.

- Networking and internships help you build relationships in your profession.

- When you are searching for a job, your online reputation is vital. Use social networking like Twitter, Facebook, and LinkedIn wisely to build and maintain your online personal brand.

- With your online job search efforts, always be prepared to give a traditional cover letter and résumé to an interested employer.

LO 11-2 Prepare a résumé that makes you look attractive to employers.

- Employers skim résumés to decide whom to interview. Employers assume that the letter and résumé represent your best work.

- Emphasize information that is relevant to the job you want, is recent (last three years), and shows your superiority to other applicants.

- To emphasize key points, put them in headings, list them vertically, and provide details.

- Résumés use sentence fragments punctuated like complete sentences. Items in the résumé must be concise and parallel. Verbs and gerunds create a dynamic image of you.

- A chronological résumé summarizes what you did in a time line (starting with the most recent events, and going backward in reverse chronology). It emphasizes degrees, job titles, and dates. Use a chronological résumé when
  - Your education and experience are a logical preparation for the position for which you're applying.
  - You have impressive job titles, offices, or honors.

- A skills résumé emphasizes the skills you've used, rather than the job in which or the date when you used them. Use a skills résumé when
  - Your education and experience are not the usual route to the position for which you're applying.
  - You're changing fields.
  - You want to combine experience from paid jobs, activities, volunteer work, and courses to show the extent of your experience in administration, finance, speaking, etc.
  - Your recent work history may create the wrong impression (e.g., it has gaps, shows a demotion, shows job-hopping, etc.).

- Résumés contain the applicant's contact information, education, and experience. Summary of qualifications, honors and awards, other skills, activities, and a portfolio reference also may be included.

LO 11-3   **Deal with common difficulties that arise during job searches.**

■ Remove any unprofessional material from your personal web page and social networking sites.

■ If you have gaps in your employment history or low experience, or if you were laid off or fired, address those problems honestly in both your résumé and your interview.

■ Seek opportunities, such as internships and volunteer work, to fill in or expand your employment history and to reinforce your skills.

LO 11-4   **Handle the online portion of job searches.**

Many résumés are now sent electronically and are posted on the Internet or the organization's website. Prepare your résumé to send both electronically and in print.

LO 11-5   **Keep your résumé honest.**

Always be completely honest in your résumé and job search. Dishonesty can keep you from being hired or cause you to lose your job later.

LO 11-6   **Write a job letter that attracts employers.**

■ When you know that a company is hiring, send a solicited job letter. When you want a job with a company that has not announced openings, send a prospecting job letter. In both letters, you should

- Address the letter to a specific person.
- Indicate the specific position for which you're applying.
- Be specific about your qualifications.
- Show what separates you from other applicants.
- Show knowledge of the company and the position.
- Refer to your résumé (which you would enclose with the letter).

■ Use your knowledge of the company, your coursework, your understanding of the field, and your experience in jobs and extracurricular activities to show that you're unique.

■ Don't repeat information that the reader already knows; don't seem to be lecturing the reader on his or her business.

■ Use positive emphasis to sound confident. Use you-attitude by supporting general claims with specific examples and by relating what you've done to what the employer needs.

■ Have at least three paragraphs in your letter. Most job letters are only one page.

■ Application essays give you a chance to expand on your best points and show your personality.

LO 11-7   **Use social networking and a personal website to create a virtual cover letter.**

Your social networking and personal website can function as a virtual cover letter to reach those employers searching for people to recruit.

Exercises and Cases

11.1   Reviewing the Chapter

1. How can you use the Internet effectively in your job search? (LO 11-1)

2. What is the role of networking and internships when you are looking for a job? (LO 11-1)

3. What is the role of social networking in your job search? (LO 11-1)

4. How can you use writing components such as emphasis and details to help set yourself apart from other candidates? (LO 11-2)

5. What are factors you should consider when preparing your contact information? (LO 11-2)

6. What are key words? How do you use them in your summary of qualifications? In electronic résumés? (LO 11-2)

7. What kinds of details make your experience look most attractive to potential employers? (LO 11-2)

8. How can activities help make you look attractive to potential employers? (LO 11-2)

9. What can you do to help get the best references possible? (LO 11-2)

10. Pick one of the common problems job hunters may face and explain how you would deal with it if it happened to you during your career. (LO 11-3)

11. Why is it more important now than ever before to be completely honest on your résumé? (LO 11-5)

12. What are some ways that job letters differ from résumés? (LO 11-6)

13. What are the differences between solicited and prospecting letters? (LO 11-6)

14. What are three tips for writing a job letter that make you look attractive to employers? (LO 11-6)

15. What are three ways to create a professional image with your letter? (LO 11-6)

16. How can you improve your online presence to make a virtual cover letter? (LO 11-7)

11.2   Reviewing Grammar

1. Most résumés use lists, and items in lists need to have parallel structure. Polish your knowledge of parallel structure by revising the sentences in Exercise B.7, Appendix B.

2. As you have read, it is crucial that your job letter be error-free. One common error in job letters, and one that spell-checker programs will not catch, is confusing word pairs like *affect/effect*. Practice choosing the correct word with Exercises B.12, B.13, and B.14 in Appendix B.

11.3   Analyzing Your Accomplishments

List the 10 achievements that give you the most personal satisfaction. These could be things that other people wouldn't notice. They can be accomplishments you've achieved recently or things you did years ago.

Answer the following questions for each accomplishment:

1. What skills or knowledge did you use?
2. What personal traits did you exhibit?

3. What about this accomplishment makes it personally satisfying to you?

As your instructor directs,

a. Share your answers with a small group of other students.
b. Summarize your answers in an email to your instructor.
c. Present your answers orally to the class.

11.4   Remembering What You've Done

Use the following list to jog your memory about what you've done. For each item, give three or four details as well as a general statement.

Describe a time when you

1. Used facts and figures to gain agreement on an important point.
2. Identified a problem that a group or organization faced and developed a plan for solving the problem.
3. Made a presentation or a speech to a group.
4. Won the goodwill of people whose continued support was necessary for the success of some long-term project or activity.
5. Interested other people in something that was important to you and persuaded them to take the actions you wanted.

6. Helped a group deal constructively with conflict.
7. Demonstrated creativity.
8. Took a project from start to finish.
9. Created an opportunity for yourself in a job or volunteer position.
10. Used good judgment and logic in solving a problem.

As your instructor directs,

a. Identify which job(s) each detail is relevant for.
b. Identify which details would work well on a résumé.
c. Identify which details, further developed, would work well in a job letter.

11.5   Developing Action Statements

Use 10 of the verbs from Figure 11.7 to write action statements describing what you've done in paid or volunteer work, in classes, in extracurricular activities, or in community service.

11.6   Deciding How Much Detail to Use

In each of the following situations, how detailed should the applicant be? Why?

1. Ron Oliver has been steadily employed for the last six years while getting his college degree, but the jobs have been low-level ones, whose prime benefit was that they paid well and fit around his class schedule.
2. Adrienne Barcus was an assistant department manager at a clothing boutique. As assistant manager, she was authorized to approve checks in the absence of the manager. Her other duties were ringing up sales, cleaning the area, and helping mark items for sales.

3. Lois Heilman has been a clerk-typist in the Alumni Office. As part of her job, she developed a schedule for mailings to alumni, set up a merge system, and wrote two of the letters that go out to alumni. The merge system she set up has cut in half the time needed to produce letters.
4. As a co-op student, Stanley Greene spends every other term in a paid job. He now has six semesters of job experience in television broadcasting. During his last co-op, he was the assistant producer for a daily "morning magazine" show.

11.7   Taking Advantage of Volunteer Opportunities

Volunteer work can improve your skills and enhance your résumé. With a partner, seek volunteer opportunities on your campus or in your city. Make a list of volunteer groups that may need help. Here are a few organizations that might help you get started:

- Big Brothers Big Sisters
- ASPCA
- Your local library or art center
- A local food pantry
- Ronald McDonald House

Present your findings to the class and encourage your friends to join you in volunteering.

11.8   Performing a Needs Analysis

Identify a specific job posting you are interested in and list its requirements. Analyze the needs of the job and identify your personal strengths and qualifications to obtain it.

As your instructor directs,

a. Work on incorporating your list into a résumé.

b. Compose bullet entries for each qualification using action verbs.

c. Identify areas in which you still need to improve. Brainstorm a list of ways in which you can achieve what you need.

11.9   Evaluating Your Online Reputation

Your online reputation is vital to your successful job search. Evaluate your reputation online using the following steps.

a. Search for your name on Google. What are the results on the first page? Do you see a positive online presence?

b. Search for your name on Google and click on the Images search tab. What pictures come up? Is there anything that could embarrass you?

c. Check your privacy settings on Facebook. What can employers see? What can your friends see?

d. Review your Twitter and Facebook posts for the past several months. What do they say about you? Do they pass the "Grandma Test"?

e. Review and update your LinkedIn profile. Do you think it will be attractive to potential employers?

11.10   Editing a Résumé

Below are a job ad and a résumé applying for that job. Using the information you have about Jennifer's two jobs (given below the résumé), critique Jennifer's résumé. Redo her résumé to improve it. Then write an email to your instructor discussing the strengths and weaknesses of the résumé and explaining why you made the changes you did.

Account Manager

Location: Aurora, IL
Job Category: Business/Strategic Management
Career Level: Entry-Level Manager (Manager/Supervisor of Staff)

Quantum National is the market leader in providing research, sales and marketing, health care policy consulting, and health information management services to the health care industry. Quantum has more than 20,000 employees worldwide and offices in 15 countries in Central and South America. Medical Innovation Communications, a division of Quantum National, currently has an opportunity for an Account Manager in our Aurora, IL, office. Medical Innovation Communications provides comprehensive product commercialization at all stages of product development: from phase 2, through national and international product launches to ongoing support.

The Account Manager has global responsibility for managing the client's marketing communications programs, assuring that the client's objectives are met in terms of program quality and on-time delivery.

Responsibilities include:

- Day-to-day client contact to identify and translate marketing objectives into strategic medical communications/education programs.
- Develop proposals, budgets, estimates of job cost, and profitability.
- Lead a team of Project Managers and Marketing Associates through guidance, delegation, and follow-up; and significant interaction with the client.
- Work with New Business Development Teams to develop proposals, budgets, and presenting company capabilities/business pitches to clients.
- Schedule the workflow of a 30-person demonstration and marketing team.

Requirements:

- Bachelor's degree.
- Ability to define and respond to client needs, working effectively under tight deadlines.
- Proven client management experience.
- Proven team management experience.
- Superior written and spoken communication skills.

Email applications and résumés to pattersj@micquant.com, and direct inquiries to J. Pattersen.

Jennifer Stanton	8523 8th Street	125 A S. 27th Ave
wildechilde@gmail.com	Ames, IA 50011	Omaha, NE 68101
cell: 515-668-9011	515-311-8243	402-772-5106

Education

Iowa State University, Ames, IA—Business
May 2017, maybe December 2017
Minor: Botany
Cumulative GPA: 2.63 / 4.0

Mid-Plains Community College, North Platte, NE—Associate of Arts
May 2013

Bryan High School, Omaha, NE
May 2010

Work Experience

May 2016–August 2016—Summer Internship at FirstWest Insurance, Des Moines, IA

- Worked with a senior account manager to oversee some medical and EAP accounts.
- Made her phone calls to customers.
- Organized meetings with customers.
- I had to write some training "how-to's" for the new billing database.

2003–2015—*Worked in family business*
Worked weekends and summers in my parents' used-book store.

Skills

Microsoft Office
Fluent in Spanish

When you ask, Jennifer tells you about her two jobs:

> At her internship this summer, the person she worked with was pretty much an absentee supervisor: Jennifer had to do all the work alone (and she's still a little bitter about that). Her department managed five Employee Assistance Provider accounts with a total of about 36,000 individual policyholders in five Midwestern states. She had to set up and maintain work schedules for 12 employees and manage the expense reports for the entire group. Four of those employees traveled a lot, so there were lots of expense reports to manage; there were so many that Jennifer had to revise the department's budget twice. She spent about four hours of every day returning customer phone calls and linking customers on conference calls with her department's employees. And those training how-to's? That turned into a 20-page how-to manual, which she wrote up and then had FirstWest's IT department turn into a website for the department to use.
>
> Her parents' family bookstore in Omaha is actually a franchise of a national chain of aftermarket bookstores: Booktopia. The store generates about $450,000 in gross sales per year and stocks about 100,000 titles (not counting Internet sales and special orders); it employs 5 full-time and 17 part-time employees. In addition to filling in as a floor clerk, stocker, and cashier—all jobs that put her customer-service, cash-handling, and "people skills" to the test—Jennifer has been handling all of the paperwork between the store and the Booktopia corporate office. (Her parents are great salespeople, but they're not good at paying attention to details. That's created friction between them and the corporate office.) That paperwork includes all of the store's quarterly and yearly budget, staffing, and marketing reports since 2003.

Note: This exercise was written by Matthew Search.

11.11 Analyzing Job Applicants Based on Their Résumés

Based on your reading of this chapter, the following job description, and the two résumés below, analyze the two applicants for the position. What are their strengths and weaknesses as highlighted by their résumés? Which of the two candidates would you select? Why?

Job description for Cost Accountant

The position of Cost Accountant is responsible for budgeting, reviewing, analyzing, controlling, and forecasting costs involving different cost centers throughout the production process, including raw material procurement, inventory management, manufacturing, warehousing, and shipping. Other responsibilities include analyzing G/L reports; ensuring compliance with Generally Accepted Accounting Principles (GAAP) and Cost Accounting Standards (CAS); conducting breakeven (BE), contribution margin, and variance analyses; and preparing periodic reports for upper management. The position requires a bachelor's degree in accounting. A certification in management accounting from the Institute of Management Accountants (IMA) will be a plus. The position also requires a minimum of two years of work experience in cost accounting at a manufacturing company.

SAM PORTER

1010, Buck St., Fairfax, VA
sporter@bestwebsite.com

EXPERIENCE

2015–2017   Abacus Engineering   Portland, OR.

Cost Accounting Trainee
- Calculated cost variance for different cost centers.
- Prepared quarterly budget reports
- Coodinated with employees at different levels for data collection

2015–till date   Bourke Winodws   Fairfax, VA

Costing Manager
- Monitored 12 cost centers
- Implemented policies that reduced costs by 25%
- Supervised a staff of three, including one cost accountant.
- I also produced multiple G/L reports for the production department as well as upper management

EDUCATION

2011–2015 Edward Young University, Perry, OH
- B.A., accounting.
- Currently pursuing CMA of Institute of Management Accounting

INTERESTS

Country music, computers, fishing, golf

Jose Cortez

1212 S. E. Avenue, Earl, PA
(111) 112-1121; jc8@pearlnews.com

Qualification Summary

Skills in **controling** and reucing costs, experience with GAAP and CAS, skills in cost analyses, project management, CMA (IMA), member of the Financial Management Association International, well-versd with ERP software

Education

- **Certification in Management Accounting**
  Graduation—2017
  Institute of Management Accountants
- True Blue University, Roald, PA
  Graduation—2016
  Degree—Bachelor of Sciences (BS)
  Major—Accounting, G.P.A. 3.55

(continued)

Experience

Silverstein Windows and Doors, Earl, PA   2017-Till date

 Cost Accountant
- Estimate, review, budget, analyze, and forecast direct / indirect and variable and fixed costs for all stages of production
- Work on the ERP system to genrate reports and data sheets giving cost analyses
- Suggested a procedure in a contract that saved the company $35,000
- Worked with the Marketing Department on the costing / pricing of lower-priced vinyl casement windows

Achievements
- Volunteered more than 100 hours for the Habitat for Humnity Award 2015–2016
- Visted door and widow manufacturing plants in Argentina, Belgium, and Japan
- Received the best employee of the month award at Silverstein Windows and Doors
- Wrote articles for *Financial Control Weekly,* a publication of Costing Professionals Association

References

 Available upon request

Note: This exercise was written by Anish Dave.

11.12 Preparing a Résumé

Write a résumé that you could use in your job search.

As your instructor directs,

a. Write a résumé for the field in which you hope to find a job.

b. Write two different résumés for two different job paths you are interested in pursuing. Write an email to your instructor explaining the differences.

c. Adapt your résumé to a specific company you hope to work for. Write an email to your instructor explaining the specific adaptations you made and why.

11.13 Critiquing Your Résumé

Answer the Résumé Checklist questions (see Figure 11.9) for your résumé. Variation: Review a class member's résumé using the same checklist questions.

11.14 Creating a Web or Paper Portfolio

Create a web or paper portfolio highlighting your professional and academic accomplishments. Include course projects, workplace samples, and other documents that support your professional accomplishments and goals.

Write an email to your instructor listing each item in your portfolio and explaining why you chose it.

11.15 Evaluating Visual Résumés

Working individually, in pairs, or in small groups, as your instructor directs,

a. Look at five of the example student résumés on VisualCV.com. What features do you like? Why? What features would you change or omit? Why? What are the advantages of VisualCV over your own web page? Disadvantages?

b. Discuss strengths and weaknesses of two résumés in an email to your instructor, a posting on the class website, or an oral presentation.

11.16 Evaluating LinkedIn Profiles

Working individually, in pairs, or in small groups, as your instructor directs, look at six profiles on LinkedIn. You could use those of your classmates, family members, or local businesspeople.

- Which one has the best résumé? Why?
- How do the profiles and résumés differ?

- Which one has the best recommendations? Why?
- Overall, which one has the best profile? Why?

Discuss your conclusions in an email to your instructor, a posting on the class website, or an oral presentation.

11.17 Analyzing First Paragraphs of Prospecting Letters

All of the following are first paragraphs in prospecting letters written by new college graduates. Evaluate the paragraphs on these criteria:

- Is the paragraph likely to interest readers and motivate them to read the rest of the letter?
- Does the paragraph have some content that the student can use to create a transition to talking about his or her qualifications?
- Does the paragraph avoid asking for a job?

1. Redeccer just added three new stores in Ohio. They also got voted best hardware store in Denton. This is where I want to start my career in supply-chain management.

2. From the time I was old enough to walk, my father involved me with the many chores and decisions that happen on a successful family farm. He taught me to work, to manage employees, and to handle large amounts of money. I believe my lifelong experience has prepared me to contribute to the continued success of your company.

3. Two years ago, my right leg was crushed in a car accident in the middle of my second semester of college. Although I had to have two surgeries and was on heavy painkillers, I successfully completed the semester with a 3.4. I know that this experience shows I have what it takes to succeed in your law firm.

4. For the past two and one-half years I have been studying turf management. On August 1, I will graduate from Western State University with a BA in Ornamental Horticulture. The type of job I will seek will deal with golf course maintenance as an assistant superintendent.

5. Ann Gibbs suggested that I contact you.

6. Each year, the Christmas shopping rush makes more work for everyone at Nordstrom's, especially for the Credit Department. While working for Nordstrom's Credit Department for three Christmas and summer vacations, the Christmas sales increase is just one of the credit situations I became aware of.

7. Whether to plate a two-inch eyebolt with cadmium for a tough, brilliant shine or with zinc for a rust-resistant, less expensive finish is a tough question. But similar questions must be answered daily by your salespeople. With my experience in the electroplating industry, I can contribute greatly to your constant need of getting customers.

8. What a set of tractors! The new 9430 and 9630 diesels are just what is needed by today's farmer with his ever-increasing acreage. John Deere has truly done it again.

9. Prudential Insurance Company did much to help my college career as the sponsor of my National Merit Scholarship. Now I think I can give something back to Prudential. I'd like to put my education, including a BS degree in finance from Ludewig University, to work in your investment department.

10. Since the beginning of Delta Electric Construction Co. in 2002, the size and profits have grown steadily. My father, being a stockholder and vice president, often discusses company dealings with me. Although the company has prospered, I understand there have been a few problems of mismanagement. I feel with my present and future qualifications, I could help ease these problems.

11.18 Improving You-Attitude and Positive Emphasis in Job Letters

Revise each of these sentences to improve you-attitude and positive emphasis. You may need to add information.

1. I got laid off at Barlons three months ago when they downsized.

2. Your company needs someone like me, who has the experience and knowledge to take your department to new heights.

3. I may not be the most qualified candidate you will see, but with your location and financial struggles, I am certainly the best you will get.

4. I understand that your company has had problems due to the mistranslation of documents during international ad campaigns.

5. Included in my résumé are the courses in Finance that earned me a fairly attractive grade average.

6. I am looking for a position that gives me a chance to advance quickly.

7. Although short on experience, I am long on effort and enthusiasm.

8. I have been with the company from its beginning to its present unfortunate state of bankruptcy.

9. I wish to apply for a job at Austin Electronics. I will graduate from Florida State in May. I offer you a degree in electrical engineering and part-time work at Best Buy.

10. I was so excited to see your opening. This job is perfect for me.

11. You will find me a dedicated worker, because I really need a job.

11.19 Evaluating Letter Content

Improve the content of these passages from job cover letters. You may need to add content.

1. I am a very hard worker. In fact, I am known for finishing the jobs of my co-workers.

2. I have always worked hard, even when most of my co-workers and my boss were hardly working.

3. I have received a 4.0 in every semester at my university. This shows my dedication to perfection.

4. My internship gave me lots of experience for this job.

5. My job duties at Saxon Sport were to create displays, start an employee newsletter, and on weekends I was part of the sales staff.

6. While at San Fernando State, I participated in lots of activities. I played intramurals in baseball, football,

basketball, hockey, and volleyball. I was treasurer and then president of the Marketing Club. I was in the Gaffers' Guild, where I made blown-glass creations. I was also in Campus Democrats.

7. I will be in Boston for a family reunion June 23–25 and will drop by your office then for an interview.

8. I feel any of my bosses would tell you that I try hard and pay attention to to detail.

9. I wish to apply for your job as a computer programmer. I have a computer science minor and two summers of sales experience at Best Buy in their computer department.

11.20 Evaluating Rough Drafts

Evaluate the following drafts. What parts should be omitted? What needs to be changed or added? What parts would benefit from specific supporting details?

1.
   Dear_____:

   There is more to a buyer's job than buying the merchandise. And a clothing buyer in particular has much to consider.

   Even though something may be in style, customers may not want to buy it. Buyers should therefore be aware of what customers want and how much they are willing to pay.

   In the buying field, request letters, thank-you letters, and persuasive letters are frequently written.

   My interest in the retail field inspired me to read Forever 21's annual report. I saw that a new store is being built. An interview would give us a chance to discuss how I could contribute to this new store. Please call me to schedule an interview.

   Sincerely,

2.

> Dear Sir or Madam:
>
> I am taking the direct approach of a personnel letter. I believe you will under stand my true value in the areas of practical knowledge and promotional capabilities.
>
> I am interested in a staff position with Darden in relation to trying to improve the operations and moral of the Olive Garden Restaurants, which I think that I am capable of doing. Please take a minute not to read my résumé (enclosed) and call to schedule an interview.
>
> Sincerely,

3.

> Dear_____:
>
> Hello, my name is Dave. I am very interested in the position of marketing guy for Applicious Applesauce. I have recently graduated from Sharman University, with a Bachelor's Degree in Marketing and Finance. I graduated with a 2.0 GPA, and took many classes in Marketing and Finance. I believe these classes will help me to grow your company to where it needs to be.
>
> I did some marketing work for my friend, Aaron, who is starting his own business. I helped promote his new business and came up with a clear marketing plan for him to follow. He is doing really well with it so far.
>
> I have no problem relocating for this job. I really want it.
>
> Thank you for your time.
>
> Sincerely,

11.21 Gathering Information about Companies in Your Career Field

Use five different websites to investigate three companies in your career field. Look at salary guides for your level of qualifications, product/service information, news articles about the companies, mission/vision statements, main competitors, annual reports, and financial reports.

As your instructor directs,

a. Share your findings with a small group of other students.

b. Summarize your findings in an email to your instructor. Include a discussion of how you could use this information in your job letter and résumé.

c. Present your findings to the class.

d. Join with a small group of other students to write a report summarizing the results of this research.

11.22 Conducting an Information Interview

Interview someone working in a field you're interested in. Use the following questions to get started:

- How did you get started in this field?
- What do you like about your job?
- What do you dislike about your job?
- What courses and jobs would you recommend as preparation for this field?

As your instructor directs,

a. Share the results of your interview with a small group of other students.

b. Write an email to your instructor containing the results of your interview. Include a discussion of how you could use this information in your job letter and résumé.

c. Present the results of your interview orally to the class.

d. Write to the interviewee thanking him or her for taking the time to talk to you.

11.23 Writing a Solicited Letter

Write a letter of application in response to an announced opening for a full-time job (not an internship) you would like.

Turn in a copy of the listing. If you use option (a), your listing will be a copy. If you choose option (b), you will write the listing.

a. Respond to an ad in a newspaper, in a professional journal, in the placement office, or on the web. Use an ad that specifies the company, not a blind ad. Be sure that you are fully qualified for the job.

b. If you have already worked somewhere, assume that your employer is asking you to apply for full-time work after graduation. Be sure to write a fully persuasive letter.

11.24 Creating a Virtual Cover Letter

Using a cover letter you have written, review your online presence. What key words do you see in your social networking profiles? What job experience, education, and skills are highlighted? How can you make your online profiles more attractive to potential employers? List what you found and identify changes you are going to make to your online presence.

11.25 Reviewing Cover Letters

All-Weather Inc. invited applications for the position of sales representative (Residential Sales). To be based in Nebraska, this person will be mainly responsible for sales of All-Weather's vinyl windows in local markets, including single- and double-hung windows and casement windows. The job description for the position reads as follows:

> The Sales Representative (Residential Sales) will be responsible for successful market penetration of identified market segments. Specifically, the duties include achieving targeted sales, conducting product demonstrations, contacting customers and other stakeholders, gathering market intelligence, preparing market and sales reports, communicating with internal customers, coordinating between customers and the Service and Installation Group, participating in meetings of trade associations and government agencies, attending company training events, and performing other duties assigned by managers. The ideal candidate will be someone with a BS degree, preferably with a technical major. Additionally, the candidate must have at least one year of sales experience, preferably in industrial products. Candidates with experience in brand marketing will also be considered. Among skills for the job, the candidate must possess computer skills, PR and communication skills, teamwork skills, and the ability to perform basic mathematical computations.

Write a response in which you discuss the strengths and weaknesses of both applicants. Judging just from their cover letter, which applicant would you prefer to hire? Why?

Antonio Ramirez aramirez@bestmail.com 164 Beet St. Houston, TX

October 12, 2017

Ms. Erin Lenhardt
1210 Polaroid Av.
St. Paul, MN

Dear Ms. Lenhardt:

Please consider this letter as my application for the post of Sales Representative (Residential Sales). I learned about your job from the journal *Plastics US* (September issue). I have a bachelor's degree in chemistry from the University of Austin, Texas, and have two years of experience selling PVC resin.

The last two years I have been a Sales Executive in Goodman Petrochemicals in Houston, TX. My responsibilities include selling Goodman's PVC resin to Houston-based PVC processors of rigid and flexible applicatons.

As you suggest in your advertisement, my degree in chemistry will help me explain to customers the important technical attributes of your vinyl windows. My focus during my bachelor's degree was inorganic chemistry, especially hydrocarbons and its practical applications. Apart from my coursework, I also interned at Bright Fenestration Products in Austin, TX.

I look forward to discussing my experience and interst in your organization with you in a face-to-face interview. I'm available for the interview any time in the next two weeks at a day's notice. I'm confident I will meet—and exceed—all your expetations for this important front line position.

Sincerely,

Antonio Ramirez

Michelle Chang
4334, Sunset Boulevard, Lincoln, NE
mchang@myemail.com

October 14, 2017

Ms. Erin Lenhardt
HR Manager
1210 Polaroid Av.
St. Paul, MN

Dear Ms. Lenhardt:

I wish to apply for the position of Sales Representative (Residential Sales) advertised through Monster.com. After acquiring a bachelor's degree in design, I joined Albatross Advertising in November, 2014, as a trainee in the Accounts Department. Currently, I'm an Account Representative handling three of our most promising brands: *LiteWait* vacuum cleaners, Nebraska Furniture Mart, and Chimney Rock Art Gallery.

My bachelor's degree in design with a major in community and regional planning not only familiarized me with demands of buildings and landscapes in our 21st-century living but also acquainted me with concepts of media and design. I joined Albatross because I wanted to see if my education has equipped me to inform, persuade, and help customers with regard to products and brands.

During my nearly two-year tenure at Albatross as Account Representative, I have created and given insightful presentations to clients. As a result of my performance, the agency has entrusted me with three of its most promising accounts, the ones that I mention above.

I would be delighted at an opportunity for a personal interview to further make my case for the job. You can contact me at my email address mentioned above.

Sincerely,

Michelle Chang

Notes

1. U.S. Department of Labor, Bureau of Labor Statistics, "Number of Jobs, Labor Market Experience, and Earnings Growth among Americans at 50: Results from a Longitudinal Survey," news release, August 27, 2017, USDL-17-1158, https://www.bls.gov/news.release/pdf/nlsoy.pdf.

2. Richard Nelson Bolles, *What Color Is Your Parachute? 2013: A Practical Manual for Job-Hunters and Career-Changers* (Berkeley: Ten Speed Press, 2013), 57.

3. National Association of Colleges and Employers, "Intern to Full-Time Hire Conversion: 'Returning vs 'Nonreturning' Students," July 21, 2015, http://www.naceweb.org/talent-acquisition/internships/intern-to-full-time-hire-conversion-returning-vs-nonreturning-interns/.

4. Teri Evans, "Penn State, Texas A&M Top the List: Recruiters Like One-Stop Shopping for Grads with Solid Academics, Job Skills, Record of Success," *Wall Street Journal,* September 13, 2010, B1; and Alexandra Cheney, "Firms Assess Young Interns' Potential: Businesses Look to Pools for Full-Time Hires, Tracking Future Employees as Early as Freshman Year," *Wall Street Journal,* September 13, 2010, B10.

5. Julie Strickland, "The Good Hires? They're in Your Network," *Inc.,* May 2013, 24.

6. Careerbuilder.com, "Number of Employers Using Social Media to Screen Candidates Has Increased 500 Percent Over the Last Decade," press release, April 28, 2016, http://www.careerbuilder.com/share/aboutus/pressreleasesdetail.aspx?ed=12%2F31%2F2016&id=pr945&sd=4%2F28%2F2016.

7. Geoffrey James, "Online Personal Branding Increases Your Hireability," *FINS Sales & Marketing,* July 18, 2012, http://sales-jobs.fins.com/Articles/SBB00014240527023040703045773943742016180012/Online-Personal-Branding-Increases-Your-Hireability.

8. Cheryl Lu-Lien Tan, "The Art of Online Portraiture," *Wall Street Journal,* October 20, 2011, D6.

9. "Facebook Costing 16–34s Jobs in Tough Economic Climate," *OnDeviceResearch.com,* May 29, 2013, http://ondeviceresearch.com/blog/facebook-costing-16-34s-jobs-in-tough-economic-climate#sthash.Yvmg7k4T.5wuXCgt6.dpbs.

10. Careerbuilder.com, "Number of Employers Using Social Media."

11. Leslie Kwoh, "Beware: Potential Employers Are Watching You," *Wall Street Journal,* October 29, 2012, B8.

12. Josh Sanburn, "How to Make Your Resume Last Longer Than 6 Seconds," *Time,* April 13, 2012, http://business.time.com/2012/04/13/how-to-make-your-resume-last-longer-than-6-seconds/.

13. Accountemps: A Robert Half Company, "Résumés Inching Up: Survey Shows Longer Résumés Now More Acceptable," news release, March 20, 2010, http://accountemps.rhi.mediaroom.com/index.php?s5189&item5210.

14. Elizabeth Blackburn-Brockman and Kelly Belanger, "One Page or Two? A National Study of CPA Recruiters' Preferences for Résumé Length," *Journal of Business Communication* 38 (2001): 29–45.

15. CareerBuilder.com, "Nearly Half of Employers Have Caught a Lie on a Résumé, CareerBuilder.com Survey Shows," press release, July 30, 2008, http://www.careerbuilder.com/share/aboutus/pressreleasesdetail.aspx?id5pr448&sd57%2f30%2f2008&ed512%2f31%2f2008; and Dennis Nishi, "'Keywords' May Unlock a New Job," *Wall Street Journal,* February 24, 2013, http://online.wsj.com/article/SB10001424127887323949404578314220242353956.html.

16. National Association of Colleges and Employers, "The Attributes Employers Seek on a Candidate's Resume," December 7, 2016, http://www.naceweb.org/talent-acquisition/candidate-selection/the-attributes-employers-seek-on-a-candidates-resume/.

17. National Association of Colleges and Employers, "Job Outlook 2013," November 2012, http://www.unco.edu/careers/assets/documents/NACEJobOutlookNov2013.pdf.

18. Roni Noland, "It's Not a Disaster if Your Old Boss Won't Provide a Reference," *Boston Globe,* March 8, 2009, 5.

19. Keith J. Winstein and Daniel Golden, "MIT Admissions Dean Lied on Résumé in 1979, Quits," *Wall Street Journal,* April 27, 2007, B1.

20. Martha C. White, "You Won't Believe How Many People Lie on Their Resumes," *Money,* August 13, 2015, http://time.com/money/3995981/how-many-people-lie-resumes/.

21. Dan Fastenberg, "The Most Common Lies on Résumés," *AOL Jobs,* April 1, 2013; and Alison Doyle, "Employment Background Checks," *About.com Job Searching,* accessed June 21, 2013, http://jobsearch.about.com/cs/backgroundcheck/a/background.htm.

22. Robert Half International, "Importance of the Cover Letter," 2013, http://www.roberthalf.com/coverletter.

23. Ibid.

24. Kathryn Dill, "Study: Half of All Available Jobs Are Never Advertised," *Forbes,* August 20, 2014, https://www.forbes.com/sites/kathryndill/2014/08/20/study-half-of-all-available-jobs-are-never-advertised-publicly/#6260c47324fe.

25. Katharine Hansen and Randall Hansen, "The Basics of a Dynamic Cover Letter," in *Cover Letter Resources for Job-Seekers,* accessed June 21, 2013, http:// www.quintcareers.com/cover_letter_basics.html.

Credits